POLITICS AND BANKING

Politics and Banking

Ideas, Public Policy, and the Creation of Financial Institutions

SUSAN HOFFMANN

THE JOHNS HOPKINS UNIVERSITY PRESS
Baltimore and London

This book has been brought to publication with the generous
assistance of the Pribram Fund.

The Johns Hopkins University Press
2715 North Charles Street
Baltimore, Maryland 21218-4363
www.press.jhu.edu

A catalog record for this book is available from the British Library.

LIBRARY OF CONGRESS CATALOGING-IN-PUBLICATION DATA

Hoffmann, Susan.
    Politics and banking : ideas, public policy, and the creation of
financial institutions / Susan Hoffmann.
        p.   cm.
Includes bibliographical references and index.
    ISBN 0-8018-6702-9
    1. Banks and banking—United States—History. 2. Banks and
banking—Government policy—United States—History. I. Title.
    HG2461 .H58 2001
    332.1'0973—dc21   00-011762

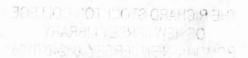

TO CHARLIE

CONTENTS

I was at my desk one morning in the fall of 1982, in the City of Cleveland's Office of Budget and Management. I had just taken the position of capital program coordinator, but the task at hand that morning was not figuring out what to rehab, build, or buy first, next, and later, as the city reentered the bond market after having been ignominiously shut out a few years earlier. Rather, I was editing the text of a modest plan for a run-down southeast side neighborhood, a project I was wrapping up in my previous role, also with Cleveland, as a neighborhood planner. My phone rang; it was Ernest Ranly, a longtime friend. On vacation from his work as parish priest in an Andean village, Ernie was in Ohio to visit his family and community. I asked about Peru. Conditions were not good, he said. People were poor and getting poorer. The government, straining to service debt it had incurred with U.S. banks, was spending little to address pressing social needs. Consequently, sympathy for the revolutionary group Shining Path was on the rise. In that moment the thought struck me that Ernie, high in the Andes, and I, at East Ninety-first Street and Harvard Avenue, had been looking at two sides of a coin. While U.S. banks declined to lend in central city neighborhoods, like the one sketched in the report on my desk, they were eager to lend in developing countries like Peru—with significant consequences for the political economy in both cases. To be sure, domestic inner-city decline and foreign guerrilla insurgency are complex problems and cannot be laid at the feet of U.S. banks, yet there is no question that banks' decisions are one critical factor in these phenomena.

That was all some time ago, but my appreciation for the centrality of the roles of private financial institutions in matters of great concern to the public only deepened throughout my career in urban planning and administration. Banks, in particular, are powerful actors whose decisions have significant political consequences; they are thus an appropriate—even crucial—subject for the attention of political scientists. Accordingly, as I turned to a new career in academic political science, I began to study this policy area. I have learned that banks not only affect politics; they are products of politics. U.S. banking institutions have been shaped—empowered and constrained—by public policy. Crucial roles in the fundamental public responsibility of providing a money supply have been delegated to them. Banks do, in large measure, what policy makers have designed them to do. This book is thus about money and banking policy.

Yet this book is also about the influence of ideas in public policy making and institutional design. My city planning career was interrupted when my husband's work with the Public Health Service took him to the Indian reservation at Winnebago, Nebraska. Casting about for work in the place in which I found myself, I started teaching government at the community college in Sioux City, Iowa, and the University of South Dakota in Vermillion. This path led back to the university in pursuit of a doctorate in political science. (I had two little girls and was pushing forty, but, well, people do these things these days.) Since my first go-round in the academy, an economic theory of politics had taken a firm hold in the study of public administration and public policy. The algebraic and geometric models I was now confronting in the literature did not capture what I had seen and lived in city hall and the neighborhoods. Certainly, businesspeople, legislators, reporters, bureaucrats, politicians, and others used public processes to serve their self-interest as they saw it, but people in various roles—public and private—also worked passionately to make policy that they thought would be good for Cleveland.

To be sure, there were sharply contrasting views of just what that public good might be. This is to say that beyond the question of whether interests or ideas drive policy making and institutional design lies the question of which ideas are influential. A grasp of contrasting public philosophies—where they come from, the values they cherish, their implications for public process, the design of their institutional children, and, yes, whose interest is served when one prevails rather than another—is crucial to understanding the policy process in the United States and the structure of the political economy. In this study U.S. banking has proven an especially fruitful arena in which to see different views in contention, for banking policy has been debated in Washington since the first Congress and in the colonial/state capitals since long before that. Further, different views have been separately institutionalized—in commercial banking, in credit unionism, and in the savings and loan framework—to a degree that is perhaps unique. Indeed, it was in noticing these "different logics" (to borrow a turn of phrase from Stephen Skowronek and Karen Orren) operating simultaneously in the institutional configuration of the political economy that this particular study was born. For me, rocking back and forth between distinctive public ideas and their institutional expressions in this policy area, in historical perspective, has been enormously helpful in coming to grips with the normative differences among classic and neoliberal, populist, progressive, and utilitarian approaches to policy making.

For help with this effort to understand U.S. banking institutions by looking for the ideas that undergird them and, conversely, to grasp the significance of alternative public philosophies by attending to what they have meant for banking, I would like to thank Charles W. Anderson and Donald F. Kettl at the University of Wisconsin–Madison. One a political theorist and the other a scholar of public administration and policy, both strongly encouraged and actively supported the bridging of subfield divides required by this project.

Others among the political science faculty at Madison also helped in crucial ways. Anne Khademian provided a foundation on which I relied in regulatory politics generally and banking policy in particular, and she was unfailingly generous with her time, her own research materials, and her exceptional talent for framing questions. Herbert Kritzer and Murray Edelman convinced me of the legitimacy and integrity of qualitative research and taught me some ways to do it. John Coleman read the entire manuscript draft and identified several points where the argument needed strengthening. From the History Department John Cooper and Colleen Dunlavy directed me to the germane work in the history and American political development literatures.

I would also like to thank John Meyer, David Siemers, and Mark Cassell, who read early drafts of some chapters and provided helpful criticism. Much of the credit for what is of value here belongs to these scholars, while responsibility for any shortcomings is mine.

Finally, I would like to thank my mother, Shirley Hoffmann, and my husband, Mark Lay, for their help with this project. My mom, a longtime volunteer in the credit union movement, brought my attention to credit unionism and the alternative way of thinking about the political economy which its institutions represent; the insights she sparked are fundamental to the structure of the argument presented here. My husband, Mark, supported my work in countless ways, and I am grateful.

POLITICS AND BANKING

1

PUBLIC PHILOSOPHIES AND REGULATORY FRAMEWORKS IN U.S. BANKING

THE POLICY AREA: DEPOSITORY INTERMEDIATION

One March morning in 1935 Marriner Eccles, recently appointed chairman of the Federal Reserve Board, was up on Capitol Hill testifying before the House Committee on Banking and Currency. "Money is created by debt," he tutored the members. "Our banking system creates money—"

Henry Steagall, the committee chair, interrupted him: "You say money is created by debt; you mean by that, bank credit?"

"Yes," Eccles responded. "I mean that the banking system, the process of loaning money, extending credit, increases bank deposits." Such deposits, he had explained a moment earlier, along with currency, are money.[1]

The idea that money is a creation of banks was a difficult one for the members of the Banking and Currency Committee in 1935. Congress had struggled with its constitutional authority to provide for money and regulate its value for a hundred and fifty years. Its members had endlessly deliberated what the stuff really is and their responsibility in the matter. Now this banker from Utah, turned public policy maker, was asserting bluntly that he knew precisely what money is and the congress members should recognize it, too.

The idea that banks create money remains a difficult one for many of us. Banks are peculiar institutions. They are financial intermediaries, as are such other classes of institutions as insurance companies and mutual funds.[2] Financial intermediaries perform the economic function of channeling funds from savers to borrowers: they allocate money. But banks are also financial depository institutions. Among financial intermediaries it is only the depository institutions that, as Eccles underscored in 1935, create money through their central and defining process of taking in deposits and making loans. While banks make up the biggest class of financial depository institution by far, savings and loan associations (s&ls) and credit unions are also depository intermediaries: economists use the term *banking* to refer to the activity of all three. While a bit daunting, with a little mathematical acumen and a lot of tenacity, the technical aspects of banking can be grasped via study of introductory textbooks in economics or money and banking.[3]

What the textbooks do not convey, indeed what they obscure, is how political the banking process is. In their central process of taking in deposits and making loans, these institutions create and allocate money. They decide where credit will flow throughout society and thus what human initiatives will flourish and which will wither. People, ventures, regions, win and lose. This is the stuff of high politics, not calculus. Money arises in an institutionalized decision process, and Herbert Simon has long since taught us that institutions' decisions embody values.[4] Consequently, the constitution of banking—the specification of its decision pathways—has been one of the most controversial and important areas of public policy in the United States since the founding. Banks make money. Public policy has made banks.

The structure and practice of depository intermediation are undergoing profound transformation. In the 1980s an institutional configuration that had not been significantly altered since the Great Depression was changing, and the rate of change accelerated in the 1990s. Within commercial banking, the largest of the three categories of depository institutions, the most obvious change is in the size of banks. Mergers and acquisitions have proceeded at a breakneck pace since federal legislation in 1994 wiped out interstate banking and branching restrictions grounded in the National Bank Act of the Civil War years, clearing the way for nationwide bank branching. In a second important change banks are reestablishing linkages with securities dealing; even before Congress finally toppled the "Glass-Steagall wall" in 1999, regulatory permissiveness had eroded this once formidable Depression-era barrier between commercial banking and investment banking. A final important change among U.S. banks is their heightened activity in international financial markets.

In addition to these changes within commercial banking, another major change in depository intermediation noted by economists and public policy makers is the apparent convergence among the three different institutional types. Formerly confining themselves largely to their special niches of business lending, home lending, and small consumer loans, respectively, banks, savings and loans, and credit unions increasingly work one another's turf. In response to the savings and loan crisis, legislative and regulatory changes have made s&Ls more like banks. Credit unions, on the other hand, successfully sought regulatory changes permitting them to act more like banks and s&Ls so that they could avoid crises. And, with the elaboration of securitization techniques and secondary markets for more and more types of debt instruments, banks have been largely relieved of the liquidity concerns that tied them to commercial lending in the past, and they have forged vigorously into home mortgages and consumer debt.

REGULATORY FRAMEWORKS

In light of a view that the three kinds of depository institutions perform the same economic role in channeling funds from savers to borrowers and expanding the money supply, some economists began advocating uniform regulatory treatment for them as early as the 1970s.[5] Historically, banks, savings and loans, and credit unions developed within separate regulatory frameworks, with distinctive rules regarding such considerations as how much interest could be paid on a deposit or charged on a loan, the terms and objects of lending, reserve requirements, and deposit insurance. By *regulatory framework* I mean a network of interacting organizations, including a distinctive type of basic actor (firm), one or more regulatory agencies, rediscount institutions, a deposit insurer, and their policies and practices. A bank, s&L, or credit union is not a solitary actor; it exists and functions within a framework of institutions that together make it work as a depository intermediary.

In the banking framework the stockholder-owned, for-profit banking corporation is the basic economic actor, chartered by either federal or state authorities. Each of three federal regulators supervises banks and plays a distinctive role in the banking framework: the Federal Reserve Board regulates the money supply; the Office of the Comptroller of the Currency (OCC) charters national banks; and the Federal Deposit Insurance Corporation (FDIC) insures deposits through the Bank Insurance Fund. Twelve Federal Reserve Banks loan money to banks and transmit monetary policy from the Federal Reserve Board.

The regulatory framework of the savings and loan industry is losing its distinctiveness from banking, but until the 1980s it was clearly separate. Most firms in the industry were nonprofit mutual associations, though some state-chartered s&ls were stock companies. The Federal Home Loan Bank Board (FHLBB) was the original federal s&l regulator, and the Federal Savings and Loan Insurance Corporation (FSLIC) was the industry's deposit insurer. Twelve Federal Home Loan Banks were the bankers' banks in this framework, borrowing funds in the capital market to loan to their member s&ls. From the mid-1930s until the early 1950s the s&l framework also included an organization called the Home Owners' Loan Corporation, which held, at one time, one-sixth of the home mortgages in the United States.

The basic economic actor in credit unionism, the credit union, is a cooperative—an alternative kind of economic organization established not for profit but, rather, to meet specified needs of its members. The National Credit Union Association (NCUA), a government corporation, is the federal regulator. Both the NCUA and state authorities charter credit unions. Deposit insurance is provided through the National Credit Union Share Insurance Fund, which is owned jointly by insured credit unions. Corporate credit unions, cooperatively owned by member credit unions, provide business services and rediscounting to those members. The Central Liquidity Facility, organizationally a component of the NCUA, is a lender of last resort.

Advocacy for regulatory uniformity and organizational consolidation within the commercial banking framework and among the separate regulatory frameworks moved from the tomes of economic theorists to the policy briefs of government officials in the Reagan and Bush administrations and continued under President Clinton.[6] Indeed, a Nixon-appointed commission recommended this direction as early as 1971,[7] and President Carter signed the 1980 legislation that took the first steps toward uniform regulation of all depository institutions.[8] The 1989 statute that framed the resolution of the s&l crisis included further steps toward organizational consolidation—abolishing the independent Federal Home Loan Bank Board and the original s&l deposit insurer. A new s&l regulator, the Office of Thrift Supervision, was set up in the Department of the Treasury, alongside the Office of the Comptroller of the Currency, which supervises national banks. A new deposit insurance fund for s&ls was established in the Federal Deposit Insurance Corporation, previously the insurer only for banks.[9]

Policy makers' proposals in 1991 to draw the separate credit union regulator and insurance fund into the banking regulatory structure as well roused credit unions to intense—and at least temporarily successful—political action to stave off such arrangements.[10]

As the functions of the three kinds of depository institutions converge and advocacy continues for consolidating their regulation, institutional actors will disappear from the political economy—indeed, some of them, the FSLIC and FHLBB for example, already have. But before what is left of the S&L industry fades into the banking framework, before credit unionism's insurance fund becomes an accounting entity within the FDIC, or before the FDIC itself disappears as banks abandon deposit insurance as a guarantee of safety in favor of brute size, the question of why policy makers built three distinct regulatory frameworks for depository intermediation as they did, in the first place, merits a hard look. This is the central question of this study.

My argument is that a crucial part of the explanation for the development of three separate frameworks is that distinctive ideas of purpose and institutional design lie at their foundations. These distinctive ideas about institutions in the political economy are encompassed in coherent systems of ideas, in public philosophies. A regulatory framework institutionalizes a way of thinking about the public world. The banking, savings and loan, and credit union regulatory frameworks are institutional manifestations of public philosophies I call *utilitarianism*, *progressivism*, and *populism*, respectively. The current deregulatory reform effort takes its ideological strength from a resurgence of "neoliberal" public philosophy.

The mapping of public philosophies onto institutions is tidier in the preceding paragraph than it is in the political economy. The S&L framework, which I interpret as an expression of a progressive perspective, included elements of populism from the outset and took on neoliberal features toward the end. While the credit union framework is a very good example of what populist public philosophy may look like in institutional expression, progressives have always seen its purpose differently than populists and tugged at its design. With its long history the banking framework reflects successful efforts to build in values from several ideological perspectives, but on the whole it has functioned much as a utilitarian would wish since 1935.

INTERESTS AND IDEAS

To claim that differing views of purpose and design have driven the development of separate regulatory frameworks for depository intermediation is to enter into the current debate among political scientists and economists over whether "interests" or "ideas" drive economic regulation.

The dominant "economic theory of regulation" explains the initiation and development of regulatory institutions and policy in the United States in terms of the axiom at the center of mainstream economic theory: all human behavior is motivated by individual self-interest. Individuals pursue self-interest regardless of whether the arena is the market or a political forum and regardless of whether their roles are to run businesses or to make public policy as appointed or elected officials. Individuals and firms will join together to seek desired regulatory treatment when they calculate that the benefits to themselves are worth the costs to themselves. Elected officials respond because the dollars and votes of those seeking self-aggrandizing economic regulation pique their self-interest. Appointed officials are motivated by bigger budgets for their agencies, promotions, and job prospects in the regulated industry.[11]

Political scientists from across the range of the discipline's subfields will recognize this economic theory of regulation as a specific application of the more general economic approach to politics. Under the various rubrics of *public choice, rational choice,* and the *new political economy,* economic theories of politics work from individual self-interest to explain political behavior, the structure and practices of public institutions, and the content of public policy.[12]

Political scientists writing in the areas of public policy and public administration who dispute the economic theory of regulation, and economic approaches to politics more generally, argue that human motivation is complex and that interest is not enough to account for institutional design and policy outcomes. Ideas must also be taken into account.

There is variation in their concept of an *idea,* but, roughly, ideas are beliefs about what would be good public policy, that is, what would be in the public interest regardless of any particular impact on oneself and about how to design institutions to achieve that. Some theorists assume, explicitly or implicitly, that private sector actors appropriately behave in accord with the dictates of individual self-interest; what they seek to demonstrate is that public sector actors, at least some of the time, understand themselves as having a different role and behave accordingly. In this approach ideas are agency officials' beliefs about what is in the public interest, derived from their professional training as lawyers, scientists, engineers, or economists.[13] For another group of theorists the *idea* that may motivate public officials is pursuit of the public interest, understood in the particular definition offered by mainstream economics and policy analysis: the greatest possible satisfaction of individual interests. In this formulation, when public officials devise policy that achieves the maximum aggregate satisfaction of individual preferences, they are acting in behalf of the public interest.[14] In a third conception of *ideas* this understanding of the public interest as maximum satisfaction of private preferences is precisely the problem that can and should be overcome by "public ideas" of the public interest. In this view citizens as well as public officials use public forums, at least sometimes, to formulate and pursue conceptions of the public interest which are broader than one in which each individual gets as much of whatever he or she wants as possible.[15]

Theorists who argue that the explanation of regulation—and, again, public policy generally—requires attention to ideas do not claim that ideas are the whole story. Particularistic interest also figures in, as do contextual variables such as technology, structural economic change, and institutional features of the political system. Idiosyncratic as well as recurrent events may have an impact. Timing counts: temporal sorting—or, less elegantly but more vividly put, "garbage can"—models of the policy process attempt to explain how policy decisions are reached given largely independent flows of streams of ideas about what constitutes a problem, potential solutions, and political processes. In these models ideas about appropriate solutions are influential when they have been disseminated among policy elites and converge with particular "problems" in a temporal window opened by events.[16]

With others who underscore the influence of ideas on public policy, I acknowledge the influence, in varying measure in different cases, of independent events, technology, particularistic interests, and other factors. But policy makers interpret events, interests, and other factors and wield technology; understanding the regulatory structures we have requires asking how they have perceived what they were doing.

The contending empirical explanations of regulation have normative implications. Scholars who make the case that interests drive economic regulation usually conclude that regulation is badly flawed. If the scholar hails from the conservative end of the contemporary ideological spectrum, this means we should not regulate and should, instead, let the market prevail; if from the liberal end, that we should regulate differently—though liberals have been short on prescriptions, since providing careful standards in legislative delegations of authority to the bureaucracy, per Theodore Lowi's advice, has been found to entail serious difficulties of its own. Scholars who argue, on the other hand, that ideas matter—whether liberal or conservative—are typically defending the legitimacy of policy-making institutions and processes and the public policy that results. In my view the normative implication of demonstrating that ideas drive public policy process and outcomes is ambiguous. That an idea has been influential does not mean we will necessarily get good policy or effective administration. Ideas of purpose may win out which are poor ideas, judged from within some other public philosophy; design ideas may be empirically mistaken, that is, not lead to the purpose intended.

Yet to claim that public philosophies drive regulatory frameworks is not only to enter the current dispute over interests versus ideas in the literature of public policy and public administration. It is also to enter a debate that is much older. Our contemporary dispute is only one of countless outcroppings of political philosophy's ancient argument over whether human institutions are naturally arising arrangements or artificial contrivances based on human ideas that may or may not correspond well with the true nature of things. Interest-based theories, whether utilitarian, as those discussed earlier, or Marxist, which locate interests in classes rather than individuals, are theories of natural or scientific causation. Arguments for the influence of ideas take steps toward the ancient idealist position.

PUBLIC PHILOSOPHIES

By *public philosophy* I mean an ideological paradigm that provides one with a basis for interpreting the social world and taking positions regarding what government should do in that world and how it should do what it does. A public philosophy is a system of ideas encompassing certain themes, among which, without trying to be exhaustive, I would highlight three as central for purposes of this study.

First, there is a foundational position on what is natural for humanity. The processes and relationships that a public philosophy sanctions as natural are privileged: what is natural is true, often confounding the empirical and the normative. Closely allied with the specification of what is natural is an epistemology, a theory of how we know the truth and how much we can know about it. To the extent that a paradigm suspects—or claims with some certainty—that we do not or cannot know what is natural, or even whether nature has a provision for the relationships at issue, it views arrangements as artificial. Current-day political philosophers speak of institutions as "constructed" if they view them as not naturally arising, whether because they believe that the institutions are aberrations from a knowable truth (as Marx might have seen it) or because they think that nature has not provided specifications in the matter at hand (as is more characteristic of contemporary critical theorists). We may think of a tension in theory between nature and construction, resulting in a continuum of positions on the extent to which institutions are natural or constructed.

A second theme in a public philosophy, a question that a public philosophy must answer, involves identifying the subject of public policy. We may think of a continuum of positions here, too. At one extreme society or the nation, conceived of as a unity, often with corporeal metaphor, is the focus of investigation and policy prescription. A public philosophy that centers its attention instead on individual persons as self-contained moral and epistemologically capable units, on what they are and what they need, anchors the other end of the continuum. In between, a public philosophy may view various levels of organization—families and communities, groups and firms, industries, economic sectors—as important subjects of public policy attention.

From a public philosophy's foundational ideas about nature and epistemology, individuals and the community, arise convictions about multiple aspects of social life. The bases of legitimate human relationships—of authority, obligation, deference—are specified. The justification for and purposes of government are identified, leading to the third major theme that I use to shape this study: a public philosophy includes a position on the proper scope and design of the private and public domains. Again, we may think of positions falling along a continuum. At one end we would find a view that most of what people do affects other people and is therefore "public," a concern of the state. The view that virtually all human action is "private," concerning only those involved and thus calling for a narrowly circumscribed state, anchors the other end of this third thematic continuum. One aspect of the public/private relationship is a theory of political economy, that is, a theory of the relationship between the state and the economic activity of production and distribution.

A public philosophy includes both normative and empirical ideas. Normative ideas are beliefs about what constitutes the good for individuals and society, what is in the public interest; they are ideas about ends, about conditions and relationships we would like to see realized in the world. Empirical ideas are beliefs about how things and people work, about nature and science, about what causes what; they are ideas of technique and engineering, of how to design organizations and processes to achieve normative purposes.

As a source of what one would project into the social world as well as a set of lenses through which to interpret what is already there, a public philosophy motivates efforts to build new institutions, reform existing ones, or dismantle institutions that are inconsistent with its fundamental tenets. An ideology may thus be constructive or destructive or both. It may enable vision, or it may blind. Any particular assessment of whether its effects are progressive or not, in the public interest or not, legitimate or not, "good" or not, depends in part upon whether that assessment arises from within the paradigm or not.

The fundamental public philosophy in the United States is liberalism. Liberalism arose historically in a project to disentangle human beings from the medieval bonds of church and state, from the web of community and society, theoretically and politically. That is, its central project was precisely to move the focus of public philosophy from one extreme of the aggregate/individual continuum to the other. At the center of all liberal theory thus stands the human individual—ontologically prior to society, independent of and equal to others, the knower of what can be known and the measure of all value.

With such an individual as the foundation, John Locke formulated the classic liberal public philosophy with which Americans are so familiar, whether or not they can name John Locke. He reconceptualized nature as a state in which humanity lives as individuals, rather than as functional parts of a social organism. Knowing became a capacity of each individual, and the truth became accessible to each, not just the select few. Given independent persons, legitimate social interaction and institutions—whether marriage, economic transactions, or government—would be based on their consent. Most human action was regarded as private; the public realm was very small. Indeed, government would be unnecessary if not for the unfortunate misconduct of some few individuals who transgress nature's (knowable) laws. Government's role is limited to protecting individuals' rights and preserving the conditions of contract. There is a bold, clear boundary between the limited public realm and the expansive private realm of society and economy. Writing almost a century after Locke, Adam Smith maintained fundamental Lockean tenets while shifting economic provisioning from the manor to the market. As individuals pursued their own interests in the market, national productivity would be optimized automatically—as if by an "invisible hand."[17]

Yet to agree with Louis Hartz that in the United States liberalism is fundamental of institutions and dominant in policy debate is not to claim that it faces no challenges.[18] Liberalism contends with challenges to its central premise of autonomous persons arising both from communitarian public philosophies and from events and circumstances. In so doing, liberalism wriggles and shifts, accommodating, finessing, co-opting normative and empirical ideas. It rearranges the emphases in its philosophic system. Thus, variants in the liberal family arise which propose large public spheres or reject the presumption of naturalness for some of the associational "contracts" that arise in the private realm or hedge on the self-evidentness of truth. Distinguishable public philosophies take shape and diverge from classic liberalism in ways that motivate advocacy of different roles for government and distinctive institutional features.

The development of the corporation as an entity acting in the political economy is among the most significant challenges with which liberalism in the United States has been obliged to contend. Classic liberalism builds society and economy on individuals, not associated entities. Locke wrote to delegitimize the powerful associations of the seventeenth century, state and church. In the eighteenth century the corporation as an entity rising for economic purposes was precisely what Adam Smith targeted for elimination. Confronted with the corporation—as an idea and as a material circumstance—liberalism in the United States diverged.

Early classic liberals in the United States, Jefferson and Jackson so prominent among them, tried to beat back the rise of the corporation. With Adam Smith they believed that natural law included economic law. And economic law indicated that transactions among free, equal, and self-interested individuals would yield the greatest good. In their view the corporation was unnatural. It was a creature of the state, and it effectively benefited particular private interests, at the expense of other private interests and the public good. It violated liberalism's public/private boundary. It did not belong in the political economy. They believed that, if governments would stay out of the economy and let natural law operate, everything would turn out for the best.

Over two hundred years classic liberal public philosophy in the United States has come to terms with corporate entities by moving them from their illegitimate perch on the public/private boundary well into the private sphere. Corporations are regarded as arising naturally in the private sphere as the result of legitimate contracts between and among individuals, not as the construct of governments. In the law and public policy corporate entities have come to be viewed as persons, vested with much the same rights and permitted to inhabit the market along with them. Despite this adjustment, current-day liberal theorists such as Milton Friedman and Robert Nozick consider their public philosophy as continuous with that of Jefferson and Jackson and retain the rest of classic liberalism's major emphases. They insist on the primacy of the private sphere, on a tiny public sphere, and a bold clear line between them. They teach that for the most part, if the state stays out of the economy, economic law will operate to yield the best results for individuals and on the whole.[19] *Neoliberalism* is the label I assign to this public philosophy that gives much the same status to corporations which classic liberalism gives to persons while maintaining the rest of the Lockean system. It is a term widely in use today; in the past *laissez faire* was widely used.

Yet liberalism carved out other paths as well. Populists refused to reconcile the corporation to the liberal paradigm. Corporate organizations controlled the allocation of resources which individuals needed to live at a basic level in the political economy as it was unfolding— they had power. To treat such an entity as a person, in their view, profoundly disadvantaged flesh-and-blood individuals. Arising after the Civil War, populism rejected the view of laissez-faire enthusiasts that the institutions of the political economy—banks, railroads, and then industrial corporations—arose naturally in favor of the view that they were artificial constructs; populists concluded, therefore, that the public may as well do the construction. Populism expanded the role of the public sphere dramatically to include regulation or proscription of relationships arising privately which would create private power as well as outright public ownership of crucial enterprises in which technology required a large scale. To retain liberalism's central focus on the individual, populism thus made major concessions along other theoretical dimensions.

Progressivism in the United States arose in the wake of populism—like populism, to respond to corporations, but to respond differently. Progressives did not hold with the populist view that the corporation should be erased from the political economy. But neither did they believe that they could finesse its presence by viewing it as a person, as neoliberals did. Progressivism was willing to permit associated entities in the political economy but admitted a power differential between corporations and individuals and inquired into terms that would legitimate the action of organizations in relationships with individual human beings. In doing so, progressive theorists and policy makers reconceptualized nature and blurred the public/private boundary.

Progressivism moved back in the direction of the preliberal philosophical view of humanity as naturally associated but with differences. Ancient and medieval political philosophers had seen all human relationship arranged hierarchically, each smaller category of association subsumed in the next higher, the whole governed from the top down by the same principles, which were knowable by the few. Progressive theorists also saw society as a whole—sometimes machine and sometimes body—but the ancient unified hierarchy was gone. Progressivism saw distinct realms of associated human action, and, while the public had an interest in all organized action, that interest—and thus the government's role—varied from realm to realm. One had to inquire into the distinctive purpose of a particular economic sector or social sphere in order to identify its optimal organization, its particular principles of governance.

As progressivism's view of humanity's natural condition shifted from the individual to the associated, so also did its epistemology. Knowing was no longer the province of an individual mind but the result of a social process. And progressivism's truth was not classic liberalism's certainty but provisional, experimental.[20]

In thought utilitarianism diverged from classic liberalism even as the United States was making a nation of itself. Jeremy Bentham, the father of utilitarian public philosophy, was roughly Adam Smith's contemporary. With the classic liberals Bentham centered the human individual as the source and judge of value. His essential departure from the classic liberal paradigm was in his answer to the question: What is the justification for state action? Whereas classic liberals answered "consent" and ended up with a minimal state, Bentham answered "utility" and opened a door for a positive state in a liberal world. *Utility* meant happiness, the good for oneself. Individuals legitimately defined and pursued their own utility, and the general welfare of society was nothing but the sum of individuals' utility. But in Bentham's view Adam Smith was quite mistaken in the belief that an invisible hand could be relied upon to work things out for the best, on the whole. Individuals' pursuit of their self-interest might have perverse consequences; thus, positive government intervention in society was justified. Government could manipulate sanctions, structuring arrangements so that individuals' pursuit of their self-interest would propel them along a path leading to their own, and thus society's, maximum utility.[21]

Bentham's thought was known in the United States, certainly by the time of Jackson, when his view that each man was a competent judge of his own good helped justify expansion of voting rights.[22] But utilitarian public philosophy became a significant influence on economic policy only in the 1930s, when welfare economists devised solutions to conceptual problems Bentham had encountered in trying to calculate utility scientifically. Formalized as welfare economics and as policy analysis, utilitarian public philosophy remains a powerful ideological influence on public policy. It shares much with neoliberalism, for with neoliberals utilitarianism has finessed populist and progressive concerns about corporate actors, treating households and firms as inhabitants together of the private sphere in calculating aggregate utility. But utilitarianism diverges from neoliberalism in doubting the invisible hand and legitimizing government manipulation of the incentives of individuals and firms where private action will not yield maximum aggregate utility.

PUBLIC PHILOSOPHIES AND REGULATORY FRAMEWORKS

What has played out in thought has played out in institutional development. In the chapters that follow I develop a narrative linking regulatory frameworks to public philosophies—institutions to ideas that undergird them—in the public policy domain of banking since the earliest days of the Republic. The narrative focuses on the organizations that make up the regulatory frameworks, on their origins and significant changes. Regarding each of these institutions I ask: What did its advocates conceive as its purpose? Given that purpose, what design did they propose to achieve it? To answer these questions, I focused on the debates over the key pieces of legislation that established or changed the organizations in the regulatory frameworks. Congress was the major forum for such debate, and I have relied on congressional floor debate, committee testimony, accounts of caucus argument, reports prepared for Congress by its own committees and others, and resulting statutes and charters. Administration officials presented much of the testimony and prepared many of the reports. Sometimes the voices in the congressional forum are those of academics, businesspeople, or other members of the public. I turn to state legislatures as well, in order to understand state banks in particular. And, stepping back from the money and banking debates, I have also looked for policy advocates' reasons for their positions, and the search for reasons leads to inquiry into contemporary public philosophies that were in play in the development of these organizations.

Chapters two through five unfold the development of the banking framework from the first Congress through the Depression. Treatment of the banking framework takes up a disproportionate share of the story because, unlike s&Ls and credit unionism, commercial banking has been with us since the beginning of the Republic. It remains dominant institutionally by far, and, philosophically, it has been a field for play of contending public philosophies from the beginning. The implications of the current moment in American public policy history, a moment in which this framework is being deregulated and the others merged into it, become clear only in the context of an understanding of why it was built as it was. I consider the institutions that have gone by the wayside: the first and second Banks of the United States, the Independent Treasury, the pre–Civil War hybrid public/private state banks; as well as the institutions that remain with us today: the private corporate bank, the Office of the Comptroller of the Currency, the Federal Reserve Banks and the Federal Reserve Board, the Federal Deposit Insurance Corporation.

Chapter two begins with the first Bank of the United States. Alexander Hamilton's brainchild was intended as a bank and became a regulator of other banks as well. Ideologically, the debate over its authorizing legislation was one episode in the epic conflict between Hamilton and Thomas Jefferson over liberalism itself. Should the individual or the nation be at the center of ideological and political attention? Hamilton's public philosophy focused on the nation, which he conceived very much in economic terms, as an integrated national economy. His Bank of the United States was a crucial tool for constructing that

unity. It was Jefferson, on the other hand, who had so clearly articulated fundamental Lockean premises in the Declaration of Independence. He envisioned a society of self-sufficient farmers and had no use
for Hamilton's economic interdependence. Moreover, Jefferson objected
not only to the purpose but to the corporate form of Hamilton's institution: in his view any corporation was a threat to individual freedom
and equality. Jefferson lost the first round as Congress chartered the
Bank of the United States in 1791. Twenty years later, however, the
institution died when legislation to renew its charter failed, leaving a
banking framework composed of some ninety state-chartered banks,
with no central government presence.

Hamilton's Bank of the United States did not fit neatly on either
side of the Lockean line between the public and private spheres, nor
did other important institutions in the history of U.S. money and banking policy. Chapters three and four highlight the theme of the relationship between the public and private spheres in explaining the rise and
subsequent disappearance of significant institutional actors.

Chapter three inquires into the rise and fall of the second Bank of
the United States and establishment of the Independent Treasury, revising the story of Andrew Jackson's bank war. Long before the Interstate Commerce Commission, the United States' second national Bank
was the first organization established by Congress as an economic regulator. Long before the Federal Reserve Board, the second Bank of the
United States was a central bank. To be sure, the first national bank
had evolved regulatory functions in practice, but Congress *intended*
the second bank as a regulator. Andrew Jackson's battle against this
institution is usually interpreted as a continuation of Jefferson's struggle
against Hamilton's bank, but this argument overlooks the fact that legislation chartering the second Bank of the United States was not a Federalist measure. It was a measure of Jefferson's Republican Party, supported by James Madison's administration and passed by a Republican
Congress. The Jeffersonian Republicans adjusted Hamilton's design in
their new national bank, explicitly constructing an agent for monetary
policy and banking regulation. Such a regulator could have been interpreted as supportive of the freedom and equality of ordinary individuals, but no paradigm adjustment was offered to help Republican policy
makers justify their action in liberal ideological terms. As a classic
liberal, Jackson fought the second bank because both its regulatory
purpose and its hybrid public/private design violated his idea of the
proper public/private relationship. The Independent Treasury rose in

its stead to handle the government's money without confounding the public's monetary affairs with private business and banking.

Chapter four examines the development of the corporate bank, the basic actor in the banking framework. In early U.S. history a corporation was regarded as a creature of the state, established for a particular public purpose. From the Revolution until the Civil War state legislatures chartered banks for a range of public purposes and with a variety of public/private hybrid designs. This approach was vulnerable to the same ideological assault—as a violation of the Lockean line between the public and private spheres—that Jackson had deployed against the second Bank of the United States. Jackson himself insisted that all banking was private activity and that state governments, as well as the federal government, should not be associated with it. Under this ideological pressure state legislatures gradually developed a model of a bank that could be justified as a private entity. It was this model that was nationalized in the National Bank Act of 1864. Banks came to be viewed as private actors in the political economy.

The National Bank Act also established the Office of the Comptroller of the Currency to handle what was left of the public's interest in the banking framework: chartering and examination of national banks. The OCC is a line department of the Treasury and thus does not violate the public/private divide, as had the first and second Banks of the United States. With the National Bank Act's tidy placement of what is private on one side of the Lockean line and what is public on the other, the banking framework institutionalized neoliberal public philosophy. It stood largely unaltered for fifty years.

Chapter five follows the congressional money and banking debates from the end of the Civil War through passage of the Banking Act of 1935, adding the institutional actors that complete today's banking framework: the Federal Reserve Banks, the Federal Reserve Board, and the Federal Deposit Insurance Corporation. The philosophical theme of nature versus construction was at the center of these debates. Appeals were made repeatedly to nature to justify conceptions of money, the role of banks, and economic arrangements generally. But first populist and then progressive analyses arose to question neoliberalism's invisible hand. Were existing arrangements "natural" or "scientific"? Could they be reformed to be scientific? Or was all money inherently a political construct?

Reinterpreted as a progressive effort to prop up economic law and a "scientific" currency in the face of calls to institutionalize discretion—

by populists on the one hand, who wanted that discretion in the government, and by bankers on the other, who wanted that discretion for themselves—the Federal Reserve Act of 1913 takes on fresh meaning. The categories conventionally applied to debate over this legislation—public versus private, centralized versus decentralized—fall into secondary roles. The original Federal Reserve Act institutionalized the approach of the progressives of the day, though it contained anemic gestures toward populism in its configuration of the Federal Reserve Board and government guarantee of the currency. A more robust populist chord was interjected into the banking framework when the FDIC was established in 1934.

The Banking Act of 1935 incorporates a significant philosophical shift and resulted in a fundamentally different Federal Reserve system. The progressives' Fed was overturned in favor of a utilitarian Fed through transformation of the Federal Reserve Board. The board had been demanded by populists but rendered an ambiguous appendage by progressives in the original arrangement. With the changes to its powers in 1935, the board became the control center of the Federal Reserve system, enabled to manipulate the incentives of banks and others in pursuit of maximizing the economy's performance, and the reserve banks became its conduits for policy.

Ideologically, then, as manifested in the banking framework, the struggle over liberalism itself gave way to a neoliberal paradigm, a brief progressive reign under the original Federal Reserve Act, and, ultimately, with the major changes in the Depression-era Banking Act of 1935, the institutionalization of utilitarian public philosophy.

It was also during the Depression that Congress dealt for the first time with savings and loan associations and credit unionism, the subjects of chapters six and seven. The savings and loan framework institutionalized a progressive public philosophy. In contrast to neoliberalism or utilitarian liberalism, progressivism views the public interest in substantive terms and posits that social and economic spheres require arrangements tailored to their particular substantive purposes. The savings and loan framework was built to serve the particular public purpose of home ownership. The basic actor in the framework, the savings and loan association, had developed in the states beginning in the 1830s. The national institutions of the framework were authorized by three statutes during the Depression, the first initiated by Herbert Hoover and passed by the Seventy-second Congress, the latter two originating in FDR's first administration and passed by the Seventy-third Congress.

This framework has largely collapsed, at great cost to the entire society, as efforts to reform it failed to take its distinctive purpose and institutional development adequately into account.

Historians have treated populism with a tragic feel. Michael Kazin interprets it as a language of political persuasion, crucial in understanding a continuing current in political opinion and behavior but "more impulse than ideology"—implicitly, not fleshed out enough to provide distinctive institutional blueprints. If Kazin is correct that this language, "whose speakers conceive of ordinary people as a noble assemblage," is given to deterioration into dialects that exclude great groups from the meeting, it would be just as well were it to lack institutional implications.[23] But Lawrence Goodwyn recognized functioning institutions constructed in terms of an inclusive populist paradigm, though only for a historical moment.[24] Credit unionism represents an example of institutions based in principles we may recognize as inclusive populist public philosophy, emphasizing economic democracy, fully developed and operating in the political economy alongside more mainstream liberal institutions.

And so there were three regulatory frameworks for depository intermediation—largely solidified in the aftermath of the Great Depression—rooted in distinctive, recognizable public philosophies. So what? Is this analysis of strictly philosophical and historical interest? Or does it have implications for the current policy debate?

In chapter eight I return to the current moment in U.S. public policy, a point at which the three regulatory frameworks are collapsing into one and that one is being substantially deregulated. It will be no surprise to see that the arguments undergirding the convergence of the three frameworks and deregulation of the economic actors that remain flow from the resurgent neoliberal public philosophy that has been reshaping the U.S. political economy.

Neoliberalism, with its simple dichotomous categories of public and private, the natural as self-evident versus the contrived, and its equally simple public policy prescriptions—loose individuals and firms to pursue their interest, minimize government involvement, and let nature's invisible hand work everything out for the best—is a powerful public philosophy. The complex institutional infrastructure of depository intermediation, built in the wake of the Depression, is collapsing before its simple logic.

Yet neoliberalism has no concept of private power, noticing no difference as units of analysis between a retired paper mill worker, living on his pension in Appleton, Wisconsin, and the Citigroup bank holding company, operating globally with seven hundred billion dollars in assets. It does not concern itself with intrinsic purpose, thus recognizes no fundamental distinction between banking, which creates and allocates money, and the fast food industry, which prepares and sells hamburgers. Nor has neoliberalism's invisible hand ever been stayed by the weight of a top heavy distribution of wealth. Yet this paradigm has framed public discourse regarding U.S. economic policy so tightly in recent years that we find it difficult to object to its prescriptions, or argue, or to conceive alternatives. Were the separate frameworks for depository intermediation really all doing the same thing? Or does it only look that way because we have just one set of conceptual lenses through which to view them?

This is why it is so important at this particular moment, and in relation to this problem, to recover other ways of thinking about the political economy and to recall the *method* of policy analysis employed here. Within public policy and public administration, fields committed to educating those who will engage practically in public affairs, for all our new sophistication we seem to be losing our understanding of what it is like to think otherwise. In articulating and grasping alternative public philosophies, we not only enable ourselves to understand the institutional moves that they drove historically; we also provide ourselves with conceptual apparatus with which to frame ongoing policy analysis and institutional design.

Money—how much of it there is, how it is allocated—is fundamental to our economy and society. It is not all of what we are about, but it affects most of what we are about in smaller or larger measure. Money arises in a complex decision process. We have built the pathways of that process over the years in ongoing political deliberation, to pursue and protect certain values. Despite the apparent finality of recent reforms, that deliberation will continue. Let us recover where we have been as an aid in mapping where we should go.

2

THE FIRST BANK OF THE UNITED STATES

FROM MANY ONE?

Alexander Hamilton spent the "greatest part" of a frosty Philadelphia night, over two hundred years ago, writing intensely.[1] A week earlier President Washington had sent Hamilton, his secretary of the Treasury, a note asking for an opinion, enclosing those already given him by Secretary of State Thomas Jefferson and Attorney General Edmund Randolph. At issue was the constitutionality of legislation incorporating a Bank of the United States, which lay before the president awaiting signature or veto.[2] Jefferson, with Randolph following his lead, argued vigorously that the act was not within the power given Congress by the new Constitution.[3] In this he sided with James Madison, who had led the unsuccessful opposition to the bill in the House.[4] Hamilton did not agree with his colleagues in the cabinet, nor with Madison, who had so recently been his most important ally in the struggle for ratification of that same Constitution. Indeed, Hamilton was author of this legislation to which the others objected. In his vision the bank was critical as a foundation for the economy of the new United States. Thus, he had spent the preceding week and that long night marshaling the full force of his stunning, if sometimes contemptuous, power of analysis in defense of its constitutionality. Hamilton dispatched his letter to the president, presumably returning with it, per the president's direction, those of Jefferson and Randolph (no copies taken). Two days later, on February 25, 1791, George Washington signed the law establishing the first Bank of the United States.[5]

The controversy between Hamilton and Jefferson over the Bank of the United States was only one episode in their epic ideological and political contest. That contest is an old story, to be sure. Perhaps its broadest lesson is my central claim—that systematic public philosophies give shape to their adherents' policy positions. That the case must be made for this hypothesis against prevailing theory perhaps provides justification enough for revisiting the antagonists' public philosophies and asking how their ideas about what would be good public policy influenced institutional design. But, as further justification, the emphasis here is not on the influence of public philosophy with regard to the fundamental political institutions of the United States, as has usually been the case in probing the Hamilton/Jefferson dialectic, but, rather, on the political economic institutions of banking. Moreover, the Bank of the United States episode is a device for drawing out particular ideas and institutional design options to which I will return in unfolding the development of money and banking institutions throughout U.S. history.

What was Hamilton's purpose in proposing a national bank? Via what design details did he expect to ensure that it would achieve that purpose? How did his proposal reflect his public philosophy? Jefferson reacted viscerally against the project—indeed, against all banking. How does his position regarding this particular institution reflect his larger ideology?

CONFLICTING PUBLIC PHILOSOPHIES

Grounded in very different public philosophies, Hamilton and Jefferson held different visions of what the political economy ought to look like. A fundamental disagreement was with regard to just what the central concern of public policy should be: the nation or the individual. Other differences, regarding such issues as the limits of the public sphere and the role of government in constructing the economy, revolved around this fundamental difference.

Alexander Hamilton thought in terms of a unified system.[6] His focus was on building a powerful nation, which he envisioned as a diverse, interdependent economy that would take a place in the world among the "enlightened commercial nations." A strong central government was crucial in this picture, not as an end in itself but as a means to the end of the nation. Hamilton intended this government would protect the nation in the international arena as well as aggressively structure and manage the domestic economy. He advanced detailed proposals for economic interventions designed for particular sectors and attempted to steer the monetary aggregate publicly. With his focus on building the nation, Hamilton would not respect any sharp divide between public and private spheres but actively use the government for economic development.

To do all that Hamilton expected of it, the central government required "energy," which we may understand as a combination of initiative, expertise, decisiveness, and authority. These emphases pointed to a strong executive branch. Hamilton knew that within the particular political culture of the United States legitimacy flowed from the people and thus depended upon authorization by a representative legislature. Nevertheless, he viewed congressional authorization of the executive at a very high level of generality, leaving maximum space for executive expertise in policy design.

Regarding human psychology, Hamilton agreed with David Hume that "every man ought to be supposed a knave" with "no other end in his actions but private interest."[7] Although he regarded this self-serving with approval, as each man's duty, Hamilton was no adherent to Adam Smith's notion that an invisible hand would automatically transform it into the public good. Such transformation could occur but only through the mediation of government and economic institutions designed with the good of the whole, which was distinct from the sum of private goods, as the *intended* outcome. The best institutional arrangements would not arise naturally or automatically, then, but required deliberate construction through public policy.

There is a twist to Hamilton's understanding of self-interest which is crucial to his theory of institutional design. Society was divided into the "few and the many," the few comprising the aristocracy of wealth, the many being the rest. The self-interest of members of the two groups was distinct. In designing institutions to yield the public interest, the self-interest of the few was to be courted and channeled. With regard to the self-interested striving of the rest, institutional design was needed not to capitalize on it but, rather, to dilute its impact.

Yet if the few as well as the many are motivated by self-interest, while the public good is qualitatively distinct from any private good or the sum of the private goods, who is it that sees the nation's interest and can create the institutional design required to achieve it? Fortunately for one interested in implementing Hamilton's vision from within his ideological paradigm, there was an inconsistency in his notion of human nature. Based on his experience in the Revolution and the Founding, he believed that there was a handful of people whose motivational structure was different from that of the vast majority. These moral supermen sought the public good and acted in terms of their understanding of it. Hamilton implicitly numbered himself among them and, explicitly, George Washington, whom he respected more than any other as military, civil, and moral leader.

At the center of Thomas Jefferson's public philosophy was not a powerful integrated nation but, rather, the individual person.[8] While Jefferson remains perhaps the world's best-known herald of the liberal idea that all men are equal and have inherent, inalienable rights,[9] there are two qualifications in his thought regarding equality and individual rights. First, these goods are not ultimate ends but are, instead, crucial means to the greatest good, which is individual human virtue. Second, Jefferson was keenly attuned to the contingency of human flourishing. The realization of equality in thought and practice, the effective exercise of rights, and the expression of adult intellect and morality depended on one's experiences in both micro- and macrosocial settings as well as on education. His vision of the political economy that would best accommodate individual freedom and equality was of an agricultural society peopled by freeholding farmers.

Jefferson did not fail to notice empirically, with Hamilton, that societies were divided into the "few and the many." But, whereas Hamilton saw the aristocracy of wealth as the manifestation of the superior capability and industry of the few, Jefferson saw them as an undeserving minority, privileged by unnatural social and economic arrangements. A strong central government could easily be bent to the purposes of this minority in constructing the arrangements through which it "saddled" and "rode upon" the majority, creating inequality and economic dependence, thereby stifling the emergence of virtue. Thus, for Jefferson the central government was to be watched suspiciously and kept on a very short leash, its legitimate scope confined largely to foreign affairs.

Also with Hamilton, Jefferson believed that, although self-interest was the dominant human motivation, there was a public interest, and it could be achieved through well-designed institutions. But, whereas Hamilton thought the self-interest of the few the basis for a distinctive aggregate national interest, Jefferson saw the public interest as nothing more than the common interest of ordinary people. This they would discover in participatory processes. Thus, Jefferson rejected the machine-like emphasis in Hamilton's institutional design. Rather, institutions must be designed not only to yield some outcome but also as social processes within which individuals would learn. Moreover, Jefferson believed that individuals should not be subject to the influences of any institution—political, social, or economic—in which they did not some-how participate. These views led Jefferson to emphasize legislative rather than executive processes, local government, and the stripping away of social and economic institutions not subject to the control of all affected.

HAMILTON'S BANK

Hamilton presented his blueprint for a Bank of the United States in a report delivered to the House of Representatives just before Christmas in 1790.[10] The bank he proposed would provide crucial infrastructure for development of the integrated national economy that was the focus of his public philosophy. The central purpose of the bank, as Hamilton projected it, was to augment the availability of capital—to create capital really—in support of economic development. The bank would also aid in administration of the central government, but Hamilton's emphasis in recommending the institution was on economic development. To be sure, when forced to defend the constitutionality of the proposed bank to Washington, Hamilton focused on its aids to government administration. Those that could be constitutionally justified included assistance in the collection of taxes, regulation of interstate trade by providing a medium of payment, and loans in anticipation of tax receipts for general and military purposes. But this focus was a tactical necessity. The weight of the report he had initially sent to the House made it clear that the central purpose of the bank was in constructing the economy.

The problem Hamilton perceived, and was trying to solve, was the inadequacy of the money supply. If his vision were to be realized, economic actors in the new United States needed credit and a medium of exchange which was reliable throughout the nation. But, according to Hamilton, "circumstances and appearances" demonstrated that there was not enough of such stuff in the United States to support development needs.

How, then, he asked, will we supply the money necessary for economic development?[11] He argued that commercial banks were the appropriate institutional device for this purpose. Two hundred years later it is difficult to grasp that Hamilton's question, What shall we regard as money? was in fact open. In a testament to his victory we learn in basic economics classes that the primary concept of money (M1) is checkable bank deposits plus cash and that the money supply is expanded through the banking system.[12] Since economics is usually held to be science, an arduous mental journey—swimming around, climbing over, elbowing through, formidable mental structures—is required before one realizes that money is a social and political construct, that it could be different, and that it is legitimate to ask what it is or should be. Indeed, this question had been the subject of extensive debate and experimentation in England's North American colonies for a century and a half before the Revolution and would remain a central political controversy in the United States for an equally long period afterward.

What to use as money had been a crucial issue throughout the colonial period because there was not enough gold and silver, the common currency of the world, in North America to facilitate domestic economic activity. Adopting the convention of native people, the first generation of European settlers used shells (wampum) for everyday transactions. The Virginians developed a system based on tobacco in which, initially, the commodity itself passed from hand to hand in payment. Later the legislature created public warehouses in which tobacco was weighed, graded, and held; tobacco certificates then circulated, instead. Other commodities served on a more limited basis in other states.[13] Much later, populist proposals for commodity-backed currency would be met with more contempt than they deserved against such precedent, derided as "corn tassel currency" by progressive policy makers.

Yet commodity money was not the alternative to banks which Hamilton felt a need to discredit. By the time he proposed a national bank, the use of most commodities had withered due to their inconveniences. Workable tobacco-based systems in Virginia and South Carolina had been terminated by two prohibitions in the new Constitution: that on states declaring anything but gold and silver legal tender; and that on states issuing bills of credit. Nor was Hamilton concerned with discrediting the use of gold and silver (specie), "the money of the world"; he simply wanted to supplement it. The approach for creating credit and a circulating medium which Hamilton wished definitively to preempt was paper money issued by the government.

The colonies had a long history with government-issued paper money by the time of the Revolution. This experience was uniquely American. European countries already relied on banks to meet private as well as government needs for capital, but banking was largely unavailable to the colonists for two major reasons. First, the large accumulations of private wealth which formed the basis for private banking in Europe did not exist in the colonies: there were no family fortunes built up over the centuries. Second, in 1741 Parliament had prohibited colonial legislatures from setting up corporations for any purpose, including banking, which was probably a specific target of this general ban on incorporation. A third obstacle to banking, found in Virginia, was the colonial legislature's prohibition on the issue of private paper intended as a circulating medium.

So, gold and silver were in short supply, and there were no banks, but a current medium was needed, nevertheless, to pay the expenses of the colonial governments as well as to support economic exchange within even rudimentary colonial economies. The legislature of Massachusetts was the first to issue paper money, in 1690, to pay the soldiers of an unsuccessful expedition against the fortress of Quebec. The money took the form of "bills"—that is, promises to pay—eventually, in specie. These bills were given by the government to the soldiers as payment for services and were made legal tender for taxes. They continued to pass from hand to hand in general circulation. Other colonies likewise issued paper money, both to pay government's expenses and to support trade. Like the first Massachusetts issue, such paper usually promised hard money (gold or silver) eventually in anticipation of tax receipts, sometimes with a small amount of interest. Another sort of government paper money entered circulation as loans to farmers and businesspeople; this paper was issued by colonial land offices, based on land security.

The challenge recognized by colonial policy makers, as by money supply managers today, was how to keep enough money in the economy to support a comfortable level of economic activity, walking the line between deflation and inflation. Clear evidence that this question was recognized in these terms is provided by debates in the legislatures and newspapers of several colonies, including Rhode Island, Virginia, and Pennsylvania—where Benjamin Franklin was the most prominent advocate of the beneficial economic effects of paper money. Experience in the various colonies was diverse. Sometimes paper money issues did prove inflationary. But often the opposite was true: paper held its value, facilitated everyday economic exchange and economic development, and was ultimately redeemed and withdrawn.[14]

During the Revolution the Continental Congress had issued paper money to cover the expenses of the war. This paper entered circulation in payment to soldiers, farmers, and other suppliers of the army (as would Civil War–era greenbacks). Initially, the money—for which redemption in specie was promised at an unspecified date—held its value reasonably well. As the war dragged on, more and more paper money was issued; the relation of the aggregate of currency in circulation to the productive capacity of the economy was not an important decision criterion in sizing these issues. Desperate political leaders were just trying to keep soldiers and garner supplies. Price inflation in terms of the "continentals" was astronomical, and they became essentially worthless.[15]

Hamilton took advantage of the freshness of this experience to discredit government's ability to exercise the restraint required to avoid inflation. Although he doffed his cap in Franklin's direction, acknowledging that government-issued paper money could work beneficially in "times of tranquility," he felt that "in great and trying emergencies there is almost a moral certainty of its becoming mischievous. The stamping of paper is an operation so much easier than the laying of taxes, that a government in the practice of paper emissions would rarely fail, in any such emergency, to indulge itself too far." Therefore, his bottom line was that "the emitting of paper money by the authority of the government is wisely prohibited to the individual States by the National Constitution; and the spirit of that prohibition ought not to be disregarded by the Government of the United States."[16]

So, more money was needed in the economy, but government should not issue it. Rather, Hamilton urged establishment of a national bank as the appropriate organizational device for this purpose. His report to the House starts with a lengthy defense of banks in general, highlighting their advantages, dismissing perceived disadvantages as temporary or not inherent, and explaining the mechanism by which they augment capital. For my story, too, a brief detour into banking history and the mechanism by which banks increase the money supply is useful here.

Banks arose in Europe in association with private commercial activity. In explaining the origins of banking, economists today often direct our attention to goldsmiths.[17] Gold and silver provided the medium of exchange in commercial transactions, but transporting necessary quantities of the cumbersome metal was difficult as well as dangerous, exposing the money to theft. Since goldsmiths maintained security arrangements for precious metals in connection with their craft, the practice of depositing specie with them for safekeeping developed. In payment to others, merchants offered goldsmiths' warehouse receipts, which could be redeemed for specie. It is a small step to the realization that the warehoused specie could be loaned to persons other than the depositor, at interest.

Goldsmiths were not the only sort of private banking available in Europe by the late eighteenth century, when Hamilton proposed his national bank. In addition to family-held banking houses, there were banking associations formed by groups of merchants. Participants pooled their specie, expecting to be lenders when their funds were idle, thereby earning some interest, and borrowers when they needed capital for a venture. Hamilton observed approvingly that such banks take "dead stock"—gold and silver employed merely as instruments of exchange—and give it life. By increasing the circulation (*velocity*, in current terminology) of money, he said, banks speed up economic activity. Commercial bank loans were for short terms, thirty to sixty days, and secured by goods in trade. The usual mechanism for such lending was the "bill of exchange," a piece of paper issued to the borrower, representing money that could be collected from the bank. Often these bills circulated like currency among the trading class.

Although they had thus originated in connection with private commercial activity, by the late eighteenth century banks existed to serve government purposes as well. Publicly chartered banks engaged in some combination of regulation, lending to governments, and lending for private economic endeavors.

The first of the great public banks was chartered by the municipal government of the commercial center of Amsterdam in 1609. Its purpose was to regulate the quality of the money supply, thereby facilitating trade. The use of gold and silver as money entailed problems for traders beyond those with transportation and security, already mentioned. Bullion had to be weighed and evaluated for purity ("assayed"). The expedient of coining the metal had developed in countries throughout Europe to address this need, but minting was largely a private operation and subject to corruption. Coins could be diminished in various ways after leaving the mint as well or else counterfeited. Further, there were so many different coins circulating in Europe that, even if they were not corrupted, determining their worth was problematic. The Bank of Amsterdam was chartered by the city to address such problems with the quality of the money. Traders took hundreds of different kinds of coins, in their variously corrupted conditions, to the bank. There the coins were weighed and valued according to the standard Dutch money. Depositors of coin received a credit on the bank's books. Deposit credit could be transferred in payment of one's debts, or a depositor or his creditor could come in and get the gold. Similar banks were established in other cities.[18]

The Bank of Amsterdam initially simply held specie and transferred it on its books among depositors or paid it out to their creditors. Banks that limited their activity in this way were called *banks of deposit*, and they did not create money. The Bank of Amsterdam was strictly a bank of deposit for a century. But, like the goldsmiths, its directors realized that they could loan out the specie that had been deposited in the bank, thus creating money for the borrower, while the same amount still stood to the account of the original depositor. The bank began lending to both the City of Amsterdam and the Dutch East India Company. Banks that did not restrict their activity to holding depositors' money and transferring it about on their books but, rather, loaned it out, thereby expanding the money supply, were called *banks of issue* or *banks of credit*. The latter, of course, is what U.S. banks do today.

Unlike the Bank of Amsterdam, the original purpose in chartering the Bank of England in 1694 was not to regulate money but, rather, to meet the needs of the king for cash. An organizational device that could augment capital for commerce and industry could surely create money for government as well. The Bank of England's charter authorized an initial subscription of 1.2 million pounds sterling. Investors paid specie for shares of this bank stock. The bank loaned all of the specie to the government. In return the government gave the bank its promise to pay, with interest. The bank had no specie on hand then but owned the government's obligation, which became the security for a note issue equal to the amount of the original subscription. These bank notes entered circulation as they were loaned out for private economic purposes. With the loan to the government and the private loans there would be twice as much money in the economy as there would have been if there were no bank.

The Bank of England gradually developed means to regulate private commercial banks and thereby the English money supply. Excessive note issue by private banks, in hopes that the notes would never return for redemption, had been largely curtailed by about 1770. This was a result of greater confidence in Bank of England notes than in country bank notes: people would circulate the notes of the Bank of England but redeem those of other banks. Private banks learned to make their loans via deposit credit, which was less subject to overextension. From the 1820s through 1840s the Bank of England would develop means for regulating lending via deposit credit as well. It learned three techniques that appeared in the arsenal of the U.S. Federal Reserve Board a century later: to signal other banks to contract or expand their lending by raising and lowering the rate it charged them for reserves; to tighten up the money supply by selling government securities (and, in the case of the Bank of England, contracting its own commercial lending); and to act as a lender of last resort for commercial banks under pressure. The Bank of England was thus a publicly constructed institutional device serving both public and private purposes: it loaned money to the government and otherwise administered public financial transactions, provided private loans, and regulated the money supply.[19]

Keeping in mind how banks thus worked to create money and capital, let us return to Hamilton's report to analyze his design for the Bank of the United States. We might think of effective achievement of the purpose of an organization as a dependent variable, and the organization's design as a set of hypotheses about how to achieve that purpose. What one conceives of as the public good, or public interest, and hence as a worthy purpose, is based in one's public philosophy. Hamilton's purpose for the bank—provision of an adequate money supply in support of economic development—flows from the center of his public philosophy, which emphasizes maximizing the wealth and power of the nation. His design for the bank also draws on his philosophical paradigm, reflecting two convictions: that the strongest and most reliable motivation on which to rely is the self-interest of the wealthy and that an institution can be engineered to transform self-interest into the public good. He also draws on convictions about theoretical relationships specific to finance and banking.

In his report to the House, Hamilton offered twenty-four "principles upon which a national bank ought to be organized." I have arranged the content of these principles into four categories: ownership, capital, assets, and governance. I use these categories here to analyze Hamilton's design for the first Bank of the United States and will press them into service repeatedly in the chapters that follow to analyze and compare the design of organizations involved in depository intermediation: state and national banks, Federal Reserve Banks, Federal Home Loan Banks, savings and loan associations, and credit unions.

OWNERSHIP

Although Hamilton viewed the provision of adequate, stable, uniform capital for economic development as critical to realization of the public interest, he did not think it could be safely entrusted to an agency within the government. Government had multiple responsibilities and could not be counted on to keep this particular purpose foremost. In the case of a war, for example, the government would view its short-term need for cash as a very high priority and was likely to loan itself all the money available, thereby shortchanging economic development and threatening confidence in the money supply.

Hamilton wanted a separate organization—an organization not subject to the cross-pressures of multiple and conflicting objectives—which would institutionalize the purpose of providing adequate, stable, uniform capital in the economy. Thus, he proposed incorporating a Bank of the United States. The explicit rationale for incorporating this bank, as for corporations generally in that era, was that government was sanctioning a vehicle for assembling private capital for a public purpose. But what Hamilton wanted from wealthy people at least as much as their money (for the bank's capital could have been gotten from the public treasury, as, indeed, much of it was) was their interest in protecting the continuity of the institution. That interest would be created through ownership. That is, Hamilton used ownership as a device for institutionalizing purpose. If wealthy persons owned the bank and could therefore profit from it, they could be counted on to see to its continuity. If continuity were ensured, the purpose for which the bank was established would not fall by the wayside.

Several of Hamilton's principles for organizing the Bank of the United States thus specified what ownership would mean for investors and how their self-interest would be served. There would be dividends on stock, paid semiannually from profits derived from lending. Stockholders could expect financing for commercial ventures on reasonable terms: it was common practice for banks to loan money to their own investors and directors, and the Bank of the United States would be no exception. This bank would be the only one chartered by the central government for the duration of its charter; this implied that it would hold the government's deposits, which would help ensure profitability because those deposits undergirded the bank's capacity to lend. The bank's notes would be acceptable in all payments to the United States, thus protecting the value of its paper. Bank stock was transferable, providing investors with liquidity; this feature was more valuable than we might realize today, for at that time financial assets such as promissory notes and personal bonds were not generally transferable under the common law.

Although he valued private ownership as a means to the bank's public purpose, Hamilton also recognized that private interest might threaten that purpose. The charter authorized an initial subscription (stock offering) of ten million dollars. This amount of equity capital was not arbitrary. The purpose of this institution was to affect the quantity of money in the economy. Hamilton's judgment was that a note issue of about ten million dollars was needed to meet business demand. He sized the "fund" (equity capital) to support that amount in notes. The directors of a chartered bank, however, might well consider it in the private interest of the stockholders not to issue the whole amount of stock authorized. Stockholders could benefit in two ways by thus holding back. First, constraining the size of the subscription could keep the stock's price up. Second, a smaller equity fund meant a smaller money supply, which would translate into a higher interest rate on loans and thus more profit. But such calculations would defeat Hamilton's public purpose: the money supply would not increase adequately. His design solution was to preclude discretion regarding the size of the initial offering: the charter would specify that the full amount of stock authorized must be issued. In periodic charter renewals Congress—not bank directors—would establish the size of the bank's capital based on its reading of economic need.

THE NATURE OF THE BANK'S EQUITY CAPITAL

The question of what assets would form the capital of the bank, or, put differently, of what investors might use to pay for their stock, was important and controversial. It was unlikely that ten million dollars in specie could have been accumulated in one depository. Indeed, if there had been that much gold and silver in the country, Hamilton might not have been preoccupied with creating money. Could some other asset be accepted in payment for stock?

In his report Hamilton noted that there were advocates of permitting investors to offer their land as equity for bank stock. Precedent for such an approach was at hand in the colonial land offices, which issued paper currency on land security. But Hamilton argued that land is not suitable backing for bank-issued paper money. To build and maintain confidence in a bank, its paper had to be redeemable in specie on demand or shortly. It was not practical to sell or mortgage pledged land to produce gold when deposit withdrawals and demands for note redemption exceeded the specie on hand. People knew that land could not be turned into money expeditiously and would not have faith in a bank so constituted. (Hamilton recognized as clearly as anyone ever has that the financial system is a house of cards resting on beliefs.) Some advocates of accepting land as bank capital conceded that a portion of the capital would have to be specie. No, replied Hamilton: those who hold money as an asset and those who hold land are not the same persons. It would not work to permit landholders to share in the profits of the bank by venturing their land, which was not what was needed, essentially becoming free riders on moneyed men, whose asset was at risk. The moneyed men would not come in.

There was, however, another asset near enough to money (that is, gold and silver) which could provide a sound basis for the issue of bank notes. Looking to the example of the Bank of England, Hamilton proposed using securities of the central government to capitalize the Bank of the United States. Congress had already implemented his recommendations for refinancing revolutionary war debt, and a reasonable market in these securities had resulted. Declaring them acceptable payment for shares in the bank would strengthen that market further. Because the securities could thus be readily sold for money if necessary, they would provide suitable capital. Private investors were permitted to pay up to three-fourths of the cost of their stock with government securities. Gold or silver was required for the remaining fourth.

The bank's charter provided that the U.S. government would buy 20 percent of the stock. The government paid for its two million dollars worth of shares, essentially, with a loan from the bank. The transaction surely created money out of air and faith, and Jeffersonians fussed about it for at least two generations. When it all shook out, the bank had the government's promise to pay, and the government had shares in the bank. One might think that this design feature was intended to benefit the government through dividends on its shares or through a role in the bank's direction by virtue of its ownership interest. But Hamilton intended the contrary: the purpose of the arrangement was to benefit the bank, not the government. "The main design of this [loan] is to enlarge the specie fund of the bank," wrote Hamilton. As the government repaid the loan over ten years, it would be putting hard money into the bank. While the government did receive its dividends, it was by charter specifically denied any role in directing the bank.

The relationship in Hamilton's design between the amount and nature of the bank's equity and its circulation (the notes it issued) warrants comment. Hamilton noted early in the report that a generally recognized safe ratio of notes to capital would be two or three to one. At first glance his charter is conservative by this standard, providing that note issue equal the size of the capital, for a ratio of one to one.

One might well wonder why he has gone to the trouble to justify the mechanism by which banks increase the circulating medium if he plans to issue only a dollar's worth of notes for a dollar's worth of capital. But the private commercial banks on which he based his generalization about a two or three to one ratio held their capital in specie, not government securities. If we consider only the hard money portion of the capital in Hamilton's bank, he has provided for a relatively aggressive expansion of five dollars worth of notes for every dollar in specie capital. Since much of the specie was never paid, the ratio was even higher in practice. "Auxiliary" capital, those government bonds that private investors used to pay for their shares, constituted the major part of the fund that supported note issue. A further 20 percent of the fund consisted of another kind of government promise to pay, the bond used to buy the government's stock.[20] Although Hamilton disguised the basis of the currency (as gold) in order to create confidence in it, given the huge portion of government debt in the capital "fund," what backed the bank's notes was largely the government's stability.

ASSETS

The Bank of the United States would augment the capital in the economy by extending credit. What sorts of loans would Hamilton have it make? (A bank's loans are assets to the bank, though liabilities to the borrowers.) With some caveats the bank was to "*trade* in nothing except bills of exchange." Bills of exchange were very short-term loans (thirty to sixty days) on actual goods in the process of trade. This restriction was consistent with the practice of private commercial bankers at that time and intended to protect the bank's liquidity. A highly political implication in practice was that the Bank of the United States would not serve people who wanted to borrow to buy land or to meet the needs of the annual agricultural cycle.

How did Hamilton reconcile his intention to solve economy-wide needs for circulating medium and credit with this restriction on legitimate objects of lending? He believed that, although the credit issued by his bank would be only to merchants, it would benefit everyone by filling the "channels of circulation" nevertheless. Other money would be freed up for lending on mortgages. Consider the consequences of such bank design if there were no other kind of money in the economy. What would happen if bank-issued paper were the money of the economy but one could not borrow that money for farms or houses?

Loans to government were strictly limited. Except for the initial two million dollar loan to the central government, intended to build up the bank's specie fund as it was repaid, Hamilton suggested in his report that loans to the central and state governments be capped at fifty thousand dollars. (Congress actually capped loans to the central government at the higher level of one hundred thousand dollars.) The public purpose of the Bank of the United States was not to provide government with cash but, rather, to pump up the economy.

GOVERNANCE

Eight of the twenty-four principles in Hamilton's report address the governance structure and process of the proposed Bank of the United States. In keeping with his view of the economy as unitary, what Hamilton was trying to do—and believed he could do—was to engineer this structure so that lending decisions would be depersonalized, based on the needs of the economy as a whole and the requirements of the bank's stability, rather than on the private interest of any individual or group.

Twenty-five directors, who were to be stockholders and U.S. citizens, would be elected annually by the private stockholders. Hamilton expected these directors to be of the commercial class, thus familiar with the conventions of commercial lending. The directors in turn would elect the bank's president. In an effort to preclude the possibility of a few big shareholders controlling the institution in their particular interest, voting rules provided for a weight of influence somewhere between one shareholder / one vote and one share / one vote. To avoid the possibility of control by a faction on the board, Hamilton insisted on rotation in office: 25 percent of the directors had to step down each year. There were provisions to allay corruption: the cashier must give bond; stockholder approval was required for director and president salaries; and directors were personally liable if they voted for lending in excess of charter provisions. The government, which Hamilton suspected of proclivity to inflation, was to have no role in directing the bank: it made no direct appointments to the board, nor did it vote its shares on any issue, though there was a provision for reporting on the condition of the bank to the secretary of the Treasury.

Hamilton's report on the Bank of the United States is among the most elegant and comprehensive applications we may ever have of the theory of administration, articulated so much later by Herbert Simon, as control of the premises of decisions to be made within an organization.[21] Hamilton's design principles mapped the decision pathways along which, he believed, the institution would create a money supply appropriate for the nation's economic development needs. He believed that it would operate impersonally, in the public interest, to achieve the purpose that was the normative heart of his public philosophy.

JEFFERSON'S OPPOSITION TO THE BANK

Thomas Jefferson did not believe that the proposed institution would serve the public interest. Although its constitutionality was hotly disputed, Congress passed legislation chartering a Bank of the United States according to Hamilton's principles and sent it along to the president. Confronted with controversial issues, Washington often called on cabinet members to argue opposing viewpoints.[22] In this case he turned to Jefferson, his secretary of state and fellow Virginian, for arguments against the bank's constitutionality.

Jefferson responded to Washington with the opinion mentioned in the opening paragraph of this chapter.[23] He began with a tirade against corporations as violations of real property law and dismissed Hamilton's central question of how to provide a money supply for economic development in one flip sentence: "I pass over the increase of circulating medium, ascribed to [the bank] as a merit, and which, according to my ideas of paper money, is clearly a demerit." Why was Jefferson railing against mortmain and alienage, descents and escheat, when Washington had asked him about a bank? Why had he not engaged Hamilton's question? For, whether or not Hamilton's design hypotheses would prove empirically accurate in the long run, he had made a masterful argument.

Jefferson's normative paradigm of the political economy was so different from Hamilton's that it did not cast up the same questions. He shared neither Hamilton's vision nor the purpose for a national bank which flowed from that vision. Jefferson was not trying to foster a diverse, interdependent economy; thus how to increase the money supply to do so was of no concern to him.

What Jefferson wanted to foster was individual equality, economic independence and moral virtue. He believed that the best socioeconomic context for realizing these ends was an agricultural economy composed of small freeholding farmers. Jefferson had expressed this conviction in his "Notes on Virginia," ten years before Hamilton presented his proposal for a Bank of the United States: "Those who labor in the earth are the chosen people of God, if ever He had a chosen people, whose breasts He has made His peculiar deposit for substantial and genuine virtue. . . . Corruption of morals in the mass of cultivators is a phenomenon of which no age nor nation has furnished an example." Conversely, he was clear that people who are not farmers are not virtuous: "generally speaking, the proportion which the aggregate of the other classes of citizens bears in any State to that of its husbandmen, is the proportion of its unsound to its healthy parts, and is a good enough barometer whereby to measure its degree of corruption."

But why is farming uniquely suited to foster virtue? Jefferson answered this question through the back door, by telling us why others are not virtuous: "[Corruption of morals] is the mark set on those, who, not looking up to heaven, to their own soil and industry, as does the husbandman, for their subsistence, depend for it on casualties and caprice of customers. Dependence begets subservience and venality, suffocates the natural progress and consequence of the arts." The culprit is economic dependence, "dependence on the whims and patronage of customers." Elsewhere Jefferson had decried dependence on employers as well. Dependence generates servility and extinguishes creative thought, leading to the "corruption of morals." But farmers are not economically dependent on other people, and their economic independence makes the space for them to follow their consciences—for virtue.

Jefferson continued with a statement of his perfect opposition to Hamilton's vision: "While we have land to labor then, let us never wish to see our citizens occupied at a work-bench, or twirling a distaff. Carpenters, masons, smiths, are wanting in husbandry; but, for the general operations of manufacture, let our workshops remain in Europe."[24]

In this agrarian vision little money is required. Farmers produce most of what they need on their farms, and their supplier provides what they cannot produce on credit until harvest time.[25] Jefferson was a "hard money" advocate, which means he believed that gold and silver alone should constitute the money supply. Extraordinary circumstances, such as war, might justify the issue of government paper money in the form of Treasury notes, but it was to be redeemed in specie and retired from circulation as soon as possible.[26] He regarded privately issued paper money as inflationary and a threat to farmers' hold on their property. (If nominal land value increased due to inflation, farmers would not be able to pay their taxes or afford land.)

Thus rejecting Hamilton's premise that a mechanism for increasing the money supply was necessary, Jefferson did not argue against the bank because it would be ineffective. He shifted ground, opposing a national bank because it would be a corporation. As a corporation, it prostrated the "laws which constitute the pillars of our whole system of jurisprudence." Most of the pillars, or "foundation laws," which Jefferson listed apply to the holding and passing of real property. Why did Jefferson regard real property law as so fundamental? And how is it that a corporation inherently violates such law?

It would be straightforward to infer the reason for Jefferson's emphasis on laws governing land ownership from the priority he placed on farming: if all men are to be farmers, real property law must ensure that land is available to them. But there is more to it. Jefferson opposed the concentration of wealth because it mitigated against equality and independence—economically, politically, and psychologically. Land was the primary form of wealth he recognized; real property law was thus fundamental because it could be used to generate or preclude the concentration of wealth.

For evidence of these views we can look to his leading role in radically revising his state's property law during the Revolution. In that context he condemned the land tenure institutions of colonial Virginia, arguing against landholding in fee tail, a device for keeping great tracts undivided within a family, and primogeniture, also designed to keep large holdings intact. He argued that these institutions effectively privileged a few families, generating an unnatural aristocracy of wealth. Their wealth had led to disproportionate political influence, as the king selected his magistrates from among their number generation after generation. The experience of living in an aristocratically dominated society distorted men's understanding of their equality and independence, on the part of the aristocrats as well as the others.[27]

Why would Jefferson argue that the Bank of the United States, by virtue of being a corporation, violated real property law? In the last quarter of the eighteenth century in the United States the corporation was not the private entity established for business purposes which we understand by that term today. A corporation was an instrumentality of the state, a delegation of state power. Each corporation was chartered by a separate act of a legislature to serve some public purpose. Incorporation was widely used by state legislatures as a device for aggregating private capital to provide public works: bridges, turnpikes, ferries, and canals. Hamilton understood his bank in this way, as a device to aggregate private funds for a public purpose. The incentive to those who invested in capital improvements, or in Hamilton's bank, was the profit to be earned from the activity, usually on a monopoly basis.

Jefferson knew this theory of incorporation but held it in contempt. What he saw in the corporation was an institutional form that, under the guise of serving a public purpose, concentrated wealth and power and bent them to private economic and political ends. Jefferson relied on the natural limits on a man—the term of his life, his capacity to work or hoard—to circumscribe the possibility of aggregating wealth. The term of a human life provided the basis of the property law reform discussed earlier: when someone dies, his property breaks up or passes in specifically authorized ways. But a corporation is not a natural man; it is a legal fiction. It cannot be counted on to die, so there is no opportunity for laws like those Jefferson advocated to come into play to break down any accumulation of wealth or power the corporation may have accrued.

Creation of an entity beyond the reach of these laws infuriated Jefferson. In a litany he railed at Washington that, because the bill establishing a bank forms a corporation, it is against the laws of mortmain, against the laws of alienage, against the laws of forfeiture and escheat.[28] Neither is a corporation limited by the capital, attention span, energy, or capabilities of a natural man. It is explicitly intended to overcome these limitations by joining people and capital. Compounding this effrontery, Hamilton's bank would be given a monopoly. And, perhaps most threatening of all, this corporation could promulgate policy in violation of the laws of the states within which it operated; people would be affected by an institution in which they had no voice. This entity was an abomination. It threatened Jefferson's most basic values. It had no place in his vision.

In answering these charges in the rebuttal he provided Washington, Hamilton took his turn shrugging off his opponent's central concerns. The bank would not violate the fundamental laws Jefferson cherished, he observed with derision: those laws simply did not apply to a corporation.[29]

THE LIFE OF THE BANK OF THE UNITED STATES

The president signed the legislation incorporating the first Bank of the United States, perhaps heeding Jefferson's closing counsel: if there is any doubt in your mind concerning this bill's constitutionality, respect the legislature's wisdom. The first national bank effectively served its purposes from 1791 through 1811, when Congress narrowly rejected a bill renewing its charter, letting the institution die.[30]

Hamilton's central purpose for a national bank was to augment the money supply in support of building an economically strong, integrated nation. As anticipated, the Bank of the United States effectively provided credit and currency in the process of its lending activity. But in response to a development Hamilton had not anticipated—the multiplication of state banks (addressed in chapter four)—the primary purpose of the national bank became more complex. In 1791, when the Bank of the United States opened for business in Philadelphia, there were four other chartered banks in the country.[31] Twenty years later, when the national bank's charter expired, there were over one hundred.[32] In this context the mission of the Bank of the United States became regulation of the money supply, augmenting or restraining, as the time and place required. It learned to regulate other banks through its handling of their notes and checks drawn upon them. These it received in the course of its own business with private parties, and, in much larger volume, through deposits of the central government. The Bank of the United States could restrain a state bank's lending by presenting that bank's paper for payment in specie (effectively reducing its reserve, in the language of a later day), or it could forbear. Because it held the accounts of the government, the biggest transactor in the economy, and about as much specie as all the other banks combined, the Bank of the United States was large enough to be an effective regulator. This broader purpose is consistent with Hamilton's intent, if we interpret his concern as provision of a money supply suitable to the nation's economic development needs, neither too small—the problem he perceived when he proposed the national bank—nor overly inflated, as could easily become the case with multiple uncoordinated state banks.

The national bank also fulfilled its secondary purpose, providing financial services to the government. The branch system that developed—permitted but not required in Hamilton's charter—was well suited to receiving public deposits, making the government's payments for salaries and other expenses, and servicing the public debt throughout the country.

The twenty-year life of the first Bank of the United States spanned Federalist and Jeffersonian Republican administrations. Secretaries of the Treasury of both parties worked with the institution. Hamilton served under Washington until 1795. Oliver Wolcott succeeded him, serving through the rest of Washington's second term and under John Adams. When the Republicans wrested the helm from the Federalists in 1800, Jefferson appointed Albert Gallatin to Treasury, and Gallatin continued under James Madison.

Jefferson himself never changed his mind about the Bank of the United States or banking in general. He viewed the national bank, with its branched structure, as a monster extending its tentacles throughout the United States—beyond the control of democratic processes, a threat to the stability of the central government. He suggested transferring the government's deposits to state banks as an interim measure and that the government ultimately hold its own funds.[33] Throughout his two terms in the White House, however, Jefferson let the bank be. He was the one, after all, who had counseled Washington to defer to the legislature—and Congress had established the national bank. (Andrew Jackson, lacking this philosophical commitment to the primacy of the legislature, would later take both steps Jefferson had suggested in his assault on the second Bank of the United States.) Further, his own Treasury secretary, Gallatin, defended the bank's usefulness. Moreover, despite his objection to the theoretical immortality of corporations, the charter of the first Bank of the United States, like the charters of most state corporations of the time, had—in current day terminology—a sunset provision. The charter would expire in 1811 if Congress did not renew it.

James Madison, on the other hand, in whose term as president the charter came up for renewal, did change his mind about the Bank of the United States. His objection in the first place, voiced from his position in the House of Representatives, had been based on the question of constitutionality, but now he argued that acceptance of the national bank in "deliberate and reiterated precedents" by the central government, local authorities, and the public rendered that question moot.[34] When Congress took up charter renewal in 1811, Madison's administration, led by Secretary of the Treasury Gallatin, argued in favor on the grounds that the bank was an effective economic regulator and fiscal agent for the government.[35]

The party of Jefferson in Congress divided three ways on the question of charter renewal. Among those who continued to share his agrarian ideal, there were two views. The first group, its members' eyes open to the headlong rush of economic expansion, agreed with the administration that the national bank's role as regulator was critical. Some of them did not like banking in general, but the state banks were a reality and should be constrained to responsibility; they noted that many of the state banks agreed that the influence of the national bank was beneficial. They also pointed out that in newer, less commercial states, often unserviced by state banks, the Bank of the United States filled in, meeting needs of common people. Congress members like John Taylor of Caroline, William Findley of Pennsylvania, and William Crawford of Georgia maintained the central focus of Jefferson's liberal ideology on the autonomous individual. But they departed from him to argue explicitly that the interest of common people was well served by the national bank.[36]

The other group of agrarians, "unreformed" or "unreconstructed" Jeffersonians, opposed recharter of the Bank of the United States because they continued to oppose all banking on philosophical grounds. They resurrected the old arguments against the bank's constitutionality.[37] Joining them in opposition to recharter was the third contingent of congressional Republicans, the free enterprisers. Here was the voice of the "interests" of the day. Led by Henry Clay, they opposed the Bank of the United States because its regulatory hand got in the way of state banks and because its dominance of U.S. government deposits kept those deposits out of state bank vaults. They voiced their objection in terms of unconstitutionality and states' rights, but their arguments have a disingenuous ring. This group made strange bedfellows with the ideologically driven die-hard agrarians, but together they defeated recharter by margins of one vote in each chamber.

The philosophical difference between Alexander Hamilton and Thomas Jefferson which I chose to highlight in this chapter has been their disagreement on the appropriate subject of public policy. Hamilton's central normative priority was on building the strength of the nation, an interdependent whole. In pursuing that purpose, he designed the first national bank. Jefferson's classic liberal thought was focused on the human individual. In keeping with his view of the conditions necessary for individual independence, equality, and virtue, he opposed the first Bank of the United States. Their contrasting positions in this particular public policy realm flowed clearly from their different philosophical paradigms. We cannot understand the establishment of the first Bank of the United States without reference to Hamilton's public philosophy. Nor can we explain its quiet death without reference to the influence of Jeffersonian ideas, articulated again by adherents in Congress.

3

ANDREW JACKSON AND THE SECOND BANK OF THE UNITED STATES

RESTORING THE LOCKEAN LINE

Although it was born in an epic clash, America's first national bank had died quietly. The reverse is the case with its successor second Bank of the United States. Despite some haggling over design details, the second national bank was born of a broad consensus that it was needed. The great confrontation flared at the end, when Andrew Jackson, self-proclaimed embodiment of the people's will, vetoed the bill to recharter the bank which had passed both houses of Congress by substantial majorities of the people's representatives.[1] Confronted with much the same issue George Washington had considered so carefully forty-one years earlier, Jackson neither sought counsel nor hesitated as he made the opposite choice.[2]

A common interpretation of Jackson's war on the second bank is that the people's champion slew the great monster of privilege on their behalf.[3] This interpretation persists despite empirical work by historians showing that the bank was effective in providing and regulating money and popular with the people, the state banks, and state legislatures.[4] The tenacity of this view may be attributable in large measure to the fact that this is how Jackson, who won, explained himself as well as to Arthur Schlesinger Jr.'s influential analogy between Jackson and FDR: in Schlesinger's view both presidents confronted entrenched economic privilege in a time of crisis on behalf of the people.[5] But I will read Jackson as an ideologue who permitted his strong presuppositions about acceptable means to blind him to the effects for individuals of institutions in practice. Roosevelt, on the other hand, learned to surrender his own suppositions about means; what suited him so well to the exigencies of his moment is that—while retaining a fix on the end of ordinary persons' welfare—he became willing to try anything. Jackson destroyed a central bank, and Roosevelt would build one.

In this chapter I center the philosophical issue of the relationship between the public and private spheres to explore the founding of the second Bank of the United States, as well as to explain its demise at Jackson's hand, and then to follow the consequences of Jackson's handiwork in the banking framework at the federal level to the eve of the Civil War. Analysis of the purposes and structure of the second national bank shows that it was what we would regard today as a corporatist economic regulator: it combined public and private interests in its structure and pursued purposes with public and private dimensions. Jackson was a classic liberal—indeed, almost a caricature of one in the purity of his public philosophy. There was no place in his worldview for such an institution. It defied the Lockean line between the public and private spheres both in its regulatory purpose, which was more than a government should do, and in its design, which did not maintain a separation between what is public and what is private. Insisting that the public and private spheres should and could be neatly separated, in theory and in institutional design, Jackson initiated and led the assault on the federal regulator. He succeeded in suspending federal government involvement with banks until the Civil War. The government dealt in specie only, not bank paper; the government's money was handled by a line agency of the Treasury Department, not by any bank. Banking was viewed as strictly private. The common people were to be protected from its hazards not by effective regulation but by using gold instead of bank paper as money.

THE SECOND BANK OF THE UNITED STATES

PURPOSE OF THE SECOND BANK

Despite the efforts of James Madison's administration and its congressional allies, Congress had permitted the charter of the first Bank of the United States to lapse in 1811. Five years later the members reconsidered and established a second national bank. Why? In that brief interval the number of state banks had risen dramatically, from 117 to 232.[6] With diverse designs and no central control these corporations, in the process of lending, issued paper notes used as currency. The notes of various banks stood in a wide range of exchange relationships to one another: in New York, local banks might accept the notes of Boston banks, although Boston banks would not take New York's; in Pennsylvania, New York notes might be accepted at a discount, but New

Yorkers would not take Pennsylvania bank notes. Even in their local circulation areas bank notes were depreciated to 90, 80, or 75 percent of par. Prices were greatly and unevenly inflated throughout the United States. There was speculation in bank stock as well as notes. In 1814, hopelessly unable to cover their excessive promises to pay hard money, most banks outside New England suspended redemption of their notes in specie. Also in the interlude between the lapse of the first national bank and establishment of the second, the second war with England raged. As gold and silver disappeared from circulation and efforts to finance the war with Treasury notes met with little success, the U.S. government accepted bank notes in payment of taxes or as bank loans in one part of the country but had difficulty paying for supplies and soldiers' salaries in other areas, where the notes were devalued or worthless. With the first Bank of the United States liquidated, there was no convenient agent for placing and servicing government debt and no medium of reliable value which the government could borrow anyway.[7]

This picture looked very much like the worst-case scenario the men in that stuffy room in the Pennsylvania State House had intended to preclude by prohibiting state issuance of bills of credit in section 10 of the first article of the Constitution. Not a few policy makers noticed that corporate creatures of the states were doing essentially that. But, while the proliferation of bank-created local currencies was disruptive to the economy and the government, such money was the only money available. Congress established the second Bank of the United States to provide a uniform currency, intending thereby to bring economic chaos under control for the benefit of the government and the people. Events, not ideology, forced their attention to this purpose, and past experience guided institutional design.

The record of Congress's debate makes it clear that providing a uniform currency, to settle the economy generally, was its central purpose in establishing a new national bank;[8] it would do this by means of direct banking and bank regulation. John C. Calhoun, who chaired the House Committee on a National Currency, presented the position most cogently. He argued that the Constitution gives Congress authority to "coin money" and "regulate the value thereof." The reality was that no coin was circulating; bank paper had become the money of the country. The founders had not foreseen the development of state banking, but they had intended to provide authority for central public regulation of the value of whatever "money" was, and bank paper was money.[9] The Republican administration shared Congress's view.[10] President

Madison had asked the legislature to "provide for a uniform currency" and to consider a national bank as the appropriate means.[11] His secretary of the Treasury, Alexander Dallas, sent a report to Congress insisting that it was the central government's obligation to provide a uniform currency and that a national bank was the way to do it.[12]

Calhoun's constitutional justification for a national bank was new. Although, as we have seen, Hamilton's central purpose in advocating the first national bank had also been to affect the economy as a whole through manipulation of the money supply, he did not claim direct constitutional authority for shaping and regulating banking. Rather, Hamilton focused on the government's need to collect taxes and make payments and on the national bank's role as the government's fiscal agent—unambiguously public purposes—making the now familiar argument that it was within Congress's prerogative to use whatever form of agency it regarded as a necessary and proper means to its legal ends. In the debates over setting up the second national bank, Jefferson's constitutional objection to the corporate form of Hamilton's bank was regarded as moot. Madison himself, who had argued Jefferson's point in Congress in 1791, had conceded in principle. Even before the Supreme Court adopted Hamilton's reasoning in *McCulloch v. Maryland* (1819), Madison declared the question precluded by "repeated recognitions . . . of the validity of such an institution" by all three branches of the government and the general will.[13] Accordingly, in considering establishment of a new national bank, its corporate form and public fiscal agency were not at issue; Congress and the administration took these for granted. They went on to accept Calhoun's argument that the Constitution gave Congress not only the authority but also the obligation to provide a uniform currency and that doing this by means of banking and bank regulation was constitutional. Hamilton had smuggled his national bank in through a back door, focusing attention on its public functions. The majority of the party of Jefferson now walked in the front gate, with the explicit purpose of regulating banking as a means to affecting the economy.

In addition to their view of the purpose for a second national bank, the documentary record clarifies contemporary policy makers' sense of the mechanisms for currency control, which had developed through experience with the first Bank of the United States. They conceived of the national bank as the regulator in a system (a "regulatory framework" in my terminology) that would include the state banks and the paper money they issued. The national bank would compel state banks to constrain credit by presenting their notes for redemption in specie or cashing drafts (essentially checks) upon them, or it could facilitate credit expansion by forbearing.[14] With regard to the extraordinary circumstances within which the second national bank would begin operation—extreme inflation and general bank suspension—policy makers expected a pair of mechanisms to reestablish order. First, the national bank would be charter bound to pay specie (that is gold and silver, or hard money) on demand. Because state banks would be competing with the national bank, this measure was expected to spur them to resume redemption as well. Second, the national bank could refuse to accept the notes of non-specie-paying banks. The national bank would be effective with these mechanisms, policy makers expected, because of its size, measured in terms of its relatively huge capital and deposits, and its presence, with branches throughout the country.

Political consensus in favor of a new national bank was broad in 1816. The second Bank of the United States was a Republican measure, but the failed effort five years earlier to renew the first national bank's charter had also originated in Madison's administration and been managed in Congress by members of the party of Jefferson. At that time, as noted earlier, Republicans had been of three minds. Unreformed Jeffersonians, opposed to all banking, joined a second group that favored state banking, but believed federal regulation unnecessary, to defeat the reformed Jeffersonians, who led for renewal of the charter. Reformed Jeffersonians such as Madison and Gallatin had concluded that banking was with us and must be regulated to ensure its consistency with the Jeffersonian concept of the public interest, which emphasized protection of the freedom and equality of individuals. The key factional shift that allowed the second national bank's charter to pass was on the part of the state banking supporters. Whether they had opposed the central bank because they did not like any regulator or because they thought state regulation would be sufficient, this group concluded, in light of the economic chaos in the absence of the first national bank, that federal regulation was consistent with state banking. Henry Clay had led them in opposition to renewal of the first bank's charter but publicly changed his position; indeed, as speaker of the House, it was he who recruited the analytically brilliant John C. Calhoun to lead for the new bank in that chamber.[15] Federalist remnants split. Some, including Daniel Webster, voted against the second bank in the spirit of partisanship; others voted for it on principle. A handful of unreformed

Jeffersonians remained opposed because they rejected all incorporated banking.

DESIGN OF THE SECOND BANK

Historians of the second Bank of the United States have emphasized the continuity of its charter with that of the first national bank.[16] While the new charter did reflect Hamilton's principles to a large extent,[17] there was a significant departure in regard to the perceived relationship between private and public interest in designing the organization. In a break with Hamilton's dicta that the public's purpose was best protected by harnessing somebody's private interest and that the board of directors of the national bank must therefore represent only the private stockholders, Secretary of the Treasury Dallas and others believed that "an interior agency" in direction of the Bank would best serve to protect the public interest.[18] Accordingly, the new charter stipulated that five of the twenty-five directors would be appointed by the president of the United States. Oversight provisions were also strengthened. Retaining the first charter's requirement for periodic reporting to the secretary of the Treasury, the second provided for congressional review as well: a committee appointed for the purpose could inspect the bank's records at any time to determine if there had been a charter violation.

Other charter changes reflected Hamilton's conception of the economic role of banking but adapted the new bank to an expanded economy. The capital of the second national bank was considerably larger—thirty-five million dollars compared to ten million dollars for the first—but the proportions of equity sold to the government versus other investors, and of specie to government securities, remained the same. There was an emphasis on redeeming the second national bank's obligations in specie on demand, intended, as discussed earlier, to regulate state banks. Branching provisions were also changed to recognize economic growth. Hamilton had been tentative about branching due to the potential loss of central board control; thus, the first bank's directors were permitted to organize branches at their discretion. In the physically expanding economy both government fiscal operations and monetary control relied on geographically dispersed capability. The second bank's directors were therefore required to establish a branch in any state in which two thousand shares were held, if the state legislature so requested and Congress approved.

Policy makers thus built an institution intended not only to handle the government's money but also explicitly to affect the economy through money and banking regulation, and they mixed public and private interests in its design. The purpose of the second Bank of the United States defied strict liberal limits on the government's role, and its design precluded placing it on one side or the other of a hard Lockean line between the public and private spheres. This was an institution rooted in events and experience but not easily justified in terms of the dominant Lockean ideology.

THE SECOND BANK IN OPERATION

By the time President Jackson vetoed renewal of its charter in 1832, the second Bank of the United States had moved through three distinct phases in operation, marked roughly by the tenures of different bank presidents. The new bank opened for business in January 1817 under William Jones (1816–19) in the midst of the economic boom that followed the end of the War of 1812. At that point in U.S. economic development both a real economy and a financial economy were already apparent. By "real" economic activity I mean the production and distribution of goods and services; the "financial economy" is the realm in which securities based on real activity are bought and sold, taking on a life of their own in the process. The boom affected both; state banks figured prominently in both; and, by regulating the currency, the resurrected national bank was intended to bring the economic free-for-all under control. In its first phase the bank achieved the immediate objective of negotiating an agreement in which state banks resumed specie payment, but beyond that it only added fuel to the economic fire it was supposed to dampen. In the real economy the national bank spurred activity and inflation by its own aggressive lending and was unwilling to use its tools for reining in state bank credit. In the financial economy speculation in bank stock had been a factor in the explosion of state bank charters, a major problem that the national bank's lenient policy on credit expansion did nothing to curb. Worse, the stock of the second national bank itself became a lush target for manipulators and speculators.

The second national bank's counterproductive economic impact in this first phase is attributable to a combination of poor management, self-dealing (decision making aimed at stockholder advantage regardless of the requirements of good management and policy), and fraud by central and branch directors. "A clique of Philadelphia and Baltimore stock-jobbers" controlled the bank, with about three-fourths of its stock in the hands of less than one hundred persons.[19] Hamilton's voting rules, intended to avoid control by a few big stockholders, had been carried forward to the second bank's charter but were simply violated. To achieve more weight in choosing directors, manipulators registered their shares in many names. Primary criteria for board decisions appear to have been achievement of large dividends and inflation of stock value. Lending was excessive, due in part to the emphasis on achieving big dividends. Further, as capital was not apportioned among the branches (eighteen of them existed by the end of 1817), there was no mechanism to constrain the amount of credit branch directors provided. The bank had very little capital to apportion anyway: after initial subscribers made their first 30 percent payment, the bank gave them loans on stock security for subsequent installments, and the 25 percent specie required by the charter was not demanded. This means that the bank's "capital" was composed largely of the promissory notes of individuals, instead of specie and government bonds. In addition to lending shareholders the money with which they paid for their initial stock subscriptions, the bank provided additional credit on the security of that stock, at 25 percent above par, so the same shareholders could buy more stock.

The most egregious outright fraud occurred at the Baltimore branch. As remains the case with intricate white-collar thievery to this day, what the culprits did is as fascinating as it is appalling. Three people— the branch president, the penniless branch cashier, and a branch director, who also sat on the main board at Philadelphia—made themselves increasingly larger loans to buy more and more stock, ostensibly on security of stock they already held. Contrary to fact, they told branch directors that such loans were authorized by the main board in Philadelphia and therefore no concern of the local board. As it turned out, no stock underpinned most of the credit: the three men were essentially printing money for themselves with which to buy more stock. Charges were brought, but the common law, developed over the centuries to address relations between natural persons, had not heard of embezzlement, nor had the statutes of the state of Maryland caught up with this particular way to steal by bilking an artificial person. This disjunction cost the Bank of the United States about $1.4 million.[20]

Both Congress and the administration had a reasonable grasp on the national bank's failure to meet their expectations; overwhelmingly, they advocated that the institution be reformed, not scuttled. Reform was thus the dominant theme of a second phase of operations under bank president Langdon Cheves (1819–23). There was a clamp-down on self-dealing, as branch directors, branch presidents, and cashiers were replaced throughout the system; lending on security of bank stock, unless with central board consent, was discontinued. Cheves made the bank's stability the central policy criterion. He suspended dividends until capital was restored in 1821 and allocated capital to the branches. He also reduced capital—by not reissuing shares forfeited as collateral on defaulted loans. He was reluctant to issue the national bank's own notes, viewing them as a potential drain on its shaky specie supply, choosing instead to offer state bank notes to borrowers. New direct lending was restricted, and existing loans were not renewed. State banks were pressed to pay balances due to the Bank of the United States. As neither the national bank's direct debtors nor those of the state banks had cash, credit retraction resulted in the second Bank of the United States owning large portions of cities and vast tracts of good farmland in the developing portions of the country and contributed to the financial panic of 1818–19.[21]

Nicholas Biddle's assumption of the helm late in 1823 marks the beginning of a third phase of operation in which the bank was finally performing as policy makers intended. With an ongoing commitment to seeing the institution work, President Monroe supported his intellectual, public-spirited friend from Philadelphia for the bank presidency upon Cheves's resignation.[22] Biddle proved gifted in the art of what was not yet called central banking. His management was both prudent, in restoring and protecting the stability of the institution itself, and creative, in designing straightforward mechanisms for providing currency and credit in accord with the needs of the changing, growing economy.

Structurally, Biddle further centralized control of the bank. Although branch directors were appointed by the central board, he seized the lead in nominating them, and although a branch president was elected by its branch directors, he developed a technique for signaling his choice, which was rarely ignored. Further, Biddle reached into each branch board to develop a strong relationship with one director, relying on him for local economic and financial information, reflections on the character of current and potential board members, intelligence regarding inner workings of the branch board, and assistance in drumming up local support for national bank policy when necessary. Finally, in an early-nineteenth-century version of the "forest ranger" approach to central policy control through front-line operating personnel,[23] Biddle targeted branch cashiers. This crucial line official was chosen from among those trained under his own eye at Philadelphia and was the central board's agent in the field.

In a management move that would prove not as helpful to the bank as his other changes, Biddle distanced himself from the secretary of the Treasury. Although the bank's formal link to the secretary—specified initially by Hamilton and carried forward to the second national bank's charter—was confined to periodic financial reporting, in practice the secretary of the Treasury had been in consultation with the bank president regarding large and sometimes quite trifling matters of policy from Hamilton's day on. Indeed, it is difficult to imagine Hamilton remaining aloof from national bank matters; likewise, hands-on Republican administrators such as Gallatin and Dallas did not sit in their offices passively awaiting accounting reports from the bank. Jackson's Treasury secretaries did not possess their predecessors' financial and administrative expertise, but the early ones did try to protect the bank politically. Because he ignored their counsel, Biddle made unnecessary political blunders. Nor did he do his institution any favors with Jackson when he isolated government-appointed directors on the bank's board from important information and decisions through their committee assignments.[24]

Contemporary reports evaluating the second national bank's performance under Biddle, triggered by Jackson's opening salvos against the institution, show clearly that public policy makers and private bankers alike were satisfied that it was effectively fulfilling its purpose of providing a uniform currency.[25] Although the currency still included an assortment of state bank and national bank notes, a dollar, in whatever form, was worth as close to any other dollar throughout the United States as people expected it to be.

The same reports show that "uniform currency" was a complex concept. It included three distinct but interrelated forms of payment medium as well as the dimension of adequacy. People expected the national bank to ensure that there was currency in an amount sufficient for everyday economic transactions. The bank was also expected to ensure that there was adequate credit available for real economic development but not so much as to permit "speculation," which was viewed as inherently inflationary. The provision of domestic exchange was also viewed as the national bank's role. While *domestic exchange* is meaningless today in the United States, it was the crucial oil of the nineteenth-century economy, with its functionally and monetarily distinct regions.

Interregional traders did not want to have to buy and sell, through brokers and at a discount, the money required to do business in different parts of the country. They wanted a medium of payment which did not lose any significant portion of its value beyond their regional economies. The domestic "bill of exchange," issued by the Bank of the United States at a small charge (compared to the cost of transporting specie or to the price charged by state banks or private money traders for a similar instrument), redeemable at national bank branches throughout the country or saleable, was the device in use. It was satisfactory to southern cotton planters, northeastern manufacturers, and the shippers and merchants between them and their markets. It also appears that the national bank was on the way to replacing state notes with its own, which would have resulted in a literally uniform currency. Thus understood as the provision of an adequate, but not inflationary, supply of credit and currency for everyday use and economic development, throughout the United States, the second national bank's purpose of providing a uniform currency was essentially what we expect of the central bank today in regulating the money supply.

Biddle achieved the bank's purpose through a combination of regulating state banks and direct banking activity. Where local or state institutional development was adequate, the Bank of the United States functioned as a regulator and clearinghouse. Where local institutional development was inadequate, which was more likely in newer states, the national bank both regulated the state banks that did exist and operated directly, providing much-needed currency for everyday transactions and credit for economic development. In most states of the South and West notes of the Bank of the United States constituted 50 to 100 percent of the total circulation of bank notes in 1832.[26] For credit purposes the national bank, with its branch system, introduced capital where needed from other parts of the country or abroad.[27] Under Biddle's direction techniques were developed for providing domestic exchange where needed throughout the economy at a minimal cost. He was also making progress in developing mechanisms to provide foreign exchange which were both less costly to U.S. traders than relying on domestic or British private houses and helped improve the U.S. balance of payments. Biddle had a great talent for seeing the whole of the expanding economy, with its functional and geographic relationships, and the relationships between financial and real activity. He essentially wrapped the bank around existing institutional development, filling in gaps locally and regionally and emphasizing devices for interregional economic integration.[28]

In addition to being a banking and economic regulator, the second Bank of the United States, like the first, was the government's fiscal agent. This means that it held government deposits, primarily from customs and the sale of public lands, and made the government's payments, mostly public employees' salaries and debt service. Money thus came in to national bank branches from customs officials in port cities in the East, New Orleans, and Charleston and from land sales offices in the West. It was paid out to bond holders in major U.S. cities and in London and to federal employees wherever they were located.

The first phase of the operation of the second Bank of the United States had been a scandal. With policy determined by self-dealing individuals, it accelerated an economic boom it was supposed to calm. In its second phase, focused on restoring its own financial stability, the national bank again intensified the swing of the economic pendulum, this time downward into deflation. In its third phase, finally, its promise as a regulator was realized through creative but prudent financial management and economic intervention. Nevertheless, the first phase would give credence to Jackson's later charge that the bank was a tool for speculators, serving strictly private purposes. The second would provide plausibility to his argument that banks deliberately caused business cycles to rob people of their real property and that the Bank of the United States was nothing but the biggest bank of all. Out of the vagaries of this experience with central banking, the stage was set for a long deliberation on the nature and proper purpose of banking and its relationship to the public interest, the management of a market economy, and private ends.

JACKSON DISMANTLES THE SECOND BANK

JACKSON'S PUBLIC PHILOSOPHY

Andrew Jackson assumed the presidency in 1829.[29] Unlike Jefferson and Hamilton, the seventh president had not digested the entire written corpus of Western political theory nor mulled over competing eighteenth-century European schools of political economy.[30] Nevertheless, his public statements and private remarks reveal a comprehensive public philosophy in terms of which he gave meaning to the world as he found it and his efforts to reshape it. In particular, he would use this public philosophy to structure the banking debate.

At the center of Jackson's public philosophy stood the individual—but how much stronger than Jefferson's, this Jacksonian version of a man! Gone was the fragility of integrity, the contingency of virtue. The people *are* virtuous and intelligent, Jackson proclaimed again and again. With such a man as the building block, Jackson could draw his own implications for the structure of the economy, the role and structure of government, and their relationship.

Agriculture dominates Jackson's economy as it does Jefferson's, but not because the economic self-sufficiency to be found in farming is the sole reliable route to virtue. Rather, at that time agriculture was where most of the economic activity was. Jacksonian men could thrive in an interdependent Hamiltonian economy, dealing with other individuals as craftsmen (*mechanics* was the contemporary term), laborers, traders, farmers—with no threat to their integrity from the preferences of these other individuals. But they could build this liberal economy themselves: the government and its unnatural corporate creatures should stay out of it. When the government interfered to incorporate a group for economic development, it conferred "privileges"—by which Jackson meant concrete financial advantages—on the persons in that group which other persons did not have, which in turn generated artificial inequality. While Jefferson's inequality had been a complex, subtle, and insidious social psychological phenomenon, Jackson's was straightforward and economic.

Jackson's strong individual was to call the tune for government as well as the economy. The Constitution had given us republican forms. Whether Hamiltonians, who thought the people incapable of direct self-rule, or Jeffersonians, who believed the people could identify the aristocracy of virtue which would rule, the founders kept the masses at arm's length. Jacksonian men did not need to be feared and tempered or nurtured and represented; they sprang onto the scene with full adult moral capacity. Thus Jackson reinterpreted the Constitution, asserting that direct democracy was intended.[31] Although he claimed Jefferson's legacy, Jackson had lost the Virginian's sense of institutional influence on individual moral development and, within the government apparatus, reversed his institutional emphasis. Whereas Jefferson viewed legislatures, with their educational and deliberative functions, as the center of government, Jackson believed them corrupt. At the federal level he asserted moral dominance in policy making for the president, who, as the only national official elected by all the people, was their voice. He expected officials within the executive branch to do what he told them to do, not to advise him on the pros and cons of what he, the embodiment of the popular will, knew the people wanted.

While Jackson insisted on the indestructible nature of the Union and the importance of the central government with a fervency that rivaled Hamilton's, he also cried states' rights as loudly as any unreformed Jeffersonian. Yet Jackson's central government was strong within very narrowly interpreted constitutional limits—protecting free white individuals to engage in their own economic pursuits, never making Hamiltonian reaches for implied powers with which to direct the economy. And his state government turns out to be little more than a foil to federal action, not Jefferson's school for virtue. What Jackson was really after was protecting individual freedom and equality from *any* government. Jackson's public sphere was very limited and strictly separate from private activity. For him constitutionality and states' rights were tactical emphases in the service of this fundamental position.

JACKSON'S OPPOSITION TO THE SECOND BANK
OF THE UNITED STATES

Viewing the Bank of the United States from within this ideology, Andrew Jackson was intent on its destruction when he assumed the presidency. He signaled opposition to the institution in his first annual message to Congress in 1829, seven years before the charter would expire, and reiterated his position in his annual messages in 1830 and 1831.[32] True to these warnings, he vetoed charter renewal in 1832. The veto did not end the bank's operation immediately, as the charter had four years left to run. Policy makers and bankers alike expected to be able to call the question again and extend the life of the regulator, but Jackson made it a central mission of his second term to ensure that this did not happen. In 1833, after disposing of two Treasury secretaries who disagreed with him, he ordered Secretary Roger Taney to remove the government's deposits from the national bank. This ended its service as the government's fiscal agent. More important, because the bank relied on manipulating the public deposits to regulate the money supply, removing them seriously eroded its ability to pursue its primary purpose.

Thus, there was broad consensus among policy makers in Washington in support of the second Bank of the United States, both at its inception and throughout the struggle to get it working; after a very bumpy start they were satisfied that it was performing well. By 1832, when Biddle asked Congress to renew the charter, there was also widespread support for the institution throughout the country: by state legislatures, by state banks, and among the people generally.[33] Jackson was thus not responding to popular demand to dismantle the bank; he had to work hard to cast it as a monster. Why, in the face of its performance and widespread elite and popular support, was Jackson intent on destroying the bank?

In interpreting Jackson's hostility to the institution, one technique would be to identify an opponent—as I did in setting Hamilton and Jefferson in opposition to each other regarding the first national bank. Many have tapped Nicholas Biddle, president of the second bank, as Jackson's foil. But in these analyses the dispute turns personal: the charming and effective, though politically guileless, Biddle brings out the spitefulness of the ignorant frontiersman;[34] or an initially reasonable Jackson, inclined to compromise, ultimately smites the insufferably arrogant, politically obtuse Biddle.[35] Choosing Biddle as the antagonist will not lead to the heart of the matter anyway, for, creative and effective as he was, Biddle was only the agent of the institution builders.

And the institution builders in Washington worked from a variety of points of view. Two of the three factions within the Republican Party supported a new national bank. Reformed Jeffersonians maintained Jefferson's focus on the individual as the measure of all value and an emphasis on the moral superiority of an agrarian order but, in practice, had begun to turn to active government to protect individuals in the face of economic diversification and integration. Long before Progressive era theorist Herbert Croly counseled the use of Hamiltonian means to Jeffersonian ends, Madison, Gallatin, and Dallas did just that in supporting a revised national bank. The Republican faction led by Henry Clay supported entrepreneurial economic development generally and state banks in particular. Federalist public philosophy had favored national economic direction from the beginning. What did these diverse bank supporters—reformed Jeffersonians, nascent Whigs, old Federalists—all share which Jackson opposed? In practice they were all willing to give the government an important role in the economy, and they all regarded the corporatist national bank as a suitable device for pursuing the public's purpose. They were willing to blur the Lockean line.

Jackson did not agree. In his public philosophy there should and could be a clear line between what is public and what is private. The government was public. The economy was private. They should not manipulate each other. Andrew Jackson destroyed the Bank of the United States because it confounded the public and the private in its structure and its purposes. In so doing, he believed, it subverted the outcomes free and equal individuals would have arrived at in government as well as in the economy.

Consider first the bank's corporate structure. When Jackson looked at this institution, he did not see Hamilton's mechanism for transforming private interest to public purpose nor Madison's revised board with an "interior agency" for representing a uniquely public interest. Rather, Jackson saw a two-way street for illegitimate crossings of the public/private boundary. With branches throughout the country and vast financial resources, the Bank of the United States could sabotage public electoral and policy processes in stockholders' private interest in a number of ways. Credit could be spread around liberally to drum up support for the bank; political affiliation could be made a lending criterion; loans or outright payments could be made to newspaper editors who would carry its viewpoint or support its preferred candidates; campaign contributions could be made; legislators could be bought with credit or bank stock. Jackson accused the national bank, angrily and often, of trespassing in the public sphere in all of these ways. His veto message underscores theoretical opportunities created by the bank's structure for private interests, domestic and foreign, to interfere with the government; his statement justifying removal of the government's deposits from the bank makes actual detailed charges.[36]

If the bank was a tool for private interests to manipulate the outcomes of public processes, it was no less a mechanism through which the public interfered with the course of private outcomes. Echoing Jefferson's criticism, Jackson believed that, when government chartered any corporation, it stacked the deck in favor of some people by giving them special privileges to monopolize and profit from a given activity. Government thus violated its obligation of equal treatment and generated artificial inequality among individuals in their private capacity. The monopoly at issue with the Bank of the United States, according to Jackson in his veto message—was on holding the public deposits. When the bank made loans based on these deposits (as one then and now would expect a depository intermediary to do), stockholders profited through dividends and gains in the price of their shares. This was not fair; any benefits derived from the people's money should belong to the people.

Jackson would thus have objected to building private incentives into a government organization even if he viewed that organization's purpose as legitimately within the public sphere. What structural arrangement would have been appropriate for government's rightful activity? Let us set aside the second national bank's role in banking for a moment and focus on its role as public fiscal agent. Jackson did not question the appropriateness of the government receiving and disbursing public funds, but, being unsure about how to structure the function, he had begun vigorously soliciting ideas for "reorganizing" the national bank immediately upon assuming office. The response was large and varied.[37] By the time of his second State of the Union message Jackson suggested a new structure.

> It becomes us to inquire whether it be not possible to secure the advantages afforded by the present bank through the agency of a Bank of the United States so modified in its principles and structure as to obviate constitutional and other objections.
>
> It is thought practicable to organize such a bank with the necessary officers as a branch of the Treasury Department . . . without power to make loans or purchase property, which shall remit the funds of the government. . . . Not being a corporate body, having no stockholders, debtors, or property, and but few officers, it would not be obnoxious to the constitutional objections which are urged against the present bank.[38]

Jackson thus envisioned a line agency of the executive branch as the appropriate institutional design for the public's business. Such a structure is consistent with a clear separation of public and private concerns as well as with Jackson's emphasis on the president, not Congress, as the people's legitimate agent. Government fiscal agency would eventually take precisely this form, with the establishment in 1840 of the Independent Treasury, within the Treasury Department, to handle government collections and disbursements.

Yet Jackson's objection was not only to confounding the public and the private in the structure of the Bank of the United States. He objected to its purpose. Banking was a private business in which the government had no part.[39] All incorporated banking was unacceptable government interference in the economy, and Jackson saw the purpose of the national bank, once stripped of public fiscal agency, as nothing more than banking. To the intense frustration of those around him the president ignored the regulatory purpose served by the national bank's banking activity. On the one public occasion when he did acknowledge it Jackson asserted without explanation that "it must be admitted by all that [the bank] has failed in the great end of establishing a uniform and sound currency,"[40] despite contemporary perceptions that the bank was performing well. People were incredulous, and a formal inquiry into the bank's performance began.[41]

The president's opposition to the national bank's purpose became clear only gradually to his advisors and to congressional policy makers. When Jackson asked for suggestions for reorganizing the bank, when he said it should be modified in its "principles and structure," when he spoke of "constitutional objections," those whom he addressed thought his argument was with its structure. They did not realize that he meant to terminate the institution's purpose vis-à-vis banking and reorganize only its fiscal agency function. That his consultants did not grasp his full meaning is clear from the reorganization scenarios they presented. The elimination of branches, increases in the government's weight in decision making through congressional or presidential appointments, increased government ownership of bank stock, provisions for state government input in bank governance and benefits from its earnings— all were suggested. Some policy makers, who did grasp Jackson's objection to relying on private incentives to achieve public objectives, supposed that he intended to continue the banking activity of the national bank wholly under public control, and they issued a detailed indictment of that approach.[42] But Jackson did not intend the government to engage directly in banking any more than he intended continued participation through the private/public hybrid Bank of the United States.[43]

Jackson's belief that incorporated banking per se violated the boundary between the public and private spheres rested on a contemporary theory of banking most systematically expounded by William Gouge.[44] Gouge, who regarded himself as a disinterested economist, worked in Jackson's Treasury Department monitoring banks and developing monetary and fiscal policy; on occasion he collaborated directly with the president. Although acknowledging that U.S. banks operated under broadly diverse charters, Gouge viewed them all as essentially the same.

The essence of banking was the issuance of paper notes that substituted for real money (specie) by corporations possessing privileges denied to individuals;[45] banking was the root of all economic evil.

To understand Gouge's criticism of bank paper we need a practical understanding of how it was injected into and moved around in the economy. Bank notes originated in the lending process. When one borrowed from a bank, he gave the banker his own promissory note, and the bank gave its notes, which it had printed itself, to the borrower. Bank notes were not money, as are the dollar bills we use as cash today; they were promissory notes of the bank—that is, the bank's promise to pay money. Bank notes entered circulation as the borrower—typically, a merchant, trader, or planter—used them to pay for commodities, mechanics' fabricated goods, or workers' services. In this way ordinary working people and farmers, who received the bank's promissory notes in payment, became the bank's creditors.

In Gouge's view this bank paper was the root of economic evil because several incentives inherently drove U.S. banks to issue more promises to pay than they could honor. First, there were profits to be earned on loans, even though the bank probably had almost no real money to lend. Bankers' claim that they served the community by gathering up capital and allocating it efficiently for economic activity was a sham. The reality was that bank owners and borrowers alike (often the same people) advocated banks to create money. Like the culprits in the scandal at the Baltimore branch of the second Bank of the United States, stockholders in state banks were likely to have "paid" most of their share of the bank's nominal capital with a personal note secured by the very shares they were buying. Yet, as soon as the bank got a supply of notes from its printer, it could—and did—begin to lend. It collected interest and principle on its loans (of money it did not have) and, to the extent it could keep its notes in circulation, did not have to pay its own obligations. Even in the rare case in which nominal capital was actually paid in, the bank was legally permitted to lend some multiple of its capital. A bank thus drew real money from the community based on nothing but paper rags and the privilege granted in its charter to print them.

A second incentive to overissue bank notes was the opportunity to seize the community's real assets. In Gouge's view banks deliberately caused business cycles, alternately inflating and deflating the currency. They printed money willy-nilly and loaned it without regard to whether borrowers were engaged in real business or "speculation." Business would boom, a false sense of prosperity would entice people to buy and borrow too much, nominal prices would rise dramatically as the money supply multiplied well beyond the level of real economic activity. Some bank or banks would then trigger deflation, calling in their loans and refusing new ones. Debtors withdrew their deposits from various banks to pay off loans. Noteholders got nervous and demanded money for their bank notes. Short on cash, more banks tightened credit. No bank paper moved into circulation to replace that which was being drawn out. As the money supply dried up, there was no medium with which frantic people could make payments on loans they had taken out when nominal prices were inflated; they lost real property to banks through foreclosure. Although many banks would fail in the scramble, a few big winners—who had possessed nothing to begin with but access to a printing press and the government-granted privilege to use it—would end up with most of the real property in the community.

The most fundamental incentive to overissue, however, was limited liability. Had the individuals who profited from banking been personally liable to their creditors, including noteholders, they would not have issued more paper promises to pay than they could honor. But there was no penalty to the stockholders when banks went bust. They did not have to pay off creditors. Gouge thus attributed the business cycle to fundamental characteristics of the banking organization.

Gouge's, and Jackson's, central objection to the banking dynamic was its impact on ordinary individuals in their private lives. Laborers and mechanics in the towns and rural farmers usually did not have bank deposits, own bank stock, or have any part in the transactions that put bank paper into circulation. Yet, once the system took hold, real money (specie) was driven out of circulation, and individuals had no choice but to accept bank promissory notes in return for their honest labor and products: they were forced to be the bank's creditors. As such, they paid the "tax" (the difference between the cost of doing business in real money and the cost of doing it in inflated, borrowed money) which supported the arrangement, but bank stockholders got the benefits, even when the system was working. Further, Gouge argued, the inflation caused by bank overissues sent prices up much faster than wages, so people lost ground in this part of the business cycle through no lack of hard work (virtue). The inevitable deflation was even worse. People lost their work as the economy contracted. Many banks would go bust; the workers and farmers left holding the worthless paper when the music stopped were robbed. Any ordinary people who had taken a loan—whether workers who had invested their whole savings in a down payment on a house in town or small farmers who borrowed to buy land or for seasonal needs—were unable to make payments, as the currency was deliberately constricted. They lost their real property and the money and labor they had invested in it, unjustly deprived of the fruits of their honest labor. In Jackson's ideology there should be a reliable relationship between work (which was virtuous) and reward, but the paper money system made a lottery of economic life.

While ordinary people lost what they had through no failing of their own, bank stockholders, protected by limited liability, got to keep what they made during the boom as well as whatever they could grab in the crash, through no merit of their own. Artificial inequality—based not on differences in individuals' willingness to work and virtue but, rather, on deliberate manipulation of the system—was the result. Once set in motion, artificial inequality would compound in generation after generation. Justice, viewed as a right relationship between virtue and rewards, would be irretrievably lost. Inequality could only occur because government interfered in the economy. Government had created the banks with their two key privileges: authority to issue a paper substitute for money and limited liability.

Many policy makers, as we have seen, confronted with the need to make provisions for money, viewed the solution to these problems as banking regulation, by means of a national bank. They had carefully designed an institution for this purpose, and it was working. But Jackson's strict classic liberal ideology could not admit this solution. In a worldview with a bold line between the public and private spheres, the option of mitigating problems caused by banking dynamics through central banking, via mechanisms understood at that time, did not exist.

Gouge's alternative solution to the economic problems caused by unregulated banking was for the government to separate itself from banking completely. Acknowledging that immediately ceasing a practice woven into the fabric of the economy would be disastrous, Gouge provided a strategy for gradually phasing out incorporated banking. Neither Congress or the states would charter new banks or renew existing charters. As existing charters wound down, banks were to redeem their entire paper circulation in hard money in annual increments as well as pay out specie for their notes on demand. Existing banks should be banned from issuing small bills, defined variously as notes in denominations of less than five, ten, or twenty dollars. This would bring gold and silver coin, real money with inherent value, back into circulation for everyday needs. For its part the federal government must not accept or pay out bank notes but, rather, must deal in hard money (gold and silver) only. Further, the Treasury Department must handle public money itself, not using any bank, through a geographically disbursed system of subtreasuries.

Ordinary people, not party to bank transactions, would be buffered from business cycles by using coin. Ultimately, banking would be legitimately practiced by individuals and private associations with no government-granted privileges. Bankers would lend their own money and issue promises to pay, such as bills of exchange, regulated by nothing but their own full liability. Banks would be for business. In this form banking was unobjectionable to Gouge and Jackson.

JACKSON MOVES AGAINST ALL INCORPORATED BANKING

JACKSON'S USE OF THE STATE BANKS

Jackson's actions throughout his second term followed Gouge's strategy for eliminating incorporated banking and replacing bank paper with specie as the money of the people. His veto of the second national bank's recharter was the first step. Transferring the government's deposits to selected state banks late in 1833 was the next. These two moves have been argued to represent not a rejection of public involvement with banking but, rather, a rejection of national government authority in favor of states' rights. But that is not how Jackson viewed what he was doing. His intent in placing the central government's deposits in the state banks was not to support state banking but to gain leverage to curb their banking practice. He told James Hamilton that he intended to use the deposit banks to "introduce a metallic currency throughout the union sufficient for the laboring class by putting out of issue and circulation all notes under twenty dollars."[46] In his final State of the Union message Jackson was talking about state banks when he urged Congress to "exert the utmost vigilance in calling into action the means necessary to correct the evils resulting from the unfortunate exercise of the power" to establish banks.[47] Three months later, in his Farewell Address, the president called on the people to be vigilant in their state governments, as well as at the federal level, against erecting banking corporations.[48]

As use of the deposit banks—"pet banks" to critics who viewed it all as a patronage move—played out in practice, Jackson's Treasury

Department made the rules until Congress spoke in the Deposit Act of 1836. This law required that the deposit banks pay specie on demand, cease issuing notes under five dollars, credit all U.S. deposits as specie, and make all payments in specie if requested by the payee. The Deposit Act thus attempted to use the deposit banks to move toward Jackson's goal of a specie currency. In an effort to reach beyond the deposit banks to discourage note issue by all banks, this legislation further provided that the government would not accept the notes of any bank that issued currency in denominations under five dollars.[49]

The Democratic Congress further supported Jackson's hard-money policy with several pieces of coinage legislation aimed at bringing specie back into circulation. An 1834 statute designated a long list of foreign coins as legal tender.[50] Devaluation Acts in 1834 and 1837 adjusted the relative values of gold and silver. Gold had been undervalued in relation to silver for about fifteen years. This legislation aimed to value gold so that it would circulate while keeping silver circulating as well due to its convenience for small amounts.[51]

Jackson's policy on payment for public lands constituted another effort to suppress the issue of bank paper money and move specie into circulation. Given the president's aggressive Indian removal policy, the availability of federal lands was high, and sales were at a frenzied pace. The proceeds, mostly in bank notes, swelled federal receipts and passed the tariff as a major source of revenue in 1836.[52] By administrative order Jackson required that the Treasury accept only gold and silver in payment for public lands. Secretary of the Treasury Levi Woodbury relayed the president's direction to government collectors and provided his rationale in the "Specie Circular."[53]

Jackson thus aimed throughout his second term to eliminate public involvement in the private activity of banking. When he retired to the Hermitage in early 1837, the national bank's federal charter had expired. The federal government no longer regulated banks nor provided a national bank currency. Measures had been taken to minimize the role of state banks in providing money as well, in an effort to make specie the money of the people and of the federal government. Jackson had called on the people to oppose state action in incorporating banks, and he was distributing surplus federal revenue to state governments, not depositing it in banks. Yet central government deposits required for transactions remained in state banks across the country. It was left to Jackson's successor, Martin Van Buren, to sever the link between the government's gold and private business completely.

THE INDEPENDENT TREASURY

The former president had been back in Tennessee for only two months when banks in New York City suspended redemption of their notes in hard money, leading to runs on banks throughout much of the country, in the Panic of 1837. Deposit banks holding the central government's funds suspended note redemption in specie with the other banks, despite conditions in the Deposit Act to the contrary. The government, which required itself to pay in specie, could not get its own legal money to pay its bills.

President Van Buren called a special session of Congress and insisted that the deposit banks' failure as government agents indicated that it was time to carry Jackson's project to fruition. To ensure the safety of its own funds, as well as to avoid fueling banks' inherent tendency to overissue on the basis of public deposits, the central government should divorce itself entirely from all banks. Van Buren asked Congress to establish an Independent Treasury (independent from banks, not the government) as a line agency in the Treasury Department, which would collect, hold, and disburse the government's money.[54]

Whigs in Congress opposed the Independent Treasury proposal and pressed, instead, for a new national bank. How could the government abandon its responsibility to regulate the general currency? Since when did the government "take care of itself and let the people take care of themselves"? The exchanges would be deranged, and money dealers would gorge themselves. Daniel Webster decried the proposal for an Independent Treasury, which "carries us back to the dark ages. . . . From an intellectual, it goes back to a physical age. From commerce and credit, it returns to hoarding and hiding; from confidence and trust, it retreats to bolts and bars . . . and to pains and penalties for touching hidden treasure."[55] The Whigs fought off the new federal agency throughout most of Van Buren's single term. But when banks in the South and West suspended again in 1839, Van Buren repeated his call for an Independent Treasury, and legislation giving it to him squeaked by in 1840.

The Whigs persisted; in 1841, with Van Buren defeated by Harrison, Whig majorities in both houses of Congress quickly passed laws repealing the Independent Treasury and establishing a new national bank. They were caught completely off guard when John Tyler, stepping into the presidency upon Harrison's untimely death, signed the bill killing the Independent Treasury—but vetoed the bank bill. The Independent Treasury was thus gone, with no bank to replace it. The Whigs quickly passed a new bank measure, essentially as drafted by Tyler's secretary of the Treasury and approved in cabinet by the president. To their amazement and horror Tyler, lacking bonds to the Whigs and courted by the Democrats, vetoed this bill.[56]

Congress and President Polk reestablished the Independent Treasury five years later, in 1846. In the interlude the Treasury Department handled the government's funds as if its authorizing law had been in effect continuously.[57]

The Independent Treasury was a line operation of the Treasury Department, just as Jackson had advocated in his second State of the Union message. It consisted of actual physical offices and vaults, subtreasuries, located in cities throughout the United States. Its officials reported to the secretary of the Treasury. Government receipts were collected and held in the subtreasuries rather than in banks; thus, no bank collected interest by lending the people's money. Nor did banks make money off the people by holding federal government bonds as capital, for Jackson had paid off the debt. The government's transactions were handled by the subtreasuries in specie only; bank currency was no longer acceptable in payments to the government nor in disbursements. The government collected, held, and disbursed its own funds through this structure until the Federal Reserve System assumed government fiscal agency in 1920.[58]

Andrew Jackson viewed banking and monetary policy through the lenses provided by his public philosophy, which included only a very narrow role for the government and a bold, clear line between the public and private spheres. The second Bank of the United States crossed that line in design and purpose: Jackson viewed the reliance in its design on private incentives as inherently corrupting of any public purpose, and to him neither banking nor its regulation were public concerns. There was no place for this organization in Jackson's normative world, and he did what he could to make the empirical world correspond. Jackson thus destroyed the national bank and, with it, central government capacity for banking and economic regulation. Public philosophy can be destructive of institutions as well as constructive. Jackson's ideas motivated his action, and he changed the institutional environment.

The fight between Alexander Hamilton and Thomas Jefferson over the first Bank of the United States had been a manifestation of their fundamental philosophical argument: Should the state's central concern be with the freedom and equality of individuals? Or should the state aim to maximize the economic development of the nation? Theirs was an argument over ends. Jackson's real argument was with his own liberal predecessors over means, though he probably never saw that. The second Bank of the United States was proposed and chartered by a president and Congress of the party of Jefferson, not by Alexander Hamilton. In response to circumstances Gallatin, Dallas, Madison, and a group within the congressional party stretched beyond the constraints of simple classic liberal ideology. In pursuing the purpose of a uniform currency—an adequate but not inflated supply of currency and credit available across the country—the second Bank of the United States protected individuals so that their accumulated property, their foothold in the system, was maintained, even as it facilitated economic development. If Jackson ever realized that was the purpose of the second bank, he did not believe that a public/private hybrid institution could achieve it.

So far I have focused on banking policy at the national level, where it was one of a small number of issues that dominated the agenda from the days of Hamilton and Jefferson through the mid-1840s. Banking policy was no less central in the states. Indeed, state legislatures were the sites at which the basic actor in the framework, the corporate bank, was under design; here also, various approaches to regulation emerged. In this chapter we leave Washington, with its Independent Treasury, and backtrack to analyze banking development in the states from the 1780s until the eve of the Civil War. The focus then returns to Washington as policy makers there pass the National Bank Act, which attempted to replace the heterogeneous state banks with uniform national banks. The philosophical theme of the relationship between the public and private spheres, used to anchor the investigation in the previous chapter, is carried forward—for Andrew Jackson's campaign to draw a clear line between the government and the economy fundamentally affected the direction of institutional development in the states as well as in Washington.

The development of state banks from the beginning of the Republic through the eve of the Civil War can be divided into two periods, marked by Jackson's veto of the second national bank's charter renewal in 1832. Before the veto states established banks with a range of public and private purposes and considerable variation in the mix of public and private elements in their design. Moreover, state legislatures pursued banking policy within a regulatory framework that, except for a few years, included a central bank that both helped provide money and regulated state banks. The states' own primary regulative vehicle was the constitution of the bank itself.

After Jackson's bank veto, with the federal government's institutional capacity for bank regulation largely dismantled, it became increasingly important for the states to act effectively in this policy area. But, even as state banking became more crucial, its legitimacy was seriously challenged by the extension of Jackson's ideological assault on the Bank of the United States to all banks. One effect is seen in the design of state banks. After the veto state legislatures groped toward a form for the bank which would permit them to retain it but view it as a private actor. As the public presence (Treasury Secretary Dallas's "interior agency") was removed from within the bank's ownership and management, the importance of outside regulation increased, leading to establishment of state bank regulatory commissions or agencies.

In an approach that has been repeated many times since, Washington eventually copied institutional models—of the corporate bank and a banking regulator—which had developed in the states. But, while in the states banks heavily charged with public purpose *and* banks designed as private actors were running at full steam, the National Bank Act passed during the Civil War adopted the model of a bank as private actor. The public's role in banking was narrowed and organizationally separated from banks, placed in a regulator that was a line agency of the Treasury Department; the regulator was a public actor. Policy makers in Washington expected that state banks would convert to national bank charters. The regulatory framework they anticipated could be interpreted to fulfill the ideological requirement that public and private concerns be segregated.

STATE BANKS BEFORE JACKSON'S BANK VETO

THE PURPOSES OF STATE BANKS

In the eighteenth and well into the nineteenth century, in accord with the dominant view of corporations in the United States, a bank was regarded as an instrumentality of the state. Voices disputing the policy of establishing banks, from a Jeffersonian perspective, were never absent, but they did not question the legal authority of state legislatures, as opposed to Congress, to create corporations.

The bank was a widely used instrument. In explaining the evolution of the regulatory role of the first Bank of the United States, I directed attention to the growth in the number of state banks from 4 to over 100 during the first national bank's twenty year tenure (1791–1811). Likewise, only five years after the first national bank was erased from the framework, the number of state banks had doubled to 232. The rate of proliferation slowed with the second Bank of the United States on the scene; nevertheless, by 1831 over 400 banks held charters in the twenty-four states that constituted the Union.[1] With some exceptions each bank was chartered separately in a special act of a state legislature.

Why had the states established these banks? The list of public purposes for which state legislatures chose a bank included: to provide credit for trade, manufacturing, and agriculture; to provide circulating medium for everyday economic transactions; to act as the fiscal agent of the state; to generate revenue for state government operations, obviating the need for taxation; to finance public improvements; and to regulate other banks in the state.

While providing credit may be viewed from William Gouge's perspective as a private purpose of lender and borrower, with unfortunate spillover effects on the public, it was—and is—also viewed as a public purpose in the context of community-wide economic development and ongoing economic health. The first banks chartered by some of the original New England and middle states were intended to meet the need for short-term commercial credit in the cities in which they operated. Thus began banking in New York, Philadelphia, Boston, and Baltimore. Before long people in these and other states sought charters for banks which would meet the credit needs of farmers, or farmers and mechanics. As the territories and states of the West developed, their legislatures chartered banks that extended credit for both commercial and agricultural activity. In the newer states of the Southwest as well as the original southern states, where the economy was dominated by plantation agriculture, banks were established to lend to planters for land acquisition and seasonal needs. Legislatures thus often made explicit policy decisions about the distribution of credit among various functions by specifying the types of loans banks were to provide; they might go so far as to specify proportions for the various types of loans. Geographic distribution of credit was also addressed deliberately through branching requirements, chartering additional banks, or allocating credit by county.

The common practice was to provide a borrower with bank notes, rather than the deposit credit of today's lending practice, so the availability of currency was a by-product of credit provision. This apparently secondary effect was sometimes equally or more important to legislators in deciding to establish banks than the need for credit. In 1792, for example, the Connecticut legislature chartered the Hartford

Bank mainly to provide currency to buy and move crops in fall and winter.[2] The need for circulating medium was especially acute in newer areas of the country—western portions of the original states and the entirety of states settled after the Revolution. Legislatures in these areas would establish banks to meet the need for currency even when many of the legislators involved were sympathetic to antibank arguments. When the original colonies/states were economically young, their legislatures could issue paper money directly in a variety of forms. But adoption of the federal Constitution had foreclosed that option. The legislative representatives of newer areas could not facilitate everyday economic transactions or nurture early economic development by directly issuing currency, as Benjamin Franklin had urged in 1729.[3] They could use the circulating medium provided by the national bank or central government issues; they could rely on "foreign" banks (banks chartered in other states) and paper promises to pay issued by private individuals and businesses; they could hope that some hard money would find its way to the frontier; or they could charter state banks, over which they could exercise some control. Before 1832, while even in the older seaboard states the weight of the simple need for currency retained influence, this consideration was dominant in establishing some of the very large banks of the Southwest. Tennessee (1820–32) and Alabama (1823–45), for example, chartered large banks with the central purpose of providing sufficient currency.[4] This factor became weighty in the states of the Old Northwest only after the second Bank of the United States was pulled out from under their rapidly growing economies.

Another purpose served by some state banks was that of fiscal agent for their state governments—handling public deposits, making disbursements, placing debt issues—as the first and second Banks of the United States did for the central government. The financial relationship between many banks and their respective state governments extended beyond simple fiscal agency, however, to providing revenue for governmental operations. Examples include the Bank of Pennsylvania, chartered in 1793, which permitted the state to "defray out of the dividends all the expenses of government without any direct tax" for forty years;[5] and Georgia's Central Bank (1828–51), which covered all of the state's expenses from 1828 to 1842.[6] More commonly, bank revenues provided not the entirety but some portion of a state's budget; sometimes they were dedicated to a special purpose, such as education. State revenue from banks took the forms of dividends, when the state shared in ownership of some or all of its banks; bonuses, which were direct payments to the state for a bank charter or charter renewal; and taxes, levied on bank capital or circulation. These were considered means of capturing some of the direct financial benefits of the banking privilege for the public.

There were banks whose primary or ancillary public purpose was to achieve revenue for a capital improvement that the legislature viewed as necessary but for which it did not wish to tax. A corporation could be set up with authority to construct the project and to conduct banking activity: the banking privilege was a source of funds for the improvement as well as an outlet for its earnings. Banking was often linked directly in this way to canal construction early on and later to railroads. Less directly, bank bonuses could be earmarked for a state's transportation improvement fund, or banks could be encouraged or required to buy stock in transportation corporations.

Several states chartered central banks to regulate banking. Like the second Bank of the United States, these state-level central banks were intended to provide adequate, reliable currency and credit through direct banking operations and by regulating other banking in the state. Also like the second national bank, there was consensus on this purpose among Hamilton's heirs (National Republicans and then Whigs), with their focus on economic development, and reformed Jeffersonians (most Democratic-Republicans and Democrats before the bank veto), who believed that banking could be useful to the common people but must be regulated to protect them. The Vermont legislature, which did not much like banks and previously had not chartered any, established a state central bank in 1806.[7] Among the original southern states North Carolina chartered a central bank in 1810,[8] South Carolina in 1812,[9] and Georgia in 1828.[10] Many of the states organized after adoption of the Constitution chartered one or more, roughly consecutive, central banks. In the Southwest, Louisiana, Mississippi, Kentucky, Alabama, and Tennessee all did so before Jackson's bank veto. States of the Old Northwest turned to state central banks only after the bank veto.

DESIGN OF STATE BANKS

The design of the four hundred–plus state banks of 1831, chartered in separate acts of twenty-four legislatures to serve one or more purposes, was not standard. To analyze their differences it is helpful to consider the constitutive dimensions introduced in chapter two to sort Hamilton's principles of bank design: ownership, capital, governance, and permissible assets. In the first three categories state banks varied in the extent of public and private participation; indeed, they lined up along a public/private continuum in each design dimension. With regard to its asset structure, the more heavily a bank was involved in agricultural lending, the more public involvement it had along the other three dimensions.

Banks set up to provide commercial loans in economically established areas fell closest to the private end of the continuum along all dimensions. Their ownership might be wholly private, yet every state took shares for the public in some or all of its banks. The nominal capital of these institutions often fell within the range of $100,000 to $200,000, though it could be less, and some were authorized up to $500,000 and more; they did not have branches. Investors were required to pay specie for their shares, although Gouge was correct in his charge that this was often not paid in; its place was held by personal notes or loans on stock security. Governance of these banks was likely to be entirely private, with directors chosen by stockholders and the president chosen by the directors. Loans were likely to be largely limited to short terms, thirty or sixty days, on goods in trade. Credit on these terms was referred to as a "discount" in contemporary discussions and was reported separately from "loans" in the accounting reports of the era. Such banks were likely to lend to theirs own directors and stockholders and to others of their political party.

A couple of state central banks hold down the opposite end of the public/private continuum in all dimensions. The Vermont State Bank (1806–12) and the Bank of Kentucky (1806–22), along with its successor Bank of the Commonwealth of Kentucky (1820–30), were owned entirely by the state; governed by directors appointed by the legislature; had no dedicated capital but banked on the whole of the state's credit; and operated to provide currency and credit widely in agricultural economies.[11] State central banks were much larger than commercial banks, often capitalized at one to three million dollars and more. Unlike the extreme in Vermont and Kentucky, they usually had dedicated capital. The capital might be raised through the sale of state bonds or composed of mortgages on real estate. In the case of banks capitalized with mortgages on privately held land, called "real estate banks," bonds were also sold to raise money that could be loaned; the mortgaged land was theoretically available in case a bank needed to produce cash, but there was little actual intent to sell any of it. In either case the state guaranteed the bonds, although debt service was usually the responsibility of the bank. A state central bank often had multiple branches in order to distribute currency and credit, thus functioning as a system rather than as a unit bank.

Between the two extremes of mostly private commercial banks and almost entirely public state central banks there existed just about every arrangement imaginable. The state shared in ownership of some banks but not in governance (beyond specifying the banks' constitutions). When the state was involved in a bank's governance, its representation on the board of directors ranged from minimal to a majority plus public selection of the president. The capital of state banks consisted of various combinations of specie, mortgages on land and slaves, and bonds issued by the chartering state, other states, or the United States. Banks were authorized to provide different proportions of commercial versus real estate and agricultural loans.

The appearance of organizational forms was not random: there were regional patterns. The older states of the Northeast and middle Atlantic regions chartered multiple small (measured in terms of capital) banks, generally without branches, which were usually for commercial lending and capitalized nominally with specie but which might be providing real estate and agricultural loans and be capitalized to some extent with mortgages. Although these states often earned income from their banks through dividends and bonuses, they were less likely to participate directly in bank governance than states of the South and West. Southern states chartered fewer, larger banks, often with branches. These banks were deeply involved in real estate and agricultural lending and fell closer to the public end of the spectrum in terms of governance, ownership, and capital composition. The original southern states of the Atlantic seaboard chartered some commercial banks, though fewer than their counterparts in the North, to operate alongside the more public giants. The newer states of the Southwest were less likely to charter small commercial banks in addition to their large central banks, and some of them went through periods of permitting no privately owned chartered banks. By 1832 the states and territories of the Old Northwest had almost no incorporated state banks, relying, instead, on the Bank of the United States.

STATE REGULATION BEFORE THE VETO

Even as they relied on banks for the public benefits they offered, policy makers in the states were aware of the hazards they threatened. Yet, rather than abandon the practice, as Jackson urged, and give up its benefits, they chose to regulate. Their primary regulative vehicle—before Jackson's veto of continuation of the second national bank—was each bank charter itself. State legislatures sought to control a bank's behavior from the inside, through the formal design of the organization, through its constitution.

State legislatures thus worked with the constituent dimensions of capital, ownership, governance, and assets positively, to create a bank that would serve their intended purposes. Legislatures manipulated the same design elements to control against the negative outcomes that concerned them: fraud and self-dealing; concentration of economic power; and Gouge's great culprit, overissue. Over time charter provisions became more detailed in the effort to protect against these potential problems.

Self-dealing by directors and stockholders was among the earliest targets of expanded charter provisions. Bank decision makers' discretion could be specifically limited in problem areas: charters limited loans on stock credit as well as loans to directors and stockholders. Charters also began to define actions that would be viewed as criminal, such as embezzlement, and to specify the punishment for charter violations. (Banking laws today remain replete with pages and pages of descriptions of what constitutes a criminal act.)

Some charter provisions aimed to prevent the concentration of economic power which had so concerned Jefferson. Based on a reading of the provisions themselves, legislatures appear to have conceived of two dimensions of this issue. First, there was the problem of potential control over any particular bank by one or a few individuals. Second, there was concern with control over banking generally by one or a couple of banks. Several techniques were intended to prevent individuals from controlling banks. Procedures for the initial stock offering could be quite intricate in an effort to ensure a broad opportunity to buy: commissioners would be appointed to supervise; books had to be opened and closed simultaneously in locations across the state; if there was oversubscription (more shares sought than existed), shares were not sold on a first-come/first-serve basis but, rather, prorated according to effective demand. The price on shares could be set quite low—often one hundred dollars and as low as twenty-five—to invite many owners. Once ownership was established, voting rules like Hamilton's for the first Bank of the United States limited any individual stockholder's weight as the number of shares that were held increased beyond certain breakpoints.

Other charter provisions aimed to prevent the second dimension of concentration of power, in which any particular bank would become too powerful. According to Albert Gallatin, this is why New York kept its banks so small in terms of maximum capital; presumably, this was the rationale in other middle states and New England, where there were also small commercial banks. Against Jefferson's fear that unlimited longevity contributed to the accumulation of power, most bank charters had expiration dates. If the bank sought renewal, the legislature could add conditions, adjusting its constitution as necessary; and it was not unusual for a legislature to refuse to renew a charter, leading to the bank's liquidation. In areas where larger banks were the norm, the level of public participation in ownership and governance was high to preclude concentrated private control of one bank by a few individuals or of economic opportunities in the state by one bank.

Whether they agreed with Gouge's contention that the overissue of paper money was deliberate or viewed the phenomenon as unintended, state legislators tried to avoid it. Manipulations of all four of a bank's basic constitutive dimensions could aim to guard against the overissue of paper money, with its general economic effects and harm to individual noteholders. Capital might be seen not only as something to lend but also as the fundamental guarantee to the noteholder. Over time various legislatures tightened up capital requirements: they increased the proportion that must be paid in specie, sometimes up to 100 percent, and they specified the time frame for paying it in, up to requiring all of it before the bank could begin operation. Governance structures were stipulated in which decision-making latitude was constrained by quantitative rules and personal penalties. Among the formulas adopted to limit bankers' lending discretion we find maximum ratios of circulation to capital, discounts to capital, and discounts to deposits. There were also specie reserve requirements. Directors were sometimes made personally liable for loans that violated such charter rules. While bank managers had latitude regarding what kind of money to pay out under various circumstances, the requirement that banks pay specie for their own notes on demand was common. In a financial

panic, however, it was customary for legislatures to suspend this requirement, though reluctantly, viewing legalized suspension as likely
to ensure stability in the long run. The obligation of a bank's owners to
its noteholders was debated. Although the unlimited personal liability
for notes that Jackson would have preferred was not a feature of incorporated banks, legislatures were likely to make stockholders liable beyond what they had actually paid in, up to the full extent of their stock
holding. Requirements regarding a bank's assets could also aim at liquidity. Charters usually specified the assets, besides its loans, which a
bank could hold; they were conservative, generally confined to the state's
own bonds, U.S. bonds, and possibly the obligations of some other states.

Initially, then, a state's banking regulation was primarily through
the charter. Over time, charters within a state converged on a model,
as legislators first copied existing charters and then gradually passed
statutes specifying standard provisions that applied to new charters,
charter renewals, and requests for increases in authorized capital. There
were statutory efforts to apply new provisions to existing charters; banks
might comply with them or litigate. Although few states took it before
Jackson's bank veto, the next step was a general banking law. Such a
statute consolidated the provisions of banking laws passed over time,
revised and updated them, and added some. Banks in many states thus
gradually came to be subject to uniform charter requirements, but a
special act of the legislature was still needed to grant each charter.

The first and second Banks of the United States provided a major
source of regulation of state banks from the outside, by which I mean
through measures other than charter provisions. Steps had been taken
in the direction of regulating banking organizations from the outside
on the state level as well. These included, for example, the beginning
of inspection and reporting requirements. Usually on an ad hoc basis,
states began requiring their banks to submit to inspection by a legislative committee or commissioners appointed by the governor, the legislature, or a court. The first standing bank supervisory commission appears to have been that established by the New York legislature in 1829.[12]
Banks might also be required to report specified information to an official of the executive or to the legislature; this report might be required
to run in a local newspaper.

In New England a regulatory system conventionally viewed as entirely private was well established by the mid-1820s. To grasp the origin and mechanism of this "Suffolk system" we need to understand
how banks made money on their notes. Recall that a bank issued notes

in the process of extending credit. A borrower spent the notes and made payments to the bank on the discount (short-term commercial credit), loan (longer-term credit, possibly on real estate), or accommodation (personal credit). If those who received the notes brought them to the bank, the bank had to redeem them in cash. But, if the notes stayed in circulation, the bank had more money on hand and could make more loans. In New England notes of Boston banks easily showed up for redemption, since the trade and consumption in which they were used largely took place in the city. Notes of "country banks" also made their way to Boston but tended to stay in circulation because it was costly and inconvenient to present them at the issuing bank for redemption. Although these notes were accepted and traded at a discount, Boston banks resented country banks' domination of the profits to be made on circulation.

The short-lived Boston Exchange Bank appears to have been the first, beginning in 1804, to make a systematic effort to buy up country bank notes in the city at a discount and send them home for redemption, thereby serving the public good by suppressing overissue, albeit through no intent but to turn a profit. In 1813 the New England Bank did the same. But it was the Suffolk Bank, chartered in 1818, which succeeded so well with its own variation on this system that it became essentially a central bank for New England. The Suffolk offered country banks the "opportunity" to keep a permanent deposit with it, plus another deposit adequate to pay off any of their notes which the Suffolk acquired. If a country bank complied, the Suffolk paid off its notes, from that bank's own balance, at the same discount at which they were received. If a country bank was uncooperative, the Suffolk sent its notes home for redemption at par in specie. By 1824 the Suffolk had sold its service as agent for redemption of country bank notes to other major city banks. This approach suppressed overissue and kept New England bank notes at par or at a minimal discount even outside New England. In 1858 the Massachusetts legislature chartered the Bank of Mutual Redemption, owned largely by the country banks themselves, with regulation through this approach as a charter purpose; it gradually supplanted the Suffolk.[13] This system, which observers persist in viewing as a private system of regulation, had become in part public as the legislature sanctioned it and chartered an organization specifically for the purpose. (Notice that the approach to constraining overissue is similar to that developed by the first and second Banks of the United States. The national central banks, however, also reversed the practice, forbearing in presentation of notes and checks at state banks to permit credit expansion when necessary.)

While Jackson was busy in Washington recruiting for his first cabinet, the New York legislature was occupied in Albany designing another approach to noteholder protection which derived from outside the constitution of the individual bank. New York's Safety Fund law of 1829 was based on the idea that all of its chartered banks comprised a system in which, in return for the publicly granted privilege of earning profit by providing the public's currency, banking organizations were mutually responsible for one another's performance. Banks with charters issued or renewed under the Safety Fund law were obliged to pay one-half of 1 percent of their capital annually for six years into a safety fund. The fund was intended to pay off the noteholders of any bank that could not or would not redeem its currency. Due to technical flaws in its design, the fund did not serve as well as had been hoped. With the alternative available after 1838 of organizing under New York's free banking law, interest in reforming the safety fund to live up to its promise waned. The approach died out in New York in 1866, when the last safety fund charter expired, but analogous approaches that involved insuring deposits rather than notes were tried in several states and would provide a model for the Federal Deposit Insurance Corporation, established at the national level in 1933.[14]

In 1831, on the eve of Jackson's veto of charter renewal for the second Bank of the United States, the bank regulatory framework thus included over four hundred state banking corporations with diverse public purposes, in addition to their private purposes, and wide variation in the mix of public and private elements in their designs. The institutional framework also included the rudiments of bank regulatory agencies in some states, with approaches including examination and supervision as well as insurance. Finally, there was a national central bank that both regulated state banks and assisted directly in the provision of currency and credit where local needs required.

National policymakers, state legislatures, state banks, and the people generally were satisfied with the system. With the exception of the Panic of 1819, corresponding to the interlude between the end of the first Bank of the United States and effective performance by the second, there were few bank failures before the Civil War. In several states no incorporated bank failed before that massive disruption of the political economy. When Andrew Jackson attacked the state banks, as when he had attacked the national bank, he worked from ideology.

STATE BANKING AFTER THE BANK VETO

INITIAL RESPONSE

In the first years after Jackson vetoed recharter of the Bank of the United States there was no significant effort in the states to follow him in rejecting public involvement with banks. Rather, in an effort to compensate for the pending loss of currency and credit which the national bank provided, legislatures increased the capitalization of existing banks or chartered new ones according to the design patterns they had already established. In the Northeast and middle Atlantic states legislatures authorized multiple small, mostly privately capitalized and governed, commercial banks. New York alone, which had sixty-four banks in 1831, chartered twenty-two more from 1832 through 1834 and twelve in 1836.[15] Massachusetts chartered thirty new banks from 1832 through 1834 and thirty-three more in 1836 and 1837.[16] Delaware, with four banks in 1831, doubled the capitalization of two of them in 1837.[17]

The original southern states also chartered additional banks, but they were fewer and larger. In South Carolina the Charleston branch of the Bank of the United States had handled almost all exchange for the state's great staple exports of cotton and rice; the legislature chartered a huge (three million dollars in capital) Bank of Charleston to fill this special role as well as four small commercial banks and two railroad banks through 1836.[18] In Virginia banking before the veto had been carried on by four "mother" banks and their multiple branches, each a self-regulating system with substantial public participation, based on the model of the Bank of Virginia, which had been established in 1804. After Jackson's veto two more such banks were chartered by 1837.[19] North Carolina responded by renewing the charters of the three banks the state had and increasing their capitalization.[20] In the Southwest we see the chartering of additional mostly public behemoths, intended for heavy involvement in agriculture, as well as smaller commercial banks. The legislature of Kentucky for example, in its 1833–34 session, chartered the Bank of Kentucky—with capital of five million dollars, 40 percent held by the state, three of eleven directors appointed by the state, and six branches—as well as two smaller banks.[21]

The situation in the Northwest was more complicated. States and territories there were economically young, and their established pattern of banking did not revolve around state banks, but, rather, there was heavy reliance on the Bank of the United States for credit and currency. They lacked indigenous capital with which to start commercial banks, and, although some had authorized state central banks in their constitutions, none had one in 1832. Indiana, Illinois, and Missouri all responded to the loss of the Bank of the United States by chartering state central banks on its model.[22]

The Bank of Indiana is regarded by banking historians as highly successful, and its form is characteristic of state central banks in the Northwest. The state subscribed half of its initial $1.6 million capital and chose the president as well as a minority of the directors. The Bank of Indiana ultimately had seventeen branches providing banking throughout the state. The central branch did no direct banking but, instead, administered the system and supervised the other branches. The bank was reorganized in 1852, eliminating the state as a stockholder, but otherwise functioned much the same until 1865, when its branches were absorbed into the national bank system as unit banks.[23] In northwestern states that had central banks there was ongoing discussion over whether to charter smaller banks as well.

Ohio, a state since 1803, and Michigan, still a territory until 1837, did not set up central banks but, rather, established multiple small, privately owned banks. Ohio was dealing with dramatic economic growth from the mid-1820s through the mid-1830s. Although there was support in the state legislature for a central bank, the members opted to charter ten smaller privately owned banks in the 1830s, in hopes of attracting eastern capital. Michigan had chartered nine banks by 1835 and added nine more in 1836.[24]

The efforts of state legislatures across the United States to fill the gap that would be left by eliminating the national bank added up to a major expansion of state banking. From about 400 in 1831 the number of incorporated state banks was up to 703 by 1836 and continued to climb to 729 in 1837.[25] State bank circulation had doubled from 1833 through 1837, and loans and discounts multiplied two and a half times.[26] This was not what Jackson had in mind.

THE PANIC OF 1837 AND THE INFLUENCE OF IDEAS

It was only with the Panic of 1837 that Jackson's view that the government should be literally and completely separated from banking began to take hold among a majority of Democrats in many states. In May 1837, two months after Old Hickory had retired to the Hermitage and his former vice president, Martin Van Buren, had taken the president's oath of office, banks in New York City suspended redemption of their notes in hard money, leading to runs on banks throughout much of the country. Recession followed the banking panic.

National Whig and Democratic leaders articulated diametrically opposed interpretations of the causes of the Panic of 1837.[27] Rooted in a Hamiltonian perspective that required active government in the service of economic performance, Whigs charged the crisis to a failure of public policy. Jackson had withdrawn the government's deposits from the national bank, destroying the capacity to prevent overissue by state banks. Placing those deposits in state banks, thereby providing a basis upon which they could dramatically increase their paper circulation, was a perverse move guaranteed to produce inflation. Requiring payment in specie for the public lands drew gold from state banks, thus undermining their stability.[28] President Van Buren himself led for the Democrats. In a straightforward application of Gouge's theory he explained to the Congress that the overissue of bank credit had caused the crisis. But inflation could not be attributed, as Whigs would have it, to the missing regulator: England had a national bank and was having precisely the same economic difficulties. Overissue was inherent in the banking system.[29]

Today's leading interpretation of the Panic of 1837 differs from both of these, emphasizing the relationships between the United States and English economies at the real and financial levels.[30] What is important here, however, is not to resolve the question of the causes of the crisis but, rather, to see how beliefs about those causes influenced institutional development in the states. Before the panic the policy question in the states—as in Congress when the second Bank of the United States was established—was how to structure and regulate banks to accomplish public purposes. Opponents of all incorporated banking were never entirely absent, but they were not influential. Both Democrats and Whigs advocated regulated banking, although the parties' positions on any particular regulatory device varied over time and from state to state. In the wake of the panic both parties advocated banking reform at first. But by the mid-1840s, with unremitting repetition of national leaders' interpretation of the Panic of 1837 and the ensuing recession, a majority of Democrats in many states moved to the Jacksonian view that banking was a strictly private activity and its ties to the public should be severed; they favored the abolition of all incorporated banking.[31] Whigs gave up on the rest of the list of public purposes for banks cited earlier but continued to insist that they were needed for economic development. The policy question in the states changed from the pre-veto focus on how to use and design banks to whether or not to have banks at all ("banks or no banks"), and it became a partisan issue.

THE MOVE TO "FREE BANKS"

The most significant institutional outcome of the state banking debates of the 1840s and early 1850s was a new model for a bank: the "free bank." This model was adopted in most states by the mid-1850s and strongly influenced the form of the national banks authorized in the National Bank Act of 1863–64. The concept of free banking was first considered in New York, where it had been advocated by opponents of the state's system of chartered banks even before Jackson's presidency. The loco foco faction of the state Democratic Party represented an urban working-class variant of fundamental Jeffersonianism. Its members objected to paper money due to its potential for inflation and thus harm to common people who held notes; they further objected to banks because, as corporations, they were monopolies. They condemned the special legislation required to establish any corporation on principle, as bestowing special privileges and as a violation of the government's obligation of equal treatment. There was also a perception of widespread corruption as charter seekers wooed legislators. With Jackson the loco focos viewed private banking, among businessmen without publicly granted charters and with full personal liability for any notes issued, as unobjectionable.

Yet New York's legislature had long since explicitly rejected the view that banking is a strictly private business. Recognizing the public effects of permission to circulate and profit from paper currency, they had restricted banking to organizations chartered for that purpose in 1804. There was no legal right, common law or statutory, for individuals or groups without charters to bank on their own credit in New York nor in at least fifteen other states with similar "restraining laws." The loco foco (and Jacksonian) objective of abolishing incorporated banking would thus require repeal of New York's restraining laws.

A second group that opposed New York's regulated banking was characterized long ago by Albert Gallatin as "speculators" and more recently by banking historian Bray Hammond as "enterprisers." This group echoed loco foco criticisms of corporate monopolies and special legislation but not with the objective of curbing bank circulation of paper money. Rather, these critics viewed banking as a profitable business in itself and a means to secure funds for other business ventures. They resented the tight control the legislature exercised over entry into banking and credit expansion through restraining laws, limits on the number of charters, and charter restrictions. To them banking as a private business meant that anyone should be able to issue paper money (though not that they should bear unlimited personal liability for its redemption). The enterprisers advocated repeal of the restraining laws and enactment of a general law positively permitting anyone to bank who met minimum requirements.

The loco foco and enterpriser views cannot be mapped onto the separate parties and were not the only views in play in New York's free banking deliberation. The loco focos were a faction of the Democrats. Enterprisers included Democrats and Whigs. A third group, including both the state's machine Regency Democrats and mainstream Whigs, continued to favor the existing system of regulated chartered banking.

Free banking had been before the New York legislature as early as 1825, when a committee studied and reported on it. At that time the idea was pushed to the back of the shelf, as the safety fund insurance approach caught on. Free banking bills were in the legislature again in 1837, when the state's banks suspended, triggering the panic. As the banking panic drove criticism of New York's chartered banks to new heights, the legislature dusted off the free banking concept and tried to figure out how to institutionalize it. The result was the Free Banking Act of 1838, amended in 1840. Commentators on that law from Albert Gallatin, who was a contemporary, to Bray Hammond, who read the record a century and a quarter later, agree that the mix of motives among the law's proponents led to an institutional outcome that undoubtedly felt Kafkaesque to the original loco foco advocates of free banking.[32]

The legislature designed the free bank with two purposes in mind. First, they intended to protect noteholders absolutely, thereby meeting loco foco concerns over the harm of paper money inflation. But the mechanism for guaranteeing notes was not the full personal liability on the part of bankers advocated by loco focos. Indeed, shareholders in a bank formed under this law were explicitly relieved of personal liability for the debts of the association, in accord with the enterprisers' preferences. The long list of devices embedded in existing charters, aimed directly or indirectly at ensuring liquidity, was also abandoned. Likewise, the Safety Fund was ignored. Instead, the legislature devised a new means for guaranteeing bank currency. In order to circulate notes, a bank formed under this law was required to deposit the bonds of specified public jurisdictions with the state's comptroller. The comptroller held the bonds, and in some circumstances the interest on them as well, in a fund to secure the notes put into circulation by the bank. If the bank refused to pay hard money to noteholders on demand, as chartered banks had in the Panic of 1837, the comptroller was to sell the bonds and use the proceeds to redeem the notes. In a related innovation banks would no longer print their own currency. The state comptroller printed the currency and provided it to each bank in an amount not to exceed the bonds it deposited as guarantee. Thus, various banks issued a "uniform" currency that was securely backed by bonds.

The other purpose of the new approach was to abolish "monopoly," the "special privilege" of a bank charter.[33] The free banking law was a general law permitting anyone to open a bank if he or she met its spare requirements, which included provision of basic information in a certificate to be filed with the secretary of state and recorded in the county in which the bank would operate and a minimum capital of $100,000, no maximum. Commercial, industrial, and agricultural lending were permitted, but no proportions were specified.

This New York legislation provided a transformed concept of a state bank. In practice state legislatures viewed banking corporations as instrumentalities of the state, established to serve various public purposes as well as the private interests of stockholders and borrowers. In removing the "special privilege" of a charter, New York's free banking law also removed the public purposes from the bank's constitution. This law made what had been the Jeffersonian/Jacksonian criticism of the corporation—that, regardless of what its advocates may claim, a bank is really operated strictly for the private benefit of its owners— the legitimate constitution of banks established under it. That is, a free bank was intended to be a private actor. Unlike the publicly constituted and regulated state banks of the past, these new banks could decide for themselves if, when, and where to bank; they could decide who could participate in ownership and how they would make decisions; they could allocate credit and currency as they would. "Free banking," Bray Hammond tells us, "was an application of laissez-faire to the monetary function."[34] An aging Albert Gallatin pointed out at the time that free banking was an application of the principle of free trade, although an erroneous one.[35]

Except for a short-lived experiment with free banks in Michigan, New York was ahead of other states in resolving the banks / no banks argument with this institutional approach. State legislatures had responded at first to Jackson's bank veto in 1832 by increasing chartered banking of the kind they already had. With the Panic of 1837 and its aftermath they tried harder to control banking. The regulatory mechanisms that had begun to develop in the pre-veto period were tightened and disseminated from state to state: internal controls, such as requirements for paid-up capital and ratios limiting note issue were made more stringent; external controls such as reporting and inspection requirements, bank commissioners or commissions, were adopted by more and more states. Likewise, an increasing number of states gathered up their banking regulations into general banking laws in the late 1830s and 1840s.

Yet, as the majority of Democrats in many states, influenced by the ideologically grounded interpretation of the Panic of 1837 repeated by their national leaders, moved from this "try harder to make banks work" position to the "no banks" position, their attack on their own state-chartered banks in Jacksonian terms intensified: banks were monopolies owing their existence to special legislation; the whole system threatened noteholders. As in New York, it was often difficult to distinguish—based on their criticisms of state banking—between the opponents of all banking and the enterprisers who wanted freer entry into banking. But, if the proposed solution to the evils of chartered bank monopoly was free banking, one could be pretty sure who was talking. Mainstream Whigs in the states did not want laissez-faire banking, but, as hopes for help from Washington faded, the clamor against chartered banks grew louder, and their perception of a need for capital for economic development continued—free banking began to look pretty good. It "presented a potential for financial expansion without the allegation of monopoly associated with state banks . . . [and] promised added security to bill holders."[36]

Jacksonian Democrats scored some victories. Of seven states that joined the union in the 1840s and 1850s four (Texas, Iowa, California, and Oregon) entered with constitutional prohibitions against banking. Arkansas, already a state before the panic, outlawed the practice when revising its constitution in 1846. Nevertheless, the enactment of no banks was both temporary and confined to western states with no institutional infrastructure for banking. By the outbreak of the Civil War, Whigs and a minority of Democrats had united to achieve passage of free banking laws in almost all states.

Under some early versions of free banking there were abuses and significant numbers of failures. Some statutes authorized low-quality bonds as backing for currency—perhaps obligations of a southern state that issued excessive debt to support public improvements. The "bankers" might have no intention of doing a legitimate banking business: they could, and did, go south to buy bonds with a small percentage down; run to the comptroller in Indiana, deposit their bonds, and claim their currency; return south to pay the balance on their bonds with the notes they had just picked up in Indiana; and open their "bank" in some remote place so that the notes could not come home for redemption. The profit in this scam was the interest on the bonds. Free banks might have virtually no specie on hand.

Such scandalous experience with early free banks after Jackson's bank veto contributed greatly, along with the earlier failures of large numbers of unincorporated banks in the Panic of 1819, to the conventional wisdom that state banking before the National Bank Act was poor. State legislatures learned, however, from their own and other states' experiences with free banks. Legislatures strengthened the free banking statutes by including many of the same internal and external controls that had applied to individually chartered banks. By the late 1850s free banks were designed much like the banks described here as falling closer to the private end of the spectrum along all constitutive dimensions. They looked like the commercial banks of the eastern states, but there was no question that they were "private" businesses, and their currency was backed by bonds on deposit with the state.

In light of the adoption of the free bank model by the federal government in the National Bank Act, which I will take up in a moment, let me underscore a crucial point that national policy makers apparently did not appreciate in turning to this model. State-level free banking operated alongside each state's individually chartered banks. Through their specially chartered banks the states continued to pursue a range of public purposes including geographic and functional credit distribution, the provision of adequate currency, and bank regulation. In this context, one in which other banks were ensuring that public availability and allocational priorities within the various states were met, free banks provided credit and currency as their private interest dictated.

To some readers free banking statutes may be begging for comparison to general incorporation laws. The development of general incorporation and free banking roughly parallel each other before the Civil War. From the beginning through the middle of the nineteenth century a transformation in the concept of the corporation generally, not just the banking corporation, from public instrumentality to private entity, was under way in practice,[37] public policy,[38] and the law.[39] Many of the arguments in the free banking debate were echoed from the controversy over the status of corporations generally. For Jacksonians corporate charters conferred special privileges, creating centers of economic and therefore political power: they were an illegitimate mixing of public authority and private purpose. But others maintained that a corporate charter did no more than provide a useful form for business organization—and, if anyone who wanted one could get one, there would not be an equal protection problem: a corporation was simply a private economic actor. By the 1850s general incorporation laws were becoming common.[40] Under them a business organization could achieve the legal and practical advantages of corporate status by meeting the standard requirements of a general law. At this time a general incorporation law provided an optional alternative to incorporation via a special charter. In this sense general incorporation is analogous to free banking: free banks operated alongside individually chartered state banks. General incorporation laws became the sole route to incorporation in the states only later, in the 1870s and 1880s.[41]

In a more important sense, however, a mix of corporations, including some sanctioned under general laws and some with individually granted charters, is not analogous to a mix of free banks and specially chartered banks. The mining, manufacturing, wholesaling, and retailing businesses that shifted from special to general incorporation had lost their public dimensions and become private concerns, operated for the profit of their owners. Yet, in a society that uses banks to originate the medium of exchange, banks are different from other businesses in that they are providing a crucial component of the infrastructure for all business—indeed, for all society. While a free bank is very much like any other corporation, legitimately making its decisions with the objective of profit for its owners, many of the states' specially chartered banks remained much more than that. In authorizing them, legislators knew they were providing economic and social infrastructure; they did so with explicit attention to having enough for everyone; and their purposes included deliberate geographic and functional allocation.

On the eve of the Civil War, then, without a central bank, it is difficult to see the United States as having one banking framework, especially because state institutions were so diverse. Each state had its banking framework, consisting of some configuration of chartered banks, free banks (essentially private businesses but with notes guaranteed by the state), sometimes a central bank, and one or more state regulatory authorities. The federal government had left the states to fend for themselves in banking policy for thirty years but was about to seize back the prerogative.

THE NATIONAL BANK ACT OF 1863–64

CONGRESS REVISITS BANKING

Banking policy had receded from center stage in Washington after 1840 as the issue of slavery became increasingly difficult to keep in the wings. Why fuss about banking, anyway? The Independent Treasury was up and running, handling the government's financial affairs in specie and occasionally Treasury notes. Fortuitous discoveries of gold had increased the stock of specie in the United States, mitigating concerns of Whig policy makers and bankers that government "hoarding" of its specie would leave business with no capital on which to bank. The divorce between the federal government and banks was working nicely.

Abraham Lincoln was elected president in November 1860. Between that time and his inauguration four months later, seven states left the Union and joined the Confederate States of America. In April 1861 the military war between the states erupted when Confederate guns fired on Fort Sumter. If it had not been absurd before to insist that the government deal only in specie, the financial requirements of the war certainly made it so. The central government's budget, quite small for decades, would now increase exponentially, and there was not enough gold in the country to cover it. Some other arrangement had to be made to provide enough of some kind of money that could be used throughout the Union.

Lincoln's Treasury secretary, Salmon P. Chase, was a former Jacksonian Democrat from Ohio and a committed hard-money man. He intended from the beginning to finance the war chiefly through the sale of bonds, which he did.[42] In accord with the Independent Treasury Act as well as his personal convictions, Secretary Chase further intended to handle the government's transactions in specie. In this he was only briefly successful. Because the banks had the only large piles of gold readily at hand, it was to them that he peddled the government's bonds at the beginning of the war. Although they would have preferred to extend their loans in the form of deposit credit, Chase insisted on gold, and from August through November 1861 major eastern banks lent the government one hundred forty million dollars in gold. Tapped out, they suspended payment of their notes in specie in December 1861. With no more gold to use, the government began issuing its own notes in 1862, as it had during the Revolution and the War of 1812; this time they were called "greenbacks."

Banking walked back onto Congress's stage in a supporting role when Chase asked for a law establishing a system of national banks in 1861 and again in 1862.[43] The central purpose, he argued, was provision of a safe "uniform currency." (Recall that the second Bank of the United States, likewise, had been chartered to provide a uniform currency and that the concept included dimensions of currency, credit, and adequacy throughout the country.) The new national banks would also help pay for the war because they would have to buy U.S. government bonds to back their currency. Congress passed the National Bank Act in 1863, which was repealed and superseded by the National Bank Act of 1864, to "provide a national currency . . . and to provide for the circulation and redemption thereof."[44]

THE DESIGN OF NATIONAL BANKS

Secretary Chase and Congress planned to achieve a uniform currency, this time, without resorting to a central national bank. They believed they could achieve a national currency through multiple national banks that would issue bond-backed currency, based on the free bank model developed in the states. The bond-backed currency was expected to prevent the overissue, the inflation, which Gouge and Jackson identified as the major culprit of banking.

The bank design specified in the National Bank Act can be analyzed in terms of the same constitutive categories—ownership, governance, capital, and assets—used to analyze the two previous national banks and state banks.

Ownership was private; the only requirement was that at least five persons join in the corporation. As with free banks under state statutes, legislative action to incorporate a national bank was not necessary. A board of directors was to submit a certificate to the bank regulator, and, upon the regulator's approval, it could begin banking activity.

The governance structure was also private, but basic rules were specified in the statute: there were requirements regarding the minimum number, residence, and election procedures of directors; directors must own at least ten shares; shareholders would have one vote per share. Bankers' decision-making authority was constrained through reserve requirements. Banks in seventeen named cities ("reserve city banks") had to maintain 25 percent reserves against notes and deposits. Half of the reserve had to be on hand in lawful money; the other half could be on deposit with a bank in a "central reserve city": New York, St. Louis, or Chicago. Central reserve city banks held their own 25 percent reserves. Banks in smaller places had to have 15 percent reserves, three-fifths of which could be on deposit in the cities named in the act. Although intended to ensure soundness, these "pyramiding" reserve requirements would later be viewed as a major flaw in the system's design.

Capital requirements for the new national banks depended upon the size of the place. The basic minimum capitalization was $100,000, but in cities with over fifty thousand people capital was to be at least $200,000, and in places with fewer than six thousand people banks could capitalize at $50,000. Half of the capital had to be paid in before banking could begin.

With regard to assets, real estate holdings and lending on real estate were both severely limited. Beyond that the statute said little about what kind of lending national banks should do. There were no requirements in the banks' constitution, like those that had existed in many states, attempting to distribute credit and currency functionally or geographically. Effectively, national banks loaned for commercial purposes.

Specification of this particular design for the new national banks is the most significant thing that the National Bank Act did. There is no question about which side of the Lockean line this bank belongs on: it is a private actor. Its design is very much like the state banks described earlier as closer to the private end of the public/private continuum along all constitutive dimensions. It is like the commercial banks of the original northeastern seaboard states but which also existed in a mix with specially chartered banks in other areas. It legitimately makes its lending decisions in pursuit of profit and legitimately pursues its own organizational interest, soundness, and continuity.

This arrangement was not going to work to provide adequate currency and credit throughout the United States for businesses and individuals. To be sure, in pronouncing these institutional arrangements inadequate to their purpose, I have the advantage over Secretary Chase provided by one hundred and forty years of hindsight: we know that the framework specified by the National Bank Act did not work well. Nevertheless, by 1860 the United States had eighty years of experience with banks and a century and a half before that with other approaches to credit and currency provision. Hindsight was available to policy makers at the time, but Lockean ideology prevented them from evaluating and understanding their own institutional experience. Banks on the model of the National Bank Act had not been the only source of currency and credit in any part of the country when that area was economically undeveloped, and such banks were not expected to stand alone in agricultural areas even when those areas were well established. Experience showed that making money work requires considerable public involvement and institutional complexity, especially in economically undeveloped and agricultural areas—as a practical matter the public and private aspects of banking were not clearly separable.

THE OFFICE OF THE COMPTROLLER OF THE CURRENCY

National banks were not the only institution specified by the National Bank Act. The statute also established a public regulatory agency, based on models developed at the state level. Is it possible that the dimensions of public purpose stripped from the state banks had been incorporated in the mission of this new organization?

The new public entity was a bureau in the Treasury Department to be headed by a new official, the comptroller of the currency. Today we call the organization the Office of the Comptroller of the Currency (OCC). Both the comptroller and his deputy were prohibited from holding any interest in any national bank. As a line agency of an executive branch department, severed from private banking, the design of this organization met Jackson's requirements for a legitimate public actor.

The comptroller was charged with bank examination and supervisory techniques that had developed in the states and had been lodged organizationally in legislative committees, commissions, or executive officials. This official was to receive periodic reports from national banks, examine banks at their own cost, and report to Congress. Recall that this sort of public supervision had become more important in the states after Jackson's bank veto, as public management and ownership interests were stripped from inside the state banks and as the central bank disappeared. The comptroller also implemented requirements associated with the new uniform national bank currency. As in state free banking arrangements, the government printed the bank notes. National banks could get this currency, which would enter circulation through their lending decisions, by depositing registered U.S. bonds with the treasurer, countersigned by the comptroller, to guarantee it. A bank was required to deposit bonds in an amount of not less than $30,000 nor less than one-third of its capital. It could issue currency up to 90 percent of the par value of the bonds it had on deposit but not to exceed 90 percent of the market value. If a national bank refused to redeem its notes, the comptroller would retire or sell the bonds it had on deposit and pay the noteholder. In a deviation from state free banking systems there was a limit, $300 million, on the total national bank currency that could be issued by the comptroller. The limit reflects the Jacksonian concern with avoiding inflation. Originally, the currency was to be distributed in proportion to population and banking capital in the states, but distribution requirements were soon lifted, and then the limit itself was removed.

Analysis of the statutory functions of the comptroller of the currency thus shows that the public's interest in the banking system had been narrowed to guaranteeing the notes that national banks issue in their own decision-making processes, ensuring the soundness of national banks, and avoiding inflation. The public concern with adequacy and distribution of the money supply, which had been addressed through the design of banks themselves as hybrid public/private entities, was lost.

As it turned out, the national banks were not up and running soon enough to make any significant financial contribution before the Civil War was over.[45] But the system was implemented, and the banks supported the secondary market for the war debt afterward.

In concluding this discussion of the transition from state banks to national banks, let us consider two questions. First, what public philosophy underlies the new banking framework specified in the National Bank Act? Second, would this new institutional framework serve effectively as a national banking system or help integrate the nation in broader terms?

How had Andrew Jackson's effort to purge the political economy of discordant institutional creatures and reinforce classic liberalism fared? With the reentry of the federal government into banking, had he lost? Had the Lockean line that he and Van Buren worked so hard to reestablish been erased? The line between the government and the economy had broken down in the reinstitution of a practice that had been particularly hateful to Jackson: public dollars would again go to banks. Because they had to buy federal debt to back their currency, banks would be paid interest from the public budget. Yet, with regard to the government's deposits, the line was largely maintained because the Independent Treasury remained in operation. National banks could be designated as federal fiscal agents, but they could not handle customs receipts, which constituted by far the bulk of the federal revenue. Thus, for the most part, national banks did not have the government's gold back as a basis for lending. With this, Jackson would have been well pleased.

The federal government was also back in the business of banking regulation, a function Jackson had viewed as beyond the public purview. Yet the design of the federal regulator complied with the ideological requirement that a government agent be wholly public. And it was a much constrained regulation, as much of the public purpose that had been pursued by the first and second Banks of the United States, and then by state banks in their absence, fell through the crack, the chasm really, between public and private organizations.

Further, the government was again constituting banking corporations, although no longer through special charter. Yet Jackson's legacy persisted in forcing those corporations to the private side of the line. If the world must be divided into public actors and private actors, banks had become private actors. Jackson taught the banks that they were private, and they came to view themselves that way. As banks thus stepped into the place in liberal theory previously reserved for individual human beings, we have the public philosophy I call, indeed so called by many today, *neoliberalism*.

Would these institutional arrangements result in a unified national banking system? When the National Bank Act was passed, there was great confidence that the heterogeneous state banks would be absorbed into one national system through conversion to national charters, resulting in one bank regulatory framework, instead of as many separate institutional frameworks as there were states. In the event state banks may not have seen the advantages of conversion, a prohibitive federal tax on their circulation went into effect in 1866, and then Supreme Court decisions outlawed state bank note issues.

For a while it looked like the approach would work. By 1867 there were 1,642 national banks, mostly state banks that had converted. As there had been 1,466 state banks in operation in 1863, the state systems appeared well on the way to extinction.[46] In Massachusetts, of 183 state banks in 1863, 178 had converted by 1865, and 4 had gone out of business; leaving only 1 under state charter in 1867.[47] Connecticut was down from 61 state banks in 1864 to 7 in 1869;[48] New York from

308 in 1863 to 52 in 1869.[49] Branches of the state central banks of the Northwest came into the national framework as unit banks. The state systems of the South, several of which had seen no failures before the Civil War, were gone. Southern banks had "loaned" their gold to the Confederate government in the early months of the conflict (by order of that government), and virtually every one of them had failed; there were thus no southern state banks left to convert to national charters. By 1868 only 247 state banks remained in operation.[50]

Yet after that states returned to chartering depository institutions with a vengeance. As state banks learned to get around the prohibition on note issue by making their loans in the form of deposit credit, state legislatures chartered thousands of state banks in an effort to meet perceived needs for adequacy, geographic distribution, and functional allocation of the money supply which national banks did not address. Eventually, states would charter savings and loans and credit unions as well. At the federal level Congress would mar progress toward the goal of a uniform national currency with the greenbacks and other forms of government paper it circulated in an effort to meet cries for adequacy and distribution of the money supply. The national bank system thus did not result in a uniform currency.

Nor did it help integrate the nation in a larger sense after the Civil War, as some policy makers had hoped. The design of the new national banks was extremely ill suited to the needs of the agricultural South, and, economically devastated as the region was, there was no local capital with which to initiate such banks, anyway. The developing West, likewise, was poorly served by the kind of banks provided for in the National Bank Act. Rather than unifying the nation, money and banking policy became a major divisive issue.

In the ideologically driven effort to separate the public from the private, much of the public purpose that had been built into U.S. banking historically—but not justified in a coherent public philosophy that could be drawn upon to defend it—was lost in the banking framework established by the National Bank Act of 1864. The arrangements would not fulfill the promise of a uniform currency or a national one.

THE FEDERAL RESERVE BOARD

WHERE NATURE ENDS

The idea that nature indicates what human social, economic, and political relationships should be is as ancient as the enterprise of political philosophy and as current as this morning's newspaper.[1] The counterview—that on the human level of being's great chain nature holds no analog to its wondrous blueprints for the physical and biochemical levels and that the social and economic order is, rather, of human design— has also been with us at least since the Sophists of Greece in the fifth century before the Christian Era. But this counterview has been marginalized throughout the history of political philosophy. Today, as postmodernism, with its critical aim of exposing the "construction" of dominant institutions, the view that all social and economic institutions are artifice probably holds more influence than ever before, and that is still not very much outside the academy.

The focus of the historic philosophical debate has thus not been on whether or not nature provides a model for human society but, rather, on what that model is and how we know it. The classic liberalism of John Locke and Adam Smith embraces nature as fervently as Aristotle and Aquinas, but with a very different view of what is natural. Whereas their ancient and medieval predecessors saw humanity's natural order as a body, an organic entity composed of fully interdependent parts, Locke saw independent, free, and equal individuals interacting via contract. Focused on economic relationships, Adam Smith identified the market as nature's mechanism for transforming the pursuit by these atomic individuals of their self-interest, as if by an "invisible hand," into economic growth and optimum distribution. To discover the order of nature, some believed, with Locke, Hobbes, and Descartes, that pure reason serves. Others thought that the natural order was to be learned through close observation—a tradition that includes such figures as Comte and Marx and most modern social science.

Like the epistemology, the language used in the debate about what is natural varies: The ancients uncovered the "natural law." Aquinas reconciled their findings with "divine law." Satisfied, John Locke interchanged *nature* and *natural law* with *God* and *divine law* without remark. Some of Locke's fellows in the Enlightenment talk less about God, more about "science." While dominant opinions about what is natural, how we know, and the vocabulary for designating it thus shift, the normative imperative that our institutions comply with nature endures. Social and economic arrangements and methodologies that can win the label *natural*, or *scientific* in the argument of the day, are likely to win politically as well.

Accordingly, debate in the United States over the shape of the economy generally, and arrangements for money and banking in particular, has been rife with appeals to nature for justification since the beginning. For Jefferson and Jackson, following Locke and Smith, natural law dictated an economy consisting of independent individuals freely contracting in the marketplace. For money nature had provided gold and silver, in Jefferson's view, and gold alone, in Jackson's; if we would only avoid artificial paper money, the supply would regulate itself in noninflationary harmony with the requirements of the economy.

To be sure, empirically, we have already seen money and banking institutions contrived by public policy—the first and second Banks of the United States and the broad range of very differently constituted pre–Civil War state banks. In telling the stories of the second national bank and the state banks, I focused on the theme of the relationship of the public and private realms, arguing that the classic liberal idea that the public sphere should be very small and clearly segregated from the private sector was effectively brought to bear to undermine and eliminate them. But there is considerable conflation in classic liberal thinking of the public with the unnatural. Money and banking institutions established by legislatures pursuing various purposes were not only intrusions of the public into the private sphere; they were also artificial contrivances, as were corporations generally.

A converse of classic liberalism's conflation of the public and the unnatural is the assumption that private arrangements are natural. I have argued that post–Civil War national banks were justified as private entities (a move so significant as to require a new label, *neoliberal-*

ism, for the public philosophy that justifies it). A private institution receives nature's sanction in classic and neoliberalism. Some other, conflicting public philosophy is required to provide the insight that both public and private institutions may be unnatural, that is, artificial constructs.

The institutions of the Federal Reserve System (Fed)—the Federal Reserve Board and the Federal Reserve Banks—were superimposed on the banking regulatory framework defined by the National Bank Act of 1863–64. Scholars have often interpreted the debate leading to the Federal Reserve Act as an argument primarily over whether the system should be publicly or privately controlled and secondarily about centralization versus decentralization. These issues were undeniably prominent, but positions on such questions of design follow from where one stands on the more fundamental philosophical issue of how far nature gets us and at what point we have no option but to make decisions. Here I will interpret the debates leading to the establishment of the Fed in 1913 and its fundamental transformation in the Banking Act of 1935 as episodes in the ongoing philosophical argument over nature versus construction.

AFTER THE CIVIL WAR

THE MONEY SUPPLY

When Abraham Lincoln's Treasury secretary, Salmon P. Chase, asked Congress to establish a new system of national banks, the immediate objective was to fund the Civil War. But the "central idea," the long-term object, was achievement of a uniform circulation.[2] In the decades after the war that goal remained elusive. The currency consisted of United States notes, the notes of the new national banks, gold and gold certificates, silver coins and silver certificates, fractional currency, and short-term interest-bearing U.S. government issues that circulated. Deposits in national and state banks were at least sometimes understood as part of the money supply.[3]

Well aware that a national bank system would not be fully functional soon enough to meet Civil War needs for currency, Congress had authorized several issues of United States notes, or "greenbacks." A total of $450 million was authorized, but the amount in circulation peaked at $433 million, varied as the notes were occasionally withdrawn and reissued, and eventually came to rest at $346 million in

1878. Greenbacks were legal tender (money that must be accepted by the creditor) for all transactions except duties on imports and interest on the central government's debt, which were payable in gold. Other circulating government paper included short-term interest-bearing securities and fractional currency (paper money that served the purposes of small change). Short-term securities were gradually taken out of circulation as they were refunded through issuance of bonds, and fractional currency was withdrawn as coinage laws were manipulated to discourage hoarding coin.

After greenbacks the notes of the new national banks constituted the second major kind of currency in use. Bank notes were backed by legal tender—greenbacks until 1879 and greenbacks or gold after that. Bank notes could be redeemed on demand in legal tender. National bank deposits, as well as their notes, were backed by greenbacks, in the sense that required fractional reserves had to be held in legal tender.

Congress had succeeded in reducing the heterogeneity of the currency in one important regard. It had expected state banks to be wholly absorbed into the national bank system, thus eliminating the plague of different notes issued by hundreds of state banks. To help the process along, several state legislatures provided for easy conversion of state bank charters to national charters, and, in the event this carrot did not work, Congress introduced a prohibitive tax on state bank notes in 1866. These notes disappeared in reasonably short order, and state banks appeared to be well on their way to absorption. But the number of state banks bottomed out in 1868, at 247,[4] then rose again throughout the country as state banks turned to the use of deposits rather than notes to originate credit.[5] In 1867, 40 percent of bank deposits were in state banks;[6] by the time the Fed was founded, in 1913, half were.[7]

Other government-issued money included gold certificates for bullion and coin deposited in the Treasury, authorized by legislation passed in 1863; gold certificates could be used in payments requiring gold.[8] Silver certificates and coin were issued by authority of the Bland-Allison Act in 1878. The Sherman Silver Purchase Act in 1890 authorized coinage of silver and issuance of "Treasury notes of 1890," redeemable in silver or gold.

The journey from these jumbled post–Civil War monetary arrangements to establishment of the Federal Reserve System in 1913 entailed an epic public conversation over what nature and science provide for money, if anything. Two theories of natural or scientific regulation of the money supply—gold and real bills—were argued. The theories were not viewed as competing, and both were ultimately built into the Federal Reserve Act. Against both, others argued that what constitutes money and the determination of its level are unavoidably constructs of, and responsibilities of, self-conscious public policy decisions.

THEORIES OF NATURAL MONEY SUPPLY REGULATION: GOLD AND REAL BILLS

In his classic and inestimably influential inquiry into the nature and causes of the wealth of nations, Adam Smith taught that a self-optimizing economy was a natural phenomenon. The "nature" of a nation's wealth consisted in commodities, in what it produced—the gross domestic product (GDP), in more current terminology. The fundamental natural force, or "cause," of the wealth of nations was individual self-interest, which, if unobstructed by misguided institutional arrangements, would lead automatically, by the invisible hand of natural law to national wealth, to productivity. There was no tension between measures that would best serve the individual and measures that would best serve the national whole.

Smith offered his conception of the wealth of nations as a criticism of the mercantilist economic theory of his day. Because real wealth lies in productivity, he argued, the mercantilist state's preoccupation with securing bullion was misplaced. When a nation produced efficiently, gold would automatically flow in through international trade; if not, gold would flow out, seeking better value elsewhere. If a state wanted to be wealthy, it should not go out looking for gold (or, by logical extension, overtly create a money supply in any way) but, rather, unleash the natural forces leading to productivity; the gold would follow automatically. Smith had made something of a straw figure, however, of the mercantilists' position. Yes, mercantilist states pursued the precious metals, but they knew that gold was just money, not wealth in Smith's sense. In the mercantile view, as developed by Smith's day, the state explicitly attended to the money supply because wealth creation—Smith's productivity—could be jump-started and facilitated if there were plenty of money around to grease the economic wheels.

The Wealth of Nations had been published in 1776, and in the United States the principals in the money debates were familiar with Smith's views on the flow of specie as a natural economic and monetary regulator. While these views were orthodoxy in theory, we have already seen variations on mercantilism in practice. Hamilton bowed to Smith rhetorically, but his Bank of the United States was all about a focus on getting money to trigger, not respond to, economic activity, even if he had to invent the money. Jefferson's Treasury secretary, Albert Gallatin, had ruminated that, regardless of how productive its fine citizens were, the natural flow of gold did not reach western Pennsylvania. And we have seen that, through state banks, states made money out of whatever they had in order to facilitate economic activity.

In the years after Jackson's assault on banking and before the Civil War, arrangements in the United States came as close to gold literally being money as they ever would. The currency of the common people was gold coin. So also was the currency of the government, which paid its debts and collected duties and other taxes in gold through the Independent Treasury. State bank statutes required gold as reserves and usually as some portion of bank capital as well. Wartime arrangements abandoned the de facto gold standard, but it is clear that the government's intention was to return to it as soon as the emergency passed.[9]

Resumption was the term for getting the country's money back on a gold standard. To return to the gold standard domestically meant that all other forms of money in use could be redeemed for gold on demand at the prewar fixed rate. The government must retire the greenbacks by paying gold for them, by refunding them with bonds payable in gold, by removing them from circulation as they came into the Treasury in the course of payments, or by some combination of these measures. National banks would redeem their notes in gold when the government's house was in order and gold was again legal tender.

The gold standard thus understood was economic orthodoxy among academic political economists of the day,[10] and to the mainstream Protestant clergy it was nothing less than God's law: from their pulpits and in their journals they interpreted resumption as honesty and justice while denouncing soft money as an invitation to extravagance and dishonesty in public and private dealings.[11] Advocates of resumption could thus appeal to God as well as science, as did the Massachusetts manufacturer Edward Atkinson when he held that hard money is ordained by "God's will and the nature of things."[12] From this point of view resumption was not a question of public versus private control over the money supply but one of whether nature's laws would reign. The view that the gold standard entails neither public or private monetary control is explicit in remarks before the Senate by John Sherman, who chaired the Banking and Currency Committee during and after the Civil War. In arguing for resumption, Sherman asserted that "a discretionary power in private persons or public officers over so delicate a subject as the national currency ought to be avoided."[13]

Hugh McCulloch, secretary of the Treasury in the immediate postwar period, wasted no time initiating movement toward resumption of the gold standard. He requested authority to retire greenbacks in his first annual report in 1865. Given a green light by the Funding Act of 1866, he moved aggressively. McCulloch was not a water boy for the interests of eastern banks in his zeal for resumption. He acted from a principled concern with inflation, which he viewed from the Jacksonian/ Gouge perspective as a cheat on the common people. But McCulloch's thinking typifies a crucial turn in hard-money ideology. In the Gouge/ Jackson scheme gold was nature's money, and the paper money of banks was the unnatural scourge leading to inflation and the evils it visits upon common people, honest business, and the economy generally. In McCulloch we see this argument transformed. It becomes an insistence that bank notes redeemable in gold are nature's money. Greenbacks—publicly issued money—became the unnatural inflationary paper that must be phased out.[14] Jackson had insisted that only gold was real money, so that neither private interests (banks) nor the government was in control; nature arranged these things. Now advocates of banks as the proper mechanism for providing currency get nature on their side. Private paper money is natural. Public paper money is an aberration.

As the orthodox notion of nature's money supply shifts from gold itself to bank notes backed by gold, we increasingly see the gold standard linked rhetorically to the real bills doctrine in the arguments of U.S. bankers, businessmen, and political economists. "Real bills" are short-term loans for commercial purposes. They are loans on actual physical goods in production, in transit, or in inventory; not long-term loans on land or capital goods nor loans for speculative purposes in public land or the stock market nor loans for government bonds. The theory is that, if commercial banks confine themselves to real bills in their lending, bank money is governed by the laws of commerce and industry, expanding and contracting in conjunction with the economy's needs automatically.[15] Both the Jacksonian fixation on inflation and the opposite concern with insufficient money would be addressed as, like the baby bear's porridge, the money supply would always be just right.

Remarks of George Coe, a prominent banker, before the House Banking and Currency Committee, illustrate the fusing of the gold standard and real bills theory in U.S. banking thought after the Civil War:

> The defects in our financial system, doubtless, are that . . . we are not upon a specie basis. . . . We are brought into this position by an extravagant issue of paper money, so called, which paper money did not originate in the natural order of commerce. . . . All paper used as money should be essentially in the nature of a bill of exchange. It must follow and grow out of trade. It cannot be injected into it by any possible means, and still preserve specie payments. Paper money consists really in orders for things exchangeable between men, whether that money be in the form of a bank-note or in the form of a bill of exchange or in the form of a bank deposit. It is drawn on things requiring exchange in the business relations among men. The consequence of that statement is this: that where articles are upon a specie basis in harmony with the world's commerce, every piece of paper issued must follow the article, and not precede it. That is a condition vital to the harmonious commerce of the country and the world.[16]

The mechanisms by which specie and real bills work together are not specified in Coe's remarks, a fuzziness extending back to the early joint appearance of the theories. According to historian of banking theory Lloyd Mints, the real bills doctrine received "its most elegant statement in all its history by Adam Smith in *The Wealth of Nations*."[17] Smith taught that, if banks stuck to short-term credit, the amount of bank currency plus specie in the country would never exceed the amount of specie that would have circulated in the absence of the bank paper.[18] He thus viewed bank money as he thought about gold, as a response to productive economic activity: productivity first, and money automatically follows. But Smith did not present a careful explanation of the mechanisms that would force any overissue of bank notes out of circulation.[19] The persuasiveness of his argument depends not on specification of a model but on an appeal to nature in a metaphor: any excess currency would "overflow the channel of circulation," which had been cut by the proper amount of specie, and return to the bank.[20]

The real bills theory effectively requires that bankers, not the government, determine the money supply. Jackson had taught the "people" and the bankers alike that banking was a private business. Yet proponents of the real bills doctrine in this period did not see themselves demanding private control of the money supply. Bankers' money creation through lending did not involve discretion; bankers were a part of the mechanism through which the money supply finds its natural level in accord with the needs of trade and commerce. It was a question of nature or artifice. The results of decisions made by bankers were assumed to be natural, while the consequences of decisions arrived at in public processes were regarded as artificial.

CHALLENGES TO NATURE'S MONEY: GREENBACKS AND FREE SILVER

The national resolve to return to gold faltered as early as 1866, when the economy slid into recession. Congress repealed the Funding Act in 1868—pulling in the reins on Treasury Secretary McCulloch's anti-inflation crusade[21]—and paused to investigate what was happening in the economy and what the monetary policy options might be. Bankers, manufacturers, traders, and political economists pulled their chairs up to the table at House and Senate hearings. The dominant opinion remained that the country must return to gold. Again and again, congress members were lectured on how wartime abandonment of the specie basis of the currency had led to a deranged economy, out of harmony with the laws of commerce. But, as a practical matter, it was recognized that there was nothing like enough gold in the country to permit the banks and the government to redeem the war-swollen volume of currency that was circulating. Resumption required deflation. The questions were: How fast should we return to gold? And, given the interrelationships among greenbacks, bank notes, and government bonds, what specific arrangements for resumption should be established?

There were dissenting voices. A "soft money" business minority favored an expanded money supply. Among those holding this view were heavy industrialists; some manufacturers, bankers, and merchants; and a handful of heterodox political economists, most notably Henry Carey. They argued from a neomercantilist perspective that a plentiful, low-interest money supply stimulates real economic activity. While people in this camp were sometimes willing to maintain the greenback circulation, their focus was on expanding national bank currency. The Jacksonian fear of inflation had been built into the national bank system through a $300 million limit on the total amount of currency it could issue. This group wanted to remove that limit and permit the banks to respond liberally to the needs of business, for investment as well as working capital.[22] This view rejected both gold and the strictures of real bills as able to regulate the money supply automatically, in accord with the needs of economic growth. Public policy needed to get out in front of the money supply and pull it, and thus the economy, along.

Greenbackism—that is, support for government-issued paper money and overt public control of the size of the money supply—among farmers developed later than minority business support for soft money. Before the Civil War, to avoid inflation, farmers had been the strongest supporters of literal hard money. As good Jacksonians, they supported the use of gold coin only and opposed banks. During the war farmers viewed government paper money as inflationary and opposed its issue. After the war farmers favored a return to gold. Their attitude began to shift only with the Panic of 1873 and the subsequent recession,[23] as they began to view the plummeting commodity prices that hurt them so badly as a consequence of artificial constraint of the size of the money supply by tethering it to gold.

Despite opposition from soft-money business groups and mounting agrarian greenbackism, the gold standard won a major battle in 1875, when Congress passed the Resumption Act. This legislation made greenbacks redeemable in gold beginning in 1879—thus allowing time for the government to accumulate gold in the Treasury—and provided for reducing total greenback circulation to $300 million.[24] Business fell in line behind the gold standard,[25] but among farmers support for greenbackism accelerated as they increasingly felt the effects of currency contraction.

As support among farmers for releasing the money supply from the strictures of the gold standard grew, "free silver" joined greenbacks in challenging gold. In turning to discuss the press for silver as another device for currency expansion, a clarification is in order: I have been using the term *gold standard* somewhat loosely. Gold had been the de facto monetary standard since the mid-1830s, when Jacksonian coinage legislation drove silver out of circulation. Silver did not circulate because the legal silver-to-gold ratio of 16:1 made it more valuable on the market than at the mint. Nominally, the United States was on a bimetallic standard—silver and gold—until 1873. In that year silver was legislatively demonetized; that is, the silver dollar was no longer a monetary standard.

At first the public took little notice of the demonetization of silver—after all, silver had not circulated in two generations. But by 1875 increased supplies of silver and decreased demand—as several European nations moved from silver or bimetallic monetary standards to a gold standard—led to a drop in its price which would have made it profitable to sell silver to the mint at the old legal ratio. But now there was no provision for minting silver. People began to notice. Mining firms and members of Congress from silver states certainly helped get the word out, but agitation for free silver was more than an expression of the self-interest of silver miners. Farmers, especially in the West and South, and their representatives in Congress seized silver—coinage of as much as possible and a return to a bimetallic standard—as a device for monetary expansion.

Some scholars have viewed the post–Civil War agrarian opposition to the gold standard as irrational[26] and reactionary.[27] Others have argued more sympathetically that farmers responded to objective material circumstances.[28] Resumption entailed price deflation of 50 percent in the decade and a half following the Civil War,[29] and prices continued to fall over 1 percent a year from 1879 through 1897.[30] The new national banks were not well designed to meet farmers' needs for credit or currency. Farmers suffered.

What I want to emphasize about farmers' monetary position is not the emotion that may have been involved or the material circumstances but the philosophical shift required to call for public construction of money, that is, for public policy that deliberately, explicitly, and self-consciously defines devices that constitute the money supply and its size. In the granges, alliances, and Populist Party, farmers and their leaders developed the "populist" public philosophy, in terms of which they could interpret what was happening to them and propose institutional solutions. I develop populist public philosophy systematically later, but note here that at its heart was a shift on the fundamental question of nature versus construction. Although I do not claim that they expressed the shift in precisely those terms, we see populist discourse move away from talk about the naturalness of its adherents' preferred arrangements and the unnatural character of someone else's (bankers'). They begin to propose alternative institutions and criticize existing ones, evidencing a conclusion that all economic arrangements are choices that serve some ends. The arrangements could be different; the ends could be different. People—not God or nature or science—decide on both. With regard to money in particular, as the authority of gold became linked to bank paper backed by gold, and to the claims of bond holders on their tax dollars, farmers rejected their own previous commitment to the idea that there was anything natural or providential about gold movements. They came to view the gold standard as a choice that, given existing institutional arrangements, operated in bankers' interest.

Viewing money as a construct, farmers arrived at some basic policy positions. They wanted decisions about the constitution and level of the money supply to be public, so they could influence the ends of monetary policy and the devices for implementing it. The economic goal they wanted to pursue was a rise in commodity prices, believing they could then better service their debts. Relying on the quantity theory of money, the approach farmers advocated for increasing commodity prices was expansion of the money supply. Free silver was just one device among others for expanding the currency. Beyond public decision making on monetary policy, farmers wanted the government, not national banks, to issue the currency and to guarantee its value.

The populist monetary position achieved some political success. In 1878 the Bland-Allison Act halted the retirement of greenbacks under way under the Resumption Act, leaving $346 million in circulation, and required the Treasury to purchase and coin $2 to $4 million worth of silver per month.[31] The Sherman Silver Purchase Act of 1890 approximately doubled the amount of silver bought at the Treasury.[32]

In the face of the silver challenge, defense of the gold standard became more shrill, binding nature's law ever more tightly to yellow metal alone. In the 1880s and 1890s many of the "sound money" arguments were no longer posed in terms of "specie" or "silver and gold," as they had been in the 1870s, but, rather, explicitly rejected the suitability of silver or a bimetallic standard in favor of gold. William Trenholm, comptroller of the currency in the late 1880s and founder and director of the U.S. Rubber Company, was an important figure in the ideological battle for nature's money. He was arguing specifically against a bimetallic standard when he wrote: "The natural laws that control the currents of the air, and the formation and condensation of clouds, are not more constant than are the natural laws that control the currents of commerce, and the distribution of capital. It is *natural law alone* that has gradually made gold the prime standard of value."[33]

With the money panic of 1893 gold standard supporters rallied politically to push back silver's advance. President Cleveland interpreted the panic as a result not of an inadequate money supply but, rather, of uncertainty over the U.S. commitment to the gold standard; consequently, he called for repeal of the silver purchase provisions of 1890. In Congress, although young congressman William Jennings Bryan gained national attention with his advocacy of silver, Cleveland's position won the day. Farm prices fell further as the economy sank into a prolonged recession.

The climax of the press for the free coinage of silver in Bryan's nomination for the presidency in 1896 is a familiar and dramatic episode in U.S. history. Also familiar is the powerful metaphor with which Bryan rejected the gold standard in the speech that cinched that nomination for him. "You shall not," he thundered before a rapt convention, "press down upon the brow of labor this crown of thorns, you shall not crucify mankind upon a cross of gold." It is unlikely that anyone would suggest that the sincere evangelist who ultimately undid himself (in the eyes of many) defending creationism did not believe that God's law governs human affairs. But it is clear that he did not view that law as extending to the details of the constitution of the money supply. In addition to denying that gold's domestic effects were God given, Bryan rejected providential claims for the international gold standard, charging that, in supporting it, Republican candidate McKinley would "surrender the right of self-government and place the legislative control of our affairs in the hands of foreign potentates and powers." He also dismissed the operations of banking institutions as the legitimate source of money: "They say that we are opposing national bank currency; it is true. . . . We [Democrats] say in our platform that we believe that the right to coin and issue money is a function of government . . . and can no more with safety be delegated to private individuals than we could afford to delegate to private individuals the power to make penal statutes or levy taxes. Those who are opposed to this proposition tell us that the issue of paper money is a function of the bank."[34] The question of who should issue and control the money supply—banks or the government, the United States or Britain, can only be posed after concluding that money is a construction based on the decisions of someone other than God.

FOUNDING THE FED

The election of 1896 was one of the handful of critical realigning elections in U.S. political history. It turned on the question of whether money is a natural or constructed phenomenon, although that question was posed in the form of gold versus silver. Bryan had predicted that the election would turn on money in 1893, when he fought to preserve bimetallism against President Cleveland of his own Democratic Party; of course, he provided leadership in making it so. Bryan called to his side of the new partisan dividing line all those who believed that the government should deliberately manipulate the money supply in pursuit of purposes chosen in democratic processes. Silverite Republicans, Populists, and Independents throughout the West and South joined him and the silver Democrats. The Republicans declared their party the protector of nature's gold standard and sound money. Goldbug Democrats, more conservative eastern Democrats, and urban industrial workers in the Northeast and Midwest moved firmly into the Republican fold.

BRYAN DEMOCRATS' POSITION: PHILOSOPHICAL POPULISM

As we know, Bryan, candidate of the Democratic and Populist Parties, was the loser in 1896. The Populist Party, so virile and confident in its rise, disintegrated with his defeat. Those who viewed the world in terms of populist public philosophy were absorbed into the Democratic Party, which became the minority in a party system that would persist until the next realignment in 1932. Less well remembered than Bryan's loss—or, perhaps more accurately, less well acknowledged—is how strong and long lived support was for him and the losing position on the realigning issue. The Commoner received 47 percent of the popular vote in 1896. He was the Democratic candidate again in 1900, polling 46 percent of the popular vote. And his party turned to him a third time, in 1908, when, with 43 percent, his popular vote count exceeded that which would gain the presidency for Woodrow Wilson in the three-way race with Theodore Roosevelt and William Howard Taft four years later.

Democrats' agitation for free silver faded as a dramatic increase in the gold supply, due to new finds and improved mining and refining techniques, expanded the currency as they had hoped silver would.[35] But the party persisted in giving voice to the fundamental populist philosophical position that monetary arrangements are a discretion-laden construct and, as such, should be controlled by public policy. The focus of their criticism shifted to the issue of control over the allocation of money, which Democrats perceived to be held by national banks and, more particularly, by "Wall Street" financiers associated with the largest national banks in New York.

Critics of the banking framework were accurate in underscoring that the structure of bank reserves specified in the National Bank Act led to a flow of money from throughout the country to national banks in New

York. Country banks, located in smaller communities, kept a portion of their reserves in banks in larger reserve cities specified in the law. Reserve city banks, in turn, kept part of their reserves in central reserve city banks in Chicago, St. Louis, or—most often criticized—New York. This pyramid arrangement facilitated channeling funds into the New York securities market. New York banks holding other banks' reserves had to be ready to disburse them to the smaller banks on demand but wanted to generate earnings on the reserves in the meantime. They therefor invested the money in "call loans" to Wall Street brokers, with which the brokers financed investors' securities purchases on margin. Call loans took their name from the fact that the big bank could call the money back from use in the stock market at any time to return it to small banks; in theory call money was as liquid as cash.

To appreciate the widespread resentment over thus channeling money from communities across the United States into the stock market, recall that this was the era of the emergence of "trusts," giant corporations formed by the merger of previously independent corporations within an industry. The railroads went first. In the 1880s railroad corporations began combining in larger entities—pools initially but huge corporations after 1887, when the Interstate Commerce Act outlawed railroad pooling.[36] Other industries followed, with the most intense wave of mergers occurring from 1897 through 1904.[37] The process was widely perceived as economically and politically threatening and was a dominant political issue from the 1880s until World War I. Creation of each new corporate trust entailed the issuance of stock. It was widely believed that these huge consolidation deals involved stock watering (issuance of more stock than a corporation is worth) and that they were not primarily motivated by technical efficiency requirements, as promoters claimed, but, rather, by commissions for promoters and unjustified profits for holders of watered stock. Many people regarded such activity as "speculation," little different from gambling; and they objected to a banking framework that channeled their money away from productive use in their communities (for farm loans, the purchase of homes, or development of small businesses) into speculation.

Yet complicity in the end sale of railroad and industrial stock was not the only, or even the most objectionable, relationship of the national bank system to the hated merger process. National banks themselves, along with some larger state banks and trust companies,[38] were combining in trusts and trustlike arrangements of various kinds. Financial institutions might combine tightly in true corporate mergers; one financial institution might control all the stock of others; a small group of stockholders might own large blocks of the stock of various institutions; or "interlocking directorates," in which a small group of people appoint one another to the boards of directors of several institutions, might be formed. The suspicion grew that a small number of huge financial combinations controlled the allocation of credit in the United States, that is, that a giant "money trust" had emerged and operated from Wall Street.

The money trust was suspected of being largely in the drivers' seat with regard to the formation of industrial and public utility trusts and, beyond that, influential in the operations of the new concerns. When a corporate merger occurs—for example, Standard Oil (1882) or American Cotton Oil (1885)—an investment banker plays a definitive role. The new concern does not sell its securities directly to the public but, rather, is paid for the lot by an investment banking firm that "underwrites" the deal. The underwriter parcels out the securities among itself and other financial firms for sale to end investors. If there was a money trust, a handful of corporations and individuals was capturing the lucrative commissions involved in this process. But, worse, this small group was suspected of carrying its influence into the operations of railroad, public utility, and industrial trusts, by holding stock and through interlocking directorates. Further, the money trust was suspected not only of channeling the nation's savings toward industrial trusts that it controlled but also of having the ability to prevent unwanted competing organizations from securing financing at all.[39]

Throughout the period from 1896 until the Fed was founded, in 1913, minority Democrats refused to regard concentrated private control over the allocation of money as natural and continued to call for reforms of the banking regulatory framework. They did not have a comprehensive alternative to the National Bank Act, but Bryan Democrats consistently demanded two related measures: government issue and guarantee of the currency; and government control of the size of the money supply. Calls for institutional mechanisms to channel credit to agriculture were also common, as were suggestions for deposit guarantee. This critique of extant arrangements, with the institutional solutions it casts up, is rooted in philosophical populism; it was articulated in politics at the national level by a large faction within the Democratic Party.

THE REPUBLICANS AND THE BUSINESS-BASED REFORM PERSPECTIVE

The Republicans, with nature on their side, had been the winners in the presidential election of 1896 and were the majority party in the alignment that ensued. Party leaders interpreted the victory as settling the money question in favor of the status quo—the gold standard and the regulatory framework provided by the National Bank Act—and kept monetary reform off the active agenda.[40] In 1900, nonetheless, they did initiate a money measure. The Gold Standard Act explicitly confirmed the gold dollar as the monetary standard of the country. Although unnecessary in light of the Resumption Act of 1875 and repeal of the Sherman Act's silver purchase provisions, this election-year declaration served to remind the voters which party defended sound money. To add punch to the Republican position, the Gold Standard Act set up a fund in the Treasury earmarked for redemption of government-issued paper money in gold.[41]

While the Republican Party in government thus regarded the money question settled in favor of a gold standard and bank-issued currency and Bryan Democrats continued to call for vaguely defined reforms intended to preempt both, progressive businesspeople and bankers developed their own critique of existing money and banking arrangements.[42] This critique did not aim to displace the banking framework as the source and allocator of money in the United States but to strengthen that framework by addressing what business viewed as its central problem: "inelasticity" of the currency.[43] Recall that the currency issued under the National Bank Act was backed by bonds. To acquire notes from the comptroller of the currency, a bank was required to buy federal bonds and deposit them with the government. The comptroller then issued notes that the bank put into circulation in the lending process or through deposit conversion.

The contemporary concept of inelasticity had two dimensions. First, when the public wanted to convert deposits into currency, there might not be currency enough to go around. There was no reason to expect that the outstanding federal debt was related to the currency needs of the country. Currency shortages ("stringencies") occurred seasonally, in connection with the fall harvest, and cyclically, in the money panics often associated with business cycle downturns. The second sense in which the money supply was viewed as inelastic was that it was not properly related to the "needs of trade." In an expression of the real bills doctrine the business critique held that money should automatically expand when business was active and contract when things cooled off.[44] Although, as I argued earlier, real bills was accepted as economic orthodoxy along with the gold standard, the business criticism highlighted its imperfect realization in the mechanisms of the national bank system.

The emerging business consensus on how to make the money supply elastic emphasized remedies of two kinds: changes in reserve arrangements and "asset currency." Under the National Bank Act, went the argument, reserves were not reserves at all because a bank was not allowed to slip below the hefty reserve level required in the statute. Regardless of the portion of its reserve held in lawful money neatly stacked in its own vault, versus that constituted by deposit credit in another bank, a bank under pressure could not *use* that reserve. Further, national bank reserves were held by each bank separately, not by the system in any way, and were thus not available to be moved around to stave off an incipient seasonal or cyclical tightening. Reserve requirements should be changed to permit pooling and use of national bank reserves. Notice that the focus of the concern with reserves here is quite different from the Democrat/populist criticism that reserve pyramiding functioned illegitimately as a mechanism for trust building and stock market speculation.

The second change needed to give the money supply elasticity, in the emerging business consensus, was a move away from the bond-secured currency of the National Bank Act to "asset currency." Asset currency would be guaranteed not by bonds but by the bank's own assets of a particular type: short-term business paper—essentially, real bills. The needs of business would drive the volume of such currency. When real production and trade were increasing, the currency would expand; when business was slowing down, the currency would contract automatically as the loans were repaid—nature again. The United States had some experience with asset-based currency, before the Fed was established, in extralegal notes of this type issued by clearinghouses. Clearinghouses were privately organized associations of banks which operated in some places to clear checks and settle interbank balances. In financial stringencies they had issued "clearinghouse loan certificates" to banks on collateral of commercial paper. This emergency currency was used in interbank transactions and took the pressure off the cash supply; it was withdrawn from circulation as soon as possible.

Since the 1890s committees designated by prominent business groups, such as the American Bankers Association and the New York

Chamber of Commerce, had been forwarding draft bills to Congress proposing changes to the National Bank Act along these lines; the Republican leadership made sure the proposals went nowhere. Senator Nelson Aldrich, powerful Republican chair of the Senate banking committee, was instrumental in this effort. But in 1907 a money panic occurred in the midst of a short, but very severe, business contraction.[45] The business community felt the bite keenly and was alarmed; the Republican congressional leadership finally focused on banking reform.

The resulting Aldrich-Vreeland Act of 1908 is conventionally recognized as an upshot of the Panic of 1907 and a step along the path leading to founding the Fed. This legislation provided for regional currency associations that could issue notes in an emergency. To get the currency, banks would rediscount specified assets with the association, either commercial paper or bonds. The procedure was modeled on the approach clearinghouses had already used, but it was currency much more broadly available. In another provision usually regarded as more important, this legislation also established the joint, nominally bipartisan National Monetary Commission to study the problem and devise comprehensive monetary reform.

The National Monetary Commission was headed by Senator Aldrich. After its members had traveled from one European capital to another interviewing central bankers; listened to domestic bankers, economists, and political scientists; and sponsored publication of thousands of pages of studies on the various aspects of money and banking—in what was not a direct commission action, a small group of men associated with it assembled at a duck hunting retreat in Georgia and quietly drafted a reform measure. This measure is referred to as the "Aldrich plan" or "Aldrich bill," taking its name from Senator Aldrich, who was there with the men and ducks. Its chief draftsman was Paul Warburg, Wall Street financier, friend of Benjamin Strong, German immigrant, scion of a German banking family, writer on monetary reform.[46]

The Aldrich proposal provided for a central bank, the "National Reserve Association," which would issue a new currency backed by gold and commercial assets. The central bank was to be capitalized at $100 million, and its ownership would be entirely private: national banks, state banks, and trust companies would subscribe 10 percent of their capital in its stock. These institutions could choose whether to join, but Warburg appears to have believed that they would not pass up the opportunity. The management, or governance, structure of the central bank was a bit baroque but boils down to private control.[47]

The Aldrich plan would not have changed the reserve provisions of the National Bank Act, except that deposits held in the central bank's fifteen branches (located in the cities where the district associations were headquartered) would count as reserves. This arrangement did not address the problem with reserves from the point of view of the Democratic critique because the concentration of system funds in New York could continue—whether through existing correspondent relations or by means of the proposed new central bank.[48] From the business perspective the Aldrich plan's central bank solved the reserve problem by creating a pool of reserves which central bank decision makers could use.

Lending by the central bank would be confined to its owner banks. It would not deal directly with businesses or individuals, as had the first and second Banks of the United States and as was the practice of European central banks. For its owner banks the central bank would rediscount paper with the characteristics of real bills. This attempt "to legislate the real bills doctrine," as Robert West put it,[49] is the feature of the Aldrich plan that I want to emphasize in relation to the central philosophical theme of this chapter—the question of whether the system is constructed in pursuit of purposes that someone chooses or is a neutral natural or scientific phenomenon.

Contemporary businesspeople and bankers generally held the real bills doctrine literally: a money supply based on short-term commercial bank assets was scientific and self-regulating. It would expand when business increased and contract automatically when business demand for money slackened. For bankers especially, who strongly supported the Aldrich plan, the theory comported nicely with their insistence that they were neutral conduits in a natural process, not powerful actors with discretion in allocating the nation's money. But Paul Warburg, the influential German banker turned Wall Street financier who drafted the Aldrich plan, and other relatively sophisticated bankers in New York did not view a banking system with real bills–based currency as wholly self-regulating. Warburg was clear that, first, public policy must create the institutional environment in which short-term bank assets could be used to influence fluctuation in the money supply and, second, that discretionary calls would be required on an ongoing basis to regulate the system, hence a central bank.[50] He further believed that only bankers were qualified to direct the system, thus the privately controlled central bank in the Aldrich plan. Bankers' agreement generally that private bankers must control the central bank may strike us as inconsistent with their view that banking was a neutral mechanism in allocating the money supply; most bankers do not seem to have noted the problem.

Just as Republican congressional leaders were finally ready to move a banking and currency reform measure, the political ground shifted under them. In the 1910 mid-term elections, with the split in the Republican Party deepening, the Democrats won a slim majority in the House for the first time since the 1896 realignment had taken hold. Democrats would insist on considering banking reform from their perspective, which regarded as problematic not only the seasonal stringency and cyclical money panics that the business view acknowledged but also the alleged money trust, which the business view ignored or denied.

In 1911 the Aldrich bill was referred to the House Banking and Currency Committee via a resolution calling for an investigation into the money trust. Committee chairman Arsene Pujo appointed a subcommittee, with himself as the chair and therefore dubbed the Pujo Committee, to conduct this investigation. Testimony and documentary evidence indicated substantial concentrated private control over credit in the United States by a few individuals and firms and their significant interrelationships with railroad, public utility, and industrial trusts. In its final report the subcommittee concluded that there was, indeed, a money trust.[51] There was more truth than paranoia to Democrats' charges. Their convention in 1912 declared the party firmly opposed to the Aldrich plan—or any central bank, which they believed would effectively legalize the money trust—and the bill died. This difference between the Democrats' position and the business reform view is what scholars who see the banking reform argument as one over centralization versus decentralization have noticed.

CARTER GLASS AND A THIRD WAY: THE FEDERAL RESERVE ACT

With Woodrow Wilson's victory in the three-way presidential contest of 1912 and the comfortable margins by which they now held both houses of Congress, Democrats had the chance, finally, to act on the money question. Pushed by reform-oriented business groups and bankers, the Republicans, as we have seen, were also ready to reform the banking system. President Wilson thus faced expectations of reform from two different perspectives, and a third, in touch with Wilson's own, was already being brought to bear on the issue. While the Pujo Committee investigated the money trust, another subcommittee of House Banking and Currency had begun work on a substitute for the Republicans' Aldrich plan. Carter Glass chaired this subcommittee; he would chair the full House Banking Committee when Congress convened in 1913, after Wilson's inauguration; and it was Glass's approach that was institutionalized in the Federal Reserve Act as initially passed.

GLASS'S PUBLIC PHILOSOPHY In Glass's public philosophy, as in that of his fellow Virginian Thomas Jefferson, the free, responsible individual comprised the center of value.[52] But not all individuals qualified as responsible in Glass's view. He had grown up during the Civil War and Reconstruction and regarded the poorer, less-educated people of his state, white and black, as pawns of an oppressive Republican regime, not qualified for political participation. As a delegate to the 1901–2 convention that wrote a new constitution for Virginia, Glass provided leadership for provisions that disfranchised blacks and poor whites. Jefferson had also denied political rights to great groups—blacks, native American peoples and women of any color. But, as indicated by the often simultaneous esteem for Jefferson and contempt for racist, classist and sexist views, it was easier for Jefferson to finesse exclusion than it would be for Glass in the twentieth century. Glass had to be straightforward about who should exercise rights, and he was. He viewed middle class white men as the persons qualified to vote and govern, not by virtue of their race and class, but by virtue of their knowledge and experience. Andrew Jackson had gone too far for Carter Glass.

Glass regarded the economy of his day with a mix of condemnation and approval. The corporations that Jefferson feared in theory had become the giant immoral trusts that directed so much of everyday life. They were an assault on equality of opportunity, and they threatened Glass's middle-class values both through the vast concentrations of wealth they represented and through the radicalism they triggered among the lower classes. Yet the ordinary run of businessmen were responsible and expert in their own fields; if the political economy could be cleared of powerful, self-serving monopolies, business could run in its natural, competitive track to the benefit of all.

While Glass retained a Jeffersonian rhetoric emphasizing limited, frugal government, he was willing to extend the reach of the state to meet the economic evils he perceived. Glass supported government action to prevent or break up giant trusts, thereby clearing the playing field for private business to compete; he was willing to regulate the railroads and utilities upon which all depend.

In Glass's public philosophy—with its positive view of business (once distorting concentrations of power are broken up), positive orientation toward government, and willingness to use the state to intervene in the economy, with its emphasis on expertise and even its reluctance to give the uneducated and incapable too much influence in public policy— we recognize a progressive public philosophy much the same as Woodrow Wilson's New Freedom.[53] There have been, and are, variations among policy makers who are considered progressive: Glass would not have gone on to the strong centralized public intervention in the economy of Theodore Roosevelt or FDR, nor did his view of the central government's role extend to providing economic and social security for individuals. Thus, the fellow laborer in the vineyard so valued by Woodrow Wilson would become FDR's implacable foe. Nevertheless, Glass was a progressive, as was Wilson, and their public philosophy is crucial in explaining the founding of the Fed in 1913.

GLASS'S PROPOSAL In an appraisal framed by his public philosophy Glass was intensely opposed to the Aldrich plan for banking and monetary reform. Its mechanism, he argued, was "so arranged that the larger banks of the country must inevitably become predominant and the control of credits continue to be exercised by a few powerful institutions in the large financial centers."[54] The Aldrich plan would only legalize the money trust. But, while Glass thus agreed with the populists in his party that there was a money trust and that government must act to break it up, he most vigorously did not agree with them that the size and allocation of the country's money supply should be controlled by public policy. The government, after all, could fall under the control of unqualified lower-class people as easily as it could fall under control of the money trust. "The political pack," he insisted, "regardless of party . . . should be sedulously excluded" from the Federal Reserve System.[55] Thus, although he shared the Bryanite revulsion of the money trust, he did not take the next step in the populist critique and conclude that someone makes up money. Unwilling to see either private (through the Aldrich plan's central bank) or public discretion institutionalized in the monetary framework, Glass turned to nature.

With the economist H. Parker Willis, whom he hired as his subcommittee's expert, Glass had begun work on a comprehensive monetary reform bill before Wilson's election. With the business reformers Glass and Willis diagnosed the central problem as an inelastic money supply. In drafting a design for a modified banking framework—a Federal Reserve System—their central purpose, repeated again and again by Glass in speeches and writings, was to provide a scientific currency. They relied on the real bills theory, viewing a currency backed by short-term bank assets as literally self-regulating in accord with the needs of business. With this purpose in mind and seeing the problem in light of his public philosophy, what design did the key congressional policy maker and his expert advisor envision for the banking framework?

The primary organizational innovation in Glass's plan for a new scientific currency was the Federal Reserve Bank.[56] The country would be divided into about twenty districts, in each of which there would be such a reserve bank, capitalized at some minimum specified amount. National banks in the district would be required to purchase stock in an amount pegged to the size of their capital. Glass also envisioned provisions for state bank membership. Only banks would buy stock; ownership of the reserve banks was thus private and in the hands of banks, as was control of reserve banks' governance. But, in an effort to remove pursuit of profit as a factor in reserve bank decision making, dividends would be statutorily limited.

Through its lending (rediscounting) operations this new type of organization in the banking framework would be the mechanism for realizing a scientific money supply. Federal Reserve Banks would lend only to member banks, not directly to business or the public. For member banks reserve banks would rediscount paper arising out of productive business transactions; these transactions might entail agricultural, industrial, or commercial purposes, as long as the paper had a maturity of thirty days or less. Paper collateralized with investment securities was not eligible for rediscount, with the exception of government bonds. These provisions were intended to encourage banks to focus their lending on the kinds of assets eligible for rediscount and to turn them away from financing stock market (read: speculative) activity. The self-regulating currency of the Federal Reserve Banks would gradually replace national bank notes. In addition to the commercial bank assets behind the new currency, there would be a substantial gold cover; Glass thus incorporated unquestioningly the other deeply entrenched view of natural regulation of the money supply.

Constitutive aspects of member banks would be manipulated marginally but in theoretically significant ways to suit them to the modi-

fied banking framework. They remained private entities, their ownership and management structures unaffected. But constraints on the
substance of management decisions, of the types noted in chapter four
as occasioned by legislatures' intent to keep banks sound, would be
manipulated. The change that Glass viewed as the most important since
the Civil War was his proposal to alter reserve requirements radically.[57]
Instead of the pyramiding arrangement that effectively channeled money
to New York, banks would deposit their required reserves in the new
Federal Reserve Banks. This arrangement would break the money trust
by preventing the movement of money's control to New York and still
provide pooled reserves (albeit regionally, not centrally) necessary to
prevent or ease monetary stringency. A second major manipulation of
management decision criteria was indirect: member banks' decisions
regarding the types of loans they would make were expected to be
molded by the new reserve banks' rediscounting practices as banks favored loans they could rediscount. With regard to capitalization, national bank requirements would not be affected, but state banks' might
be: state banks could join the system if they met the same capitalization requirements as national banks.[58]

Note that Glass's initial scenario did not include a new central organization. There was no central bank, as there was in the Republicans'
Aldrich plan, for Glass believed it would subject the money supply to
private control by the money trust. Discretionary private control would
not result in a scientific money supply, expanding and contracting as
necessary in response to the legitimate, nonspeculative, needs of business. Nor was there any new public central organization in Glass's original concept—no new Treasury Department division or any entity akin
to the ultimate Federal Reserve Board. Glass envisioned that the existing Office of the Comptroller of the Currency would certify, supervise,
and examine Federal Reserve Banks, a role analogous to the one it played
vis-à-vis national banks. occ would not have discretion over the size
and allocation of the money supply.

Glass's plan reflects his progressivism. In sketching the contours of
his public philosophy earlier, I noted his willingness to see both government and business as positive and to use government in the economy.
Progressive public philosophy is developed more fully in the next chapter. But here note that the emphasis on the science of social and economic relationships, so strong in Glass's thinking about this particular
policy problem, is central in progressive thought. Progressives believe
that through inductive research within a community of inquiry, sci-

ence, we can discover empirical regularities in economic and social relationships. They also believe that society can use that knowledge to make things work better. They thus move away from classic liberalism's assumption that nature's laws are automatically self-realizing for the greater good. With many progressives of his era Glass believed that there is a correct, scientific, natural configuration for economic relationships; his shift was in the conviction that public policy might have to establish institutional mechanisms to enforce or maintain such relationships. Progressives today are often more self-conscious about the extent to which institutional arrangements they advocate, with mechanisms designed based on social scientifically observed regularities, serve goals subject to dispute.

Progressive public philosophy also framed the analysis of business and banking groups advocating monetary reform. They had engaged in social research to figure out how money works. Indeed, Glass and Willis relied upon the research conducted by privately supported reform groups.[59] Such groups shared Glass's purpose of creating an elastic currency, based theoretically on the real bills doctrine and a gold standard, and they would use positive government to adjust economic institutions. Yet I have distinguished their position from that of Glass and Wilson: the diagnosis of banking and business-based reformers did not regard the money trust as a problem to be solved through banking reform, and their proposed institutional solution included a wholly privately controlled central bank.

Within progressivism, as in any of the paradigmatic public philosophies outlined in this study, there are differences in degree. Glass's faith that a scientific money supply—once the government had cleared obstacles to its operation—would prevent seasonal and cyclical money panics without further intervention was greater than bankers', and his confidence in discretion was less, whether that discretion was placed in private or public hands. These ideological differences explain the central design difference of Glass's plan from the business-backed reform plan: its lack of a central board, whether public or private.

WILSON'S AGREEMENT WITH GLASS Believing that it would be futile to proceed with his approach to banking reform unless the president-elect sanctioned it, Glass met with Wilson in December 1912, well before the inauguration. Wilson viewed the problem in much the same terms as Glass. He did not doubt that there was a money trust or that banking reform was crucial to loosen its grip on the credit resources of the country, thereby providing a "new freedom" to business. Wilson had called for a scientific currency from the stump, and he was supportive of the broad outlines of the design Glass offered toward that end. In one difference with Glass's design, Wilson asked that a provision be drafted for an "altruistic" board that would be the capstone of the system. Glass suspected that big bankers had gotten to the president-elect to seek a centralizing entity. Nevertheless, the two were substantially in agreement. Wilson encouraged Glass to continue work on the bill—which was eventually submitted as the administration's measure with Wilson's full and active support.[60]

DEALING WITH BRYAN AND BUSINESS Scholars have written a great deal about the twists and turns along the route from Glass's proposal, as discussed with Wilson the day after Christmas in 1912, to the Federal Reserve Act, which the president signed a year later, the day before Christmas in 1913.[61] Let us frame a summary of that journey by asking: Did the Federal Reserve Act specify a banking framework that substantially complied with Glass's purpose and design? That is, may we conclude that the ideas Glass held drove the Fed's initial institutional design?

Recall that, in keeping with the populist view of the monetary system as a construction, the design features Bryanite Democrats had long regarded as essential were two: government control—*control* meant the locus of discretion in the system—and government (not bank) issue and guarantee of the currency. Bryan himself, who was secretary of state at the time, as well as the viewpoint he championed, remained influential as administration figures deliberated currency reform before the bill's introduction. A measure without Bryan's support might not pass, and Wilson expected that his outright opposition would not only doom the bill in Congress but would also disrupt the party. Accordingly, Wilson invited Bryan to meet with him in May 1913, personally explained the plan, and asked for Bryan's support. At that point the plan specified that Federal Reserve Banks would issue the currency and appoint the vast majority of members of the Federal Reserve Board. Bryan vigorously opposed both features as unwarranted private control. He insisted on government-issued notes and a board consisting of public members only.[62] Both Senator Robert Owen, a Bryan Democrat who chaired the Banking Committee in the Senate, and Treasury Secretary William McAdoo agreed with Bryan.

Wilson decided to support these two demands—whether for strategic reasons or through conviction can be debated, although Wilson historian Arthur Link is convinced of the latter.[63] Accordingly, the president asked Glass to modify the bill. Glass resisted both changes. He insisted that Federal Reserve notes were bank, not government, obligations. Guaranteed as they were by the member banks' rediscounted paper, the assets of the reserve bank that issued them, the reserve banks jointly, and a substantial gold cover, the government's guarantee would not be reached (that is, the government would never have to make good on the notes) and effectively meant nothing. Wilson agreed but argued that, "if we can hold to the substance of the thing and give the other fellow the shadow, why not do it?"[64] Glass was thus persuaded to concede in calling the Federal Reserve notes government obligations, but he regarded the substance of his design unaffected: government issue and guarantee of Federal Reserve notes were mere "textual blemish."[65] Not a dollar of the currency, he repeatedly assured himself and various audiences, would ever be issued except on application of a Federal Reserve Bank. The philosophical significance of Glass's position, again, is that scientific currency arises as banks respond to real business needs for short-term financing, not in arbitrary government issue of notes such as greenbacks.

Glass also resisted the president on the composition of the Federal Reserve Board. The draft design for this entity had gone through a couple of iterations since Wilson had asked Glass to add a central board to his proposal. Initially, Glass specified a board with a large majority of its members chosen by the Federal Reserve Banks.[66] But by the time Wilson explained the bill to Bryan the proposal was for a board with a majority of representatives appointed by the president as well as some representation by bankers. As just noted, Bryan insisted it be changed to include only presidential appointments. Glass wanted bankers on that board, going so far as to march a group of very prominent bankers over to the White House to take his side. Wilson held firm in support of Bryan's position. Glass gave in and altered the draft bill to provide for presidential appointment of all Federal Reserve Board members.

Glass's opposition to Bryan's demand was based directly on his philosophical commitment to a scientific, self-regulating currency; he believed that a public board would interfere with nature if it exercised discretion in manipulating the size and distribution of the money supply (which is, of course, what populists wanted). Bankers, on the other hand, were experts in the scientific laws of banking; a board composed of bankers and chosen by bankers would ensure no discretionary deviation. In conceding on this institutional design point, did Glass lose? He thought not: there were no provisions for the Federal Reserve Board to exercise policy control over the size and allocation of the money supply. Its role was to certify, supervise, and examine the reserve banks in a relationship analogous to that of the comptroller of the currency and national banks. Glass was satisfied that the board did not threaten the scientific ebb and flow of the money supply in response to the needs of business.[67]

Glass was thus sanguine about writing both of Bryan's populist institutional requirements into the Federal Reserve bill before it was introduced in Congress. He was sure that in the context of the framework's design that neither government issue and guarantee of the currency nor a board composed of all presidentially appointed members meant discretionary public policy control over the size and allocation of the money supply. Both details only "[gave] the other fellow the shadow," in Wilson's words.

Banking community opposition to the design features of Glass's plan (although not its purpose in establishing a scientific, elastic currency) was active at all stops in the legislative journey through Congress. Bankers wanted their central bank and tried at every turn to push the bill's provisions back in the direction of the Aldrich plan. Bankers also wanted reserve requirements that would continue to encourage the movement of funds to big banks. Finally, bankers and banking experts offered many suggestions for alterations that would help banks do business and facilitate operations of banks and reserve banks; details of this sort were welcomed into the plan, both to gain banker support and because Glass was genuinely concerned that the institutions he proposed operate effectively. But the final Federal Reserve Act gave nothing to the bankers that Glass regarded as altering his design in substance. In reporting the final bill back to the House, after conference, Glass declared that "the conferees on the part of the House . . . have the pleasure of reporting the bill back without one single fundamental alteration of its structure."[68]

The central purpose of the Federal Reserve Act, as passed in December 1913, was "to furnish an elastic currency." The driving idea behind the legislation was that this currency would be scientific. A scientific phenomenon involves no discretion or power; it is amoral; it is simply the way things are; it is true. The new currency would self-regulate: within the institutional context specified in the legislation, the level and allocation of the money supply would adjust itself automatically to the legitimate needs of business. Bankers would not control it; uneducated farmers would not misallocate it to themselves.

As adjusted by the Federal Reserve Act, the banking regulatory framework included existing institutions, banks and the Office of the Comptroller of the Currency; and two new ones, Federal Reserve Banks and the Federal Reserve Board. The design of each of these institutions followed Glass's plan, with the exception that the number of Federal Reserve Banks was settled at twelve, rather than twenty.[69]

REFOUNDING THE FED

Most people, among the interested public as well as policy elites, expected that the banking regulatory framework as modified by the Federal Reserve Act would mitigate cyclical swings in the U.S. economy, preventing huge booms and massive crashes and even possibly little booms and mild crashes. Things did not work out that way. The economy boomed in the 1920s, crashed hard in 1929, then lay there contracting further and further well into 1933.

In response to the Great Depression, Washington policy makers engaged in the most intensive and self-conscious spurt of institution building at the national level since the Constitution was written. Banking and money was only one of several policy areas in which major construction was under way in the mid-1930s, but, because money's mechanisms affect all areas, reforms here are arguably among the most fundamental of the era.

Beyond emergency and stopgap measures initiated by the Hoover and Roosevelt administrations,[70] policy makers took two major legislative runs at the banking framework in response to the Depression: the Glass-Steagall Banking Act of 1933 and the Banking Act of 1935. Some scholars have viewed the 1935 legislation as a continuation of reform begun in 1933;[71] others have noted differences in the design emphases of the two laws but have not identified the fundamental philosophical shift that accounts for those differences. My argument is that, while the Banking Act of 1933 rested on the same ideological foundations as the Federal Reserve Act of twenty years earlier, the Banking Act of 1935 introduced institutional modifications rooted in explicit rejection of the Federal Reserve Act's central idea that, without ongoing discretionary intervention, the money supply, its size and distribution, would regulate itself in accord with the needs of the economy. The Fed of 1935 is not the Fed of 1913; it is based on a different fundamental idea.

TRYING HARDER: THE GLASS-STEAGALL BANKING ACT OF 1933

After passage of the Federal Reserve Act, Carter Glass left the House of Representatives to serve briefly as secretary of the Treasury under Wilson then returned to Congress to represent Virginia in the Senate. It is there that we find him in the 1930s—powerful, respected, and feared: in the seventy-third Congress (1933–34) Glass chaired both the Appropriations Committee and the subcommittee of Banking and Currency, which controlled all important banking legislation. His leadership in establishing the Federal Reserve System and his prerogatives regarding any changes to it were widely acknowledged. Accordingly, it was Glass who led the reform effort that culminated in the Glass-Steagall Banking Act of 1933.[72] He called on H. Parker Willis, who had worked with him to draft the Federal Reserve Act, to draft a banking reform bill, which he introduced in 1931. Versions of the bill moved on and off the Senate agenda until its eventual passage in June 1933.

Since establishment of the Federal Reserve in 1913, the world had not gone the way Glass had anticipated, and he was determined to get it back on track. The heart of the Banking Act of 1933 was a renewed effort to disconnect member banks from the stock market and focus them on lending in response to the real needs of trade. The Federal Reserve Act was supposed to have accomplished this, but banks and bankers thwarted Glass's design and, in so doing, he believed, were responsible for the stock market boom in the 1920s and the crash in 1929, which in turn had triggered the Depression.[73]

CHANGES TO MEMBER BANKS' PRACTICE AND STRUCTURE Two thrusts of the 1933 legislation—its prohibition of interest on demand deposits and the "Glass-Steagall wall"—aimed directly at member bank practice and structure. In 1913 the Federal Reserve Act provision that Glass had viewed as the most important change since the Civil War was its requirement that banks hold their reserves in the Federal Reserve Banks. This provision was intended to break up the correspondent relationships that channeled funds into the stock market through big banks in New York. But banks had sidestepped this obstacle: in response to generous interest rates on their deposits offered by money center banks, smaller banks simply maintained correspondent relationships in addition to their newly required reserve bank deposits. Trying again to dam up this channel to the stock market, the 1933 legislation prohibited banks from paying interest on deposits.[74]

Second, member banks had been getting around regulatory prohibitions on investment banking and brokerage by using investment affiliates. As the public suspected and investigations by the Senate Banking and Currency Committee in 1932 and early 1933 (the Pecora hearings) confirmed, commercial as well as investment bankers were engaged in scandalous, if not illegal, activity in the securities market. Like the Pujo money trust investigations twenty years earlier, the Pecora hearings heightened public demand for reform and muted banker resistance. For Glass the paramount aspect of his 1933 reform was outright prohibition of any affiliation between commercial banks and securities firms.[75] Member banks were not permitted to underwrite securities; they could not own or be owned by investment banking firms nor have interlocking directorates with them nor even provide correspondent functions.[76] The Glass-Steagall wall thus erected between commercial banking and securities dealing stood fortress-like for a long time but began to crumble in the 1990s and finally collapsed with the Gramm-Leach-Bliley Act of 1999.

CHANGES TO FEDERAL RESERVE BANKS In the renewed effort to prevent banks from lending for speculative purposes, the Glass-Steagall Banking Act of 1933 took aim at the reserve banks as well as the member banks. The Federal Reserve Act's rediscounting provisions were intended to focus banks on short-term lending for productive purposes: only such loans would be eligible for rediscount at the reserve bank (with some exceptions). Like efforts to disconnect banks from "speculation" in the stock market, however, the positive effort to turn them toward "productive" loans had not worked out as planned. Member banks quickly realized that they could take eligible assets to the Federal Reserve Banks for rediscount and use the money thus borrowed as the basis for ineligible loans on stock security. Glass wanted reserve banks to refuse to rediscount (lend) for member banks that did this, but reserve bank officials insisted that they could not control "quality," that is, the kind of loans member banks made with resources provided by the reserve bank. In the Banking Act of 1933 Glass told reserve banks they would have to control quality: reserve banks must monitor the kinds of loans member banks were making as well as their investment portfolios. Any bank that had rediscounts with its reserve bank was not permitted to increase its loans on stock security or put its money in the call loan market.[77]

The 1933 reforms included another theoretically significant move on the Federal Reserve Banks. Recall that these new organizations in the banking framework were the key institutional innovation of the Federal Reserve Act, intended to resolve the currency elasticity problem by rediscounting member banks' commercial paper and by providing reserve pooling. Glass had envisioned them as a neutral mechanism in scientific currency expansion and contraction, not a locus of policy control. But the reserve banks had developed extrastatutory structures and practices through which they pursued policy objectives in the money market.[78] With the complicity of the other eleven reserve banks, the New York Federal Reserve Bank had effectively acted as a central bank in the 1920s, much like the institution envisioned by the banker-supported Aldrich plan. It had acted alone and in concert with the other reserve banks in pursuing policy objectives in the domestic money market, and it had coordinated its actions with European central banks to effect recovery in their money markets after World War I.[79] In the 1930s the New York reserve bank no longer provided leadership; all twelve banks participated more equally in the major extrastatutory policy institution they had developed, the Open Market Committee.[80]

Glass did not want the reserve banks to make monetary policy—whether it was New York acting as a central bank, any one reserve bank acting in its own district, or a committee including leaders from all of the reserve banks that tried to make such policy. For this reason the Banking Act of 1933 took control of open-market operations away from the reserve banks, and provided a statutory basis for the Federal Open Market Committee for the first time. Its membership included all twelve reserve bank governors—thus pulling the body away from New York's influence. To prevent the body of twelve from becoming a central bank and to preclude any one bank from undertaking policy on its own, supervisory control of the Open Market Committee was vested in the Federal Reserve Board.[81] Federal Reserve Banks also lost the authority to conduct any transactions with foreign banks except with permission and under regulation of the Federal Reserve Board.[82]

CHANGES TO THE FEDERAL RESERVE BOARD In addition to adjusting member banks and reserve banks, the Banking Act of 1933 tinkered with the Federal Reserve Board. In the twenty years since the system had been established there had been a tug of war between the board and the Federal Reserve Bank of New York, and between the board and reserve banks generally, over matters of policy. In this struggle bankers had tried to strengthen the reserve banks, while the Treasury and Congress pressured the board for policy moves. Since the statute had not intended to provide for discretionary monetary policy, it provided no guidance in settling this dispute. The board lost out in such encounters because, while neither the board nor the reserve banks had a statutory basis for discretionary control, the reserve banks controlled the levers of day-to-day system operations. By the early 1930s, impotent to deal with the Depression as the banking system and economy collapsed around it, the Federal Reserve Board was a pathetic entity with little authority and less respect.

The 1933 legislation included changes to the board's role, but it would be a mistake to interpret them as efforts to make it a locus of policy control—that is, a central bank. Glass did not want discretion in the Federal Reserve Board any more than he wanted the reserve banks to have discretion. Rather, a strengthened board was intended to keep the system on the real bills track. The board was given more authority over reserve banks so that it could stop them from exercising discretionary monetary policy, not so that it could exercise monetary policy in their place. To keep bank resources out of the stock market, the board was given more supervisory authority over the practices of member banks and reserve banks. To keep the government from seizing control, the Federal Reserve Board was moved physically out of Treasury's building, and the terms of the board members were lengthened from ten to twelve years.

CREATION OF THE FEDERAL DEPOSIT INSURANCE CORPORATION

The Banking Act of 1933 also created the Federal Deposit Insurance Corporation (FDIC). This was not Glass's idea. Indeed, the new organization is an ideologically discordant feature in the banking framework. While Glass attempted to preserve money's value through institutional restraints that kept it on a scientific course, the FDIC provides a guarantee that one's money will not be lost; it was demanded by those who disbelieved that money was a scientific phenomenon. As such, deposit insurance in 1933 is analogous to federal guarantee of bank notes in 1913.

Indeed, while through Bryan's agency populist thinkers had won a federal guarantee for notes in the Federal Reserve Act, guarantee of deposits, although discussed, was rejected at that time. The call for deposit insurance in 1933 came again from populist thinkers, among the public and in the Congress. There was no natural guarantee that their deposits would hold value; they wanted an artificial one from the government. As Glass had insisted in 1913 that Federal Reserve notes were bank obligations but compromised on the point to save his legislation, so in 1933 he insisted that deposits were the responsibility of the bank but again compromised. He accepted deposit insurance when Representative Henry Steagall, chair of the House Banking Committee, insisted on it as the price of his cooperation in passing the Banking Act of 1933.[83]

The institutional reforms in the Glass-Steagall Banking Act of 1933 were thus rooted in the same central idea as the Federal Reserve Act, that the money supply would self-regulate—if only unscientific practices could be squelched. On one hand, with his renewed effort to disconnect them from the stock market, Glass was still fighting the bankers. On the other hand, to achieve his major objectives, he had to compromise with the populist outcroppings of the moment and accept the FDIC.

A SHIFT IN IDEOLOGY: THE BANKING ACT OF 1935

Senator Glass was trying to shore up a Federal Reserve System based on the theory that the domestic money supply would self-regulate in response to the productive needs of business in a world in which that theory made less sense than it ever had. Money's tendency to find its way into wicked, nonproductive, inflationary speculation remained; as we have seen, this was the perception that the reforms of 1933 primarily addressed. The real bills theory had been seriously assaulted from another quarter as well. The huge body of federal government debt issued by the Treasury during World War I was not anticipated when the Federal Reserve Act was passed. This debt constituted both a wildcard that could inflate the money supply meaninglessly and a lever through which deliberate monetary policy could be effected. This lever was the tool the Federal Reserve Banks had "discovered," experimented with, and learned to use. Moreover, even if the money supply could somehow be made to respond only to business's legitimate demand, the Depression convinced at least a few people that money might contract nicely as business demand for credit dried up, the economy shriveled, and hungry people lived in cars and shanties. Would that mean that the monetary system was working?

Like real bills, the gold standard also proved incapable of automatic, beneficent regulation of the money supply; it had not ensured any reliable relationship between the amount of gold in the country and the money supply nor between the money supply and productive economic activity. As the Federal Reserve System was coming on line in 1914, Europe had gone to war. Gold first flowed rapidly away from the United States, as belligerents drew down all they could. Then it reversed course and flowed in even more rapidly as Europeans sought a safe haven for their assets, presenting massive inflationary potential. In the Depression large amounts of gold were hoarded domestically, while the Federal Reserve was drained by foreign withdrawals.

Despite the lack of fit between the world and the ideologically driven institutional arrangements specified in the Glass-Steagall Banking Act of 1933, there was no clamor for further changes to the banking framework from the public or from policy elites. Why, then, did another major banking reform law follow in 1935?

MARRINER ECCLES: A PERSONAL SHIFT IN PUBLIC PHILOSOPHY In September 1934 President Roosevelt asked Marriner S. Eccles of Utah if he would consider the post of governor of the Federal Reserve System. Eccles was not a typical brain truster by any stretch of the imagination. Indeed, his story before the Depression seems unlikely for a person who would not only challenge a basic component of the country's public philosophy on the ideological level but also successfully institutionalize his counterview in arguably the most important actor in the U.S. economy. Eccles was an enormously successful hands-on businessman from Utah who had held significant to controlling ownership interests and management positions in firms in logging, construction, railroads, coal, electric power, sugar, milk, and banking. He tells us that he shared a laissez-faire public philosophy with the other businessmen in whose company he spent his days and with the businessmen in the East to whom they looked for leadership.[84]

Yet, as the Depression deepened and he coped with its effects in his businesses and with the human misery with which he became so intimate as director of relief for Utah, Eccles slid into a frame of mind unusual among his peers: questioning, ruminating, analyzing cause and effect in new ways. He rejected the view of neoliberal business and financial leaders who said that nothing should be done about the Depression, who argued, he tells us, "that a depression was the scientific operation of economic laws that were God-given and not man-made. They could not be interfered with. Depressions were phenomena like the one described in the Biblical story of Joseph and the seven kine, fat and lean. . . . [I]n time . . . the economy would right itself." "But was that true?" he asked. "Did economics itself proceed on the basis of God-given laws? Was human interference with them equivalent to blasphemy? My own reaction was that all such talk was naive. . . . [Economics] is all man-made. . . . The moment the production and distribution of wealth moved beyond a hermit's cave and affected two or more people, economics became artificial in character, in the sense that it was subjected at once to man-made rules and regulations."[85]

Eccles thus explicitly rejected the view that the economy was a natural phenomenon and could be counted on to correct itself. The money supply, in particular, even given the Herculean efforts of the Federal Reserve Act to keep it in productive channels, would not automatically facilitate overall economic health. Business might get nervous and not seek to borrow. Bankers might find it in the interest of their institutions to hold onto their assets, rather than make loans. Nor would a gold standard ensure that anyone would be willing to spend money— gold could be hoarded just like bank money. Thus, contra Adam Smith, the pursuit of self-interest might not lead to the wealth of a nation. Eccles developed a macroeconomic analysis that has been characterized as that of "a Keynesian who had never heard of Keynes";[86] he concluded that federal government action to infuse money into the economy was the way out of the Depression.[87] Like the independent-minded British economist whose works he had not read, Eccles supported direct government spending—what has come to be called fiscal policy. But he was even more enthusiastic about using monetary policy to loosen up the money supply. Money was sitting in the banks: let's get it out and get it working. But the Federal Reserve Act, as amended through 1933, did not provide institutions or procedures for the aggressive (or wimpy) pursuit of monetary policy.

INSTITUTIONAL CHANGES This iconoclastic banker from Utah agreed to accept Franklin Roosevelt's appointment as governor of the Federal Reserve Board in November 1934, on condition that the president would support him in a fundamental transformation of the banking framework.[88] Determined to use the Federal Reserve System to conduct discretionary monetary policy rather than to respond passively to the demands of business, Eccles was on a collision course with Carter Glass. Eccles prepared a bill, introduced as an administration measure, which would make the changes he considered necessary in the design of the organizations in the banking framework. Glass could see that the bill would knock science from the driver's seat in favor of human decisions, and he fought for major changes at every step of the process. At this early phase in his Washington career Eccles was not adept at politics; it was only with FDR's support and quiet maneuvering that a much revised bill, retaining enough of what Eccles wanted to satisfy him, escaped from Carter Glass's Banking and Currency subcommittee to become the Banking Act of 1935. This statute contained three titles. Title I made the FDIC permanent, and Title III made noncontroversial minor banking changes. Title II contained Eccles's ideologically significant changes, and it is on this that we will focus.[89]

Changes to the powers of the Federal Reserve Board constitute the substantive center of the Banking Act of 1935. Although he tried, Eccles failed to win an explicit statement that the board's purpose is to manage monetary conditions actively (rather than merely to constrain member banks and Federal Reserve Banks from violating the dictates of the real bills doctrine). But, in recognizing the tools of monetary policy and giving the board the authority to wield them, the new legislation nonetheless effectively changed the board's purpose. The Banking Act of 1935 transformed the Federal Reserve Board from a passive supervisory entity into a central bank with broad discretionary authority.

Due to the changes Eccles championed, today the Federal Reserve Board has three tools for manipulating the money supply: the discount rate, open-market operations, and reserve requirements.[90] When the Federal Reserve Act was written in 1913, the rediscount rate (today termed the *discount rate*) was the sole mechanism for manipulating the money supply which U.S. policy makers clearly recognized. The individual reserve banks had authority to set the rate for their own districts, but they were expected to do so in response to business needs, not as a tool with which to pursue self-selected economic policy objectives. Nevertheless, the New York Federal Reserve Bank had manipulated the rediscount rate in the United States' major money market to effect national monetary policy objectives; there had been efforts by the several reserve banks to coordinate their rates; and the board had tried, with little success, to influence reserve bank rates. Eccles's bill would have authorized the board to impose rediscount rates on the reserve banks: as passed after struggling with Glass, the legislation authorized the board to instruct them to reconsider their rates.

Open-market operations—the buying and selling of U.S. government securities—has become the Federal Reserve Board's most powerful tool for effecting its monetary policy objectives. But open-market operations were not anticipated in the Federal Reserve Act of 1913 and only became possible with creation of the national debt that financed World War I.[91] It took several years for the reserve banks to observe the effects on the money markets of dealing in these securities and to grasp the potential of such operations; thus we speak of having "discovered" this policy tool. Glass's Banking Act of 1933 had left open-market operations in the hands of a Federal Open Market Committee composed of one representative of each reserve bank. Although the Federal Reserve Board had authority to approve or disapprove what the committee proposed, it could not initiate action, and any reserve bank could decline to participate. Eccles wanted to vest this powerful tool in the board alone, with a strictly advisory committee of five reserve bank presidents.[92] After the struggle with Glass on this point, the Banking Act of 1935 specified a revised Federal Open Market Policy Committee to include all seven members of the board plus five reserve bank presidents, the five to rotate. Further, all reserve banks were required to participate in the operations on which the committee decided. This arrangement effectively gave control to the Federal Reserve Board, which was Eccles's objective.

The authority to manipulate member bank reserve requirements is the third monetary policy tool Eccles won for the Federal Reserve Board in 1935. Throughout this study I have classified reserve requirements as a design feature under *governance* because reserve requirements function as a constraint on bankers' discretion in decision making. To protect noteholders and depositors, as well as the soundness of individual banks, reserve requirements had been statutorily established for the first and second Banks of the United States, for state banks in the several states, and for national banks in the National Bank Act and the Federal Reserve Act. In 1935 Eccles wanted to delete fixed statutory reserve requirements entirely and give the Federal Reserve Board discretion to manipulate them as a monetary policy tool. When the Banking Act of 1935 passed after the sparring match between Eccles and Glass, the board gained authority to adjust reserve requirements but within limits. Eccles was satisfied that he had effectively won all three monetary policy tools for the Federal Reserve Board.

Beyond providing it with these three major policy tools, Eccles's bill also gave the board authority to tinker with constitutive aspects of member banks beyond their reserve requirements. So that the board could steer banks' choice of assets, Eccles asked for authority to specify what kinds of loans would be eligible for rediscount. He wanted to be able to use eligibility requirements, at the board's discretion, to move the banks toward categories of lending deemed especially beneficial for overall economic health.[93] Removing statutory eligibility requirements that had forced banks to focus on short-term commercial loans struck at the theoretical heart of the Federal Reserve Act. Eccles got a small part of what he wanted in this regard in the Banking Act of 1935. Securities that were statutorily ineligible could be rediscounted, albeit at a higher rate, if the reserve bank approved. In a closely related change Eccles sought to relax statutory limitations on real estate loans and to give the board discretion regarding the terms of such loans. While he succeeded in getting expanded permission for banks to lend on real estate as well as to buy such loans, the more permissive terms were fixed in the statute. The board also gained authority to tinker marginally with capital requirements for member banks.

While empowering the Federal Reserve Board for discretionary policy action, the Banking Act of 1935 also ensured that the Federal Reserve Banks would no longer figure as competitors for policy control of the system but, rather, would be neutral conduits for board policy. As already noted, reserve banks were stripped of authority to set open-market policy and required to participate in the operations upon which the FOMC decided. Further, the legislation adjusted their governance structure. The Federal Reserve Act had provided that the Federal Reserve Board select the chairman of each reserve bank's board of directors, who would be the chief executive officer of the reserve bank. In practice the reserve bank boards had ignored the central board's authority by creating the extrastatutory position of governor, whom they selected themselves as the effective chief executive officer.[94] Eccles recaptured Federal Reserve Board authority over selection of reserve bank CEOs in the Banking Act of 1935; the law combined the statutory office of chairman of the board with that of the extrastatutory governor in a new "president" and gave the Federal Reserve Board authority to approve the president chosen by each reserve bank's board of directors.

The Banking Act of 1935 changed nomenclature in the system in ways that highlighted the altered roles of the Federal Reserve Board and the Federal Reserve Banks. The chief officers of the reserve banks would no longer be called governor, as just noted, but rather president. This change is laden with significance for bankers. The chief officer of European central banks had long been called governor. Stripping reserve bank chiefs of this title underscored the fact that they did not set monetary policy. Concomitantly, the Federal Reserve Board was renamed the "Board of Governors of the Federal Reserve System," and all seven of its members were retitled "governor," underscoring that the board is the central bank. The head of the board would henceforth be the "chairman" of the Board of Governors of the Federal Reserve System.

Beyond changes to the powers of the board, Eccles's bill proposed one change in its structure: with the intention of strengthening the influence of the president of the United States over monetary policy, Eccles sought authority for him to be able to remove the chairman at will. On this the brazen new Fed chairman from Utah lost. The Banking Act of 1935 did not give the president such authority, although he retained power to appoint all board members and the chair to fixed terms; instead, the law changed the board's structure in ways that Glass wanted. Its size was reduced from eight to seven members, and member terms were increased from twelve to fourteen years. The secretary of the Treasury and comptroller of the currency lost their ex officio positions. These changes provided the board some distance from the Treasury and the president, as Glass wanted, but also increased its own discretion, which had been Eccles's fundamental objective.

Recalling President Wilson's assessment of the respective outcomes for Glass and Bryan in 1913, in 1935 it was clearly Eccles who won "the substance of the thing" by a huge margin, while Glass was the "other fellow," who had to settle for the "shadow." Indeed, Bryan himself regained ground as the public board on which he had conditioned his support for the Federal Reserve Act, viewed initially by Glass as a nonessential but benign appendage, was transformed into a powerful, public central bank with discretionary authority to manipulate monetary policy. One wonders whether Eccles recognized his debt.

A PHILOSOPHICALLY UTILITARIAN BANKING FRAMEWORK To thank Bryan for keeping open an institutional door through which Eccles entered is not to claim that philosophical populism became fundamental to the revised banking framework. To be sure, there are populist influences, most prominently government guarantee of money—whether a dollar bill or a deposit. The banking regulatory framework is extensive and has a long history. Compromises have been made. It is not philosophically pure.

Nevertheless the changes made to the U.S. banking framework in 1935 were radical and altered its institutions in such a way that the working of the system as a whole is now best understood in terms provided by utilitarian public philosophy. Eighteenth-century philosopher Jeremy Bentham was the father of utilitarianism. Roughly contemporary to Adam Smith, he shared the classic liberal conviction that the human individual is the source and judge of all value. Also with Smith, he believed that individuals pursue their self-interest in the marketplace, and that is as it should be. Bentham's essential departure from classic liberalism was precisely Marriner Eccles's disagreement with the neoliberal businessmen and bankers of his day: Bentham did not think that individual pursuit of self-interest in the market would necessarily yield the best outcome on the whole, for everyone. Sometimes the market fails. There is no invisible hand, or at least it does not perform reliably. For Bentham, as for Eccles, state action was justified where nature ends, to ensure optimal outcomes.

So, what does a utilitarian government do? Bentham was a radical liberal. The good for an individual is what that individual thinks it is, what makes one happy—the more happiness one achieves, the better. Being a mathematical sort, Bentham tried to quantify happiness. He measured it in units called "utils," thus the term *utility* for individual good, or happiness. Society's good was strictly the sum of individuals' utility. That is to say, the general welfare, the public interest, had no quality different from, or independent of, individual interest; the public good consisted strictly in the "greatest good for the greatest number," or "maximum aggregate utility." It was the state's job to maximize aggregate utility. For Bentham a primary way the state did that was to manipulate behavioral incentives through law and public policy. The state became a beneficent overseer.[95]

As utilitarian thought has made its way into economics, it is not just the incentives of individual human decision makers which are manipulated but also those of firms, of corporate entities. Thus, like neoliberalism's marketplace, the utilitarian marketplace also consists of both individuals and firms. Utilitarianism works nicely placed, essentially, over the top of neoliberal institutions. Mathematized in mainstream economics, utilitarianism attempts to keep high the gross domestic product and other aggregate indicators of utility.

To manipulate behavioral incentives—or, in Herbert Simon's language, decision premises—is precisely what Eccles empowered the Federal Reserve Board to do. With its monetary policy powers, with its clear lines of authority, with the Federal Reserve Banks as its policy conduits, the Fed adjusts the premises taken into account by thousands of individual banks when they lend and millions of individuals and firms when they borrow. Eccles's changes made the banking framework a system and gave the board the capability to transmit incentives throughout that system. The Fed does not manipulate all the premises in any one lending or borrowing decision, but it does manipulate some of the premises in all of them. In making their decisions, banks make and allocate money. The Fed's reach extends throughout the U.S. economy in a way that no other institution's effects do: it is the ultimate Benthamite overseer.

6

PROGRESSIVISM AND THE S&L FRAMEWORK

CENTERING THE PURPOSE

In the 1990s and early 2000s the formerly distinctive institutions of the savings and loan regulatory framework are being absorbed into the banking framework. Legislation in 1989 replaced the spectacularly failed Federal Savings and Loan Insurance Corporation with a new Savings Association Insurance Fund, located within the FDIC, the longtime bank insurer. The same statute replaced the Federal Home Loan Bank Board, the former independent S&L regulator, with a new Office of Thrift Supervision (OTS), which joins the bank regulator, the Office of the Comptroller of the Currency, in the Department of the Treasury. Surviving savings and loan associations are now constituted more like banks or have actually converted to bank charters.

Scholarly explanations for the expensive failure of the framework include macroeconomic forces and technological innovation; ineffective regulation; unsound practices and fraud; politics-as-usual; and "moral hazard," which means a proclivity to make excessively risky decisions due to insurance, in this case, federal deposit insurance.[1] But this chapter is not an effort to review or resolve the debate about why the framework failed. Its central question is, rather, why, if the whole edifice is so readily absorbed into the banking framework, had a comprehensive separate set of interacting institutions been built in the first place?

The short answer is that the savings and loan framework was built for the particular public purpose of promoting home ownership in the United States, which was not well served by banks. Now the choice to own a home may appear a private matter, and surely it is. But the idea that the benefits of home ownership extend beyond the individuals involved has been carefully fostered at least since Americans began leaving their families' farms for wage labor in the textile mills of New

England. In the nineteenth century prominent community members viewed home ownership as a way to build character, encourage thrift, strengthen family life, and generate community responsibility among workers who no longer owned or controlled their means of production. By the early twentieth century national leaders took for granted that home ownership served these values and believed further that it made better citizens and even enhanced national security. Today urban planners try to preserve or rescue city neighborhoods by increasing owner occupancy. Advocates of articulating the s&L framework believed that home ownership was intrinsically good for individuals, communities, and the nation—and that the banking framework was largely irrelevant in advancing this public purpose.

The argument of this chapter is that, with its special-purpose character, the savings and loan framework is an institutional manifestation of progressivism, a public philosophy that centers the identification and pursuit of particular substantive public purposes. I offer first a sketch of the progressive paradigm and then a closer look at the thought of one progressive policy maker—Herbert Hoover. For it was Hoover who led the way in making home ownership a national public purpose and in attempting to redesign the financial infrastructure nationwide to promote that purpose. In 1932 he initiated the first of three federal statutes that established the national institutions of the s&L framework. After stepping back from Hoover's day to analyze the century-long development of savings and loan associations which had already occurred in the states, we take up the institutions framed by each of the three foundational federal statutes.

PROGRESSIVISM

The paradigm that I label *progressivism* was grounded in the pragmatic philosophy of John Dewey, Charles S. Peirce, and William James. John Commons and Thorstein Veblen spun out its implications for political economy. It framed the journalistic commentary of Herbert Croly and Walter Lippmann.[2] And, most important for this study of the relationship of ideas to institutions, early in the twentieth century it motivated concrete measures advocated by such public policy makers as Theodore Roosevelt, Robert LaFollette, and Woodrow Wilson.

Progressive philosophers and policy makers had a distinctive interest in the substantive purposes of various social, economic, and political organizations. They were interested in both the efficiency—which meant, for them, effectiveness—and the reliability with which orga- nized activity served its purpose. While they believed in market mecha- nisms, they did not think raw market competition a sure or final guar- antee of effectiveness or reliability. The purpose of an organization or activity might justify departure from classic liberalism's insistence on contract and the market. Reference to purpose weaves itself, in pro- gressive thought, through all three of the themes we have in play: the tensions between the individual and the social/economic system as a focus for public policy, those between nature and construction as an explanation for how the social world comes to be as it is, and those between the public and the private as the justifiable sphere of action.

INDIVIDUALS AND ASSOCIATION

Progressives viewed their thought as beginning not with the axiomatic principles of classic liberalism—the "self-evident" autonomy, equal- ity, and freedom of human individuals, from which is deduced the fur- ther self-evident rule that all adult human association must arise through contract—but, rather, in the world around them.

And the reality presented by the late-nineteenth/early-twentieth century United States was an increasingly interdependent social and economic system. Yet, in insisting that public philosophy adjust its focus to bring the associated world into view, progressives did not dis- count the Jeffersonian emphasis on individual development in favor of Hamilton's focus on policy that benefits the nation as a unitary actor. They tried to overcome this historic dialectic. How could individuals be supported in realizing their full human potential within an intricate web of socioeconomic interdependence? How could the nation be strong and effective as a nation if each person were out marching to the beat of her own drummer? While progressives shared a view that, empiri- cally, an associated world was the overwhelming reality, some of them viewed that world with grave reservations—and focused on trying to protect individuals within it, while others gushed poetic over it—justi- fying ever-larger and stronger organization, in the economy and of the state, on the basis of efficiency.

Progressivism's argument with classic liberalism was not only that the focus of our thought—our analysis, our policy attention—must shift from the individual to associated humanity but that the very locus of that thought was not in lone, separated individual minds but in a com- munity of inquiry. Thought begins in the material world and is a cooperative undertaking. Association is always already here—in both society and epistemology.

Progressive thought regarding the appropriate focus of public attention was far richer than individuals, on the one hand, and nation, on the other. Progressives saw multiple units of analysis: nation, sector, group, person—any of which might merit critical examination and perhaps public policy intervention. At the highest level of aggregation progressivism preached the unity of the nation. This emphasis was, perhaps, inconsistent with progressivism's view of itself as grounded in material circumstances, perhaps more normative than empirical. Coalescing around the turn of the century, progressivism sought to overcome the still politically potent divisions left by the Civil War as well as the new divisions arising with wave after wave of immigration. With both humanitarian and imperialistic faces, progressivism's effort to establish national identity played itself out largely in the international arena and is beyond the scope of this study.

In viewing domestic social and economic arrangements, progressives were greatly interested in the sector as a focus of inquiry. In this their thought reflected the corporatism of German political economy. Both physical and social design—technology and organization—did and should vary from one economic sector or social realm to another: structures and processes that worked best for banking might be quite different from those suitable for, say, the railroad industry or the education of children. Identifying the best practice in a sector depended not on abstract principles but on the particular purpose and mechanisms of the sector. Thus, policy making and implementation required specialized knowledge of the area in question—and we see the root of the characteristic progressive emphasis on expertise.

For progressives the social world included groups of various kinds: corporations, voluntary associations, trade groups, benevolent societies, local governments. Politically, progressives' benign view of groups was a counter to emerging populist criticism of the political economy. Populism (considered systematically in the next chapter) viewed a particular sort of group—the corporation—as unnatural and a threat to individual freedom. Populists wanted corporations excised from the political economy. By viewing the corporation as just one of many kinds of groups in the social world, progressives finessed populist concerns. Corporate organization was not necessarily a threat to individual freedom. The great efficiency of rational corporate organization could enhance human powers—evaluation of any organization depended upon its purpose. Moreover, progressives believed that corporations were, or could be made to be, increasingly managed in the public interest.

Progressivism thus saw a social world composed not just of liberalism's autonomous individuals but of multiple social units—groups and sectors, communities and the nation. Yet, despite its insistence that individuals only exist—unavoidably, empirically—within a vast network of interdependence, progressivism regards itself as liberal, not conservative, public philosophy. While interdependence was Thomas Jefferson's worst nightmare—the ultimate threat to individual development—for progressives complex interdependence supports individuals: within an efficient system the particular contributions of all contribute to reliable generation of the material and social security that undergirds the particular growth of each.

NATURAL OR CONSTRUCTED?

Progressivism thus views complex human association as natural. As with any philosophy, what is natural is good. But, in contrast to conservatism, which also considers complex association as humanity's natural state, progressivism is willing to tinker deliberately with social and economic institutions to help nature along. There is always the possibility that existing institutional arrangements could be enhanced or perfected or that they have gone wrong, have been diverted from their essential purposes and forms, and must therefore be corrected.

As the basis for progressive manipulation of economy and society, the social sciences emerged and flourished. Progressives rejected deductive method based on axioms (for example, "individuals are motivated by self-interest") and insisted that science must be inductive, grounded in the world. They were characteristically optimistic in studying the social world, confident that they could identify its scientific mechanisms. Carter Glass and Woodrow Wilson thought about their intervention in banking in this way: the "science" of money and banking could be identified, and the Federal Reserve Banks would channel behavior in the banking sector back into accord with scientific principles.

As the progressive spirit matured, some progressive policy makers became bolder in their efforts to engineer social improvement and economic progress. Could they move beyond the correction of mistakes in existing institutional arrangements, to generate organizations and institutions *de novo* where no arrangements had arisen for serving some intrinsically worthy ("natural") human purpose? Many believed they could, thus sliding along the nature-construction continuum toward construction. But, even when their efforts at social and economic reform became quite vigorous—as in the construction of the electric power, telecommunications, and transportation industries, and the s&l framework—progressives did not see themselves as constructivist. They did not recognize that they may have imputed or invented the purposes of the institutions they engineered. Science was the study of nature, the way things really are, truth. Nature picked the purposes, the ultimate being human progress; the progressives only uncovered them and sometimes helped nature along its path.

THE PUBLIC AND THE PRIVATE SPHERES

Progressivism denies classic and neoliberalism's firm boundary between the public and private spheres. The public may have an interest in any organized activity. Reflecting its corporatist bent, progressivism conceives of the public interest in substantive terms within separate realms of activity. Each sector has its purpose. The public has a greater or lesser or different interest in the various sectors depending on their purpose and mechanisms.

This substantive view of the public interest is distinctive. It contrasts with a classic liberal view that insists that the state simply maintain conditions that permit maximum individual autonomy in all adult relationships, accepting any pattern of organized action which emerges from the free choices of autonomous individuals as good. Progressives insist that systematic study of such organizations might make them better. Progressivism's public interest contrasts, likewise, with a neoliberal view of the public interest in maximum freedom for corporations, as well as individuals, to pursue their particular interest in whatever way they choose. How much corporate latitude should be permitted depends on the industry. How critical is its product to basic human needs? What potential does its technology have for damaging the natural environment? Also quite different from progressivism's substantive view is the utilitarian definition of *public interest*—the greatest possible sum of individuals' and firms' idiosyncratic utilities, operationalized in dollars as maximized economic output. Progressivism does not regard all economic activity as productive. Some things should not be done even if somebody profits. Progressivism allows that a smaller GDP might serve the public interest better than a larger one—if much of the total were accounted for by, say, tobacco products, home security devices necessitated by social disintegration, a wide range of choices in hand guns and the health care system utilization entailed in their use, and exotic military weaponry.

That the public has an interest in the substantive purpose of a sector and the processes it employs in pursuit of those purposes does not necessarily mean that the state has a role. Private groups take their responsibilities seriously; they engage in social science, learn how to improve their own performance, and act on that knowledge in society's interest. Progressives like business. They also, however, like government. Progressivism's government is not the necessary evil it is in classic liberalism and neoliberalism. Depending on the public's interest in a sector and the sector's particular mechanisms, government's role might simply be to study it to identify best practice and then distribute the findings. Government might regulate the practices of organizations or the quality of their products. It might develop and promote a particular industry. The state might go so far as to constitute organizational actors that had not arisen without public intervention and the pathways of their interorganizational relationships. In tandem with their emphasis on the unity of the nation, progressives were especially interested in using the national government to shape economy and society.

Progressive public policy has been criticized for its justification of the corporation and of integration of some economic sectors in monopolistic and oligopolistic arrangements. Further criticism has taken the progressive state to task as a champion of private interests seeking to solidify their advantages, rather than of the public interest in organized activity, and as technocratic in itself. In critical analyses progressivism has been termed *corporate liberalism, corporate capitalism, interest-group liberalism,* and *conservatism.*[3]

I share reservations about the optimism of progressive thought and the paternalism and elitism its emphasis on expertise entails as well as the failures of some of its institutional children. Yet I wish to offer the defense that, as public philosophy, progressivism (usually) knows its answers are provisional. This is an advantage it shares with populism, over neoliberalism and utilitarianism, as a framework for ongoing evaluation of public policy and institutions.

HERBERT HOOVER'S PUBLIC PHILOSOPHY

Although the conventional wisdom surely gets in the way of seeing Herbert Hoover as a shining example of progressivism, I ask you to suspend disbelief long enough to entertain the argument of this section: that progressive public philosophy is clear in Hoover's writing and his career. Indeed, Hoover's work brings progressivism alive in a way that the earlier abstracted discussion cannot.

It is so difficult to think of Hoover as a progressive largely because FDR's political strategists effectively portrayed him as a laissez-faire do-nothing, fiddling as Rome burned. The portrait endures despite the efforts of revisionist historians to reestablish his progressive credentials.[4] Hoover had the misfortune to be out front when the economic system slowed dangerously, disastrously, in the Depression. In his efforts to sustain, reinvigorate, and even reshape economic processes, Hoover used the national government and the presidency assertively by comparison to his predecessors.[5] But in the extraordinary circumstances with which he attempted to cope, what he did was not enough. Nonetheless, consider Herbert Hoover's beliefs and his actions.[6]

Like other progressive thinkers, Hoover both accepted the empirical reality of an interdependent social and economic system and insisted on the absolute necessity of individual freedom and equality. He believed that an efficient national economy was *for* individuals, to facilitate their human growth and development. He also believed that all progress originates in the thought and efforts of individuals; thus, equality of opportunity to realize their potential was crucial in enabling individuals to function *for* the system. Hoover believed that individuals are motivated by a combination of self-interest and altruism which he called "American individualism" and that the American social and economic structure was moving in a direction that brought out that altruism in the service of the public interest.

Again with other progressive thinkers, Hoover saw and valued multiple units of analysis between the individual, on the one hand, and the nation, on the other. Many distinctive kinds of groups—families, communities, local governments, business entities, trade associations, voluntary associations for social improvement—figured in his thought. Groups interacted with one another in guildlike relationships within their own spheres. Caught up in Hoover's appreciation of the roles and contributions of groups, I often think I hear the hands-off conservative associationalism of Frederick Hayek.[7] But then something abruptly reminds me that this is the Great Engineer talking, a public policy maker who was entirely willing to manipulate human organization as well as physical organization, from the top down and the bottom up, in pursuit of purpose.

Hoover was literally an engineer by profession. As such, he was well aware that discoveries in hard science lead to technological development but not automatically. Technology—the application of increasing knowledge of relationships among things to achieve purposes—requires human agency, deliberate engineering. With followers of the scientific management theorist Frederick Taylor, Hoover knew further that the alignment of human organization to the requirements of technology was also not automatic: building institutions required purposive manipulation. But Hoover was more than a Taylorite. When he studied social and physical science to identify optimal approaches to social organization, he seems to have been sensitive to the requirements of human development, not stopping at mechanical and logistical elegance.

Through a series of quasi-public positions in which he successfully devised organization for dealing with massive disasters, Hoover made his transition from engineering to public service during World War I. As he self-consciously fleshed out a public philosophy in which to ground his ongoing public service, Hoover's thought developed to include the progressive insistence on an active national government. In his view the federal government should conduct social science research to identify or devise good practices and organizational arrangements and go on to change the institutional infrastructure of society and economy. He emphasized reliance on publicity and education as the means by which the federal government should bring about change, believing that voluntary compliance was likely. He preferred to avoid federal legislation, although he did not shrink from it on occasion. While Hoover firmly supported government regulation of utilities and other industries, he drew the line sharply at government ownership. Public ownership smacked of socialism or communism. These public philosophies, in Hoover's view, lost sight of the central importance of individuals; their institutional creations would fail to kindle the spark of human individuality, creativity, excellence, at the basis of all progress.

Hoover's approach to his job as secretary of commerce from 1921 through 1928 clearly reflects his progressive public philosophy. As sardonic as the observation may feel now, in light of what happened next, Secretary Hoover held the optimistic view that the United States was close to eliminating poverty. In pursuing that vision, he expanded his department in an aggressive effort to bring management of the entire U.S. economy under his control. He repeatedly won appropriation increases from the stingy Congresses of the Harding/Coolidge era to expand existing Commerce Department bureaus and to create new ones, and he seized bureaus from other departments when he could.

Hoover's approach to managing the economy was a progressive's approach: he studied different sectors separately, inquiring into their mechanisms, and planned within them in their own terms. The organization of his Commerce Department reflected this corporatist, sectoral way of thinking. Each departmental division was a think tank specializing in a particular area—mining, fishing, aeronautics, radio broadcasting, to name a few of those he regarded as economic. He also conducted research and proposed policy in realms that he distinguished as social: most prominently, child welfare and housing. Each division was staffed by experts and interacted with private groups operating in its area of responsibility. Commerce Department staff conducted economic and social scientific research on a scale unprecedented in U.S. government. On this basis they devised and promoted reforms in structure and practice throughout society and economy. This progressive approach, remnants of which may show up under the rubric *industrial policy* today, presents a clear contrast to the utilitarian macroeconomic management with which we are currently more familiar. Utilitarian economic managers try to maximize aggregate GDP (without triggering inflation) through monetary policy and, if there is room for discretion in the budget, fiscal policy.

Once Hoover and his staff knew the shape of the reform they wanted in a particular area, it was a favorite technique of his to organize a conference or commission on a grand scale. These conferences were usually intended more for publicity, education, and persuasion than for generating solutions. They were means for achieving voluntary compliance with the experts' proposed social and economic reforms and for drumming up support when legislated change was seen as essential.

HOOVER'S PROGRESSIVISM AND HOME OWNERSHIP

Nothing better demonstrates Herbert Hoover's substantive sense of the public interest, his sector-specific approach to public policy, his emphasis on social science and research, his confidence in expertise and belief that fundamental social change could be engineered, and his willingness in the end to move to legislated reform—in short, his progressivism—than his ongoing effort to promote home ownership in the United States.

At the outset of his tenure as secretary of commerce Hoover established a Division of Building and Housing to foster a public interest in home ownership, for he was concerned that "the sentiment, 'Own your own home,' was losing force." Based on broad-ranging research, Hoover and his housing division staff promoted reforms in local zoning and building codes, residential architecture, the production of building materials, and the organization of the building trades. They produced educational material for the public on house plans, choice of locality, and financing options. Hoover created a voluntary organization, Better Homes in America, to support his department's ideas.[8]

Hoover carried his concern with home ownership into his presidency. In 1930 he announced a President's Conference on Home Building and Home Ownership, coordinated and staffed largely by Commerce Department personnel. He appointed experts from all over the country to thirty-one committees, which spent fifteen months engaged in "nationwide research and preparation of ideas" regarding "the different segments of the problem"—from subdivision layout and taxation to design and construction to furniture and landscaping.

When the conferees convened in Washington for several days in December 1931, Hoover told them that the central purpose of their work was "to consider . . . in what manner can we facilitate the ownership of homes and how can we protect the owners of homes?" He went on to explain why he viewed home ownership as a crucial public purpose: "every one of you here is impelled by the high ideal and aspiration that each family may pass their days in the home which they own. . . . This aspiration penetrates the heart of our national well-being. It makes for happier married life, it makes for better children, it makes for confidence and security, it makes for courage to meet the battle of life, it makes for better citizenship. There can be no fear for a democracy or self-government or for liberty or freedom from homeowners no matter how humble they may be."[9] Hoover had already concluded that the major obstacle to achieving this great national purpose was a deficient U.S. financial structure. Indeed, he had already publicly proposed major reform of the institutional infrastructure and called on Congress to legislate it.[10]

BUILDING AND LOAN ASSOCIATIONS

When Hoover convened his home ownership conference late in 1931, he and the Commerce Department housing staff were well acquainted with an institution that had been facilitating home ownership in the United States for a hundred years: the building and loan association.[11]

The first building and loan association in the United States was organized in 1831 in Frankford, Pennsylvania—now a part of Philadelphia. According to the minutes of its first meeting, the purpose of the Oxford Provident Building Association was to enable its members to build or purchase homes.[12] While most of the members were wage earners in textile manufacturing, the initiators were a physician and two industrialists, who had established the area's first textile works.

The bylaws of the Oxford Provident specified a design tailored to its purpose. So that each could ultimately buy or build a house, the thirty-six members agreed to pool their savings. Saving took the form of buying shares of stock. Each member subscribed to one or two shares and paid for them with five dollars down and three dollars per month. This capital, plus collections for fines and interest, formed the association's fund for lending. When adequate funds accumulated, the trustees called for bids for one or more loans. The member offering the highest premium got the loan and built or purchased his house, which was not to be "at a greater distance than five miles from the market house in the Borough of Frankford."

Members of the Oxford Provident met monthly to conduct its affairs and make their payments. They elected a treasurer and thirteen uncompensated trustees; the trustees in turn elected a president and a secretary. The first U.S. building association thus continued for ten years, until all who wanted homes had been accommodated, and then dissolved itself, disbursing funds among the members.[13]

THE PURPOSE OF BUILDING AND LOAN ASSOCIATIONS

Between 1831, when thirty-six people thus formed the Oxford Provident Association so they could acquire homes for themselves, and 1931, when Hoover declared home ownership a purpose of significance to the nation and a proper object of the attention of the central government, building and loan associations had spread throughout the United States. Their central purpose was to facilitate home ownership among people of modest to middling means—which included most people in the United States—through suitably structured financing. Building and loan associations had a second purpose: the encouragement of saving, or "thrift." For it was the savings of ordinary people which would provide the funds for financing the homes of ordinary people.[14]

Institutional antecedents of building and loan associations had been focused on that second purpose: safe saving for working people. Among them Britain's "friendly societies" are cited by chroniclers of the building and loan movement as its ancestors.[15] Beginning in the eighteenth century, people of small means joined together in these societies, making regular small payments so that in times of unemployment, illness, or other difficulties they could draw out small loans or annuities. This basic arrangement was modified to undergird home ownership in Britain as well as in the United States.

The mutual savings bank is also frequently cited as a forbear and relative of the building and loan association.[16] Beginning in 1816, state legislatures chartered these institutions so that people of small means could safely save modest excess earnings and achieve a reasonable return. With their distinctive purpose mutual savings banks were constituted differently than state and national banks. They were owned by the savers, without capital besides their savings. Earnings and losses were shared among depositors. Assets were restricted to only the safest of investments: real estate mortgages, and high-quality bonds. Mutual savings banks did not issue notes that circulated as money nor accept demand deposits. The vast majority of such banks has always been in a few states in the Northeast.[17] For mutual savings banks the relationship of means and ends was reversed from that in the building and loan associations: their central purpose was safe saving, and they held mortgages because they were regarded as the safest of securities.

THE DESIGN OF BUILDING AND LOAN ASSOCIATIONS

To analyze the design of building and loan associations, as they developed through 1931 to serve the purpose of facilitating home ownership, let us call up the constitutive categories we have used to consider various kinds of banks: capital, ownership, governance, and assets. Their liabilities are also important.

CAPITAL The role of capital in a building and loan association was essentially as a fund for purchasing homes. A building and loan's capital was accumulated as members bought shares of stock, for which they paid in small amounts over long periods of time. By 1931 four major variations on building and loan design had arisen: terminating, serial, permanent, and stock associations. Their fundamental difference was in the timing of the purchase and withdrawal of shares.[18]

The Oxford Provident, discussed earlier, was a terminating association. In this design all of the stock was issued at the same time and matured at the same time, about ten years later. If someone wanted to join in the interim, he or she had to buy the shares of a member who wished to leave. There were penalties for early withdrawal. Terminating associations might or might not charge interest on home loans; thus, there might or might not be dividends on shares. Any earnings were distributed only when the association liquidated.

The serial plan developed in the 1850s. In this scheme new series of stock were issued quarterly, semiannually, or annually. This arrangement made it easier for new members to join and gave members more time to avail themselves of their right to a home loan. Members received dividends at the expiration of their series. The serial plan was still in wide use in the 1930s, though terminating associations had died out.

By about 1880 a "permanent plan" emerged, providing yet greater flexibility for putting money into a building and loan and taking it out. In this arrangement one could join by purchasing a share at any time. Gradually, practices developed whereby a member could make any size payment on shares at any time. Prepaid shares came to be permitted, and members were permitted to leave their shares in the association beyond their maturity, thus earning interest. Although notice of thirty, sixty, or ninety days might be required, penalties for withdrawal virtually disappeared. Members no longer had to wait until their stock series matured to receive dividends, as net earnings were periodically distributed.

What was happening with this development in institutional design was an unlinking of borrowing and saving at the level of the individual member. Initially, every member of a building and loan both saved and borrowed for his or her house. But over time, as it became easier to deposit and withdraw savings, the associations drew in funds from persons who sought a safe place to save and a modest reliable return but did not take a home loan. By 1931, among twelve million savings and loan members in twelve thousand associations throughout the United States, two million had home loans, and ten million were simply savers.

As saving alone became the motivation of many for joining a building and loan association, dividends (earnings on shares) became more important. In the terminating, serial, and permanent plans, dividend rates varied with the practices and performance of the association. To provide a guaranteed dividend level a final variation on capital arrangements developed in a few states by the 1930s. These "stock associations" issued two different kinds of shares. Most members held regular shares, which they could purchase and withdraw when they wished, effectively, a savings account. A special class of nonwithdrawable stock was also issued. This stock generated a fund to ensure dividends on regular shares and to cover losses if there were any. If there were especially large earnings, these too would accrue to the special stockholders.

OWNERSHIP Except for a limited number of stock associations, building and loans up through 1931 were mutually owned. Mutual ownership is a device that works well in a progressive approach; it means that an entity is intended not for profit but, rather, specifically to achieve some substantive purpose. Mutual financial institutions might be philanthropic: people with more resources attempting to do something for people with less. Philanthropic second mortgage entities, for example, had been organized in a few U.S. cities. Or mutual institutions might be organized on a self-help basis by people attempting to help themselves achieve some purpose through cooperation with one another. In either case establishment of a mutual entity represented a decision not to leave provision of what was wanted to the market—these entities were not intended to maximize anyone's profit but to achieve their substantive purpose.

As self-help mutuals, building and loan associations were owned by all the people using their services. Savers were not creditors to the association (like the depositors in a bank), nor were borrowers debtors (like borrowers from a bank). They were all members. Any earnings achieved by the association (except in the limited number of stock associations) were distributed equally among the members.

GOVERNANCE As we saw in the example of the Oxford Provident Association, early on there was considerable participation by the membership in the governance of building and loan associations. But over the decades, as shares became more and more like bank deposits, members lost their sense of ownership and no longer participated in decision making. They routinely proxied away their votes for the board of directors in the process of signing up for shares, without even realizing they had voting rights.[19]

By the end of the nineteenth century building and loans were often initiated and controlled by business interests in the community: real estate brokers, insurance agents, and contractors.[20] Lawyers and bankers were involved. Although they did not profit directly from a mutually owned building and loan, local businesses could benefit from the housing development facilitated by the financing it provided. Yet there is considerable indication in the congressional hearings of the early

1930s that providing service for the people and the community remained
a strong motivation among directors and managers; this intent to provide
service for other people, for their good, is characteristic of progressivism.

ASSETS AND LIABILITIES In 1930, 88 percent of building and loan
associations' aggregate assets of $8.8 billion were in mortgages on owner-
occupied homes,[21] accounting for about a third of the home mortgages
outstanding in the United States. The structure of these mortgages was
the crucial innovation that facilitated home ownership for wage workers.

The significant features of building and loan home mortgages were:
a long term, amortization, and a high loan-to-value ratio. Throughout
the building and loans' first century (1831–1931) borrowers typically
repaid their loans over a term of eight to twelve years. Amortization
meant that a payment of the same size was made periodically, monthly
or weekly, such that at the end of its term a loan was completely paid
off, principal and interest. Technically, borrowers' payments were payments on shares of stock in the association, not directly booked on
their mortgages. When they had paid for shares such that the amount
of the shares—plus earnings on those shares—equaled the value of the
mortgage, the mortgage was canceled; thus, the loan's term was not
precise but reasonably predictable. A "high loan-to-value ratio" meant
that building and loan mortgages were given for a large portion of the
home's value, ranging from about 65 to 75 percent in 1930. A borrower
may have already saved the down payment in the association before
securing a loan.

Long-term, self-amortizing, high loan-to-value mortgages with more
liberal terms than those just explained are familiar today, but it was
the building and loan movement that devised them, and only building
and loans made them before Depression-era changes in the financial
system.[22] Mainstream home financing was structured quite differently.
A typical "straight" first mortgage loan was for 40 to 60 percent of the
appraised value of a home. Its term was likely to be one, three, or five
years, during which time only interest was paid. At the loan's expiration the principal was due in full. In ordinary times the loan was usually
renewed, although there was no guarantee that it would be. Renewal
entailed paying fees again, and renewed mortgages might be subject to
call at the lenders' discretion. Such straight mortgages were offered by
insurance companies, mutual and stock savings banks, state banks and
trust companies, and individual investors. The mortgage banker played
a pivotal role in the system, placing mortgages in communities through-

out the country, mostly for insurance companies but also for other institutions and individuals. Straight first mortgages were regarded as very safe securities, accounting for their presence in the portfolios of the most safety-conscious of financial institutions.

To get a straight first mortgage of 40 to 60 percent home buyers were expected to have a down payment of about 20 percent, leaving a considerable gap, which many covered with a second mortgage. Terms on second mortgages were very demanding, with high principal payments, a short term, up-front charges of 18 to 20 percent of the principal, and interest rates up to 10 percent. They were offered by marginal participants in the financial industry. Indeed, the second mortgage business, usually unregulated and often in violation of state usury laws, had a tawdry reputation.[23]

Mainstream home financing of this kind was not within the reach of most Americans, or they overextended themselves to secure it. Major institutions did not lend on older homes, low-value homes, or homes in lower-income neighborhoods.

Beyond their mortgages building and loans had a small volume of other assets. They had some cash, often kept on deposit in state or national banks. By 1931 many had a reserve or contingent fund, also likely to be on deposit in a bank. The practice of building a reserve fund developed as associations' began to pay out dividends periodically, instead of waiting until a series of stock had expired. It became prudent to regularly hold back some portion of earnings to pay losses or expenses or to level off dividends in a dry period. A final asset held by building and loans, in some states, was a small amount of conservative government securities.

Building and loan associations had little by way of liabilities. Member savings were capital to the association, not liabilities, like the savings and demand deposits of a bank's clients are to a bank. This is to say, there were no demand deposits in a building and loan association. Indeed, savers' subscriptions were not technically savings deposits but capital. By 1930, however, building and loan members often had no clear sense of the different status of their funds in a building and loan compared with demand or savings deposits in a bank.

Some building and loans incurred the liability of bank loans. They might borrow from banks occasionally to meet a spike in withdrawals. Or some associations regularly took bank loans during construction season and repaid them during the rest of the year, when member payments on stock exceeded the demand for new home loans.

STATE REGULATION OF BUILDING AND LOAN ASSOCIATIONS

Recall from the discussion in chapter four that state legislatures began early to regulate state banks through the provisions of their corporate charters. By contrast, building and loan associations operated without state regulation of any kind for decades, largely as voluntary unincorporated associations, under their own constitutions and bylaws. Gradually, some building and loans were organized under general laws.[24]

New York was first, in 1875, to pass a general law regulating building and loan associations. Other states did not follow until the late 1880s and into the 1890s, when, spurred by the emergence of national building and loan organizations, regulation became widespread.

The "nationals" appeared in the mid-1880s and operated interstate. Although some were responsibly conducted, the form was largely a racket. At a time when it was extremely difficult to get credit to buy a home, people were persuaded to invest in the national building and loan associations by promises of rather fantastic returns, with hope of getting their turn for a home loan, and by confidence in the safety record of local building and loans. But national building and loans were designed to put much of subscribers' money in promoters' pockets, and they made few loans. While their number grew rapidly, to 240 in 1893, the nationals disappeared in the recession that began that year. The national associations damaged the building and loan reputation, and in some areas where they had been active local associations failed in their wake. The United States League of Local Building and Loan Associations (later the United States Savings and Loan League) was formed in 1892, with the initial objective of securing state legislation prohibiting or regulating interstate operation. The motivation for starting the league was progressive: an effort to ensure that good practice was enforced.

Once under way, state regulation of building and loan associations passed through the same stages as state banking regulation had. There was reporting by associations to designated state officials. Permissive examination often followed and then mandatory examination. State officials gained the authority to rule on requests for forming new organizations. The officials involved might be banking or insurance regulators or separate building and loan commissioners.

Building and loan associations themselves thus sought regulation, through their state building and loan leagues and the U.S. League. They expected regulation to prevent problems—whether arising from dishonesty, carelessness, or ignorance—and to ensure good practice in safe associations.[25] By 1932 only South Carolina and Maryland did not regulate their building and loan associations.[26]

THE IMPACT OF THE DEPRESSION

In 1930 there were twelve thousand building and loan associations in the United States, with twelve million members. They held $8.8 billion dollars in assets, mostly mortgages on the homes of working people. Thousands of local leaders had participated in the organization and management of the associations and in the state leagues formed to seek regulation in the interest of promoting good practice; they believed they were pursuing a social good. Also in 1930, the surreal spell that was the Great Depression was settling in on the United States. It brought hazards and opportunities to the building and loan movement.[27]

As the Depression deepened, building and loan associations encountered difficulties and failures increased. There were heavy withdrawals by savers who needed their money or feared for the stability of financial institutions. Building and loans typically borrowed from banks to meet exceptional withdrawal pressure, but, with liquidity concerns of their own, banks would not lend to them now. Indeed, the banks called in credit they had previously extended to building and loans. Associations that had their cash or reserves in banks sometimes lost them or could not readily access them as the banks failed. By 1931 building and loan borrowers were having trouble paying on their mortgages; many stopped. In company with all real estate the value of the collateral on building and loan mortgages was declining precipitously.

Nonetheless, the vast bulk of building and loans battened down the hatches and came through the Depression intact. Because they did not hold demand deposits, they did not have to pay savers on demand and were not considered insolvent if they could not. They paid out gradually as funds became available on performing mortgages. To avoid foreclosures they restructured mortgages by extending the term and reducing the payment, or they accepted just the interest for a while, or they forbore altogether if there was hope that a borrower would once again be able to pay. To the extent that they did foreclose, building and loans maintained the value of their assets by not dumping foreclosed houses on the severely depressed real estate market, as banks so often did. As local institutions, building and loans were in a good position to keep foreclosed properties, manage them, and sell them only after the market had recovered.

Yet, hunkered down as they were, though surviving, building and loans were not in a position to do much to help the economy. The mainstream system of home financing had been problematic without the strain of the Depression, and with it the system disintegrated. Borrowers could not make the demanding periodic payments on their second mortgages. On first mortgages most borrowers, whether still employed or not, could hardly be expected to pay off the principal balance upon expiration. In normal times they would have refinanced, but now there was no refinancing available. The rate of foreclosure accelerated sharply in 1929, again in 1930, and continued up in 1931 with no end in sight. People were losing homes in which they had considerable equity. Real estate values plunged as foreclosed properties were dumped on the market for what they would bring. Thousands of desperate home owners, left in the lurch by dominant financial institutions, sought help from building and loans. But the alternative organizations had no funds with which to make new mortgages.

THE FEDERAL HOME LOAN BANK ACT: FEDERAL HOME LOAN BANKS

In this context, late in 1931, President Hoover asked Congress for legislation establishing a new institution in the U.S. financial system: the Federal Home Loan Bank. Up to twelve such banks, in regions throughout the United States, would loan money to building and loan associations and other financial institutions on the collateral of their home mortgages. The flow of funds thus released was expected to enable lenders to meet withdrawal pressure, refinance mortgages, and even make some new mortgages, giving a boost to the market for new and existing homes. Congress responded by passing the Federal Home Loan Bank Act in July 1932.

THE PURPOSE OF FEDERAL HOME LOAN BANKS

Although the emergency gave Hoover the opportunity to get his home loan rediscount bank measure passed, his purpose in advocating formation of such institutions was not centrally to relieve emergency conditions. Before the Depression was upon him, Hoover had already concluded that deficiencies in the financial structure constituted the major obstacle to advancing home ownership. He intended his home loan banks for the "long-view purpose" of promoting home ownership by strengthening certain financial institutions, especially building and loan associations. To be sure, the president also expected his proposed reform to address the present emergency. Among its purposes he included relief of the strain on mortgage lending institutions, thereby relieving pressures on home owners, and the revival of construction, thus increasing employment. The emergency was an opportunity to seek fundamental reform that he had wanted anyway.[28]

THE DESIGN OF FEDERAL HOME LOAN BANKS

The mechanisms of the Great Engineer's new banks were intended to reform the country's financial structure, in the service of home ownership, in two ways. First, the building and loan–style mortgage was encouraged (and, indeed, would ultimately become standard), making home ownership more feasible for the individual purchaser. Second, new institutional channels would be created to facilitate the flow of society's financial resources into home ownership. Analysis of the design of the home loan banks, based on the statute as initially passed, demonstrates how they would do these things.[29]

Modeled in part on the Federal Reserve Act, the Federal Home Loan Bank Act provided for eight to twelve separately capitalized, regional rediscount banks. These new banks would loan money to home financing institutions relying on initial capitalization from two sources: the member institutions themselves and the federal government. To use a Federal Home Loan Bank's services an eligible institution—building and loan association, savings bank, or insurance company—had to become a member of the Federal Home Loan Bank in its district, or an adjoining district, by buying stock in it. To the extent that eligible institutions did not provide the minimum necessary capital (as determined, subject to a statutory floor, by the Federal Home Loan Bank Board in the process of organizing the banks), the United States government would buy stock in each Federal Home Loan Bank. Given the economic and financial circumstances in which the home loan banks were being organized, it was expected that the government would be the major stockholder in the beginning.

How did Hoover reconcile his proposal for government purchase of the vast bulk of the Federal Home Loan Banks' stock with his insistence that public ownership was beyond the limit of appropriate government economic involvement? His progressivism included a strong role for the government in constituting, as well as regulating, the organizations of the economy and their interrelationships. In order to originate and firmly establish an institution as crucial as mortgage rediscount banks, government ownership was acceptable on the temporary basis provided for in this statute. In the long run, Hoover emphasized, the Federal Home Loan Banks would be privately owned by their member institutions, as the Federal Reserve Banks were owned by their member state and national banks.

As a design feature of the system, what did it mean for the member institutions of a Federal Home Loan Bank to "own" it? In the progressive view ownership was intended not so much as a profit opportunity but, rather, to create an ongoing responsibility for, and interest in, maintaining these institutions. Hoover referred to the ultimate private ownership of the home loan banks as "mutual," with its connotations for nonprofit service. Effectively, ownership gave member institutions a role in the governance of the Federal Home Loan Banks and the opportunity to use the services they were established to provide.

Each Federal Home Loan Bank was to be governed by a board of eleven directors. The Federal Home Loan Bank Board, also created by the statute, would appoint two of them. Member institutions would elect nine, three each from large, medium-sized, and small institutions. All nine of the member-elected directors were to be chosen from among the officers and directors of member institutions. The usual term for a director would be three years, and the board would select its own chairman and vice chairman.

Composition of the boards of directors for the Federal Home Loan Banks did not excite the intense controversy that surrounded this question in the case of the Federal Reserve Banks. The requirement that the vast majority of the board, nine members, be directors or officers of mortgage-lending institutions is an example of the characteristic reliance on expertise in the particular matter at hand in progressive institutional design. Some small sentiment surfaced in the hearings on the home loan bank bill for having a class of directors to represent general business interests within each district, as with the Federal Reserve Banks, but that did not catch on. The role of the central Federal Home Loan Bank Board's two appointees on each home loan bank board of directors was understood as representation of the public's interest.

Federal Home Loan Bank boards of directors would run their banks within regulatory parameters established by the Federal Home Loan Bank Board. This central board was responsible for organizing the system and for regulating the home loan banks.

The Federal Home Loan Banks' central function was to get money to member mortgage lenders. Accordingly, their major asset would be loans, termed *advances* to member building and loans, savings banks, and insurance companies.

To secure an advance a member would borrow against home mortgages it had already made. Details regarding the features of mortgages which would be eligible as collateral were a crucial mechanism through which the statute aimed to reform home mortgage–lending in the United States. Mortgages with certain characteristics—long term, full amortization—brought a larger advance than other mortgages. This provision attempted both to encourage all eligible financial institutions to make this type of mortgage and to strengthen building and loan associations, the exclusive source of such financing at that time. Because the president and Congress were trying to address the emergency, existing mortgages on the terms standard before the Depression were not ineligible as collateral, but they secured a smaller advance.

To ensure that the funds supported home ownership and not rental housing, eligible mortgages were on residences for one to three families. Nor was the system supposed to serve the wealthy: the $20,000 limit on the value of the mortgaged property made working- and middle-class home mortgages eligible for rediscount.

Defaulted mortgages could not be rediscounted under the original Federal Home Loan Bank Act. Although Hoover favored their inclusion, building and loan movement representatives resisted in the interest of the institutional stability of the Federal Home Loan Banks. Including defaulted mortgages would have made the system more helpful in the emergency circumstances in which it was born but would also have loaded home loan banks' portfolios with very shaky securities, which would have threatened the viability of the new rediscount institutions from the outset as well as the viability of the local building and loan associations that capitalized them.

In addition to extending advances to their members on the basis of mortgage collateral, Federal Home Loan Banks could lend to and borrow from one another. They could also hold deposits in other home loan banks. These mechanisms served to move available money around the country. In "normal times" one area of the country would have surplus funds seeking safe investment, often the Northeast, while another area—California, for example—had insufficient funds to meet the demand for new housing. The Depression would not last forever, and the legislation's framers were trying to put a system in place for the long haul. Finally, a home loan bank might hold conservative securities as assets, including the bonds of other home loan banks.

On the liability side of their balance sheets Federal Home Loan Banks were empowered to sell bonds to the public and to use the funds borrowed in this manner to make advances to their member institutions beyond what was possible based on their own capital and member deposits. Advocates of the legislation hoped these securities would be attractive in the U.S. financial market, as similar securities were in European countries. As it worked out, Federal Home Loan Bank bonds did provide an easy and safe way for individuals and conservative financial institutions to invest in home mortgages, thus channeling society's savings into home ownership.

Another Federal Home Loan Bank liability of significance was deposits. Member institutions could maintain excess cash and reserves, which they had previously placed in commercial banks, on deposit with their Federal Home Loan Bank. Having lost their assets in failed and closed banks, creating their own deposit institutions was very important to the building and loans. Bankers, even those who supported the idea of mortgage rediscount banks, opposed empowering home loan banks to take member deposits.

THE POLITICS OF THE FEDERAL HOME LOAN BANK ACT:
IDEAS AND INTERESTS

Hoover had wanted a grander mortgage rediscount system than he actually proposed and saw enacted in the Federal Home Loan Bank Act. With European models in mind, he envisioned a facility that would serve all financial institutions engaged in mortgage lending, including commercial banks, and which would rediscount mortgages on "productive" real estate, beyond those on owner-occupied homes. The president had more liberal terms in mind as well, including a willingness to rediscount defaulted mortgages. But, when he floated his idea in meetings with financial leaders, most of those representing institutions that made straight home mortgages were opposed. Savings bankers were lukewarm. Only the building and loan people were reliably enthusiastic. They had floated proposals of their own for a national home mortgage rediscount bank before Congress a couple of times, first in 1919, and two or three states had established their own mortgage rediscount banks before the Depression.

Hoover had found no support for his grander mortgage rediscount bank proposal in Congress either. In October 1931 a group of thirty-two congressional leaders from both parties—whom he had called together in an effort to elicit support for his financial relief proposals generally—rejected the idea. Hoover was not expecting much cooperation from the seventy-second Congress. The Democrats had the House, and, even though the Republicans had a majority by one in the Senate, he felt that conservatives in his party were aligned against him with the Democrats.

Without support from major financial institutions or Congress, Hoover scaled back his proposal. While savings banks and insurance companies were included as eligible members from the first draft of the bill on, Federal Home Loan Bank design was tailored to meet the needs and policy direction of building and loan associations. The president believed that the building and loan people could muster substantial influence in Congress.[30]

Congressional hearings on the Federal Home Loan Bank bill were extensive in both the House and the Senate, permitting identification of advocates and opponents of the measure and their arguments. Indeed, as Hoover had anticipated, building and loan people—through their individual associations, state leagues, and the United States League—became his chief allies in winning passage of a Federal Home Loan Bank Act. In those days, before the presidency included institutionalized congressional liaison capacity, the statute would not have made it without them. Through their United States League building and loan representatives worked closely with Commerce Department officials to draft the initial bill and with an unofficial committee of the House to draft a substitute measure more to their liking. They orchestrated substantial support for the measure during the hearings, drumming up telegram campaigns and gathering data and preparing analyses requested by the administration and congressional committees.

In addition to building and loans, support for the Federal Home Loan Bank bill came from real estate boards across the United States and their national association and from the building and home supply industries. Supporters often raised concerns about the mechanics anticipated by the bill and asked for changes, but they agreed with the central purpose of the measure—to promote home ownership by restructuring the financial system—and with its broad contours.

Their arguments in favor of the bill were chiefly in three areas. First, they emphasized the advantages of the amortized mortgage as the key to home ownership for people of modest and middling means and wanted to see it become more widely available. Second, they insisted that the proposed Federal Home Loan Banks were needed as a permanent part of the country's financial infrastructure. Home mortgage lenders needed a reserve, or rediscount system, even in normal economic times. This would strengthen the institutions making amortized mortgages. Finally, supporters of the home loan banks believed that they would help in the emergency. By borrowing against their "frozen" assets, building and loans would be able to meet the withdrawal requests of savers, restructure current mortgages, and, just possibly, refinance some of the home owners left out in the cold with their expired straight mortgages.

Two additional arguments in favor of the bill were voiced by leaders in the building and loan movement and experts from the Commerce Department. One was the intent to use the home loan banks to standardize good practice on the part of the individual building and loan associations throughout the states. Second, there was an intent to create an institutional mechanism for moving available mortgage money around the country, from areas where it was not in demand at the moment to areas that were in deficit.

Opposition to the president's proposal was strong and organized. It came chiefly from insurance companies; mortgage bankers, who were agents for major financial institutions; and commercial banks, both state and national, as represented by individual banks, state banking associations, and the American Bankers Association. Their central argument was that the home loan banks were not needed; indeed, the reform that Hoover and the building and loans advocated was a mistake. Standard straight mortgages were sound finance. There was trouble now because people who should not have bought homes did so and because the real estate market had inflated ridiculously and required a natural correction. Once "liquidation pursued its course," the existing system would "adequately finance real estate [that] warrants financing, on a sound economic basis."[31] This is a version of the argument that nature (read: the existing financial system) provides the best of all possible worlds; the government should not deliberately route society's financial resources.

Some opponents of home loan discount banks did allow that temporary special liquidity measures for home mortgages made sense. These should be provided, they argued, by the Reconstruction Finance Corporation, recently established to deal with emergency financial conditions.

A second major argument advanced by opponents of establishing Federal Home Loan Banks was that their design was unworkable in various ways. The bonds would be unmarketable. The banks would be too expensive to initiate or to run. Eligible institutions could not afford the stock. Many supporters of the legislation suggested changes to make the system's mechanisms work better, but, for opponents, groping for reasons why the home loan banks would not work appears to have been another approach to fighting establishment of an institution they regarded as unneeded.

The charge that the rediscounting operation of the home loan banks would lead to "overbuilding" was the third major argument advanced by opponents. Funds newly available to building and loans through Federal Home Loan Banks would be used to finance new homes. New construction was undesirable: there had already been too much speculative land subdivision and home construction. People who should not be building a home because they could not afford it (assuming a straight mortgage, substantial down payment, and second mortgage) would get themselves into a bind. Too much of this activity had already gone on and was, indeed, the real reason that people were losing their homes now, not Hoover's imagined deficiencies in the financial system. Overbuilding would devalue the property of current home owners and depreciate securities (held by the legislation's opponents) based on those homes.

Beyond these three major issues, other opposition arguments included ostensible concern for government revenues—Federal Home Loan Bank bonds would be tax exempt and would compete with other government bonds—and an objection to government involvement in business. Finally, there was a charge, with a disingenuous ring coming from representatives of the major mainstream financial institutions, that, while the Federal Home Loan Bank System would strengthen and preserve certain institutions—building and loan associations—it would not do anything to help individual hard-pressed home owners in the emergency.

Hoover stayed on top of the home loan bank bill's progress. Although he had always found it distasteful, he worked Congress members and the leadership to the end. An effort by the chairman of the responsible Senate subcommittee to bottle up the bill particularly angered Hoover. He called upon his remaining Republican allies in the Senate, who maneuvered the bill out around the subcommittee. The Federal Home Loan Bank Act passed in July 1932 with bipartisan support over bipartisan opposition.

Thus, despite vigorous opposition by powerful financial interests, fundamental reform of the financial system was enacted. This reform was quintessentially progressive: it was motivated by pursuit of a particular substantive purpose believed to be in the public's interest—promotion and preservation of home ownership—and it was engineered in detail to work in this particular policy area.

THE HOME OWNERS' LOAN ACT:
FEDERAL SAVINGS AND LOAN ASSOCIATIONS

In March 1933, only eight months after the Federal Home Loan Bank Act had passed, the Senate held hearings on a bill to repeal it.[32] In the meantime Hoover had been defeated by Franklin Roosevelt, who had just taken office. The central theme in FDR's campaign had been that the federal government must act to help individuals directly in the face of the Depression emergency and, conversely, the charge that Hoover's approach only helped big, monied institutions. Accordingly, members of Congress and prominent administration officials, labeling them "Hoover creations," indicted the Federal Home Loan Banks as aiding financial institutions (the building and loans) while doing nothing to help hard-pressed individuals.

An expectation that the Federal Home Loan Banks would directly refinance mortgages for individuals had spread widely among Americans, with good reason. The authorizing statute contained a provision, inserted by amendment on the Senate floor, that, as long as the government held stock in them, the banks must directly refinance the mortgage of any home owner who could not find another lender. Further, in the November 1932 congressional campaigns incumbent candidates had trumpeted the new institutions as a source of direct relief for desperate constituents facing foreclosure. Thousands of citizens—not only home owners but those with farm and apartment building mortgages as well—descended on the Federal Home Loan Banks in those first months seeking refinancing. But these institutions had been designed strictly as rediscount banks. They had no mechanisms for direct lending, despite the statutory provision requiring that they do it.

The task of defending the new institutions fell to Federal Home Loan Bank Board members and staff. They underscored the accomplishments of the young system. In a few months the first board, appointed by Hoover, had created twelve districts and organized the twelve banks. The banks were up and running, pumping cash into the moribund economy by providing advances to members. Their activity had been particularly welcome during the bank holiday in early March: while the building and loans used some of the money available through the new rediscount banks to refinance mortgages expiring with other institutions, most of it was used to meet the withdrawal demands of savers, providing them with much needed cash.

Bank board officials argued that not the Federal Home Loan Bank Act but only its direct lending provision should be repealed. They made the case that the Federal Home Loan Bank System was designed to put home ownership in the United States on a secure footing over the long haul. But the home ownership picture had deteriorated considerably even since the legislation was passed in mid-1932. The home mortgage disaster had burgeoned at the rate of a thousand foreclosures per day, and there was no end in sight. The new rediscount banks, capitalized with the resources of small savers in local institutions, would be sunk at the outset in an effort to refinance all this. Bank board officials argued that the disaster should be met with a temporary, government-financed approach that did not threaten the savings of small savers or the stability of local home financing agencies.

Momentum for repeal of the Federal Home Loan Bank Act fizzled. Congress backed off, giving bank board personnel a chance to devise a plan that would comply with the new FDR administration's urgent emphasis on rescuing individual home owners from foreclosure. Their plan had two prongs, both of which kept home ownership clearly in view as the central purpose. In the emergency the federal government would provide assistance directly to individuals, as FDR would have it, on a scale massive enough to abort the disintegration of home ownership then under way. But the government would also act to expand the private institutional infrastructure, so that it could better facilitate home ownership over the long haul, as Hoover would have had it. Congress enacted this plan in June 1933 as the Home Owners' Loan Act.[33]

The Home Owners' Loan Act is important to this study primarily because of the second prong, the long-term institutional innovation it added to the savings and loan framework: federally chartered savings and loan associations. But a brief discussion of its approach to the emergency at hand is in order as well. The statute established a temporary entity, the Home Owners' Loan Corporation (HOLC), to enable people to keep their homes in the midst of collapsing private real estate and financial markets. The HOLC was entirely capitalized and owned by the federal government. Its board of directors was the Federal Home Loan Bank Board, effectively making it part of the bank board. It bought home mortgages that were in default or close to it from private lenders:

banks, savings banks, insurance companies, mortgage bankers, individuals, and building and loan associations. It paid for the defaulted mortgages not with cash but with federal government bonds and then extended a new, restructured mortgage to the home owner. A new HOLC mortgage was for up to 80 percent of the property's value, fully self-amortizing over fifteen years, and at 5 percent interest. In addition to the amount required to pay off the old loan, it included sums necessary to pay taxes and other liens on the property and to cover essential maintenance and repairs; this gave home owners a clean slate and a home they could keep if they could just make the modest monthly payments.

The Home Owners' Loan Corporation was popular and successful. It bought defaulted mortgages for three years, from mid-1933 through mid-1936. At its peak it owned one-sixth of the mortgages on owner-occupied homes in the United States. Its operations advanced the building and loans' innovation of the long-term, self-amortizing home mortgage as the key to home ownership for wage workers. The HOLC was liquidated in 1951, its remaining mortgages sold to savings and loans and other lenders. In the end it had cost taxpayers nothing; indeed, it returned a small profit to the Treasury.[34] With the central purpose of preserving home ownership, the HOLC functioned compatibly within the S&L framework. In addition to saving homes for individuals, it stabilized and preserved building and loans by buying their difficult mortgages.

The second kind of institution authorized by the Home Owners' Loan Act, the federally chartered savings and loan association, was meant as a permanent addition to the S&L regulatory framework, to fill a serious gap identified by the Federal Home Loan Bank Board as the Federal Home Loan Banks began to operate. In an effort to comply with the direct financing requirements in the statute and to guide the home loan banks in dealing with the throngs of people at their doorsteps seeking refinancing, the bank board had devised a procedure that might be expected to work within the system's design. Federal Home Loan Banks were directed to sort out the home owners from the ineligible loan seekers, identify the credit-worthy among them, and refer them to member lenders in the home owners' locale.[35]

But this procedure did not work. Member building and loans did not have resources sufficient to the need, and other kinds of financial institutions were pulling out of home mortgage lending altogether. Upon investigation the bank board learned further that one-third of the counties in the United States had no local home mortgage entity of any kind. But the building and loan system worked through institutions on the local level. The bank board therefore proposed that the federal government charter building and loans to articulate and strengthen the institutional infrastructure of home ownership. The Home Owners' Loan Act referred not to "building and loans," however, but to federal "savings and loan associations," triggering the shift to the term familiar to us today for the basic actor in the S&L framework.

The idea of federal chartering had been under discussion among building and loan movement leaders before the housing market collapse, entirely aside from emergency needs. Advocates wanted federal chartering because they expected it to contribute to standardizing best practice, reflecting the progressive concern for effectiveness and reliability. They believed that federal charters could be used to improve and reform appraisal practice and to strengthen supervision in states where it was weak. Advocates of federal charters for S&Ls hoped for widespread conversion from state to federal charter.[36]

Opponents of federal chartering in the U.S. Building and Loan League, the state leagues, and among the directors of the individual associations viewed it as a violation of the local character of their institutional approach.[37] Local control was a crucial value with them as a means to the end of home ownership. "Foreign" capital—money from financial institutions such as insurance companies, chartered in other states, and national banks, chartered by the federal government—had not met their needs. They had started building and loan associations because they did not want their town's savings to end up in New York through the relationships in the banking framework. They did not want home financing in their community to depend on decisions made in insurance company home offices. Nor did opponents of federal chartering want federal government control of their associations or competition from associations that were federally chartered.

Under the circumstances, however, the gaps in the fabric of the regulatory framework at the local level were glaring. Federal Home Loan Bank Board personnel and movement leaders who recommended federal chartering viewed it as a way for the central government to help fill in those gaps, without violating the local character of the framework's practice. As designed in the Home Owners' Loan Act, a federal savings and loan could only be organized by local people, but the bank board was authorized to provide a particularly crucial stimulus: capital. The government could buy shares in a federal S&L, matching local private investment dollar for dollar up to a limit of $100,000. The S&L

would begin buying out the government's stock after five years, eventually leaving the association as a private entity. Herbert Hoover would have approved.

Federal s&ls would be private but closely regulated in terms of structure and practice. The bank board would charter, regulate, and supervise them, in a relationship like that of the Office of the Comptroller of the Currency to national banks. Federal s&ls were required to join a Federal Home Loan Bank, as national banks had to join a Federal Reserve Bank. State-chartered Federal Home Loan Bank members could convert to federal charters if they chose.

While leaving much of the detail regarding structure and practice of the new associations to the bank board, Congress specified their purposes in section 5 of the Home Owners' Loan Act: "In order to provide local mutual thrift institutions in which people may invest their funds and in order to provide for the financing of homes, the Board is authorized, under such rules and regulations as it may prescribe, to provide for the organization, incorporation, examination, operation, and regulation of associations to be known as 'Federal Savings and Loan Associations,' and to issue charters therefor." The statute confined the bulk of a federal s&l's lending to within fifty miles of its main office and to homes appraised at twenty thousand dollars or less. Beyond that, constitution of the organizations was regulated in the charter, devised by the new Federal Savings and Loan Division of the bank board.

The first standard charter vastly reduced the types of shares s&ls could offer from the broad variety that had developed over a century among state-chartered institutions. Completely eliminated were the various stock ownership options permitted in some states: federal s&ls were all mutual associations. They could not be owned by a few people who were primarily interested in profit or in financing their own speculative activity in real estate. (In the 1980s discontinuing this restriction would contribute to the s&l debacle.) The first charter also reduced the type of share savings accounts which could be offered.

With regard to federal s&ls' assets, the standard charter modernized the form of loans. It encouraged s&ls to use direct reduction loans in place of the old-fashioned sinking fund approach that was still dominant practice in state associations. In the older approach borrower payments were not applied directly to the loan but, rather, accumulated in a savings account. When those payments and the dividends they had earned equaled the loan plus the interest on it, the loan was canceled. With the newer direct reduction loan, payments were booked directly against the loan, reducing it regularly. The standard charter also required a reserve equal to 5 percent of total assets.

Through this first standard charter and revisions that followed in 1936, 1949, and 1952, S&L practice and structure was, indeed, standardized and professionalized, as advocates had hoped. In this process a view of the S&L framework as an "industry" was deliberately fostered, to replace the earlier sense of the building and loan "movement."[38] The sense of ownership on the part of shareholders, already weak by the Depression, was largely obliterated with the gradual change in federal charters to the terminology of *savings accounts* and *interest*, rather than *shares* and *dividends*.

THE NATIONAL HOUSING ACT: DEPOSIT INSURANCE FOR S&LS

PHILOSOPHICAL TENSION IN THE NATIONAL HOUSING ACT

With the National Housing Act of 1934 Congress created the Federal Savings and Loan Insurance Corporation (FSLIC), the final major institution in the pre-debacle S&L regulatory framework.[39] Unlike the statutes creating the Federal Home Loan Banks and federal S&Ls, the National Housing Act was not centrally concerned with preserving and promoting home ownership but, rather, with stimulation of the macroeconomy. FSLIC was an add-on, the purpose of which, while inconsistent with the utilitarian premises underlying the rest of the statute that created it, was entirely consistent with the progressive public philosophy motivating the S&L framework within which it would function. Deposit insurance was a means for ensuring a flow of funds into S&Ls for home ownership, even as Congress created other mechanisms that could draw money away from them.

In the Banking Act the year before (1933) Congress had created the Federal Deposit Insurance Corporation to insure bank deposits. The approach was effective in triggering a flow of money back into banks, but much of it came at the expense of building and loan associations. Not only were savers putting new savings, which might otherwise have gone into building and loans, into insured banks, they were also withdrawing matured shares from building and loans and moving the funds to banks.[40] Commercial banks were not making home loans. For S&Ls to serve their purpose and channel money into home ownership, they had to get some of those savings accounts back.

Although many within S&L circles opposed deposit insurance, circumstances forced them to consider the option. Debate had begun in earnest while bank deposit insurance was in the making. Advocates argued that, if banks had deposit insurance, building and loans must have it, too, in order to attract funds with which to make home loans. In good progressive form advocates also viewed an insurer as a means for extending federal examination and supervision over state associations and for improving state regulation where it was weak, in pursuit, again, of standardizing best practice. Federal Home Loan Bank Board personnel and the leadership of the U.S. Savings and Loan League worked out a design for insurance which was regarded unenthusiastically in the industry as the way to do it, if it had to be done.[41]

The point at which it had to be done was hard upon them. For, as S&L people debated deposit insurance, the Roosevelt administration developed the bill that would become the National Housing Act of 1934. According to Marriner Eccles's account of the genesis of this proposal and to supportive testimony from a parade of Roosevelt administration luminaries during congressional hearings, its primary stimulus was concern over continuing very high levels of unemployment.[42] Administration officials knew that the building trades were the sector hardest hit by unemployment, accounting for a third of aggregate unemployment nationwide. They knew that in normal times most building activity was in housing. And they knew that a revival in construction would ripple out through the economy, jump-starting the still moribund durable goods industries and stimulating everything from lumber to transit to furniture and appliances.

But Roosevelt himself, in late 1933, was still trying to balance the budget. He shrank from suggestions of more direct spending on the Civil Works Administration to keep people employed. He cringed at the idea of ever more government credit as well, through the HOLC, to stimulate new housing construction. Eccles came to the rescue with the argument that, instead of spending public money to get things moving, the government should shake money out of the banks. Roosevelt liked his thinking. In Eccles's scenario bank loans would lead to construction, construction to employment, employment to monetary velocity, and velocity to reflation of the economy as a whole. And it was reflation as a whole which he was after; home ownership was not Eccles's aim.

As special assistant to the secretary of the Treasury at the time, Eccles got himself appointed chairman of a working group to draft a bill that would incorporate this logic. The first link in the chain was to shake money out of the banks. How would they do that? The banks were fat with money and happy to stay that way. They were maintaining very high degrees of liquidity, so, even as deposit insurance brought everybody's hoard out from under the mattress and into the bank, banks did not lend. The only asset banks were buying was government bonds, which accounted for as much as 40 percent of their portfolios. Why, complained Eccles, did the government have to sell bonds to get money from banks and then spend it to make anything happen? What would it take to get banks to make loans themselves and, in the order of things, expand the money supply, increase velocity, and make the world go?

Out came the Benthamite overseer in Eccles, whom we met in the previous chapter. Banks were not around to ensure full employment; they were not there to promote home ownership, nor were they concerned with Eccles's utilitarian end of reflation of the economy on the aggregate. Banks were there to make money, and in the current circumstances they kept it once they had it. That is to say, they were risk averse. To trigger the chain leading to reflation, banks' self-interest had to be piqued. Banks needed to see that they could make profits safely. Incentives must be created.

Crafted by Eccles, the bill that became the National Housing Act of 1934 was a complex set of institutional maneuvers in accord with the simple utilitarian logic that, to achieve the public good, the government manipulates self-interest. Its first title aimed at construction employment in the modernization of any buildings, not just homes. To entice lenders to make unsecured modernization loans for up to twenty thousand dollars, up to 20 percent of the loan was insured by the government. The second title of the National Housing Act was the "heart of [the] program," according to Eccles. It attempted to stimulate lending for new construction—of small houses by individuals or large-scale rental projects by corporations—through the incentive of mortgage insurance. The insurance was paid for privately by the borrower in the loan payments. But the program would be run by a new public agency, the Federal Housing Administration, and there was a guarantee of public funds if the insurance fund were inadequate. To induce borrowers to borrow, only a particular kind of mortgage, one that borrowers would find attractive, was eligible for insurance. This was a mortgage structured according to the principles that had been worked out in the building and loan movement, but it pushed those principles further: an FHA-insured mortgage would be self-amortizing, over a longer term, with a higher loan-to-value ratio, and a lower rate than the standard building and loan mortgages. Title III of the National Housing Act provided for government-chartered private corporations to buy the mortgages once the banks made them, yet another incentive to banks to make such mortgages. (As it turned out, the only such secondary mortgage entity for decades was not private but, rather, the government-owned Federal National Mortgage Association.)

Behind closed doors leaders of the Federal Home Loan Bank Board and the savings and loan industry were horrified by this plan. Bank deposit insurance was already draining savers' dollars out of s&Ls and into banks, where those dollars just sat. Now, to get the banks to lend that money, this legislation would take borrowers away from the building and loans in pursuit of the lower rates that mortgage insurance would make possible. Leaders in the s&L framework saw that they would lose control of resource allocation, functionally and geographically, to the banking framework—which had never served well the substantive public purpose for which the s&L framework existed.

Deposit insurance for s&Ls was the price demanded by the Federal Home Loan Bank Board chairman and industry leaders for grudging support of—or, more accurately, restraint in their opposition to—the National Housing Act of 1934. They hoped that deposit insurance would enable s&Ls to recapture savings at dividend levels that would permit their mortgage rates to be competitive with bank rates. Accordingly, Title IV, inconsistent with the utilitarian thrust of the rest of the National Housing Act in Eccles's view, created the Federal Savings and Loan Insurance Corporation (FSLIC) to protect the progressive s&L framework, with its substantive public purpose.

DESIGN OF THE FEDERAL SAVINGS AND LOAN INSURANCE CORPORATION

FSLIC was a government corporation intended to insure accounts in savings and loan associations, initially up to $5,000. Its $100,000,000 capitalization was drawn from the Home Owners' Loan Corporation, and thus FSLIC was wholly owned by the HOLC. It was regulated, supervised, and managed by a board of trustees composed of the members of the Federal Home Loan Bank Board.

Insurance was required for federal savings and loans but was optional for state-chartered associations. To the extent that state s&Ls sought insurance, the objective of standardization (ensuring effectiveness and reliability) was advanced as many of the same requirements that applied to federally chartered s&Ls were brought to bear on them, including periodic examination, a geographic limit on loans, development of a reserve fund, and prohibition of fixed dividends.

The insurance fund was built with premiums paid by participating s&Ls. Although the premium was later reduced, the initial statute required payment of one-fourth of 1 percent of each association's insured deposits plus creditor obligations annually, until the FSLIC achieved a reserve equal to 5 percent of its exposure. After that, additional premiums could be assessed if the reserve fell below 5 percent or if there were losses to cover. In the meantime FSLIC could issue bonds to cover losses.[43]

THE S&L FRAMEWORK: 1934–1970S

With the addition of the deposit insurer in 1934, the s&L regulatory framework was in place largely in the form it retained until the Depository Institutions Deregulation and Monetary Control Act of 1980. The regulatory framework included the Federal Savings and Loan Insurance Corporation, federally and state-chartered savings and loan associations, the Federal Home Loan Banks, the Federal Home Loan Bank Board, and the Home Owners' Loan Corporation.

There were marginal changes. As intended from its inception, the HOLC was phased out in the early 1950s, having functioned effectively as a dike to hold back the floodwaters of foreclosure while home ownership was stabilized. The independent Federal Home Loan Bank Board was drawn under line control in 1939 and headed by a commissioner instead of a board during the war as an economy measure, but its board was restored in 1947 and its independent status in 1955. Its regulatory and enforcement powers were increased in 1966. FSLIC bought its stock back from the government and, with no stockholders, remained essentially a division of the Federal Home Loan Bank Board.[44] The maximum insurable deposit was up only to fifteen thousand dollars by 1966, from five thousand dollars in 1934, and was at forty thousand dollars in 1979. Savings and loan asset powers continued to be constrained almost exclusively to mortgages for owner-occupied homes. Ownership of all federal s&Ls remained mutual, although some states permitted stock ownership.

The mechanisms of the s&L framework were deliberately and elegantly engineered to channel social resources into home ownership, and they served their purpose effectively for forty-five years. Savings and loan associations drew in the resources of small savers through savings accounts made attractive by interest rates marginally higher than their alternatives and by the guarantee of deposit insurance. The resources of large investors—including individuals, insurance companies, pension funds, banks, and government instrumentalities—were drawn in through the bonds issued by the bank board on behalf of the Federal Home Loan Banks. The bonds made it safe and convenient for big investors to finance home ownership without having to engage directly in mortgage lending and servicing.

Savings and loans associations turned those resources into home mortgages on standard terms that worked for moderate- and middle-income people. They financed the postwar housing boom and the suburban expansion. Home loan banks successfully channeled funds—member deposits as well as bond proceeds—within and among regions from institutions and areas with surplus resources to those in deficit. This mechanism was crucial to the growth of newly developing parts of the country, most notably California.

Progressivism is referred to as "pragmatic"—sometimes in criticism and sometimes in defense—because it justifies arrangements based on whether they "work," that is, achieve their respective purposes. The s&L regulatory framework protected and promoted home ownership effectively for a long time.

The construction of the s&L framework provides a striking example of progressive public philosophy in action. Progressives in government and in the industry thought home ownership was an intrinsically worthy public purpose—good for individuals, for community health, and for national stability—and they believed that they could engineer institutions specifically to realize it. And they did. Commitment to home ownership as a national public purpose, along with the conviction that institutions can be designed to serve particular purposes—in short, progressive public philosophy—explains why the framework was built, segregating a stream of capital dedicated to a special purpose, and why it continued for decades.

It does not explain why the arrangement failed so disastrously after 1978. A vast literature identifies a list of factors that contributed to the collapse of the s&L industry and argues over their priority; as noted at the outset, settling that debate is not the task here. In the concluding chapter, however, I will suggest that steps taken to shore up the s&L

framework as it began to crumble were rooted in a different public philosophy than the progressivism in terms of which it was built.

In the next chapter I turn to the third, and smallest, regulatory framework for depository intermediation in the United States: that of the credit union. Like the current banking and s&l frameworks, credit unionism has deep roots in Depression-era reforms, although, unlike the larger frameworks, much of its institutional elaboration occurred later, especially in the 1970s. Institutionally, credit unionism bears substantial parallels to the banking and s&l frameworks, with its own basic actor, deposit insurer, rediscount institutions, and regulatory agency. Philosophically, a different central value will be seen to animate its structures—the populist effort to guarantee individuals some level of control over their own resources.

7

Credit unionism has been, and remains, the smallest by far of the three regulatory frameworks for depository intermediation. In 1934, when credit unions were first recognized in federal law, they had total resources of about fifty million dollars.[1] That was less than 6 percent of total S&L resources and was barely registerable on any scale that would tally up banks' capital and assets.[2] In 1997 credit unions' $362 billion in assets accounted for 5.7 percent of the total assets of all depository institutions, while S&Ls had 16 percent, and banks had the lions' share, 78.3 percent.[3] Yet credit unionism's little market share represents continuous soundness and steady growth,[4] while the S&Ls' current share is the net result of disastrous decline and retrenchment from a peak of about a third in the late 1980s. Although banking has picked up most of what the S&Ls lost, bankers are alarmed at credit unions' gains.[5]

Bankers and their trade associations are strong proponents of the view that depository institutions are converging and should therefore be brought under uniform regulation. From this perspective credit unions increasingly do the things that banks do. While they continue making their traditional small unsecured loans, they also make loans on residential real estate and even small business loans. They offer credit cards, retirement accounts, and "share draft" accounts that function effectively like checking accounts. Why, then, should their insurance fund be structured differently than the bank insurance fund? Why should there be a separate credit union regulator cluttering up the government's organization chart? Why should credit unions have special tax advantages? Why should they be exempt from costly and bothersome Community Reinvestment Act obligations?

Why, indeed, is this whole separate regulatory framework here at all, if credit unions do much the same thing that banks do? It exists because credit unionism is rooted in a different public philosophy than either the dominant banking regulatory framework or the declining s&l framework. But, even if we concede that different ideas motivated development of separate institutions, does that matter anymore? Does it justify continued maintenance of an alternative regulatory framework? Bankers say it does not.

The institutions of depository intermediation are essentially decision pathways for creating and allocating money. Pathways constructed in response to different ideas, and thus decisions based on different premises, will yield different distributional outcomes. Unlike what has happened in the s&l framework, the ideas that distinguish credit unionism from banking appear to continue to mean something in the governance and operation of the institutions of the framework. Thus, even if credit unions deal in similar financial products, there is an alternative ideological and institutional locus of control and at least a possibility that money will be allocated differently. The "convergence" observed by adherents to the dominant public philosophy may be apparent only from their point of view. And it may depend not upon "natural forces" or "economic laws" but upon explicit legislative and regulatory choices.

POPULIST PUBLIC PHILOSOPHY

Credit unionism is an institutional expression of populism. I use the term *populism* to label a coherent public philosophy—a set of propositions which provides a basis for interpreting the social world and for taking positions regarding what that world should look like and what the government's role should be. Thus, I take populism as rational, providing bases for criticism and constructive action, in the same sense as other public philosophies—classic liberalism, neoliberalism, progressivism, and utilitarianism—linked in this study to institutional development.

It is necessary to underscore the concept of a public philosophy in connection with the label *populism* because other meanings have been assigned to the term, meanings that I do not intend to evoke. Prominent journalists, scholars, business leaders, and public policy makers—during and after the Progressive Era—were fond of calling populist thinkers irrational and dismissing their institutional critique and their positive program.[6] Some called historical populists "racist," ignoring contemporary progressivism's own biases and apparently unaware of the efforts toward inclusive thought and action of some populist leaders.[7] Building on the confusion so generated, current-day scholars and journalists are wont to label as *populist* demagogic politicians who play to the fear and darker prejudices of ordinary people,[8] or they use *populism* to refer to irrationality and prejudice among those people.

The case that the historical populists developed a systematic public philosophy and institutional program and struggled toward inclusiveness in defiance of the pervasive ideological and institutional racism of the political economy has been made persuasively.[9] Nevertheless, with all the baggage attached to the term, perhaps I would make my own intended meaning clearer by finding a different label for the public philosophy institutionalized in credit unionism. How much to fight over a word or a symbol is a thorny question in any case. Often of tactical or strategic significance in politics, such a struggle may degenerate into pedantry in intellectual history. Moreover, weighing heavily in the balance on the side of surrendering the term *populism* to the haze is that I do not intend to argue that historical populists, in the "populist moment," included credit unions per se in their institutional program. Rather, what I will show is that credit unionism is a later expression of the same ideas that had guided the historical populists. Early credit union leaders spoke not of populism but of a crusade for "economic democracy." Thus, to avoid the negative connotations of *populism*, I could call the public philosophy at issue *economic democracy*.

Nevertheless, I have labeled the ideas that undergird the credit union framework *populist* for two reasons. First, I want to retrieve the full critical and constructive leverage of this alternative public philosophy. This requires seeing the circumstances that gave rise to its insights and the institutional approaches it advocated. Retrieval of the paradigm in its moment of emergence brings back into focus important questions, and answers, which have fallen off the radar screen of public debate. The second reason I choose the label is to dispel the conclusion of populism's defenders that economic democracy simply lost in the struggle over the shape of the political economy. The scholars who rescued the integrity of the populist worldview, who defended its rationality, its realism, and its usefulness in working toward individual thriving and social generosity, conclude sadly that it had no lasting institutional influence.[10] But institutional offspring of the emphasis on economic democracy at the center of populist thought, although minor and surely threatened, are among us in the political economy. We will only see them if we recall the public philosophy that gives them meaning. And we can only effectively defend them in its terms.

POST–CIVIL WAR AGRARIAN EXPERIENCE

The people among whom the populist variant of liberal public philosophy developed in the United States in the decades after the Civil War believed that freedom rested fundamentally on access to what they needed to be economically productive. But, as the economy took on the organizational shape it did in those decades, farmers in the West and South came to see their freedom as usurped. The rise of the corporation, or trust, was the central reality on their screen. Resources without which they could not work, as well as routes to market for their products, were privatized, becoming inaccessible to them on terms they could meet. Corporate organizations enclosed the commons and foreclosed the market.

Railroads first were recognized as usurpers of economic freedom. Farmers had expected the railroads to be public highways, connecting them to the market. Thus, they subsidized railroad construction generously through the bonded indebtedness and taxation authorized in their state legislatures and municipalities. But railroads did not work like public highways: the cost of shipping commodities might equal more than half the price a farmer could get for them. Moreover, also in the spirit of providing a public improvement, the federal government had subsidized railroad development with great grants of public lands. Land was the absolutely fundamental resource required for economic productivity in the agricultural United States. As the availability of free and low-cost land came to an end, the railroads' control over vast tracts was increasingly viewed as an illegitimate usurpation of the commons. Further, the egregious abuses by railroads—"transit" pricing, stock watering, fraud, control of state legislatures—as well as pedestrian mismanagement and competitive fumbling are well recorded.[11] Here let it be enough to say that farmers were not irrational to conclude that they had been cheated.

Farmers found themselves powerless in individual dealings with corporations of other sorts as well. Large grain elevator companies were critical. It was convenient for railroads to load from big shippers with elevator facilities; they refused to stop and load from individual farmers and even from the flat warehouses of smaller local dealers. Farmers were forced to sell to the elevator company in their area at the price offered. They could not themselves sell on the major markets, where big shippers got much better prices than they gave the farmers. Adding insult to injury, it was common enough that grain dealers graded farmers' product inaccurately, further lowering the price. There was no recourse. Implement dealers were also critical, for there was no farming without plows and wagons. Combined in trusts, they set the price, and, selling on installment, they set the interest rate. Farmers had no choice but to pay.[12]

Gradually, however, in the face of long experience, populist thinking closed in on banks as the most problematic of all the corporations. Banks were like other corporations in controlling access to crucial resources—money and credit—needed to participate in the economy, but they were more fundamental. Their practices reinforced market control by railroad and industrial corporations because those entities could get credit from banks, while farmers could not.[13]

The worst of it was in the South, which had been relegated to the financial Stone Age by the Civil War. Virtually all state banking had collapsed with the Confederacy. The new national banks could only be established with gold and bonds of the Washington government, and there was precious little of such capital in the postwar South.

With no place for southern farmers to turn for money to produce a crop, the crop lien system emerged as the dominant economic and social reality in their lives. In this system the farmer gave a lien on his cotton crop to a "furnishing merchant," or "advancing man," who provided supplies on credit until that crop came in. Because no one else would deal with a farmer who had no cash and whose crop was mortgaged, the farmer was obliged to seek everything he needed from his furnishing merchant—production needs such as seed, fertilizer, and implements as well as household goods, including cloth, lamp oil, bacon, and flour. When he harvested his cotton, the farmer sold it to the furnishing man, and his account was settled up. There were multiple opportunities for unfairness. When a farmer bought, the furnishing merchant sold at an inflated price of his choosing and then charged interest, also at a rate set by him. When the farmer sold, the furnishing merchant again controlled the price, grading the cotton himself. When the farmer settled up, it was on the basis of bookkeeping controlled by the furnishing man. The farmer generally remained in the red, going home from the settling each year with the next year's crop already mortgaged. Eventually, much of the land was deeded over to the furnishing man by farmers, who never seemed to make enough on their cotton to pay out. Southern land ownership reconcentrated as former freeholding farmers became sharecroppers, "plows" on the Man's land. Because there was no place to get money to get off this merry-go-round, black and white people from Virginia to Texas sank further into a new twentieth-century peonage. The banking system did not work for southern farmers; indeed, it did not exist for them.[14]

Nor was there any bank financing for farmers in the West—the Dakotas and Minnesota, Nebraska, Kansas, Iowa, and Oklahoma. There it was the land and the equipment that was mortgaged to get money for next year's crop or to make payments on the mortgages for last year's crop. Land and chattel mortgages were held not by banks but by loan companies, capitalized with money from outside the region, at short terms and high rates. Both became impossible to service as the money supply was squeezed and commodity prices dropped; foreclosure on land and equipment was common in the cyclical crashes of the 1870s, 1880s, and 1890s.[15]

As crushing as the nonexistence of reasonable credit for producing a crop was, post–Civil War money and banking policy was even more devastating as farmers turned to sell their product. In a severely deflationary policy the government, through the national bank system, pressed the country back onto the gold standard. Despite explosive growth in the real economy and the population, greenbacks were held constant, and bank note circulation contracted. Commodity prices therefore declined continuously from 1870 through 1897 throughout the South and the West.[16] Farmers received ever lower prices for their commodities, because money was scarce, and paid ever more for their production resources, as a function of the rates they paid for credit, because money was scarce.

FARMERS' ACTIONS

In an effort to interpret an experience that must have felt surreal and to devise solutions to their problems, farmers were organizing themselves by the early 1870s. The Grange, the Patrons of Husbandry, and the Wheel helped prepare the ground, but the Farmers Alliance was crucial in congealing a comprehensive populist public philosophy and spreading it.[17] Alliances were organized at subcounty and county levels which associated on a statewide basis and joined together, in turn, under the broad umbrellas of a Northern Alliance and a Southern Alliance. With its stronger central apparatus the Southern Alliance eventually overshadowed the Northern. Although formal merger was not declared, programmatic unity was achieved as the alliance became overtly political nationally by 1892; the Knights of Labor and other reform organizations joined with the Farmers Alliance to form the People's Party, also called the Populists.

Self-education was a central activity of the local alliances. Each chapter had its "lecturer," who was responsible for suggesting and developing topics for discussion. The alliances went beyond earlier farm organizations' instruction in good agricultural practice to probe the mechanisms of the political economy. Assuming that ordinary people could understand these matters, farmers studied economic theory, monetary policy, finance, and business practice. They debated, developed positions, learned to speak and to argue; leaders emerged. The Southern Alliance was evangelistic; it dispatched its leaders as organizer/lecturers to spread its developing analysis. Also critical in developing and disseminating populist public philosophy was the National Reform Press Association, a thousand editors and their reform newspapers strong.

Beyond education doing business was a central action focus for the alliance. Although its members regarded corporate business as unjust, illiberal, and exploitive, the Farmers Alliance was not opposed to business in itself or to the benefits of organized action. Local and state alliances began by designating a business agent, who bundled member orders for such production needs as wagons and plows and negotiated on behalf of all to secure terms better than an individual farmer could get. The experience of business agents in dealing with the dominant structures of the economy fed back into the developing populist critique.

Alliance chapters went on to develop their own cooperative business organizations for buying inputs and selling their product. Cooperative stores carried production and household needs, selling at the minimum mark-up required to operate the business. In the South the alliance organized cooperative cotton yards where cotton was gathered and graded in sufficient quantity to deal directly with international buyers, thereby bypassing the advancing man. Western chapters organized cooperative grain storage facilities so they could grade, store, and sell their own grain or hold it off the market awaiting optimal pricing.

Yet, where the technological realities of the economic infrastructure required massive capital investment and extensive human organization, as with the railroads and public utilities, the historical populists called for public ownership. Likewise, the money and banking system must be directly controlled by the government. Populists saw the privatized financial system as the fundamental flaw in the structure of the economy. In establishing the national bank system, they argued, the federal government had abrogated the people's sovereign power to issue money. National banks were private corporations, making their decisions, like industrial corporations, based on the profit motive. They did not—indeed, there was no element in their design to suggest that they would—attempt to make their decisions based on the needs of ordinary people and of the economy to function smoothly. Populists called for the end of the national bank system and its replacement with government-issued notes, "in sufficient volume to do the business of the country on a cash system; regulating the amount needed, on a per capita basis as the business interests of the country expand."[18]

How to pursue these political demands was problematic in the post–Civil War party system, with corporate business interests leading both major political parties. Initially, the Famers Alliance, while viewing itself as nonpolitical, urged its members to support only candidates—of either party—who "are thoroughly identified with our principles and who will insist on such legislation as shall make them effective."[19] By the late 1880s significant numbers of people with populist views were elected to state legislatures, executive offices, and Congress. As the alliance became more overtly political, it pursued several paths: joint slates with the dominant party in some areas; local third parties; or, in the South, capture of the Democratic apparatus at some times in some places. In 1891–92 the alliance opted for a national third party, the People's Party, and was joined by the Knights of Labor and other reform groups. The People's Party was explicitly ideological, explicating much of the populist critique and institutional program in its first platform, the Omaha Platform, of July 1892.

POPULIST IDEAS

As farmers thus studied, talked, and acted from the Civil War through the turn of the century; as alliance business agents and lecturer/organizers traveled, observed, and learned; as political action was taken, systematic populist public philosophy developed as an alternative to the dominant neoliberal public philosophy of the Gilded Age. We should note at the outset that, although farmers' organizations provided the venue for this development, populism did not understand itself narrowly as an agrarian perspective. Populist thinkers viewed theirs as a system that made sense of the world from the viewpoint of the "plain people," the majority of whom were farmers at that time. In populist speaking and writing, the *producing classes,* or *producers,* included wage workers in factories as well as farmers. *Industry* included agriculture.

The People's Party included the Knights of Labor as well as the Farmers' Alliance. Its platform proclaimed that "the interests of urban and rural labor are the same, their enemies are identical."[20] As public philosophy, populism can be abstracted in terms of our three themes—the unit of analysis, nature and construction, and the appropriate scope of the public and private realms—to provide a framework for the evaluation and design of public policy, in its historical moment and in ours.

Like all liberal public philosophy, populism begins with an emphasis on freedom for human individuals. Liberalism's end is that each of us achieves our potential. And freedom is a means to that end. In liberal philosophy, historically, freedom to create oneself—or to find oneself, if you prefer—has carried a very strong economic emphasis. From John Locke's claim of a natural right to the resources one could use productively and to ownership of what one makes with those resources to Adam Smith's insistence on unrestricted access to the market to Thomas Jefferson's visceral rejection of the economic dependence of any person on other persons, there is an assumption that, if we have the freedom to claim what we need to be economically productive, we will be able to work out the rest of what we require to thrive. Populism yanks liberalism's sometimes wandering spotlight back onto the fundamental character of economic freedom, understood as the ability of ordinary people to control their own economic circumstances.

Yet powerful economic entities—corporations, or trusts, in the moment of populism's emergence—may preempt access to the grounds of productivity and seize control of the terms of distribution of the product. Rejecting corporate organization, however, does not entail nostalgic insistence on returning to a simpler economy composed of atomic individuals. Populism embraces the benefits of organization but proposes that business organizations be constituted differently. The cooperative is the populist institutional solution. A co-op is a business entity in which participants pool their own resources for the purpose of providing themselves with goods and services they choose. This contrasts with the purpose of a corporation, which populists viewed as a return to capital at the expense of working producers and consumers, not for their benefit. A cooperative has no profit-seeking capital but only member contributions necessary to undertake the activity at hand, and it distributes gains among the members. Its governance is participatory, both to direct the co-op and to provide education and experience to members, empowering individual members. Cooperative business organization enables participants to gain a measure of control over the resources they contribute and the resources the co-op generates.

To keep liberalism's most central emphasis on individual human development and the freedom it requires in focus, in the face of historical social and technological choices, populism abandoned the classic liberal insistence on a sharp division between the public and private spheres, both empirically and normatively. Empirically, concentration of wealth in the economy spills over into the public sphere, jeopardizing political democracy. Thus, normatively, the constitution of economic relationships is a public concern. And, because economic issues are fundamental to individual thriving, the structure of the economy should be the central concern of public policy. Government does and should define permissible terms of economic organization. Government should own basic economic infrastructure. And, most fundamentally, government does and should control the money system because it underlies all other economic relationships.

Government that defines the terms of economic association permissible in the private realm, that owns and operates huge organizations providing crucial economic infrastructure, that creates and adjusts the money supply, the most fundamental economic relationship of all, is not the limited government of Locke or of Jefferson and Jackson. In the words of the preamble to the historic Populist Party's first platform, populists believed "that the powers of government—in other words, of the people—should be expanded . . . as rapidly and as far as the good sense of an intelligent people and the teachings of experience shall justify, to the end that oppression, injustice, and poverty shall eventually cease in the land."[21] Yet, even as populists call for a broader role for the government in the economic sphere, they know that government can become the tool of particular interests. Thus, government must be kept under the control of ordinary people. Historical populists called for the secret ballot; initiative and referendum; direct election of senators, president, and vice president; a limit of one term for the president; women's right to vote; and civil service reform to put an expanded federal government beyond the control of any political party.

The neoliberal public philosophy of the post–Civil War decades justified corporate concentration of economic power as a "natural" dynamic, analogous to (the contemporary understanding of) biological evolution, which led to the survival of the fittest. Likewise, as we saw in chapter five, monetary arrangements featuring bank-issued currency backed by gold rested primarily on the claim that gold was nature's money. Populism was shrill in its rejection of nature's sanction for arrangements that denied economic freedom to ordinary people. In insisting that controlling the terms of economic association and the design of money in particular are responsibilities of government, populism takes the position that the economy is a construct of public policy. Populism recognizes no natural law specifying that the way things are is the way they must be. The world can be different. Populism thinks it should be different.

PUBLIC PHILOSOPHY AND THE ORIGINS OF U.S. CREDIT UNIONISM

While there have been banks in the United States since the Revolution and savings and loan associations since the days when Andrew Jackson was fashioning nails for the coffin of the second Bank of the United States, credit unions appeared in the political economy only in the twentieth century. They arose as an institutional device through which ordinary working Americans could gain control of their own resources to meet their own saving and borrowing needs, which had gone unmet by the older depository intermediaries.

The average run of people, whether on farms or in the city—hourly, salaried, or self-employed—were of modest means. They had tiny sums to save and borrowed small amounts. Several themes recur among their reasons for seeking small loans. Before health insurance illness often caused financial crisis; a loan covered physician or hospital services or else rent and groceries when it was a family's primary wage earner who could not work. Temporary unemployment for other reasons might also lead to borrowing for necessities. A small loan might be sought to set up a household or for one large durable household item. Sometimes a person borrowed to launch a small business—for a beautician's chair, a typewriter, or other tools of a trade. People sought small loans to pay for training and education. Once credit unions were available, people often borrowed to refinance loans originally taken for reasons such as these.[22]

Banks did not serve this sort of need. Even S&Ls, which accepted small savings, did not make small loans. To the extent that small loans could be found, the field was held by pawnbrokers and by individuals and loan companies that took security in the form of chattel mortgages or a claim on wages or salary. Serious abuse was widespread as, in the face of state usury limits, the small loan business was conducted at the edge of the law or beyond it. Known collectively as "loan sharks," providers of small credit charged 6 to 40 percent per month and more for money, plus various fees, and were quick to garnishee wages and foreclose mortgages.[23] The tragic anecdotes, repeated by contemporary reformers, are endless: individuals who paid 1,000 percent interest and were then sued for principle, who lost their jobs when employers found out about entanglement with a loan shark, or who committed suicide after trying to cope with the debt of an unreliable friend for whom one had cosigned.

THE PROGRESSIVE RESPONSE TO THE SMALL LOAN EVIL

When progressive reformers in the early twentieth century looked at these circumstances, what they saw was the "small loan evil." Some among them—most prominently, New York's Russell Sage Foundation—tackled that evil in their characteristic social scientific way. They studied the problem, empirically assessing its dynamics and scope, and sought to identify or fashion appropriate institutional solutions. At the 1911 meeting of the Academy of Political Science Arthur Ham, director of Russell Sage's Division of Remedial Loans, read a paper sketching their findings and advocating a characteristically progressive solution. We should, he insisted, bring the small loan business out of the shadows with appropriate regulation. To attract legitimate capital legislators should realize that state usury levels of 6 and 7 percent must be set aside in favor of an interest rate that would allow a reasonable return and cover the costs involved. The state should license or incorporate lenders in this area and supervise and inspect them.[24] Indeed, by the time Ham spoke, Russell Sage had already identified fourteen "remedial" loan companies—for-profit companies established for "philanthropic" purposes, meaning that they intended not to gouge people but to provide small loans at reasonable rates. The foundation administered a federation of these companies and promoted the idea for replication. Ultimately, Russell Sage developed a model statute for state regulation of small loan companies, suggesting an interest rate limit of 3.5 percent per month, or 42 percent annually. State statutes based on Russell Sage's model had been widely adopted by the early 1930s.[25]

Another institutional remedy for the small loan evil, noted briefly by Ham in his remarks at the American Academy of Political Science in 1911, was the credit union. Leaders and historians of the U.S. credit union movement trace the ancestry of its basic actor to the buying cooperative set up by the weavers of Rochdale, England, in 1844. But, most directly, they claim the cooperative credit societies that developed in mid-nineteenth-century Germany as forebears. Because commercial banks served only large landholders and producers, Hermann Schulze-Delitzsch (1808–83)—a reform-minded lawyer, judge, and legislator—organized craftsmen and small shopkeepers into "people's banks." While Schulze-Delitzsch's organizations spread in the towns, a retired civil administrator named Wilhelm Raiffeisen (1818–83), moved by suffering among farmers in the countryside, was organizing similar, but separate, rural credit cooperatives. The fundamental constitutive features of these organizations remain clearly recognizable in American credit unions. All members were owners, in that they bought small shares to generate a fund from which they made loans to one another. Governance was democratic, each member having one vote in the general meeting, regardless of the number of shares owned. Subordinate committees handled everyday management, supervision and inspection, and lending decisions. Loans were made on the basis of character. The forms and practices of German cooperative credit directly influenced the development of cooperative credit institutions throughout Europe.

The beginning of viable cooperative credit organizations in the United States hinged significantly on the work of the Canadian Alphonse Desjardins. Appalled by the abuse of ordinary Canadian people by loan sharks, whose practice was much the same as that of their counterparts in the United States, Desjardins studied European institutions that provided banking services for small borrowers. On the basis of European models but rejecting the need for separate urban and rural forms, Desjardins organized the first Canadian credit union in 1900.

In the United States Desjardins helped to draft the 1909 Massachusetts statute enabling the state to charter credit unions. This first state credit union law originated with Massachusetts' progressive bank commissioner, Pierre Jay. Jay had stumbled across an account of European people's banks, sought out Desjardins in Canada to learn more about the institution, and concluded that this would be a good means with which to combat the small loan evil. Progressive businessmen and organizations in the state assisted in lobbying for the statute and promoted the organization of credit unions. The first U.S. credit union, however, was organized shortly before Massachusetts passed its law. With assistance from Desjardins, St. Mary's Cooperative Credit Association in Manchester, New Hampshire, had begun its work in 1908 by authority of a special act of the state legislature and continues to operate today.[26]

Among the original progressive proponents of credit unions was Boston businessman and philanthropist Edward A. Filene. Being active in a long list of domestic and international social and economic reform efforts, Filene was friendly with and advised presidents from Woodrow Wilson to FDR. While little involved personally in organizing credit unions, Filene brought his considerable prestige to bear in advocating the institution, and, more important, he provided most of the funding necessary to promote credit unionism from 1915 through 1935. His contributions—individual and through the Twentieth Century Fund, which he endowed—totaled over a million dollars.[27]

Progressive reformers had thus discovered the credit union in the context of their study of the small loan evil. Through their progressive lenses they saw an institution particularly suited to the purpose of providing small loans for working people, delivering them from the hands of unscrupulous loan sharks. While I am about to urge that it is populist thinking that best explains the origins of U.S. credit unionism and that a populist analytic scheme better enables us both to "see" credit unions and to justify their continued vigorous presence in the political economy, it is nevertheless true that progressives in business and government helped get them started.[28] It is also true that progressive terms are heard in the policy debate around credit unions today.

POPULISM AND THE TAKE-OFF OF CREDIT UNIONS

There was another way to view credit unions at the beginning of the twentieth century, as at the beginning of the twenty-first. Roy F. Bergengren, the organizer who took credit unionism out of the conference rooms of the Chamber of Commerce in Boston and the Russell Sage Foundation in New York and built a national grassroots movement, saw them in this other way—as did grassroots leadership in the movement and its crucial advocates in Congress.

Bergengren, a young lawyer who was not making a very good living given his proclivity for taking the cases of the poor, came on the scene in 1920, when, after a decade of lackluster results from the efforts of progressive groups to organize credit unions, the strong-willed philanthropist Filene intervened. Filene charged one of his personal employees to prepare a study identifying problems and then personally hired

Bergengren to try again to light a fire under credit unionism.[29] Bergengren viewed credit unions within the context of his public philosophy, which he referred to as "economic democracy" and which, as we look at his work and his words in the next pages, we will recognize as populism.

In Bergengren's view the central purpose of credit unions had to do not with the object of their lending, small loans, but with the locus of control over the allocation of resources.

> A credit union is a cooperative credit society in the business of supplying its members with cooperative credit. It accomplishes this end by first furnishing its members with the machinery which enables them to accumulate savings in a common pool. These savings the members of the specific group manage through officers chosen by and from their number. The money is invested in loans to members of the group exclusively, and only for provident or productive purposes, and at reasonable rates of interest. All of the net earnings . . . are divided among the members of the society in question as dividends on their savings in the common pool. *There is no exterior capital and no one outside the specific group in question may have anything to do with the credit union in question directly or indirectly.* In all matters each member has a single vote, whatever his share holding.[30]

In laying out this skeletal description, Bergengren has covered all the categories—ownership, capital, governance, and assets—which I have been using to analyze financial intermediaries throughout this study. I will take up this analysis in more detail, but here it is useful to note what Bergengren underscored: no one else "may have anything to do with the credit union." The "machinery" has been designed to put members in control of resources to meet their own needs. For the same reason that a cooperative was populism's choice for the constitution of organized actors in the political economy, it is Bergengren's choice for the constitution of a depository intermediary.

The credit union for Bergengren was thus not a social service agency intended to provide small loans to poor dependent people. It was machinery that empowered "the average worker . . . and the small farmer" to help themselves by helping one another.[31] With the populists Bergengren insisted repeatedly throughout his career that "average" people are entirely capable of understanding and managing financial affairs.[32] To be sure, people must learn these skills—and the credit union as cooperatively constituted was their tool for that: members learned to manage their own financial resources and leaders emerged who learned to manage the financial institutions of the credit union movement.

Populist thought attended centrally to the locus and effects of control not only of individual business organizations but also of the economy as a whole. With the populists Bergengren placed the structure of the economy at the center of public concern:

> Political democracy can be most securely buttressed by economic democracy. . . . Logically, it should come to pass eventually that the masses of the people . . . will control in credit unions an appreciable segment of the national wealth. When they do, the great danger to our democracy that is contained in the trend to the control of a greater and ever greater proportion of the national wealth in an ever-decreasing number of people will be forever eliminated. There will result from this new accumulation of democratically controlled wealth safeguards of the American economic system that will be the soundest guarantee of . . . political democracy.
>
> We have always, in America, accepted the ideals of political democracy. *Economic democracy is attained by applying the principles of political democracy to the affairs of the market place.* The two— political and economic democracy—are . . . essential to each other. . . . Our Crusade seeks only to protect our political institutions, in all of their freedom, by economic institutions which will be equally free.[33]

Bergengren thus echoed populists' fundamental criticism when he argued that "great danger" lay in the "trend to the control of a greater and ever greater proportion of the national wealth in an ever-decreasing number of people." Such inequality threatened political democracy itself. The corrective was economic democracy, which would be "attained by applying the principles of political democracy to the affairs of the market place," that is, by cooperatively constituted business organizations, instead of profit-seeking corporations. Bergengren made bank control fundamentally problematic in the claim that the "soundest guarantee of political democracy" will be the democratic control of "an appreciable segment of national wealth" by the people themselves in credit unions, as opposed to banks.

Bergengren pressed forward the populist logic that economic institutions are not natural phenomena but artificial constructs, calling on legislatures to provide the basis in law and policy for cooperative business organization, as it had for corporations. In 1921 he and Filene established the Credit Union National Extension Bureau (CUNEB). CUNEB consisted essentially of Bergengren's labor and Filene's money; its mission was to spread credit unionism across the United States. On his first day Bergengren made a list of five objectives for the organization, which remained under the glass of his desktop until 1935. "Get the laws" headed the list. "The first big job of the Bureau [was] to build the basis in law on which the cooperative credit structure should be reared."[34] In pursuing this objective, Bergengren crisscrossed the country by rail from 1921 through 1934, securing passage, with local people, of twenty-eight state credit union laws and revision of several others.[35] In 1934 he organized the successful effort to secure a federal enabling statute.[36]

Once there was an enabling law in a state, Bergengren tackled the second and third objectives on that desktop list. Objective two was to organize a sample of viable credit unions, and number three was to continue CUNEB's assistance until there were enough credit unions to form a self-supporting state league. Bergengren's approach echoed the populist institution of the traveling lecturer/organizer. As he personally organized the first few credit unions in a state, Bergengren identified grassroots leaders and recruited them to fan out and organize more credit unions.[37]

To democratize governance of the credit union movement, and thus put CUNEB out of business, was Bergengren's aim from CUNEB's first day. Objectives four and five on that desktop list were to organize self-supporting, self-governing state credit union leagues and then a national association of those leagues. The state and national leagues would assume the tasks of promoting the movement, deciding how to develop it, and handling attendant financial responsibilities. Turning over the reins to the movement itself became increasingly urgent to Bergengren as philosophical differences with Filene, who controlled the purse at CUNEB, manifested repeatedly. One such dispute, highlighting an important philosophical difference between progressive and populist approaches, surfaced as Bergengren moved to organize the national association. Filene opposed starting a credit union association without the help of experts in "organizing large financial institutions." Bergengren was adamant that credit unionists did not need experts, especially bankers, to guide the terms of their national association: the people in the movement were quite capable of designing their governing association. Bergengren won. He organized a meeting of credit union leaders from throughout the United States at a YMCA camp in Colorado in 1934. Without banker assistance they established a constitution for the Credit Union National Association (CUNA). The Filene-financed, Bergengren-staffed CUNEB wound down over a couple of years as CUNA assumed leadership of the credit union movement.[38]

The governance structure that was established for governing credit unionism as a movement continues today. Credit unions in a particular state participate in choosing directors for the state league, and they finance its activities; state leagues, in turn, participate in choosing directors for the national association. It is through this structure that positions are developed on matters involving government and on internal matters.

Beyond a forum for position development state leagues and CUNA provide services to credit unions. They interface with legislative, executive, and judicial processes at the state and national levels. They educate credit unions' volunteer boards and committees in technical aspects of running financial institutions and in credit union philosophy. They provide business development assistance that individual credit unions could not afford. And they have developed an array of support organizations that permit individual credit unions to do vastly more than they could alone. In the movement's view of itself the idea that people help themselves by helping one another extends beyond the individual credit union. Credit unions should help one another too, and state leagues and CUNA are crucial in institutionalizing this idea.[39]

Motivated by his public philosophy, Bergengren was the crucial individual behind the effective take-off of U.S. credit unionism after 1921. But did the grassroots leadership he recruited share his worldview, with its emphasis on ordinary people gaining control of their own resources to help themselves? Indirect evidence of grassroots leaders' views can be found by noting whose side they took when ideological differences between Bergengren and Filene flared into the open in a dispute over the constitution of credit unions. In 1933 Filene was actively attempting to drum up support in Washington for channeling government money to credit unions, to be pumped out in loans for consumer spending. Bergengren opposed government capital for credit unions on the grounds that it violated cooperative principles: it was contrary to the principle of self-help, and accepting government money could be expected to weaken self-governance. Sidestepping his hired man, Filene took his case directly to the grassroots credit union leadership in a cross-country tour. His views were roundly rejected in state after state, while Bergengren received widespread support.[40]

Bergengren viewed his first objective to "get the laws" as substantially fulfilled in June 1934, when Congress passed the Federal Credit Union Act in the closing hours of the second session of the Seventy-third Congress. That busy Depression-era Congress was awash in New Deal legislation, but the Federal Credit Union law was not an administration measure.[41] It originated with Roy Bergengren, the credit union organizer from the field. And, although Bergengren justifiably claimed credit,[42] there would have been no statute at that time without the initiative, hands-on commitment, and persistence of an influential populist advocate in the Senate. A young populist supporter in the House was less crucial but no less ideologically committed.

Over Filene's opposition Bergengren had decided to move in 1933 for a federal credit union law. He viewed the special session that year as an auspicious moment politically: FDR had enforced a national "bank holiday," and banks looked very bad. Little credit unions, by contrast, growing throughout the Depression and with no involuntary liquidations to date, looked good. Moreover, Bergengren anticipated establishment of the credit union national association soon and wanted to hand over the reins with authority to organize credit unions anywhere in the country. Thirty-eight states had credit union laws, but a handful of those had been so influenced by small loan companies as to render them difficult to use, and in some states regulators were hostile. A federal law would provide an alternative and, of course, could be used in the states with no credit union law at all.

Bergengren turned to Senator Morris Sheppard, who personally helped him draft the bill, introduced it in the Senate, testified in its behalf before the Committee on Banking and Currency (of which he was not a member), prodded the committee until it reported favorably, and was the legislation's chief spokesman on the Senate floor. After the bill stalled in the House, passing that chamber only hours before Congress would adjourn, Sheppard seized the ball again. With no time for a conference, he walked onto the Senate floor, conferred with fellow Texan Vice President Garner, who was presiding, and then asked the Senate for and received unanimous consent of the amended bill, unread. Bergengren dubbed Sheppard "father of credit union federal legislation."[43]

Bergengren had identified Sheppard because he knew that the senator had an interest in cooperative credit; he does not appear to have realized, however, that he was tapping into a comprehensive support-ive public philosophy.[44] Sheppard represented Texas, a cauldron of his-torical populism. During Sheppard's childhood and adolescence the Texas Farmers Alliance had organized substantial cooperatives for buy-ing and selling and was influential in founding and building the People's Party. Sheppard's father was a member of the House of Representatives who had supported William Jennings Bryan. Upon his father's death a very young Morris Sheppard won his seat in the House in 1902. He revealed his philosophical colors to the chamber when he blasted the trusts in his maiden speech, interpreting the growth of huge corpora-tions as a threat to the people, to freedom, and to justice. In 1908 Sheppard hit the campaign trail hard for Bryan for president, his region generating more funds than any other. Moving on to the Senate in 1913, Sheppard kept his focus on the grinding unresolved difficulties of the farmers he represented. In 1915, as an alternative to the progressive measure that became the Federal Farm Loan System, Sheppard had of-fered a bill for agricultural credit cooperatives modeled on the German institutions started by Raiffeisen; his scheme would have provided more control over their credit institutions to farmers themselves and less to the federal bureaucracy.[45]

For help in the House Sheppard turned to fellow Texan, Democratic Representative Wright Patman. The younger man was not on the House Banking Committee, where the credit union bill stalled while Chair Henry Steagall awaited FDR's endorsement (which came in the elev-enth hour), but he wrote to all Democratic members of the committee, urging that it "should be enacted without delay. It will serve a useful purpose all over the Nation and especially in communities not served by small banks. I am sold on this legislation one hundred percent."[46] When the bill was finally reported favorably, Patman rose with a strong endorsement in the debate on passage: "I wish to commend the Com-mittee on Banking and Currency for bringing this bill out. It is spon-sored by Senator Sheppard, of Texas. . . . This is his bill. I think it is one of the most important and meritorious bills we have had before us for consideration at this session of Congress."[47] The bill was little under-stood by House members generally. Aside from Banking Committee members, Patman was the only person who spoke knowledgeably about credit unions on the floor. His understanding of what Bergengren and Sheppard were doing and his support for their approach to economic problems were rooted in his public philosophy. Undoubtedly well aware of the meaning of the term, Patman has labeled himself a populist.[48] He was still a lesser player in 1934, but he would become a critical congressional champion of credit unionism, personally initiating legislation to strengthen its institutionalization and protect its philosophical foundations long after Roy Bergengren and Morris Sheppard had passed from the scene.

The evidence is thus good that a populist public philosophy underlies credit unionism. While Bergengren did not call himself a populist, he reflected that way of seeing the world and acting in it in his writing and his work, and the grassroots leadership supported him. Crucial advocates in Congress were avowed populist thinkers with direct links to historical populism.

THE BASIC ACTOR: THE CREDIT UNION

As with banks and s&ls, it is within a framework of interacting organizations that credit unions realize their distinctive public philosophy in the economy. The individual "natural person" credit union is the basic actor in the credit union regulatory framework.

THE PURPOSE OF A CREDIT UNION

The question of credit unions' purpose is in hot dispute in the public policy debate as I write. I have argued that the purpose of a credit union, from within a populist public philosophy, is to empower ordinary people to achieve some control over their own financial resources. But from a progressive perspective, held by many both in and out of Congress when the statute was passed, credit unions can be viewed as special-purpose financial institutions—a component in a scheme in which banks serve commercial credit needs, s&ls provide home loans, and credit unions make small consumer loans for people of small means. The language of the Federal Credit Union Act, as passed in 1934 and as it remains, permits either interpretation. A federal credit union, the statute declares, is a cooperative association organized "for the purpose of promoting thrift among its members and creating a source of credit for provident or productive purposes."[49]

In more recent years the credit union movement tackled this ambiguity, which persisted within the movement itself, head on and clearly recovered a populist view of credit unions' purpose. In 1968–69 CUNA undertook an extensive deliberative process aimed at devising a plan for comprehensive "recodification" of the Federal Credit Union Act. In hearings across the country, credit union members, volunteers, and staff; representatives of the state leagues; and state and federal regulators debated the purpose and constitution of credit unions.[50] With regard to purpose, the outcome was a proposal to add to the existing language of the statute that a credit union is for the purpose of "providing an opportunity for its members to use and *control* their own money in order to improve their economic and social condition."[51]

Historically, the term *self-help* has also been used to characterize the purpose of credit unions by their advocates in Congress and in the movement; it continues in use today, but, without having done an actual count, my reading is that talk of self-help is declining and appeal to the possibility for members to "control" their own finances increasing. The two terms label the same concept. The term *choice* is increasingly relied on to characterize the purpose of credit unions as well: credit unions offer consumers a choice. Not to have choices regarding one's savings and where one acquires financial services is not to have control. *Choice* is thus a third label for the same concept I have in mind in using *control.*

CREDIT UNION DESIGN FROM 1934 TO THE 1970S

The ambiguity regarding credit union purpose could remain unconfronted for many years because the same institutional design served, whether a participant in the policy debate regarded the purpose of credit unions to be providing small savings opportunities and small loans for poor people or economic empowerment of average Americans. The average run of folks were of modest means, and small savings options and small loans on reasonable terms, not provided by existing financial institutions, were among their first needs in an effort to gain control over their own finances.

To make loans a fund must be generated. Under the Federal Credit Union Act of 1934 at least seven people—a traditional but arbitrary number according to Bergengren—subscribe to at least one share each in the amount of five dollars. The statute has also required, since the beginning, that credit unions retain earnings to build a reserve fund against bad loans. It is the reserve fund, or retained earnings, which accountants regard as equity capital, or simply "capital," in comparing credit unions with other financial depositories. Share capital, on the other hand, is treated, for accounting purposes, like deposits in a bank.

Credit unions are owned mutually by all their users, called *mem-*

bers or *member/owners* in credit union parlance. The function of ownership is not to provide an opportunity for profit-making by supplying a good or service to nonowners, as is the case with for-profit corporations. Rather, membership in a credit union is intended to provide members an opportunity to pool their own resources, under their own control, so they can help one another with financial services. Credit unionists talk about "mutual self-help."

Credit unions thus do not have stockholders and depositors, the former requiring dividends on their stock and the latter expecting interest on deposits. Rather, everyone who puts in money is a member. Member funds are "shares," held in share accounts. In the language of ownership members earn "dividends" on their shares, not interest on deposits. For decades, to help ensure that people did not join credit unions primarily in pursuit of maximizing return on invested funds, the standard federal credit union bylaws limited dividends to 6 percent annually. With limited member dividends and no separate class of stockholders demanding a return to capital, the particular form of credit union ownership reduces pressure to achieve profits as a factor in the institutional decision calculus, permitting decision makers to focus on providing the services their membership wants on fair and attractive terms, even if different choices would result in higher returns.

Ownership of any particular credit union is limited in a way that is unique among financial institutions—to groups having a "common bond." A common bond is a relationship of some sort, a common interest, shared by people forming the credit union. In the 1930s, whether or not a state statute required a common bond, the practice was to organize state credit unions among employees of a particular organization, members of parishes or other associational groups, or residents in communities or rural districts. The central function of the common bond was to ensure financial viability. It facilitated sound credit decisions because the loan committee knew the borrower. Lending decisions based on character reduced the costs of small lending, obviating the need to investigate credit history and take security. The common bond reduced delinquency and default due to the felt obligation to repay one's fellows. A second function of the common bond was that it facilitated organizing credit unions.

Reflecting contemporary practice, the original Federal Credit Union Act required that credit unions be formed by "groups having a common bond of *occupation,* or *association,* or . . . within a well-defined neighborhood, *community,* or rural district." Regulators thus came to classify credit unions based on their common bonds as "occupational," "associational," or "community." The term *field of membership* refers to the pool of persons who could potentially join a credit union because they share its common bond.[52]

Membership in a credit union entitles one to a role in its governance. The democratic structure under the Federal Credit Union Act rests on the foundation of one member / one vote in the annual meeting, regardless of the number of shares, and an explicit prohibition of proxy voting. The statute originally specified that members elect a board of directors, a credit committee, and a supervisory committee. The board of directors made policy for the credit union, including loan terms and declaration of dividends within statutory and regulatory constraints, and elected the credit union's officers, including the treasurer, who was the general manager. The credit committee decided on loan applications. The separate supervisory committee, a majority of the members of which were not on the board of directors, provided an internal check on operations and policy. They conducted audits; reviewed passbooks; monitored compliance with legislation, regulation, the bylaws, and charter; and had authority to suspend officers, directors, and members of the credit committee, subject to a vote of the membership.

Volunteerism in the governance structure of a credit union is a crucial constitutive feature, intended to ensure decisions focused on member needs, not profits. It is also crucial to making a reality of the credit union movement's contention that ordinary people can manage their own money; CUNA and state leagues devote considerable resources to training volunteers. Under the 1934 statute members of the board, supervisory committee, and loan committee were unpaid. Officers, including the chief operating officer, could be paid if a credit union so chose in its bylaws. In practice staff was mostly voluntary.

Under the Federal Credit Union Act as passed in 1934, permitted loan assets of a credit union were tightly constrained. Unsecured loans could be for up to fifty dollars and two years; the rate was statutorily limited to 1 percent per month on the unpaid balance to ensure that it would be much lower than the small loan companies' 42 percent. Loans secured by note or shares in the credit union could be made in amounts larger than fifty dollars. To keep the safety of shareholders' funds at the forefront, rather than return on shares, investment assets were very conservatively restricted to U.S. government securities or securities fully guaranteed by the United States and to deposits in state and national banks, which had deposit insurance by that time.

CHANGING CREDIT UNION DESIGN

Credit unions continued very much the same from the 1930s into the 1970s. They offered one way to save, the standard share account, and one kind of loan, small, mostly unsecured.[53] Statutory changes in capital, ownership, and governance arrangements were marginal. Unlike many savings and loan associations, credit unions did not court outside capital, discourage member participation in governance, or undertake deliberately to shed the view of themselves as a "movement" in favor of seeing themselves as a business or industry.[54]

In the mid-1960s, however, active participants in credit unionism increasingly questioned credit union service offerings. The average run of Americans were not "poor" anymore. Their savings—not worth banks' bother in 1930—became the object of vigorous competition among banks, s&ls, and, later, the new money market mutual funds. On the loan side there were now multiple legitimate sources of small credit. These developments rendered traditional credit union saving and lending services less critical. Yet average people needed financial services more than ever. Checking accounts, once a tool of businesses, became a virtual necessity for households too, as U.S. society moved away from the use of cash. And, with inflation running at the unprecedented levels triggered by the guns and butter economic policy of the Vietnam War years, ordinary people needed interest-bearing account options for their money—just to maintain its value. They needed not only simple savings accounts but also basic investment services, like retirement accounts. And people continued to seek credit for education, housing, major purchases, and launching small businesses.

In this context CUNA undertook the movement-wide recodification process. Completed in 1970, its goal was to produce a recommendation for completely overhauling the Federal Credit Union Act, which required a focus on the fundamental question of the purpose of credit unions and led to recovering the clear view that a credit union exists to provide "an opportunity for its members to use and control their own money in order to improve their economic and social condition." The design changes that CUNA decided to pursue were driven by consideration of what it takes to serve that purpose in the current economic environment, rather than that of the 1930s.

Movement leaders expected to pursue their recommended changes as a package, in one run at Congress. But, as it turned out, credit unionism was swept into the broader regulatory and legislative battles reshaping depository intermediation in the 1970s. Prepared with their comprehensive recodification program, credit union leaders, their congressional allies, and the grassroots membership rode the waves quite nicely, emerging with virtually everything they wanted. But the changes came in pieces—most significantly, in the Housing and Urban Development Act of 1974, amendments to the Federal Credit Union Act in 1977, and the Depository Institutions Deregulation and Monetary Control Act (DIDMCA) in 1980.[55]

Statutory changes after 1970 enabling credit unions to expand and update their products and services fall into the analytical categories of *assets* and *capital*. Loan asset authority increased dramatically to include home improvement loans, mobile home loans, residential mortgages, and self-replenishing lines of credit—which, along with authority to raise rates on loans depending on economic conditions, put credit unions in a position to offer credit cards. For the traditional unsecured loan the cap on principle was removed entirely, the maximum maturity was increased to twelve years, and the 12 percent limit on interest rate—in place since 1934—was increased to 15 percent. It also became easier for credit unions to loan money to other credit unions, facilitating more responsive member service.

With regard to investment assets credit unions gained authority to invest (up to 1 percent of capital plus surplus) in securities of any organization offering services to credit unions, such as insurance and data processing. This change appears, perhaps, arcane, but it is of great consequence as its purpose is to permit the movement to build up support services for credit unions (such as share draft processing and a secondary market for home mortgages) in support of their vastly increased services for members.

In the analytic category of *capital* credit union savings options increased dramatically. (Please keep in mind that credit union share capital, the ownership stake of all members in their credit union, functions like the deposit liabilities of a bank.) For forty years federal credit unions had offered exactly one type of share account, essentially a passbook savings account. Its rate was limited to 6 percent by federal regulation (an advantage over banks, limited to 4.5 to 5.5 percent under Regulation Q). In the 1970s credit unions gained federal legislative authority to offer savings accounts with various maturities and rates as well as certificates of deposit. To enable them to attract household funds as the competition became tougher, the credit union regulator began to loosen up on the permitted interest rate in 1973.

Further diversifying share account options, and perhaps most significantly, credit unions began to offer share draft services. A draft on one's shares in a credit union is essentially a check. Thus, credit unions broke through to providing transaction accounts for households, a fundamental financial need in the contemporary economy. Moreover, these were interest-bearing transaction accounts, like the negotiable order of withdrawal (NOW) accounts being introduced by mutual savings banks in New England. A handful of state credit unions in Rhode Island were first to offer share drafts in 1970. In 1974 the federal regulator permitted a limited number of federal credit unions to experiment with share drafts and in 1978 issued rules under which any federal credit union could offer the service. By that time about half the states permitted share drafts for state credit unions, mostly by regulation as opposed to statute. In 1980 Congress provided explicit statutory authority for share drafts in DIDMCA.

Credit union asset powers and share capital arrangements have thus expanded considerably, such that credit union members provide for themselves, with their own resources, a broad range of financial services of their choosing. What has not changed is the source of credit union resources: what they have to work with continues to be member share deposits and retained earnings.[56]

Although credit unions' distinctive common bond feature was initially a device for ensuring financial viability and expanding the movement,[57] "for some members of Congress and in common parlance outside the credit union movement, the term 'common bond' came to be understood as a means to restrict credit unions to a narrowly defined niche with limited scope."[58] For decades federal regulators interpreted the common bond narrowly, requiring personal acquaintance among credit union members and sometimes placing arbitrary numerical limits on fields of membership. In the economic circumstances of the 1970s and early 1980s restrictive regulatory interpretation had perverse effects. The preponderance of credit unions had common bonds of "occupation," their field of membership often confined to a single industrial plant. Such credit unions were frequently forced into liquidation in the spate of plant closings which occurred through that period. Further, establishment of new credit unions was hamstrung as regulators and organizers realized that in the contemporary economy five hundred people were required to form a minimally viable association but that many, many workplaces did not have five hundred people. The common bond thus worked against both economic viability and expansion, its initial objectives.

Regulatory interpretation of the common bond loosened minimally in the 1960s and throughout the 1970s, but in 1982 it shifted dramatically. The decision was made to permit membership in a single federal credit union to consist of multiple groups, each group with its own common bond. The regulator offered two reasons for this change. First, "some groups were too small either by themselves or when grouped together to support a viable credit union." Permitting multiple group credit unions facilitated serving people who otherwise could not have qualified for a charter. Second, permitting diverse groups to join together in a single credit union provided the diversification necessary to protect against economic difficulties, such that a credit union would no longer be forced to liquidate when one plant closed or one industry slumped.[59] The expanded interpretation is thus justified in terms of the common bond's original functions: financial viability and expansion of the availability of credit union services.

The foregoing changes in asset, capital, and ownership features have resulted in increased credit union size and complexity, challenging credit unions to develop necessary professionalism while maintaining democratic governance and volunteerism. Paid professional management and staff have increased considerably in credit unionism, although, as late as 1989, a third of credit unions still had some volunteer staff.[60] Nevertheless, the basis of each credit union's governance structure continues to be one vote per member in the annual meeting, regardless of the number of shares, with no proxies allowed, and policy making remains entirely with the volunteer board of directors that members elect. The loan committee remains voluntary but has become optional: lending decisions may be delegated to professional loan officers under board policy. The independent, volunteer supervisory committee continues to monitor operations and policy, but it is likely to hire outside auditors.

Reconstituted as they have been since 1970, credit unions have increased their presence in the political economy dramatically. In 1998 seventy-seven million Americans belonged to credit unions, up from twenty million in 1970, and total assets had increased from $15 billion to $362 billion.

NATIONAL CREDIT UNION ADMINISTRATION

Credit unionism's expansion since 1970 can be attributed to the introduction into the credit union framework of an independent federal regulatory organization as well as to the changes in the constitution of individual credit unions. Indeed, the new regulator has been instrumental in advancing some of those constitutive changes. The National Credit Union Administration (NCUA) was created in 1970 at Wright Patman's initiative. Then chairman of the House Banking and Currency Committee, Patman was well positioned to secure a major organizational change he viewed as necessary to protect the philosophical underpinnings of credit unionism and thereby expand its presence. Although its members were surprised by Patman's move, the organized credit union movement, represented by CUNA, supported it enthusiastically.

BOUNCING AROUND THE BUREAUCRACY

Patman was reacting to what he viewed as a history of credit union regulation which was out of step with the movement's philosophy. Since passage of the Federal Credit Union Act thirty-odd years earlier, the supervisory bureau had been a waif in the line bureaucracy. Echoing state laws that placed credit union supervision with banking regulators, Bergengren and Sheppard's initial bill had provided for chartering by the Federal Reserve Banks and supervision by the Office of the Comptroller of the Currency. But neither the Federal Reserve system nor Treasury would accept any responsibility for credit unions, seeing these odd associations as outside their missions.[61] According to Bergengren, finding a department willing to accept jurisdiction proved one of their "most difficult early problems."[62] A. S. Goss, a longtime credit union activist from Washington state,[63] came to the rescue. Goss was then president of the Federal Land Bank, in the Farm Credit Administration (FCA). He suggested that the FCA would provide a sympathetic home and persuaded his superiors to concur.[64] Accordingly, the initial statute gave jurisdiction to the FCA. Goss's optimism proved unfounded, as the evangelical, populist Credit Union Division rested uneasily within the ideologically progressive FCA.[65]

In 1942 the Credit Union Division was transferred to the Federal Deposit Insurance Corporation by executive order, based upon a Bureau of the Budget finding that it had "no relationship to the basic function of the FCA." But the FDIC, the banking framework's deposit insurer, with its adversarial relationship to banks, did not view the evangelistic spirit of credit union regulation as congruent with its mission either. The FDIC established labyrinthine procedures for dealing with credit unions and opposed virtually all revisions CUNA sought to the statute. As the FDIC's hostility became clear, Patman, without success, sought legislation that would move the Credit Union Division to the Federal Home Loan Bank Board.[66]

CUNA itself eventually mounted a drive to move the credit union regulator. It targeted the Federal Security Agency (FSA), expecting the entity that ran Social Security to be more hospitable because its programs aimed at the "security and economic status of people." CUNA drafted a bill, enlisted congressional sponsors, fought President Truman's Bureau of the Budget, pulled out the stops for a grassroots telegraph blitz on the White House, and succeeded in securing legislation making the move in 1948. Patman's involvement included writing to President Truman to urge him to overrule his Budget Bureau. In 1953 FSA (renamed the Social Security Agency [SSA]) was absorbed into the new Department of Health, Education and Welfare (HEW), and the Bureau of Federal Credit Unions went along.[67] CUNA was satisfied enough with these arrangements, and credit unionism grew.[68]

THE NATIONAL CREDIT UNION ADMINISTRATION:
A SEPARATE, INDEPENDENT AGENCY

Despite CUNA's quiescence, Congressman Patman opened hearings on a bill to create a separate agency to regulate credit unions. With unabashed enthusiasm for the peculiar financial institutions, he proclaimed that credit unions "have really worked for the people, and they have been doing a wonderful service, filling a great need. I have often said and I truly believe that outside of the church the credit unions provide the greatest good to humanity."[69] But Patman's enthusiasm did not extend to SSA and HEW regulation of credit unions. His central disagreement with administration officials went straight to the ambiguity over credit unions' purpose. Administration officials saw credit unions through progressive lenses, as a social welfare service providing small loans for disadvantaged people. Repeatedly, they defended their handling of credit unionism by pointing to projects for disadvantaged groups, and they defended placement of the credit union bureau within HEW because it was in "close proximity to the social welfare programs."[70]

But this was exactly what Patman saw as problematic: he viewed credit unions as financial institutions, not social agencies; he saw them serving ordinary people generally, not just the disadvantaged. In the course of a long diatribe aimed at Social Security Commissioner Robert Ball, Patman charged: "Now, you compare your work in the credit unions with what is being done for the Latin Americans and the Indians and many other projects. I do not think that is material here. This is something that is bigger than that. This involves poor people, middle income people."[71] Fernand St. Germain, who would succeed Patman in the chair, agreed: "I think wherever we can help [the poverty class in this country] we should. However, my concept, my understanding of the credit union movement is that it was established by wage earners."[72] Likewise, Frank Annunzio maintained that it is "the average American citizen who participates in a credit union."[73]

Patman and other committee members hammered administration officials for their failure to be advocates for organized credit unionism. You take actions the movement does not support, they charged.[74] We don't see you bringing us bills responding to credit unions' priorities.[75] Credit unionism could have reached more people if you had done things differently.[76] "It is . . . quite clear," concluded Patman, "that the Department of Health, Education, and Welfare does not take a great interest in the operation of the Bureau of Federal Credit Unions."[77]

In advocating creation of a new regulator, Patman's purpose, his committee's, and CUNA's was to achieve philosophically consistent regulation, an evangelistic regulator. Patman was explicit. "We should have," he insisted, "a federal credit union agency that is administered by those who believe in the philosophy of the credit unions."[78]

A more inopportune moment for proposing a new, separate, federal agency can hardly be found in the history of the organization of the U.S. federal government. Richard Nixon was president, and he placed a high priority on organizational consolidation for presidential management and policy control. In the area of depository intermediation, in particular, Nixon's Hunt commission was proposing to collapse existing agencies into one super–banking regulator under Treasury control, even as Patman was proposing an additional and independent organization. In testimony that had been cleared through Nixon's Budget Bureau administration spokesmen consistently opposed an additional agency.

With conciliatory rhetoric Patman proposed that the desired independent agency have a single administrator, appointed by the president, with advice and consent of the Senate, and removable at his pleasure. This would give the president his rightful control. It would also raise credit union regulation from under three layers of bureaucracy to the status it deserved, like regulation for the s&l industry and banking. Patman's bill also contained, at CUNA's behest, a "National Credit Union Board of Governors." This board would have nine members, all with credit union experience, to provide the administrator with policy guidance. In appointing this board, the president would give special consideration to nominations from CUNA. Such a board would provide considerable policy control to CUNA.

As Congress ultimately constituted it in 1970, the National Credit Union Administration was indeed an independent agency headed by a single administrator who was appointed by the president and served at his pleasure. But the strong board requested by CUNA and included by the House was weakened in the Senate; it became merely advisory, appointed by the president with no requirement for nominations from the movement. There would be no appropriation for the NCUA; the new agency was funded entirely by credit unions, as its predecessor bureau had been since 1953.

RESTRUCTURING THE NATIONAL CREDIT UNION ADMINISTRATION

The ink on the statute establishing the NCUA had scarcely dried when CUNA began asking Congress to restructure the new regulator. The single administrator design did not work as advocates of a separate agency intended. As the first administrator, President Nixon had appointed Herman Nickerson, a Marine Corps general with no credit union experience. Tension ran high between Nickerson and CUNA from the beginning; CUNA formally asked Nixon to remove the administrator in 1973, a request the president ignored.[79]

The NCUA was restructured in 1978 by the broader Financial Institutions Regulatory Act. The new design was recommended in a study that the agency itself commissioned to identify how it would best be structured to meet growing responsibilities. The consultant concluded that a single administrator, serving at the president's pleasure, was too easily prey to political pressure and that anticipated increases in the NCUA responsibility would be best met by a board to share the workload. The new board would have three members, not more than two from the same political party. They would be appointed by the president for fixed, staggered six-year terms. The president would designate the chair, who would serve as the agency's administrator. The former advisory board would be discontinued. The design was intended to give the board some independence from the president as well as from the organized movement and to permit it to be responsive to Congress. In addition to establishing the new board, Congress upgraded the personnel structure in the agency to bring it more in line with that in other depository institution regulators.[80]

NATIONAL CREDIT UNION SHARE INSURANCE FUND

In the credit union regulatory framework the organization that insures member shares is the National Credit Union Share Insurance Fund (NCUSIF).[81] Congress established the share insurance fund in September 1970, shortly after creating the separate regulator earlier that same year. Organizationally, NCUSIF is administered by the NCUA (the federal credit union regulator); as an accounting entity, it is a fund in the U.S. Treasury; as a distinctively constituted component in credit unions' regulatory framework, it is owned by the credit unions whose shares it insures. Its purpose is to guarantee that individuals will not lose the money in their share accounts in credit unions, analogous to the purpose of deposit insurance for accounts in banks and S&LS.

CREATING THE NATIONAL CREDIT UNION SHARE INSURANCE FUND

Whether to ask Congress to constitute such a fund was debated within CUNA from 1934 until 1970. The core arguments against federal share insurance flowed easily from credit unionism's central emphasis on facilitating people in the control of their own resources. There was a concern that the requirements attendant upon federal share insurance would intimidate the volunteers involved in establishing credit unions, thus imperiling organization of new credit unions and denying this organizational tool to people who would benefit. Even existing credit unions, with their volunteer boards and part-time staffs, would be jeopardized by the cost of share insurance and associated accounting requirements. Further, federal control through a share insurer was viewed as having a strong potential for overreach: it could impinge on the self-governance of individual credit unions and threaten state regulation of state credit unions.

Moreover, argued the opponents of federal share insurance, as financial institutions for the "common man," "credit unions historically have always been vitally concerned about the security of shareholders' savings."[82] They had taken steps, with their own resources, to serve the same purpose of protecting member deposits. State leagues and CUNA had organized "stabilization funds," to which credit unions contributed to provide shaky credit unions with funds and other help. Bonding programs to prevent loss through actions of credit union personnel were extensive. Two states had established insurance funds. The very constitution of the individual credit union, with its unique common bond and conservative investment assets, emphasized safety for member funds, not risk taking for profit. Indeed, the record was that member losses of credit union share accounts had been very small. Until 1970 CUNA remained officially opposed to federal share insurance, through resolutions taken at its annual meetings.[83]

Yet the minority within CUNA in favor of federal share insurance had been growing. Particularly adamant were people associated with large federal credit unions. As these credit unions became more complex, their leadership worried about economic forces beyond their control. They wanted the same ultimate failsafes built into the credit union framework which banking and s&Ls had—share insurance and a central bank. Some of them felt so strongly that these measures should be legislative priorities that they formed the National Association of Federal Credit Unions (NAFCU) in 1967 to pursue them, regardless of CUNA's position. A very small number of credit unions were NAFCU members, but they represented a disproportionate share of credit unionism's assets.[84] NAFCU's central argument was that federal insurance was necessary to guarantee member funds, especially because members were depositing larger amounts than in the past. The movement's internal approaches to guaranteeing member shares were not good enough because any loss to members was too much. NAFCU argued further that federal credit union members believed their funds were federally insured anyway and that this was a reason to provide credit unions with the same insurance as other depository institutions had.[85]

The fight within the movement over share insurance was aired before Congress during hearings on Patman's bill for an independent regulator. Senator Wallace Bennett, who heard the argument from his seat on the Senate Financial Institutions Subcommittee, took NAFCU's side and followed up with a bill to establish share insurance shortly after the independent agency measure passed.

At that point CUNA's annual meeting voted to reverse position and support federal share insurance. The issue was thus no longer whether to have share insurance but, rather, how to design the fund. Like NAFCU,

Bennett saw credit unions becoming like other depository intermediaries. He used the FDIC and the FSLIC, the banking and s&L deposit insurers, as models in drafting his proposal, which the NAFCU fully endorsed. CUNA, on the other hand, insisted that credit unions were unique among financial depositories and that their share insurer should reflect their differences; Wright Patman introduced a share insurance bill in the House reflecting CUNA's position.

Differences between Bennett's NAFCU-supported approach and Patman and CUNA's bill were in three areas. First, taking into account the small size of many credit unions, CUNA wanted lower cost and less burdensome reporting than Bennett proposed. Second, CUNA's proposal provided less mandatory and discretionary authority for the federal administrator than Bennett's in several areas. Most significantly, whereas Bennett proposed a standard insurance arrangement in which credit unions would pay premiums as an expense, CUNA demanded something quite different: credit unions' payments to the insurance fund would be *investments* in it, not premiums, and insured credit unions would own the fund.

CUNA's positions once again reflect the organized movement's central concern with maintaining credit unions as an institutional mechanism through which members control their own resources. CUNA could shift its position to support share insurance by viewing it as the ultimate guarantee of the safety of member funds, thus philosophically consistent. But that share insurer had to have a design that was consistent as well. A mutually owned insurance fund fit, reflecting the historic commitment to pooling resources to help one another and to advance credit unionism. The fund would be there if a credit union were in trouble. But, at the same time, a member-owned fund, with mechanisms for transferring gains and losses back to individual credit unions, would keep each credit union's responsibility clearly in view. If a credit union went under, all insured credit unions would feel it directly. If few credit unions failed, the fund could generate dividends for members. And, if a solvent credit union liquidated, as they so often did before expansion of the common bond concept, it could have its equity back to return to its members, taking its share of losses or gains.

As Congress constituted the share insurance fund in 1970, CUNA lost on the core constitutive feature of fund ownership by insured credit unions. Credit unions were to finance their share insurance by paying premiums calculated as a percentage of insured accounts, just like banks and s&Ls financed their deposit insurance. Share insurance became mandatory for federal credit unions and permissive for state-chartered institutions. Corporate credit unions were, and are, also eligible for share insurance, although only up to the same limit per account as natural person credit unions.

RESTRUCTURING THE NATIONAL CREDIT UNION
SHARE INSURANCE FUND

Under its initial design the NCUSIF worked well through 1979, increasing its capitalization steadily, even though, unlike the FDIC and FSLIC, it did not have a loan from the government upon startup. But in the early 1980s credit union losses increased with the rash of plant closings and the general economic conditions that contributed to them, resulting in severe stress on the share insurance fund. In response, CUNA, NAFCU, and NCUA asked Congress to revise the share insurer's design, incorporating the ownership principle originally advocated by CUNA; Congress complied in 1984. In the revised arrangement insured credit unions pay in to the NCUSIF 1 percent of their total insured deposits, an amount that is adjusted annually. This 1 percent deposit constitutes each credit union's investment in the share insurance fund and is carried as an asset on its books. It is also the core of the NCUSIF's capital, which is enhanced with retained earnings. If there is stress on the fund, the NCUA may call for a premium payment in addition to the deposit; the premium is an ordinary expense to credit unions. Since recapitalization with these 1 percent deposits in 1985, the NCUA had called for the annual premium only once through 1997. Ordinarily, the share insurance fund's investments yield enough income to maintain its reserve ratio (1.3 percent of insured deposits), cover operating expenses and costs due to credit union failures, make additions to retained earnings, and sometimes pay dividends to its credit union owners as well.

Credit unionism's uniqueness is striking when we consider how this approach contrasts with solutions to deposit insurance crises in the S&L and banking frameworks a few years later. When S&Ls' insurer went broke in the late 1980s, Congress gave the massive bill for resolving failing thrifts to taxpayers. When the bank insurance fund dipped into the red in the early 1990s, Congress shored it up with loans from the Treasury. But in 1985, when credit unions' insurer was in trouble, Congress constructed an organizational mechanism through which the movement drew, in good populist tone, upon its own resources to solve its own problems.

BANKERS' BANKS FOR CREDIT UNIONS

CORPORATE CREDIT UNIONS

The credit union regulatory framework includes an interesting and integral institution—the "corporate" credit union, of which there are currently forty-one—which lacks a direct functional analog in the banking and s&l frameworks. Corporate credit unions provide liquidity to member depositories and thus are something like Federal Reserve Banks and Federal Home Loan Banks, the rediscount institutions in the other regulatory frameworks. But they do considerably more as well. Corporate credit unions are credit unions for credit unions. Their purpose is to provide services to the natural person credit unions that are their members. Those services include liquidity loans but also investment assistance, transaction accounts, and share draft processing. Functionally, they thus resemble larger banks that sell correspondent services to smaller banks as well as rediscount institutions.

Corporate credit unions were constructed within the particular context of the credit union regulatory framework. When federal credit unions were created in 1934, Bergengren and Sheppard anticipated liquidity needs. Their initial bill called for federal charters for "central" credit unions for each state, which would have access to Federal Reserve Banks' rediscount windows. At the insistence of FDR's Treasury Department all authority for such state-level liquidity facilities and any sort of access to Federal Reserve Banks were stricken from the bill. It fell to the state credit union leagues, in cooperation with CUNA, to devise corporate credit unions to meet various needs of credit unions, one of which was liquidity. The majority of corporate credit unions are thus creatures of state law and subject to state regulation, but they have recently come under federal regulation by the NCUA as well. Federal regulation became a factor as federal credit unions, which were initially forbidden to join state-chartered corporate credit unions, gained that ability and as federal chartering of corporate credit unions began. Another avenue for federal regulation arose with share insurance, which is extended to corporate credit unions.

Corporate credit unions are constituted in a manner consistent with the populist philosophy that underlies credit unionism. Like the framework's basic actors, natural person credit unions, corporates are nonprofit cooperatives owned by their members; they are essentially organizational devices by means of which credit unions gain control of resources with which to meet their own needs by pooling what they have, helping themselves as they help one another. Corporate credit unions are particularly crucial to small credit unions. In addition to volunteer policy making, many small credit unions continue to be staffed in part or whole by volunteers or by part-time staff; through their corporate credit union they can professionally invest idle funds and safely provide sophisticated financial services to their members. Also like other credit unions, corporates have fields of membership, usually consisting of credit unions and credit union service organizations in a particular state or group of states.

Corporate credit unions build up core capital through retained earnings, like other credit unions. They also have a special class of share capital—"membership capital share deposits"—withdrawal of which is restricted, thus providing a secondary capital cushion. Finally, effective in January 1998 in accord with new NCUA regulations, corporate credit unions may have paid-in, nonshare capital. Regulators have introduced this option because they recognize the important role of corporate credit unions in the framework and want to strengthen their thin capitalization; paid-in capital is inconsistent, however, with cooperative organizational constitution. Its potential adverse impact would be to center maximization of return as a decision-making criterion, rather than member service. In an effort to preclude that impact NCUA regulations provide that paid-in capital will have no voting rights. It remains to be seen whether corporate credit unions will make much use of this option (in 1998, only one had paid-in capital) and, if they do, whether it damages their integrity as service providers for member/owners.

A distinctive feature of corporate credit unions' governance, historically, was strong management interlocks with the state leagues that established them. The leagues had democratic governance structures, and many designed corporates to function as their agents. In 1994 the NCUA prohibited interlocks between state leagues and their associated corporate credit unions.

A look at corporate credit union assets, which include loans to members and investment assets, shows that, historically and today, member credit unions have used their corporates far more for investment services than for liquidity. Those investments currently are short term and high quality: federal agency securities, corporate debt, and, increasingly, asset-backed securities.[86]

U.S. CENTRAL CREDIT UNION AND THE
CENTRAL LIQUIDITY FACILITY

Corporate credit unions served their members' limited demand for liquidity lending for decades. Nevertheless, by 1970, anticipating growth, the organized movement placed a priority on gaining the ability to redistribute funds around the country as well as the liquidity that could be provided for credit unions by a single central bank and lender of last resort, with access to government borrowing if necessary. Caught up in the substantive twists and turns and the timing of the profusion of depository institution legislation Congress considered in the 1970s, credit unionism now finds itself with essentially two central banks, plus access to the Federal Reserve. Rethinking is under way.

When a central liquidity organization became a priority for CUNA, the association turned again to Wright Patman, who introduced bills in 1970, 1971, 1972, and 1973. Failing in Congress each time, CUNA itself organized the U.S. Central Credit Union in 1974, which is chartered under Kansas law.[87] U.S. Central is a credit union owned by natural person credit unions through arrangements with their corporate credit unions. It is a significant actor in the credit union framework, providing investment and liquidity services to corporate credit unions.

Despite the existence of U.S. Central, credit unionists continued to press Congress for a federally chartered liquidity facility with authority to tap the Treasury in the ultimate liquidity crunch—for neither U.S. Central or corporate credit unions or natural person credit unions had such access. They succeeded in 1978: as part of restructuring the NCUA to enable it to meet anticipated expansion of credit unionism, Congress established the Central Liquidity Facility (CLF). The CLF is a government corporation within the NCUA, capitalized by member credit unions (state and federal credit unions are eligible and usually join through their corporate credit unions as agent) and managed by the NCUA board.

The CLF, however, has been used very little. It was organized four years after Kansas chartered the U.S. Central Credit Union, which had taken off nicely, expanding its operations to meet credit union needs. Then, two years after the CLF was established, in the Depository Institutions Deregulation and Monetary Control Act of 1980, Congress finally gave credit unions the access to the Fed discount window which Senator Sheppard and Roy Bergengren had asked for so long ago. Both the General Accounting Office and the Treasury have recommended disbanding the CLF.

ADDITIONAL ORGANIZATIONS IN THE CREDIT UNION FRAMEWORK

In the credit union movement's view of itself, as articulated by CUNA, the basic idea of people pooling their resources so that they can control their allocation to provide themselves with needed services extends beyond individuals joining in a credit union to credit unions joining in larger organizations. Through CUNA and the leagues credit unions have developed a network of organizations which enables them to provide member services far beyond the capability of individual credit unions.[88]

Two credit union service organizations predate the corporate credit unions, extending back to the 1930s, when Bergengren was still active on the staff of CUNA. The CUNA Supply Cooperative was initially a printing operation, organized to provide credit unions with specialized forms for record keeping and reporting at less cost than individual credit unions would have paid to local printers. Its successor, the for-profit CUNA Service Group, provides a broad range of business and financial services. These include marketing assistance, credit and debit card programs and an IRA program, in addition to forms and office supplies.

The CUNA Mutual Insurance Society was also founded during CUNA's very early days; it was an insurance company through which virtually all credit unions carried "loan protection insurance" for their borrowers. If a borrower died, the loan was paid off—protecting both the borrower and the credit union members who had made the loan. CUNA Mutual has become the CUNA Mutual Insurance Group; its nine subsidiary companies offer a range of insurance products to individual credit union members and to credit unions as well as other business services. CUNA Mutual continues to be mutually owned by the insured.

The CUNA Mortgage Corporation is a newer entity in the network of credit union service organizations, developed after credit unions' entry into home mortgage lending in the 1970s. To reduce the risk of mortgage lending and to provide liquidity, CUNA Mortgage buys the mortgages credit unions originate and pools and sells them. CUNA Mortgage Corporation is owned by the CUNA Service Group and CUNA Mutual. The result of credit unionism's interconnection and mutual assistance through this array of organizations was noted in a study by the Federal

Reserve Bank of Kansas City: "it may be more realistic to view the credit union industry as one financial network with thousands of branches rather than thousands of small intermediaries."[89]

CHALLENGES FROM BANKING:
WHO SAYS WHAT CREDIT UNIONS' PURPOSE IS?

In expanding successfully, credit unionism has brought upon itself an ongoing, vigorous challenge from organized banking, which had largely left it alone until the late 1970s. Bankers' trade associations reject credit unionism's view that changes in its framework maintain its central purpose in the face of new economic circumstances. Rather, bankers insist that Congress established credit unions for the purpose of providing small loans to clearly bounded groups of poor people. They argue that credit unions should be confined to that purpose, or, if they are not, they are banks and should not have separate institutions or be permitted distinctive design features.

THE COMMON BOND

The most recent struggle between bankers and credit unionists over credit unions' regulatory framework has been over the common bond. As already noted, the NCUA began easing interpretation of the common bond in the 1970s and loosened it dramatically in 1982, permitting multiple groups with their own common bonds to join in one credit union. The rationale was that this move would strengthen financial viability and facilitate expansion of credit unions, precisely the original functions of the common bond. The expanded interpretation of the common bond was effective in undergirding credit union strength and expansion. Alarmed at the competition, bankers and their trade associations argued that the NCUA lacks authority to permit multiple group credit unions and won the point in *AT&T Family Federal Credit Union v. First National Bank and Trust Company*, decided by the Supreme Court in 1998.

Late in 1996, well before the Supreme Court dealt the death blow to broad regulatory interpretation of statutory common bond language, CUNA, with NAFCU, geared up a major campaign to amend the Federal Credit Union Act to permit broader common bonds explicitly and thus preserve and expand access to credit unions for individuals.[90] The "Credit Union Campaign for Consumer Choice" followed a format that has become familiar whenever CUNA mobilizes to defend or construct the institutions of the credit union framework. In this format proposed legislation is formulated, bipartisan sponsorship is recruited in both houses of Congress, and sustained grassroots contact is organized. Credit union members write letters. Credit union volunteers and state league directors visit their representatives and senators in Washington, arriving armed with materials prepared by the leagues and CUNA. Sometimes thousands of people show up at the Capitol. When presidents have been the problem, they have received stacks of telegrams. This grassroots approach dates back to 1934, when Bergengren mobilized credit union members from throughout the United States to press Congress for the Federal Credit Union Act. As with the first and all intervening grassroots mobilizations to expand and protect the credit union framework, the Campaign for Consumer Choice was successful. The Credit Union Membership Access Act, passed with bipartisan support and signed by President Clinton in August 1998, amends the Federal Credit Union Act to permit vastly expanded fields of membership explicitly, shoring up the legal foundations of credit unionism's institutional infrastructure.[91]

THE SEPARATE SHARE INSURANCE FUND AND REGULATORY AGENCY

In 1991 bills containing several versions of big bank-supported reforms to the regulatory frameworks of depository intermediaries were in Congress. The bill introduced by House Banking Committee Chair Henry Gonzalez provided for absorbing the NCUA (the separate credit union regulator established in 1970) into a new combined regulator of all depository institutions, and it placed the credit union share insurance fund in the FDIC. The Bush administration bill contained a milder assault on credit unions' separate institutions; it would have placed a Treasury representative on the NCUA board and required credit unions to give up ownership of their share insurance fund.

CUNA and the Michigan League mounted a grassroots mobilization, aptly named "Operation Grassroots," to defend credit unionism's various distinctive constitutive features, including the separate regulatory agency and the unusual design of its insurance fund. Congressional advocates of credit unions' positions succeeded in deleting provisions from the banking reform bills that would have begun integrating separate credit union institutions into the banking framework. But, as it turned out, the Bank Insurance Fund (BIF) slid into the red at about this time. Broad industry reform was stripped from pending measures, leaving only intensive care for the BIF to pass in 1991. The separate credit union framework was unmolested for the moment.[92]

SHARE DRAFTS

From 1974 through 1980 credit unions' authority to offer share drafts (essentially, checking accounts) was the most active front in the battle with bankers over the credit union regulatory framework. As outlined earlier, federal and state regulators gradually permitted expansion of the service until 1980, when Congress provided an explicit statutory basis for credit union share drafts in the Depository Institutions Deregulation and Monetary Control Act.

In the interim the American Bankers Association brought suits relentlessly in both state and federal courts challenging regulators' authority to permit share drafts—and bankers were winning. CUNA launched one of its characteristic grassroots efforts to secure credit unions' power to provide share draft service, this one dubbed "SOS: Save Our Share Drafts." Fernand St. Germain, who responded with a bill in 1979 amending the Federal Credit Union Act to permit share drafts, mused: "Never in my nineteen years as a legislator have I seen so much mail on a subject . . . . For the first time in my nine years as chairman of the Financial Institutions Subcommittee, members come up to me on the House floor and ask when I'm going to give them a bill to vote on."[93] As they have consistently, Congress took credit unions' side in this confrontation with banks, responding with temporary legislative authority for credit union share drafts from December 1979 through March 1980 and permanent authority in the Depository Institutions Deregulation and Monetary Control Act in 1980.

TAX EXEMPTION

Credit unions are exempt from federal income taxes as well as state income taxes, for the most part, while banks and S&Ls are not. Bank trade associations argue that this particular feature of credit union design constitutes an unfair competitive advantage, but, despite repeated challenges, they have not yet succeeded in persuading Congress to rescind it.

State credit unions existed before federal income taxation was introduced. They were not mentioned in the Income Tax Act of 1913, but in

1917 the attorney general ruled them tax exempt because they shared the mutual and nonprofit features of s&ls and mutual savings banks, which were explicitly tax exempt under the statute. The Federal Credit Union Act did not address the issue of taxation when initially passed in 1934, but in 1937 it was amended to exempt federal credit unions from federal income taxes. With very few exceptions the states followed the federal government and exempted state and federal credit unions from state income taxation.

Seeking new sources of revenue for the Korean War and lobbied by bankers' representatives, Congress rescinded the income tax exemptions of s&ls and mutual savings banks in the Revenue Act of 1951. They reasoned that these institutions had drifted away from the mutual ownership and nonprofit features that justified their special tax status. At the same time, the tax-exempt status of federal and state credit unions was explicitly reaffirmed; as grounds for this exemption, the Internal Revenue Code specified their constitution as nonprofit mutual organizations with no capital stock.[94]

Over the years members of Congress and representatives of credit unionism alike have justified tax exemption on the basis of the small size of credit unions (based on restrictive common bonds), their limited product offerings, and their special public purpose in serving poor people.[95] As credit unions have grown, become full-service financial institutions, and reaffirmed their mission to serve not just poor people but the ordinary run of Americans, bankers' groups (joined by s&l lobbies after s&ls lost their tax exemption) have insisted that credit union tax exemption is no longer justified.

All state and federal credit unions, however, remain mutual, nonprofit cooperatives with no capital stock. These populist features—not small size, limited product offerings, and exclusive service to the poor (progressive justifications)—are the historical, legal bases for credit union tax exemption. If the movement wishes to continue to defend its tax-exempt status effectively, it is crucial that it be clear about the justification for the distinctive features of its regulatory framework. Some recent arguments still slide back and forth between the two quite different sets of theoretical justifications for tax exemption.[96]

Precisely because they do remain true mutual associations, tax exemption is important to the safety and soundness of credit unions. Credit unions do not issue stock, as do investor-owned financial depositories. They build up an analog to banks' capital—which, as we have seen, serves such purposes as absorbing losses, buffering against withdrawal pressure, maintaining dividends in a period of slow earnings—by retaining earnings. Taxing their earnings would hamper building capital.[97]

The credit union regulatory framework is animated by populist public philosophy, that is, a central concern with building institutions through which ordinary individuals gain some control over the economic resources they have and some ability to claim those they need. Admittedly, philosophical ambiguity about credit unions—about whom they existed to serve and what they would do for them—existed for decades. Thus, here I have highlighted the beliefs of credit union leaders and key public policy makers, from the beginning, that credit unions were for ordinary people generally, to provide the financial resources they needed. In 1970 the organized movement itself clarified that its purpose was to provide "an opportunity for its members to use and control their own money in order to improve their economic and social condition."

With that clarification credit unionists have worked with Congress to transform the credit union framework. They created a separate regulatory agency sensitive to credit unionism's distinctive ideas and a separate, distinctively constituted share insurer. These institutions, in turn, supported the effort to transform individual credit unions from the source of small loans into providers of a full array of financial services needed by average Americans. On this basis credit unionism weathered difficulty in the late 1970s and early 1980s to expand considerably, even as the s&l framework contracted. Today credit unionism constitutes a viable philosophical and institutional alternative to commercial banking.

WHITHER BANKING REGULATION?

And so there were three. Three differently constituted institutions—banks, savings and loan associations, and credit unions—operated in the U.S. economy as depository intermediaries. They existed and functioned within separate sets of interacting institutions, or "regulatory frameworks," each with its own basic actor, regulators, deposit insurer, rediscount institutions, and other organizational actors. These regulatory frameworks continued through the 1970s largely in the shape imprinted by the major Depression-era structural reforms. All three kinds of intermediaries performed the function of channeling funds from savers to borrowers, thus allocating society's resources; in this sense to view them as the same is reasonable.

Yet the decision premises built into the structure and processes of the separate frameworks by public policy facilitated achievement of different goals in the allocation of social resources. In the dominant banking framework banks' mission was to do what they expected would prove most profitable for themselves as corporate entities and for the businesses whose endeavors they financed. It was up to the Fed to manipulate incentives so that this pursuit of self-interest would maximize aggregate well-being, the goal of economic policy from the utilitarian standpoint. Savings and loan associations allocated money to support home ownership, regarded as intrinsically good for people and society. Strongly shaped by a progressive philosophical perspective, the s&l framework as a whole was built quite deliberately to channel some of society's resources toward the pursuit of this particular substantive good. Credit unions focused on providing individual persons with control of their own money for their own purposes, projecting populism's central ideological concern into society's financial apparatus. The credit union framework provides an institutional alternative that permits people to partition their money from the nation's capital pool, to be allocated by different people and according to different criteria than those prevailing in banks.

To be sure, the mapping of distinctive public philosophies onto separate regulatory frameworks is not pure. Among those who argue that particularistic interests drive public policy the case has been made that in the politics of structuring public agencies, design outcomes are products of maneuvering and compromise and thus do not coherently institutionalize any policy makers' preferences.[1] From the ideas perspective taken here it can be similarly argued that diverse views contend in institutional design. Indeed, at the level of the policy domain of depository intermediation as a whole, this historical analysis demonstrates that to be the case. Within the separate frameworks, however, especially the minor frameworks, we have seen considerable ideological coherence. The dominant banking framework, with its long history and broad scope, reflects, in varying degree, neoliberal, populist, progressive, and utilitarian emphases, but on the whole its current design permits it to be manipulated systematically in pursuit of a utilitarian economic outcome.

In 1980, with the Depository Institutions Deregulation and Monetary Control Act (DIDMCA), Congress took the first steps along a path leading toward elimination of the distinctions among banks, savings and loans, and credit unions and, beyond that, between depository intermediaries and other financial institutions. The burden of this excursion through policy history has been to show that policy makers' ideas about what will be good public policy are a significant part of the explanation for the regulation we have had in this policy area, characterized by the presence of three separate regulatory frameworks. Likewise, advocacy for reforms that aim to unify the regulation of financial institutions draws strength from a public philosophy: the resurgent neoliberalism of the current era. From a neoliberal point of view the minor depository frameworks that institutionalize competing ways of thinking about the economy are mistakes; so also are ideologically inconsistent elements built into the dominant banking framework in historical moments when faith in the automatic realization of the best of all possible worlds wavered.

Here I will first briefly review the resurgence and increasing influence of the neoliberal paradigm for policy making in the United States and then outline the reform agenda that criticism in its terms set out for the regulation of depository intermediaries. Finally, based on the historical and ideological analysis presented in the previous chapters, I will identify reservations about relying upon neoliberalism as the guide, or as the exclusive guide, for institutional design in this policy area.

THE RESURGENCE OF NEOLIBERALISM

The revival of the neoliberal paradigm as a credible framework for the evaluation of economic policy and a guide for institutional design benefited considerably from the economic circumstances of the 1970s. These were not good years for the United States economically. Inflation mounted, and interest rates rose in waves, cresting as high as 21.5 percent in 1980. Yet economic growth slowed to a glacial pace after 1973, with productivity increases that were tiny compared to those that had been achieved routinely since World War II. Wages stagnated with gross domestic product, and the income gap between the affluent and the ordinary, which had been closing by several measures, began to widen. *Stagflation* was the term attached to the unprecedented simultaneous occurrence of inflation and economic slowdown.

What was to be done? The neoliberal criticism of the shape the economy had taken since the Progressive Era and the Depression, largely relegated to the academy for decades, gained ground.[2] From this point of view much about existing economic arrangements was not in the public interest. Fundamentally, the problem was that the economy was not operating efficiently: scarce resources were not allocated such that the gross domestic product (the wealth of the nation, to recall Adam Smith) was as large as possible. The cause of the problem was clear: markets, nature's mechanism for allocating resources optimally, had been obstructed throughout the economy by government regulation. The solution, likewise, was simple. The free market should be restored— or, in more general philosophic terms, natural law should be respected. Accordingly, government must back out of the economy, away from direct provision of services as well as regulation, thus recovering the bold, bright Lockean line between the public and private spheres.

The special sectoral regimes that were the institutional children of progressive public philosophy proved highly vulnerable to this criticism. Regulatory agencies staffed by experts and relying upon considerable input from the regulated industry had long been criticized by scholars from the left as tools of the regulated industry, established to serve not the public's interest in effective and reliable performance—as the progressives would have it—but, rather, the particularistic interests of the regulated firms. Neoliberal scholars agreed that the public interest was not served, yet their solution was not the intensified oversight and increased popular participation in regulatory processes which left-leaning critics urged but, instead, the elimination of government regulation and restoration of market discipline. The public's interest would be served as competition led to improved economic performance, lower prices, and more choices for consumers.

Like progressives' sector-specific institutional interference with markets, the macroeconomic manipulations of the philosophically utilitarian by means of fiscal and monetary policy also came under assault; these measures were viewed as ineffective at best and, more likely, counterproductive. Neoliberals did not have to work very hard to discredit fiscal policy, as deficit politics made it largely unavailable in any event. The more significant debate was over monetary policy. While among utilitarians there has been a fresh search for the most effective tools and appropriate targets, neoliberal "monetarists" urged the elimination of discretionary monetary policy altogether in favor of growth in the money supply at a preannounced rate under a set of rules.

The market and a limited public sphere are powerful public ideas in the United States. Within only a few years, from about 1975 through 1980, there was significant pro-competitive deregulation in the airline, trucking, telecommunication, securities, and railroad industries.[3] In the 1980s, as the neoliberal critique gained steam, it undergirded privatization of services that had been directly produced in the public sector, and it justified chipping away at economy-wide environmental, consumer, and worker protection regulations on the grounds that they were not efficient.

THE NEOLIBERAL REFORM AGENDA FOR DEPOSITORY INTERMEDIARIES

Within the context of the difficult and poorly understood economy-wide dynamics of the 1970s and intensifying in the 1980s, depository intermediaries experienced their particular troubles. Rising interest rates, coupled with the availability of new computer technology, led to the appearance of a new kind of financial institution, money market mutual funds. These new funds had a serious adverse impact on depository institutions through the liability side of their balance sheets. In the process termed *disintermediation*, when market interest rates passed the ceilings that depository intermediaries were permitted to pay, individuals and firms chose money market funds and other alternatives, instead of traditional deposit accounts. As deposit flows slowed, banks sought out alternative, higher-priced sources of funds—Eurodollars, large denomination CDs, and federal funds (loans from other banks), while s&Ls, without these options, dramatically slowed mortgage origination. Depositories were suffering on the asset side of their balance sheets as well. Savings and loan associations, as we know far too well, had long-term, fixed rate mortgages in their portfolios which, as interest rates rose, paid less than the cost of capturing new deposits. Not as universally recognized but at least as significant a factor in the thrift industry decline, in the 1980s extensive securitization enabled various financial institutions to move into mortgage loans. Banks were losing borrowers too: as their credit became more expensive because they were paying more for funds to lend, the commercial and industrial firms that were banks' best customers increasingly turned away from them to borrow directly in the money market.[4]

As in other economic sectors, the pro-competitive deregulation favored from a neoliberal perspective gained ground as the solution to banking's woes. Writing in 1982, economists Thomas Cargill and Gillian Garcia succinctly level the neoliberal criticism of depository intermediation as it stood in the 1970s.[5] The financial system, they stipulate, is supposed to provide an efficient flow of funds throughout the economy. The mechanism for achieving such efficiency is competition among financial institutions in the market. But in an overemphasis on stability Depression-era reforms deliberately hampered competition, thus rendering the financial system inefficient by creating "heterogeneity" among depository intermediaries, ignoring their "similar economic and functional operations."

Cargill and Garcia point approvingly to the 1971 report of President Nixon's Commission on Financial Structure and Regulation (the Hunt commission), which had already developed this fundamental critique. They underscore the "new philosophy" reflected in the report, the basis of which is the "competitive market principle." That philosophy was summarized in the commission's statement of its objective as "to move as far as possible toward freedom of financial markets and equip all institutions with the powers necessary to compete in such markets . . . . each institution will be free to determine its own course. The public will be better served by such competition. Markets will work more efficiently in the allocation of funds and total savings will expand to meet private and public needs."[6]

On the basis of this "new" philosophy the Hunt commission rec-ommended a far-reaching reform program. First, interest rate ceilings on deposits should be phased out.[7] Different ceilings among the three types of intermediaries distorted the market for allocating money, ren-dering it inefficient, and any rate ceiling hampered depositories' com-petition with nondepository financial institutions. Second, banks should no longer be the only depository allowed to provide checking accounts. s&Ls should be able to compete with their NOW accounts, and, if credit unions wanted to offer checking beyond a minimum percentage of their deposits, they should be able to convert to s&L or bank charters. All institutions thus offering demand deposits should be subject to uni-form reserve requirements under Fed authority in order both to level the competitive field and to provide leverage for monetary policy. Third, depositories should have broader asset powers; that is, they should have more leeway in their investment and lending activity. At the time, a crucial implication of this thinking was that s&Ls should be able to move outside of the home mortgage business and banks should be able to move in. Fourth, to create a level playing field—that is, an undistorted market—rules should be made more uniform for depositories through some consolidation of the regulatory and supervisory functions of dif-ferent agencies and through combination of the deposit insurers. Fifth, barriers to entry into banking (such as restrictions on branching and interstate banking)[8] and barriers to banks' entry into other financial services and products (the Glass-Steagall wall between banks and secu-rities firms), both viewed as restraints on market competition, should be relaxed. And, finally, all depository intermediaries should be subject to the same federal taxation.[9]

This deregulatory reform agenda constitutes an outline of the pro-gram pursued ever since and largely accomplished by the end of 1999. I will use it in the next few pages to sketch the profound changes in banking regulation which have occurred, but permit a qualification at the outset. I label this a philosophically "neoliberal" agenda. While the Hunt commission report was unambiguous in declaring a neoliberal philosophical perspective as the justification for its program, its opera-tional recommendations were more nuanced, qualified based on con-cerns that we have seen arise historically from within other evaluative systems. The report made mention, for example, of the undesirability of excessive concentration of wealth and the need to transmit mone-tary policy effectively. What I see in reviewing the policy debate is that reservations on the part of advocates for deregulatory reform fell away over time and the details of the reforms on their agenda became far less qualified, often as unambiguously neoliberal as the outline given here implies.

Major efforts to begin to legislate the deregulatory reform agenda articulated by the Hunt commission failed in 1973 and 1975, as Congress balked at viewing the depository intermediation structure it had built through neoliberal lenses, with special reluctance to leave housing finance reliant upon a free market in money. But, riding the crest of the deregulation wave of the late 1970s, a significant portion of the package was enacted in the Depository Institutions Deregulation and Monetary Control Act of 1980 (DIDMCA). President Carter signed that statute, and the Reagan, Bush, and Clinton administrations all advanced proposals consistent with remaining portions of the banking reform agenda.[10]

In keeping with the first three recommendations on the reform agenda, DIDMCA phased out interest rate ceilings on time and savings deposits, permitted S&Ls and credit unions to offer checking accounts, and expanded depositories' asset powers. Banks entered the home mortgage business; S&Ls got authority to offer consumer and business loans, and credit unions were permitted to deal in home mortgages and credit cards. The statute also raised the deposit insurance limit from $40,000 to $100,000 per account. In 1982 the Garn–St. Germain Act loosened up further in the same directions.

In terms that I have used in this study, what these first big steps in depository deregulation did was to begin stripping away differences in the constitution of the basic actors in the three frameworks, differences that had been built in historically because—contrary to the neoliberal assertion that these institutions all serve the same economic function—they were not, empirically, intended to do the same thing. But neoliberalism's logic is uncompromising: only one design for a depository intermediary serves the public interest—a profit-maximizing economic actor. If an institution allocates money based on any other than a profit-maximizing criterion, it damages economic efficiency. It is a violation of the public's interest to channel money into housing in Parma, Ohio, if that money could be more profitably invested in Peruvian government bonds or commercial real estate in downtown Cleveland. Beyond stripping away differences among depositories, DIDMCA began removing limits on the behavior of banks which interfered with their neoliberal mission of competing hard, with one another and with other kinds of financial institutions.

Further legislative enactment of the reform agenda stalled in the 1980s as much of the s&l industry collapsed and its insurance fund went bankrupt, attributable in part to DIDMCA's and Garn–St. Germain's efforts to make s&ls profit maximizers instead of home ownership facilitators. Likewise, banks, competing more aggressively, as the neoliberal model would have them do, got into serious trouble. Their biggest problems stemmed from excessive lending in developing countries and in urban commercial real estate development. Several large banks failed by the late 1980s, and the bank insurance fund dipped into the red in 1991. Congress's next statutory actions in 1989 and 1991[11] thus concentrated on dealing with the s&l and bank insurance funds, respectively. In addition to infusions of money, these and other statutes after 1992 tried to protect deposit insurance through strengthened supervisory power to close, merge, and otherwise manage the imprudent and stiffened penalties for the criminal. These moves are often termed *reregulatory*; this is something of a misnomer, as they did not move back toward the kinds of constitutive regulatory distinctions that DIDMCA had broken down but, rather, moved toward stronger enforcement powers, as depositories exercised their new competitive freedom.

Even as they reregulated in this sense, some in Congress pushed forward toward the next objective on the deregulatory agenda—consolidation of regulators and deposit insurance funds. The 1989 savings and loan bailout law abolished the Federal Home Loan Bank Board, which had been the s&l regulator, and the Federal Savings and Loan Insurance Fund, the original federal s&l deposit insurer. Although this law replaced both agencies with new ones, the moves add up to consolidation. The new Office of Thrift Supervision (OTS) is not independent, like its predecessor, but is part of the Treasury, alongside the OCC, the national banks' regulator. Likewise, the new Savings Association Insurance Fund (SAIF) is located in the FDIC with the bank insurance fund. Further consolidation, both across the separate frameworks and within the banking framework, remains a live issue. Proposals for complete absorption of OTS into OCC and for collapsing SAIF into the bank insurance fund reappear regularly; as s&ls have failed or essentially become banks, it may be only a matter of time until their separate regulator and deposit insurer disappear. So far, credit unionism—whose advocates have maintained a focus on the distinctiveness of their purpose—has successfully defeated similar efforts to collapse its regulator and insurance fund into the banking agencies. Within the dominant banking framework Congress has legislated more uniformity in the supervisory approaches of the Fed, FDIC, and OCC but has not combined the agencies.

Although regulators had already loosened up with regard to interstate banking and branching, Congress did not legislate this next major item on the banking deregulatory reform agenda until 1994. The Hunt commission had called upon state banking regulators to ease barriers to entry, thereby promoting competition, by relaxing branching and merger restrictions within states. By the 1990s deregulation advocates had transformed this recommendation into the bolder proposal that federal law facilitate bank expansion and combination across state lines. The Bush administration formally proposed the move in 1991. But it was Democratic committee leaders who provided the initiative and stamina to win passage of the Riegle-Neal Interstate Banking and Branching Efficiency Act in 1994, before the fall elections that put Republican majorities in charge of both houses of Congress. Riegle-Neal eliminated remaining barriers to bank expansion across state lines, creating the possibility—indeed, the virtual certainty—that privately owned banks would operate nationwide. The law was not fully effective until 1997, but merger and acquisition frenzy among banks rushing to get big—and therefore more competitive in the global market, according to one rationale for the move—immediately followed its passage.

Late in 1999, after several false starts and to the surprise of even longtime observers, Congress ticked off the last major institutional change on the banking reform agenda outlined by the Hunt commission almost thirty years earlier: demolition of the "Glass-Steagall wall" erected by the Banking Act of 1933 between commercial banking and securities dealing. Here again, as the neoliberal perspective had gained strength, the proposal had become far bolder. The Banking Act of 1933 permitted banks to underwrite governments' general obligation bond issues; the Hunt commission recommended undermining the Glass-Steagall wall only to the extent of permitting banks to underwrite public revenue bond issues as well. The Gramm-Leach-Bliley Act of 1999 (GLB) permits banking organizations to underwrite and deal in private securities generally. And, in addition to removing the barrier between the banking and securities industries, Gramm-Leach-Bliley also removes the prohibition, dating from the Bank Holding Company Act of 1956, on banks dealing in insurance products.

Beyond further consolidation of regulatory agencies and deposit insurance funds, the last item outstanding on the deregulatory reform agenda is the question of whether to levy federal income taxes on credit unions, as on banks and s&Ls. As with efforts to collapse their separate regulator and insurance fund into banking agencies, income taxation of credit unions has not stayed in any bill long enough to pass out of committee in the House or Senate. It is not currently on the active agenda but will undoubtedly return.

Washington policy makers from both parties and at both ends of Pennsylvania Avenue have cooperated in thus legislating the bulk of the banking deregulation agenda outlined by the Hunt commission in 1971. They envision the emergence of privately owned banking organizations with nationwide presence and diversified financial services firms that deal in securities and insurance as well as traditional commercial bank products and services. These organizations will easily move money around the country and globally as they compete in the deregulated marketplace. Benefits are expected to include greater profitability for banks, increased micro- and macroeconomic efficiency, convenience and better service for customers, a more stable banking system due to nationwide banks' ability to protect themselves against regional downturns, and thus protection for the bank deposit insurance fund. Policy makers who advocate deregulated U.S. banking expect it to serve the public interest.

WHY NOT NEOLIBERALISM?

The logic of the banking deregulatory reform agenda compels both the elimination of the minor depository frameworks and stripping of ideologically inconsistent elements from the dominant banking framework. This agenda is one of many current expressions of neoliberal public philosophy. By *neoliberalism*, to reiterate and underscore, I mean a public philosophy that insists on a clear boundary between an expansive private sphere that includes the economy and a tiny public sphere occupied by a limited state, emphasizes the market as a natural mechanism for achieving optimal resource allocation, and does not distinguish between human persons and corporate entities as participants in the market. This is a powerful public philosophy in the United States. For many it inherits the moral authority of the classic liberalism of Jefferson's announcement of U.S. independence, Locke's second treatise on government, and Adam Smith's great statement of the path to

the wealth of nations; indeed, for many it is the same public philosophy. I have distinguished it from classic liberalism, however, insisting
on the separate label *neoliberalism*, because it admits corporate actors—
some of which, these days, rival or surpass the size and capability of
some nation-states—into the private sphere on much the same grounds
as individual human beings.

Why should there be concern about making policy for money and
banking in neoliberalism's terms? The current direction benefits from
the power of the deeply held ideas of the market and limited government, despite limits to their applicability. Like any public philosophy,
neoliberalism functions both empirically, providing policy makers' with
a framework to aid perception and interpretation of what there is in
the social world and how things work, and normatively, prescribing
the direction for reform. Applied to this policy area, neoliberalism falls
short as an adequate paradigm: a view of the social world through its
lenses neither captures what we have nor provides an adequate guide
for where we should go.

EMPIRICAL SHORTCOMINGS

Empirically, neoliberalism does not serve well as a paradigm for understanding the history of institutional development or the mechanisms
in this policy domain. To account for banking policy history it has been
necessary to think in terms outside of neoliberalism's conceptual
scheme. Consider two of the philosophical tensions used throughout
this study in probing policy makers' views: the relationship between
the public and the private spheres and nature versus construction.

Through neoliberal lenses the world is seen as divided into distinguishable public and private spheres. But, in trying to understand the
relationship of the state to the economy in the banking policy area,
insisting on a neat public/private divide obscures more than it illumi-
nates. Historically, U.S. banks and other depository intermediaries have
been creatures of public policy. Banking "regulation" should thus be
understood not as limitations placed on inherently private economic
actors by the state but, rather, as including, from the beginning, the
construction of the basic actors of depository intermediation—banks,
s&Ls, and credit unions—and ongoing manipulation of their processes
and structures. Government constitutes these institutions; it does not
simply prod their behavior from the outside.

If the basic actors of depository intermediation are not clearly private, neither do other organizations in the regulatory frameworks fall wholly on the public side of a Lockean line. The major rediscount institutions—Federal Reserve Banks and Federal Home Loan Banks—were specified by Congress to serve a public interest in the stability of the banking system. But they rest in part upon private capital, accommodate private viewpoints in their governance, and provide business services to their member firms. Deposit insurers are public entities, created to protect the public's interest in safety. But their funding arises, under usual circumstances, not from congressional appropriations but from charges to insured institutions, and, in serving their public purpose, deposit insurers benefit depositories as businesses by helping them attract funds. Although depositories may complain about the intrusion of the public regulatory agencies (OCC, FDIC, Fed, OTS, NCUA) which charter, supervise, and examine them, depositories' business interest is nonetheless served by regulatory enforcement of good practice.

The public and private sectors thus interpenetrate at the level of any one of the organizational actors in depository intermediation. And this interpenetration is even more complex when the regulatory framework as a whole is taken as the unit of analysis, as, indeed, it must be if we are to understand how banking works. For banking is not accomplished by banks alone but by banks within their institutional context; likewise, a credit union would have very restricted capabilities if not embedded in its institutional framework. The institutional frameworks of depository intermediation fulfill public purposes while simultaneously generating private earnings and meeting private needs.

Even more fundamental to neoliberalism than its insistence that the public and private spheres can be separated is its position on the question of nature versus construction. Neoliberalism situates itself firmly at one end of the philosophical continuum: just as nature has laid down laws according to which physical and chemical systems behave, so there are laws according to which the economy operates. We have seen the appeal to nature show up repeatedly in two related, but distinguishable, ways in money and banking policy development. First, there is something that *is* money; nature has a provision for the stuff. Second, the market—nature's device for automatic optimal allocation of society's scarce resources generally—can be relied upon to produce the optimal allocation of money.

Thinking in liberal and neoliberal terms, policy makers throughout U.S. history have tried to identify what money really is and then insist that only such money be used. Gold and silver—specie—were the money nature had provided in Jefferson's view. No, Andrew Jackson corrected him, only gold was really money. Well, argued former Jacksonians and Whigs alike after the Civil War, bank paper was real money as long as it was backed by a gold reserve and issued only in support of commercial activity. Later revision permitted that gold may be dispensed with domestically—and, later still, internationally too. For today's neoliberals real money issues in a decision process that occurs within financial institutions that are unrestricted in their choice of assets, privately owned, strongly capitalized, and managed in pursuit of profit.

Yet other policy makers throughout U.S. history, in efforts to facilitate day-to-day exchange for individuals and economic development in the nation or their particular locales, ignored or defied the imperative to comply with nature and worked furiously to contrive arrangements for money. There was paper money issued by colonial and then state governments; such money was backed by land, tobacco in a warehouse or other commodities, or a promise to pay gold or silver in the future. There was paper issued by the national government, backed by the promise to pay gold or silver on demand or at some time in the future. There was paper issued by state banks—capitalized with specie, claims on land or slaves, bonds of state governments, or national government bonds—in the process of making loans based on a variety of constraints built into bank governance and asset structures by state legislatures. And there was paper money issued by national banks, which were capitalized with specie or federal government bonds and operated under governance structures and asset restrictions that have varied over time. There is now deposit credit issued by banks, s&Ls, and credit unions as well as paper money guaranteed by the federal government but moving into circulation through depository intermediaries.

The history of the policy area thus strongly suggests that there is no natural provision for money: we begin unavoidably with convention, and it is not self-evident what the convention should be. What is clear is that whatever provisions we make for money, policy choices lie at its core, influencing its level and allocation. Thus, the concept of a private market for money's optimal allocation is problematic. In the process of constructing money, allocative objectives—functional, geographic, and distributive—are built into the form of the money itself. It is thus not possible to disentangle the allocation of money from the prior process of inventing it. That is to say, once we see that there is no peculiarly natural, neutral mechanism for money, it is clear that there is no absolute market efficiency in its allocation, only, it is hoped, effectiveness relative to the purposes we choose to pursue through the financial system.

Thus, neoliberal concepts, taken as empirical—and much of mainstream economics and the policy analytic technique it undergirds do just that—work poorly to illuminate the institutional development that has occurred in this policy domain.

SHIFTING THE NORMATIVE FOCUS

To be sure, there are advocates of neoliberal reforms who would be undaunted by the charge that neoliberalism provides a poor model for description, for they recognize—in company with political philosophers—that neoliberalism is, essentially, a normative paradigm. In its terms government *should* back out of involvement with banking, and the proper purpose of banks—as, indeed, of the entire financial system—should be the efficient allocation of capital. A depository institution should maximize its profits in the market, for on this basis money finds its most productive use, maximizing output with society's scarce resources. Public policy's central concern is to ensure that there is a market. Populist, progressive, and utilitarian variants of liberal public philosophy, with their distinctive reservations about the market, highlight other normative concerns for policy consideration. Moving into these alternative perspectives, what values appear threatened by banking deregulation?

POPULIST VIEW From a populist viewpoint ensuring that capital allocation is left to market forces was not historically, and is not now, the central goal for money and banking policy. Historical populists and their current-day philosophical heirs call neoliberals on the move that let corporations into the market. They reject claims that market allocations can be optimal, given the power differentials between persons and corporate organizations as market participants. They shift the normative focus to distributive concerns—to ensuring that the money system works to meet the currency and credit needs of individuals and to avoiding the concentration of wealth.

For populist thinkers government has the responsibility to provide for a medium of exchange in forms available to everyone for day-to-day transaction needs. Before the saving, borrowing, channeling, and efficiency on which neoliberal money and banking policy focuses, we all need to have something to use as money. In the late nineteenth century this view figured in the press for government paper currency and free silver—people needed an adequate medium of exchange whether or not there were banks in a particular location. Today, as banks are deregulated, the basic concern for an available transaction medium is expressed in opposition to ATM charges for access to cash from one's own account and in advocacy for requiring banks to provide "no frills" checking accounts and low-cost check cashing for people without checking accounts. Banks resist these directions; they see themselves—indeed, in the neoliberal paradigm, should see themselves—as businesses that provide services to make money, not governmental or social service agencies. But from a populist viewpoint, if deposit account balances and drafts on them are the money public policy provides, public policy must provide universal access to them.

This populist concern for availability of individuals' money is not entirely distinct from the concern for its safety as a goal of public policy. Historical efforts to ensure safety have shown up in institutional devices both outside and inside the banking framework. Outside the banking framework historical populists advocated direct government issue of the currency. Inside the banking framework government guarantee of notes, introduced in 1913, and deposit insurance, dating from the Depression, reflect the concern for guaranteeing the absolute safety of individuals' funds. More recently, laws passed in the 1960s and 1970s to compel full disclosure of loan terms—the Home Mortgage Disclosure Act, the Real Estate Settlement Procedures Act, and the Consumer Protection Act—reflect ongoing concern that market competition cannot be relied on to protect individuals in dealings with banks.

The populist goal of constructing a money system that works for individuals extends to the concern that suitably structured credit, as well as currency, be available for individuals' personal and small business purposes—regardless of whether those purposes would constitute the most profitable use of resources from a lender's perspective. Historically, this emphasis accounts for the rise, outside the commercial banking system, of the credit union framework, as competition among mainstream financial institutions did not meet the credit needs of individuals.

Within the banking framework the requirements of the Community Reinvestment Act of 1977 (CRA) reflect ongoing skepticism that competing banks will meet the credit needs of individuals, especially individuals in less-affluent communities. CRA requires a bank to provide evidence, during routine supervisory examination and the special examinations that occur when merger and branching requests are at stake, that it tries to meet the credit needs of people in the place where it is physically located and from which it draws deposits. The statute is strongly supported and fiercely protected by community-based organizations and consumer advocacy groups. From a neoliberal viewpoint CRA is the epitome of unwarranted public intervention in the market. Senate Banking Committee Chair Phil Gramm has engaged in a vigorous personal crusade to cut back its reach. Being a staunch proponent of restoring markets, Gramm appears to be motivated by his ideology, as banking lobbies have not pressed the issue during his tenure at the Banking Committee helm.[12]

A surprising though little noticed bit of newer institutional development, intended to shore up small community banks, also reflects the populist concern that huge, distantly headquartered corporations will not meet individuals' needs for personal and small business credit. The Federal Home Loan Banks, the rediscount institutions in the old S&L regulatory framework, were not eliminated in 1989 when that framework lost its separate insurance fund and independent regulator; rather, they were reconstituted, as Congress opened membership in them to commercial banks engaged in housing finance. Gradually, the value of the Federal Home Loan Banks to small banks was recognized: with loans on very attractive terms from Federal Home Loan Banks for liquidity management and portfolio expansion, small banks have a fighting chance to cope with ongoing disintermediation and to survive in the face of consolidation in the financial services industry. In the Gramm-Leach-Bliley Act of 1999—even as they cleared remaining barriers to such consolidation—Congress recognized, buttressed, and extended this role for the Federal Home Loan Banks by authorizing them to lend to small banks, even if those banks are not engaged in housing finance.[13] The philosophically inconsistent provision was a price advocates of Gramm-Leach-Bliley's central thrust paid for support among some members of the House of Representatives.

Deregulation advocates dismiss such populist concerns for availability of currency and credit on the grounds that vigorous competition in the marketplace will automatically result in better service for consumers. Competition will yield more convenient access to deposit accounts—through branches, ATMs, and online banking—as well as lower fees on consumer services, even as it results in macroeconomic efficiency. Credit will be more available than ever as the breakdown of regulatory barriers permits not just depository intermediaries but also other firms to make loans, money will move easily around the country, and consumers will benefit.[14] Based on historical and current experience,[15] historical populists and their current-day philosophical heirs reject the assumption that a free market in which corporations play will work things out for the best. They demand that government make institutional provisions that aim directly to meet the basic needs of individuals.

Moving from a micro- to a macroeconomic perspective, the populist goal of avoiding the concentration of wealth, and thus of private power, is entirely lost from view in the neoliberal approach. No one doubts that interstate banking and branching will lead to significant concentration in the banking industry as the old state and national regulatory limits on size and reach are stripped from the dominant banking framework. Acquisitions of whole banks by other banks has regularly commanded newspapers' financial pages since 1994; and since 1997 there has been a rapid move toward consolidating separately capitalized and managed whole banks into regional and nationwide branch networks under one ownership and board of directors. Nor is there any question that demolishing the Glass-Steagall wall will lead further to the combination of banks and other kinds of financial firms in giant diversified financial services corporations. Dismissing as fiction the idea that these structural developments are market driven (natural, inevitable), populists demand that government, which enables the private concentration of wealth by means of the institutional infrastructure it provides, also make available infrastructural possibilities for dispersion.

Credit unionism's escape (so far) from the neoliberal-prescribed fate of s&ls—that is, from being rolled, if gradually, into a consolidated banking framework—is one response to the populist demand; its institutional apparatus remains available for groups of people who want to hold their capital outside the merging stream and control its allocation. The quiet transformation of the Federal Home Loan Banks to serve, among other purposes, as an institutional support mechanism for small community banks may also aid in preserving outposts of locally controlled capital.

PROGRESSIVE VIEW Progressivism values efficiency, but in the progressive ideological framework *efficiency* does not mean achieving the largest possible product from a fixed stock of scarce resources, regardless of the composition of that overall product. Rather, it means effective, reliable performance in particular realms of human activity, and some realms are more important than others. Although progressives view markets positively, they do not assume that market mechanisms will be equally effective and reliable in all areas. There is a role for government, one that varies depending on how a particular sector works and how important that sector is for society.

Such thinking undergirded the deliberate construction of the s&L regulatory framework in pursuit of the substantive social and economic good of making home ownership more available. Mainstream financial institutions were not reliably channeling money toward this purpose; people in local communities and policy makers in Washington engineered a regulatory framework that did. Is demolition of much of that framework a great loss from a progressive point of view? While applying a progressive perspective to the disassembly process may have averted, or at least abated, the carnage of the s&Ls' passing from the political economy, one could conclude from that same perspective that they are no longer needed to support housing finance.

As late as the 1970s, policy makers did not have confidence that money would flow into housing without the Federal Home Loan Banks and their bonds, so convenient for institutional investors, and the s&Ls on the corner, so available to ordinary people. But in the 1980s technological advances facilitated widespread securitization of home mortgages. Now that residential mortgages can be sold readily in a secondary market, various kinds of financial institutions—including credit unions, finance companies, and banks—can initiate them. Individual and institutional investors can invest in them, since what they actually buy is a saleable security based on a pool, rather than a mortgage that must be held to maturity. Many observers believe that securitization achieves the purposes that the s&L system was serving from a progressive perspective. (It is important to note, however, that defenders of the still-functioning Federal Home Loan Banks, both in the banks and in depository institutions that use them, are convinced that continued operation of these mutual institutions effectively keeps the cost of home ownership lower than it would be in their absence.)[16]

Yet even if savings and loan associations are no longer needed to ensure that people can get home mortgages, did we have to have a catastrophe as the mechanism of housing finance changed? Confessing the immeasurable benefits of hindsight and the limits of a brief discussion, consider, nonetheless, that efforts to rescue s&Ls were strongly shaped by neoliberal precepts. From that perspective, as s&Ls were getting into trouble in the 1970s, the problem was that they were not permitted freedom in the market. Neoliberal solutions were to permit s&Ls to pay market rates to attract deposits and to broaden their asset powers, permitting them to compete for more kinds of business. As many s&Ls used these new capabilities to get into deeper and deeper trouble on both sides of their balance sheets, resulting in declining net worth, a further neoliberal solution was to abandon mutual nonprofit ownership and attract capital by permitting small numbers of individuals to own s&Ls for profit. This is largely how the crooks got into the picture (although, to be sure, most s&L owners were not crooked but, rather, were decent people trying to cope with dynamics beyond their control with incongruous institutional tools); outright fraud is estimated to account for 10 to 15 percent of total s&L insurance fund losses.[17]

As the situation continued to deteriorate in the 1980s and it became clear both that s&Ls were in trouble and that other financial institutions could serve their purpose, a decision to phase them out could have been made. But phasing out s&Ls would likely have required extensive, long-term public involvement by some latter-day Home Owners' Loan Corporation (the Depression-era government agency that bought one-sixth of the mortgages in the economy, restructured them, and closed down without losing a penny of taxpayer money); that is not a solution that appears from a neoliberal point of view. In the end, after trying a list of market-style and private solutions for too long, extensive public involvement, through the Resolution Trust Corporation, was needed anyway—at a huge financial loss to the government.

Through progressive philosophical lenses the great concern with recent moves in banking deregulation is for demolition of the Glass-Steagall wall, the former barrier between banks and securities dealing.[18] Progressives have not been throwing in flags on interstate banking and branching. The value underlying both positions—support for interstate banking but opposition to combining commercial banking with investment banking—is reliability. For progressives, who do not share the fear of bigness in itself that arises in the populist paradigm, big banks would enhance the reliability of the financial system, while diversified financial services firms threaten it. Carter Glass advocated interstate banking and branching in the 1930s as a source of strength and stability for banks but could not overcome opposition from the more philosophically populist House. The 1994 banking and branching legislation can be seen from Glass's viewpoint: banks with nationwide presence can weather problems in local economies, move money among their own units as necessary for liquidity, and internalize mistakes made in lending strategy.

While interstate banking and branching may thus be viewed as supportive of reliable banking performance, removal of the Glass-Steagall regulatory wall between banking and securities markets threatens the reliability of the financial system and the real economy. For progressives banks' special ability to increase the money supply should not be linked to activity in the securities markets.

In neoliberal theory this special ability is axiomatically exercised in a clear relationship to increased real economic activity: competitive banks allocate capital efficiently, and the "efficient" allocation of capital means the allocation that creates the most wealth. Securities markets, likewise, channel capital to its most productive use in the real economy by definition, and securities' prices accurately reflect the value of underlying productive assets. Concern about bank participation in securities markets, whether as underwriter or broker, simply does not arise.

Yet for progressives, based not in axiom but on historical experience, there is not a natural or mechanical or lawful connection between securities and the value of the underlying assets. There may be—much of the time there is, but there does not have to be: "the connection of the financial economy to the 'real' economy of factories, farms, and firms is an imperfect fit."[19] In the 1920s frenzied trading in investment trusts pulled these securities' prices out of any recognizable relationship to the value of the underlying swampland in Florida.[20] In the 1980s corporate raiders destroyed real institutional productive capability as a by-product of securities manipulation. Today, beyond bonds and ordinary equities, mutual funds, and old-fashioned hedging instruments (futures), increasingly complex financial instruments are traded in securities markets. Derivatives, for example, include relatively straightforward securities resting on pools of mortgages but also very risky devices tied to indexes and interest rates, so abstract that few people understand them or their relationship to real assets. And all of these instruments are churning faster and faster in the secondary market. Is it reasonable to assume that they reflect the productive capacity of real assets?

From the progressive viewpoint, as a practical matter, without an institutional barrier between commercial banking and securities, banks face too many temptations to inflate the money supply beyond the value of the real economy and to allocate money based on criteria other than what is likely to be most productive. And, while they are at it, a populist would add, they are likely to bilk individual consumers and violate their privacy. Permitted back into the casino (securities dealing), banks will gamble again. In so doing, experience shows that they threaten the soundness of individual banks, the reliable performance of financial markets, and, ultimately, the performance of the real economy. Few would argue anymore that banks' relationship to the securities market was the only cause of the Great Depression, but the institutional economists still out there remind us that it was one of them.

That said, a progressive perspective allows the possibility of a positive view of the huge diversified financial services firms that are arising in an institutional context devoid of the Glass-Steagall barrier. But such firms, regardless of their structure (as bank holding companies or banks with operating subsidiaries, both permitted under the Gramm-Leach-Bliley Act), can be expected to contribute reliably to improved economic performance only under increasingly sophisticated regulation, that grounded in an understanding of the unique role of banking in the political economy and the particular empirical dynamics that make banking unlike any other industry. Even were there murmurings of agreement with this caveat among policy makers, while neoliberalism is ascendant, it is unlikely that a commitment to the ongoing expense entailed in keeping a large cadre of highly trained regulators ahead of the financial game could be sustained politically.[21]

UTILITARIAN VIEW Those who think about public policy in utilitarian terms share, with neoliberals, a normative emphasis on maximizing the overall economic product. Sharing also a theory of human motivation and economic behavior, both groups expect to achieve the public's interest through market exchanges. They would thus construct the same institutional environment, up to a point, and neoliberal moves to strip away institutional obstacles to the market built in by populists and progressives are consistent with a utilitarian point of view. But, while neoliberals assume that market allocations will be efficient—so that the market itself becomes the end of economic policy—utilitarians recognize scenarios in which the market fails. Thus, maximizing utility becomes the explicit goal of economic policy, indeed, of all public policy. To maintain and improve overall economic performance, utilitarians would empower government for discretionary manipulation of the incentives of economic actors. The Federal Reserve's capacity for discretionary monetary policy is one tool for this purpose.

Is the Fed's ability to influence self-interested behavior in the economy, in the interest of maintaining aggregate performance, threatened by the substantial achievement of the banking deregulatory reform agenda? Early moves, to the contrary, actually enhanced the benevolent overseer's reach. Yet whether techniques will be identified through which the Fed can effectively manipulate incentives in the new institutional environment and whether discretionary authority to wield them will be legitimized are open questions.

As noted earlier, with the Depository Institutions Deregulation and Monetary Control Act of 1980, Congress took the first big statutory steps in pursuit of banking deregulation. But, as the phrase *monetary control* implies, the legislation had a second major purpose: it aimed to improve the Fed's effectiveness in the conduct of monetary policy. In the eyes of many, fiscal policy—another utilitarian tool—was discredited in the wake of the war in Vietnam and the stagflation of the 1970s as a means for tinkering with the macroeconomy; and federal budget deficits were beginning to make it largely unavailable in any event. Participants in the policy process of various ideological stripes were taking a fresh look at the possibilities for monetary policy. Neoliberal "monetarists"—who would banish the utilitarian's discretion from the conduct of monetary policy in favor of a steady, rule-driven increase in the money supply (an effort to simulate natural constraints)—were important in opening this discussion. But, even as the potential for monetary policy in macroeconomic management gained new luster and the search was actively on for the most effective approaches, the Federal Reserve Board's leverage was slipping.[22] Deposits in s&ls and credit unions were becoming a more significant part of the money supply but were beyond the reach of the Fed's reserve requirements. Banks also were evading control: to escape costs, many left the Federal Reserve system. (Membership had always been optional for state banks, and national banks could leave by converting to state charters.) DIDMCA addressed this erosion by subjecting all depositories—s&ls and credit unions, state banks as well as national banks—to the Federal Reserve Board's reserve requirements. Because access to Fed services was extended along with Fed control, all depositories effectively became Fed members. Whether monetary policy continues to be exercised with the strong discretionary hand that Marriner Eccles fought to institutionalize or becomes more rigidly rule driven, as neoliberals would have it, extending Fed reserve requirements to all depositories improved its leverage.[23]

But do the structural changes in the banking industry threaten the possibility for the discretionary public tinkering with money which is so essential, in the utilitarian view, to maintaining overall economic performance? We are moving into a new and very different institutional environment. While depository intermediation will remain important, direct borrowing in the securities market is increasing considerably; in the ultimate deregulated scenario banks are supplanted by generalized financial services firms engaged in both approaches as well as the development and sale of insurance products. These firms will be large enough to internalize their liquidity needs. They will operate globally, moving money out of and into different national economies in pursuit of profitable opportunities. In this new institutional environment maintaining discretionary leverage over the money supply may well require new fulcrums in the "private" economy as well as public regulators with an international reach. Whether the ideological environment will permit the new and extended regulatory development required from this perspective is an open question.

So, then, while from a neoliberal perspective the deregulatory reform of banking in the United States is expected to serve the public's interest, with benefits for the economy as a whole and for individual consumers, reservations about this direction and concern for the values we may be sacrificing arise from the viewpoints of other public philosophies. Will the basic needs of individuals in all communities—for access to their own funds, a home loan, a small business loan—be met? Will the consolidated financial system perform reliably? Will the U.S. government be able to steer it?

The central argument of this narrative is that policy makers' ideas about what is good public policy are a crucial part of the explanation for institutional design and public policy. Particularistic interests also figure in, although identifying them has not been the quest here. Likewise, idiosyncratic events and ongoing conditions influence policy. But at this moment in the enterprise of political science it is an appreciation for the influence of ideas which needs shoring up. Interests, events, and conditions all must be interpreted, and public philosophy provides a framework for interpretation as well as prescription.

Yet the claim that ideas of the public's interest, not just the pursuit of selfish interests, motivate policy making, is not a claim that we may therefore conclude that the result is "good" public policy. Ideas can be destructive of institutions and policy directions that have served well from other points of view, as well as constructive.

Neoliberalism is a powerful public philosophy. It draws moral authority—through a sleight of hand but effectively, nonetheless—from the classic liberalism at the foundation of our political culture. The emphases neoliberalism imports from classic liberalism, on maintaining a bold line between a limited government and an expansive private sphere and on confidence in the market as nature's mechanism for resource allocation, have influenced public policy in the United States since the founding, not only in building institutions and charting policy directions but also in undermining and destroying functioning institutions rooted in different premises.

Counter-ideas have also been in play historically and have influenced the shape of the current-day political economy. Banking may be unique, or at least unusual, in the degree to which different public philosophies were separately institutionalized in distinct regulatory frameworks. But, for just that reason, studying this policy domain is especially helpful for seeing that there have been, and are, different ways to think about the political economy and that institutional expressions that appear outdated or unnecessary from one point of view make sense as efforts to protect values cherished from another.

Neoliberalism is again ascendant. The force of its logic has been deployed to undermine public education, demoralize the civil service, minimize the sense of national responsibility for the particular problems of big cities, and constrain environmental regulation. In its terms savings and loan associations were inherently inefficient because maximizing profit was not their object, and credit unions do the same thing as banks.

If we have reservations about the direction in which neoliberal public philosophy is taking the political economy, arguing with its prescriptions in each policy area is one approach we can and should take. But that approach strongly suggests the story of Sisyphus and his rock, for the belief that neoliberal prescripts will work in any particular policy area rests partly on the power of the paradigm itself, rather than the empirical reality of mechanisms in that policy area.

We will have to take on neoliberalism itself, to show its limits as a framework for policy evaluation and design. And that requires more than charging that those who argue in its terms are the handmaidens of particularistic interests. That charge is only partly true and does not suggest alternatives. Neoliberalism has ideological coherence and justifies moves that at least some of its adherents sincerely believe to be in the public interest. To counter its influence we will need to recover and restate, reinvigorate and elaborate, coherent alternative public philosophies and the institutional alternatives they present. There is no question that money is effective stuff in a political struggle, but, ultimately, we need to fight ideas with ideas. Indeed, money is nothing but the institutional expression of ideas that have won.

Notes

Chapter 1: Ideas and Institutions

1. House Committee on Banking and Currency, *Banking Act of 1935: Hearings on H.R. 5357*, 74th Cong., 1st sess., 1935, 216–17.

2. Roger LeRoy Miller and David D. VanHoose, *Modern Money and Banking*, 3d ed. (New York: McGraw-Hill, 1993), 90–91.

3. For example, Paul A. Samuelson and William D. Nordhaus, *Macroeconomics*, 14th ed. (New York: McGraw-Hill, 1992); Frederic S. Mishkin, *The Economics of Money, Banking, and Financial Markets*, 5th ed. (Reading, Mass.: Addison-Wesley, 1997); Miller and VanHoose, *Modern Money and Banking*.

4. Herbert Simon, *Administrative Behavior* (New York: Macmillan, 1947).

5. Thomas F. Cargill and Gillian G. Garcia, *Financial Deregulation and Monetary Control: Historical Perspective and Impact of the 1980 Act* (Stanford: Hoover Institution Press, 1982); Cargill and Garcia, *Financial Reform in the 1980s* (Stanford: Hoover Institution Press, 1985).

6. Task Group on Regulation of Financial Services, *Blueprint for Reform: The Report of the Task Group on Regulation of Financial Services* (Washington, D.C.: GPO, 1984); U.S. Treasury, *Modernizing the Financial System: Recommendations for Safer, More Competitive Banks* (Washington, D.C.: GPO, 1991); Frank N. Newman, "Consolidating the Federal Bank Regulatory Agencies," proposal requested by Senate Committee on Banking, Housing, and Urban Affairs, November 23, 1993.

7. *Report of the President's Commission on Financial Structure and Regulation* (Washington, D.C.: GPO, 1971).

8. The 1980 law is the Depository Institutions Deregulation and Monetary Control Act (DIDMCA). For a summary of its provisions, see VanHoose and Miller, *Modern Money and Banking*, 239–40. For a longer discussion, see Cargill and Garcia, *Financial Reform in the 1980s*.

9. The 1989 legislation is the Financial Institutions Reform, Recovery and Enforcement Act (FIRREA). For a summary, see Miller and VanHoose, *Modern Money and Banking*, 246–47.

10. The Federal Deposit Insurance Corporation Improvement Act (FDICIA)

passed in 1991. Early drafts of the legislation would have consolidated banking regulation in one agency and collapsed the credit union regulator and insurance fund into the banking framework. As the contemporary crisis in the Bank Insurance Fund (BIF) deepened, however, virtually everything beyond salvaging the BIF was stripped from the bill.

11. The classic statement of this theory is George Stigler, "The Theory of Economic Regulation," *Bell Journal of Economics and Management Science* 2 (Spring 1971): 3–21.

12. For literature reviews and overviews of economic theories of politics, see Martin Staniland, "The New Political Economy," chap. 3 in *What Is Political Economy?* (New Haven: Yale University Press, 1985), 36–69; and James A. Caporaso and David P. Levine, "Economic Approaches to Politics," chap. 6 in *Theories of Political Economy* (Cambridge: Cambridge University Press, 1992), 126–58.

13. James Q. Wilson, ed., *The Politics of Regulation* (New York: Basic Books, 1980); Robert A. Katzmann, *Regulatory Bureaucracy: The Federal Trade Commission and Antitrust Policy* (Cambridge, Mass.: MIT Press, 1980).

14. Roger G. Noll and Bruce M. Owen, eds., *The Political Economy of Deregulation: Interest Groups in the Regulatory Process* (Washington, D.C.: American Enterprise Institute for Public Policy Research, 1983); Martha Derthick and Paul Quirk, *The Politics of Deregulation* (Washington, D.C.: Brookings Institution, 1985); Edith Stokey and Richard Zeckhauser, *A Primer for Policy Analysis* (New York: W. W. Norton, 1978).

15. Robert B. Reich, ed., *The Power of Public Ideas* (Cambridge, Mass.: Harvard University Press, 1988); Steven Kelman, *Making Public Policy: A Hopeful View of American Government* (New York: Basic Books, 1987).

16. The classic statement of the garbage can model of decision making is Michael D. Cohen, James G. March, and Johan P. Olsen, "A Garbage Can Model of Organizational Choice," *Administrative Science Quarterly* 17 (March 1972): 1–25. March and Olsen review the logic and literature of garbage can models in *Rediscovering Institutions: The Organizational Basis of Politics* (New York: Free Press, 1989), 11–14. John W. Kingdon adapts the model to public policy choice in the federal government in *Agendas, Alternatives, and Public Policies,* 2d ed. (New York: HarperCollins College, 1995); and Derthick and Quirk's explanation of successful adoption of the idea of procompetitive deregulation in *Politics of Deregulation* may be read as a temporal sorting approach.

17. John Locke, *Second Treatise of Civil Government* (1689; rpt., Chicago: Henry Regnery, 1955); Adam Smith, *An Inquiry into the Nature and Causes of the Wealth of Nations* (1776; rpt., New York: Alfred A. Knopf, 1991).

18. Louis Hartz, *The Liberal Tradition in America: An Interpretation of American Political Thought since the Revolution* (New York: Harcourt, Brace and World, 1955).

19. Milton Friedman, *Capitalism and Freedom* (Chicago: University of Chicago Press, 1982); Robert Nozick, *Anarchy, State, and Utopia* (New York: Basic Books, 1974).

20. The public philosophy that I have labeled *progressivism* is the subject of Charles W. Anderson, *Pragmatic Liberalism* (Chicago: University of Chicago Press, 1990).

21. Jeremy Bentham, *The Principles of Morals and Legislation* (1789; rpt., New York: Hafner Press, 1948).

22. Arthur M. Schlesinger Jr., *The Age of Jackson* (Boston: Little, Brown, 1945), 330–31.

23. Michael Kazin, *The Populist Persuasion: An American History* (New York: Basic Books, 1995).

24. Lawrence Goodwyn, *The Populist Moment: A Short History of the Agrarian Revolt in America* (New York: Oxford University Press, 1978).

CHAPTER 2: THE FIRST BANK OF THE UNITED STATES

1. "Opinion of Alexander Hamilton," February 23, 1791, in *Documentary History of Banking and Currency in the United States*, ed. Herman E. Krooss (New York: Chelsea House, 1969), 1:279.

2. George Washington to Alexander Hamilton, February 16, 1791, in ibid., 1:278.

3. "Opinion of Thomas Jefferson," February 15, 1791, in ibid., 1:273–77.

4. "Speech by Representative James Madison Opposing the Bank Bill," February 2, 1791, in ibid., 1:262–70.

5. "Act to Charter the Bank of the United States," February 25, 1791, in ibid., 1:307–14.

6. Primary sources on which this sketch of Hamilton's public philosophy relies are his five reports on public finance and economic development, in Alexander Hamilton, *Alexander Hamilton's Papers on Public Credit, Commerce and Finance*, ed. Samuel McKee Jr. (New York: Liberal Arts Press, 1957); secondary sources are Clinton Rossiter, *Alexander Hamilton and the Constitution* (New York: Harcourt, Brace and World, 1964); and Lynton K. Caldwell, *The Administrative Theories of Hamilton and Jefferson: Their Contribution to Thought on Public Administration*, 2d ed. (New York: Holmes and Meier, 1988).

7. Hume is quoted in Rossiter, *Alexander Hamilton*, 128.

8. This sketch of Jefferson's public philosophy draws on primary sources including "Notes on Virginia," in *Basic Writings of Thomas Jefferson*, ed. Philip S. Foner (Garden City, N.Y.: Halcyon House, 1944), 50–181; "Autobiography," in ibid., 409–85; "Bill to Abolish Entails, 1776," in ibid., 27–28; "A Bill for the More General Diffusion of Knowledge, 1779," in ibid., 40–46; "A Bill for Establishing Religious Freedom, 1779," in ibid., 48–49 ; "A Declaration by the Representatives of the United States of America, in General Congress Assembled," in ibid., 21–26.

9. In his draft of the *Declaration of Independence* Jefferson wrote of "*inherent* and inalienable rights"; Congress revised his phrase to the familiar "*certain* inalienable rights" (my emph.). Jefferson, "Declaration by the Representatives of the United States," 21.

10. Hamilton, "Report on a National Bank," in McKee, *Papers on Public Credit*, 53–95.

11. Ibid., 72.

12. See, for example, Samuelson and Nordhaus, "Money and Commercial Banking," chap. 10 in *Macroeconomics*.

13. John Kenneth Galbraith, *Money: Whence It Came, Where It Went* (London: Andre Deutsch, 1975), 47–50.

14. Ibid., 51–57; Bray Hammond, *Banks and Politics in America, from the Revolution to the Civil War* (Princeton, N.J.: Princeton University Press, 1957), 11–28.

15. Ibid., 29.

16. Hamilton, "Report on a National Bank," 72.

17. For example, Miller and VanHoose, *Modern Money and Banking*, 112–13.

18. Galbraith, *Money*, 7–17.

19. Ibid., 28–41.

20. In discussing the extent to which the bank's capital fund adequately backed its note circulation, we should note a confusion involving bank deposits which plagued U.S. banking policy for a long time. As Hamilton was doing here, public policy makers and private decision makers alike concerned themselves with the relationship of equity capital to the size of the bank's note issue. Their objective was to ensure enough specie capital to redeem any notes presented for payment. Deposits held an ambiguous position in a bank's ledger. Deposit credit might represent hard money brought to the bank for safekeeping. Such gold was used precisely like gold paid in as equity capital: if someone brought in a bank note for redemption, gold on deposit was used to pay. Alternatively, deposit credit might represent a loan: there was more lending via deposit credit in early U.S. banking than contemporaries or later commentators usually recognize. In either case deposits were not recognized as liabilities— that is, as monies owed someone, a potential reduction of the bank's capital— in the same sense as notes. Hamilton exhibits this confusion in his report, when he says that the bank's "total debts shall never exceed capital stock . . . credits for deposits excepted."

21. Simon, *Administrative Behavior*.

22. Jefferson to Martin Van Buren, June 29, 1824, in Foner, *Basic Writings*, 791.

23. "Opinion of Thomas Jefferson," in Krooss, *Documentary History*, 1:273–77. Jefferson's response to Washington is brief; I interpret it against a backdrop of his other writing. In addition to the works cited in note 8 I rely on several letters: Jefferson to Elbridge Gerry, January 26, 1799, in Foner, *Basic Writings*, 641–47; Jefferson to Albert Gallatin, December 13, 1803, in *The Writings of Thomas Jefferson*, ed. Andrew A. Lipscomb and Albert Ellery Bergh (Washington, D.C.: Thomas Jefferson Memorial Association, 1904), 10:436–39; Jefferson to John Eppes, June 24, 1813, in ibid., 13:269–79; Jefferson to Eppes, September 11, 1813, in ibid., 13:353–68; Jefferson to Eppes, November 6, 1813, in ibid., 13:404–32; Jefferson to Albert Gallatin, November 24, 1818, in *The Writings of Thomas Jefferson*, ed. Paul Leicester Ford (New York: G. P. Putnam's Sons, 1892–

99), 10:114–16; Jefferson to William C. Rives, November 28, 1819, in ibid., 15:229–32; Jefferson to Gallatin, December 26, 1820, in ibid., 10:175–78; and Jefferson to Henry Middleton, January 8, 1813, in ibid., 13:202–3.

24. Jefferson, "Notes on Virginia," 160–62.

25. Jefferson boasted that in his "country" (Virginia) the annual economic cycle worked beautifully with almost no money. The farm supplier was the key to this cashless utopia. He provided what the farmer needed for planting and household purposes in the spring, entering a credit to the account of the farmer. In the fall the farmer delivered his crop to the same merchant. Jefferson to Eppes, November 6, 1813, 13:404–32. Jefferson apparently did not recognize the dependence built into this relationship. After the Civil War, in the absence of any alternative institutional infrastructure for providing agricultural credit, it was precisely the farmer/supplier relationship that led to the impoverishment of small farmers throughout the South and the consolidation of landholding. As the scruples of the "furnishing merchant" evaporated, farmers sank deeper into the red with him year after year, until ultimately they either sold their land to pay him off, or the land was taken. See Goodwyn, *Populist Moment*, 20–25, 72.

26. Jefferson to Eppes, June 24, 1813, 13:276–77; Jefferson to Eppes, September 11, 1813, 13:353–69.

27. Jefferson, "Autobiography," 430; "Bill to Abolish Entails," 27.

28. Jefferson, "Opinion of Thomas Jefferson," 1:273.

29. I have been discussing the purpose for which Hamilton wanted a national bank and the reasons Jefferson did not. Whether the bank was constitutional is a separate question from the focus here, but, because so much of the debate over the bank was cast in the language of constitutionality, a summary of that issue is warranted. In the opinion Washington requested of him, Jefferson made two arguments against the bank's constitutionality. First, the Constitution does not include establishment of a corporation among the enumerated powers of the central government. Second, neither is the power to establish a corporation implied under the authority "to make all laws *necessary* and proper for carrying into execution the enumerated powers." A national bank may be a convenience in laying taxes, borrowing money, and regulating commerce, but it is not "necessary" in the sense that there is no other way to accomplish these objectives.

In his rebuttal Hamilton argued that the authority to establish corporations, or to choose any other means toward legitimate ends, is an inherent part of sovereignty. While in our federal system the central government does not have power in all areas, it is sovereign in those areas in which power is enumerated, and its power to employ appropriate means toward enumerated ends is implied. Jefferson's construal of the word *necessary*, he continued, was too narrow. If a particular means, such as a corporation, could reasonably be expected to serve a legitimate end of the government, it can be said to be necessary. Chief Justice Marshall would later borrow liberally from Hamilton's reasoning to establish the doctrine of implied powers in *McCulloch v. Maryland* (1819).

30. This description of the bank's life draws on Hammond, *Banks and Politics*, 144–226, in addition to the primary sources noted.

31. The Bank of North America had been chartered in 1781 by both the Continental Congress and the State of Pennsylvania, with a special relationship to the general government under the Articles of Confederation. Massachusetts had chartered a bank at Boston in 1784; Maryland one in Baltimore in 1790; and the Bank of New York, which had begun operation in 1784, got its state charter in 1791.

32. J. Van Fenstermaker, *The Development of American Commercial Banking: 1782–1837* (Kent, Ohio: Kent State University Press, 1965), table A–1, 111.

33. Jefferson to Gallatin, December 13, 1803, 3:436–39.

34. Madison is quoted in Hammond, *Banks and Politics*, 210.

35. Albert Gallatin, "Treasury Report on the Bank," in Krooss, *Documentary History*, 1:362–68.

36. "Speech by Senator William Crawford Favoring the Bank Recharter," in ibid., 1:393–95.

37. "Speech by Representative William Burwell Opposing the Bank Recharter," in ibid., 1:369–85; "Speech by Representative John Eppes Opposing Recharter," in ibid., 1:386–92.

CHAPTER 3: ANDREW JACKSON AND THE SECOND BANK OF THE UNITED STATES

1. The votes were 28 to 20 in the Senate and 107 to 85 in the House. *Abridgement of the Debates of Congress*, 11:753; and *Register of Debates in Congress*, 8:1074, cited in Jean Alexander Wilburn, *Biddle's Bank* (New York: Columbia University Press, 1967), 6.

2. According to James Alexander Hamilton (Alexander Hamilton's son), Jackson himself had contrasted his style of decision making based on his own convictions with Washington's penchant for weighing cabinet members' views. See Hamilton to Timothy Pickering, July 3, 1828, in James Alexander Hamilton, *Reminiscences of James Alexander Hamilton; or, Men and Events, at Home and Abroad, during Three Quarters of a Century* (New York: Charles Scribner's Sons, 1869), 77. With regard to ignoring the cabinet on the bank issue in particular, Jackson told Hamilton that he had decided to open his assault in his first annual message even though the action was "contrary to the opinion of so great a majority of [his] cabinet." Jackson to Hamilton, December 19, 1829, in ibid., 151.

3. The classic statement of the view that Jackson fought the second Bank of the United States on the people's behalf is Schlesinger's in *The Age of Jackson*. In this class conflict perspective Jackson took a stand against capital on behalf of urban workers and small farmers. Historians of the consensus school countered that Jackson opposed the bank as either the champion or the dupe of the rising breed of entrepreneurial capitalists who sought to throw off central control of the economy. See Richard Hofstadter, "Andrew Jackson and the Rise of

Liberal Capitalism," in *The American Political Tradition* (New York: Vintage Books, 1948), 45–67. In *Banks and Politics in America* (Princeton: Princeton University Press, 1957), 300–323, Bray Hammond similarly interprets Jackson's fight against the second Bank of the United States as motivated by advocacy for laissez-faire capitalism, though ultimately counterproductive as it paved the way for control of banking by a concentrated private interest in New York.

As I read Jackson, the class conflict scholars are correct that he viewed himself as champion of the common man. But consensus historians are also correct in recognizing that Jackson was not opposed to entrepreneurial capitalism—the common man could be an entrepreneur; they miss the crucial point, however, that Jackson insisted that individuals, not government-sanctioned corporations, be the entrepreneurs. But, whether Jackson opposed the bank on behalf of individuals as farmers and laborers or individuals as businesspeople, neither school has made the argument of this chapter: that Jackson could not see that a publicly designed banking regulator helped individuals—whether farmers, workers, or entrepreneurs—because he could not accept institutional design that violated his ideological insistence on a clear separation between the economy and the (very limited) government.

4. Wilburn, *Biddle's Bank*; Hammond, *Banks and Politics*, 300–323; Robert V. Remini, *Andrew Jackson and the Bank War* (New York: W. W. Norton, 1967), 41; John M. McFaul, "The Monsters in Conflict? State Banks and the Bank of the United States," *The Politics of Jacksonian Finance* (Ithaca: Cornell University Press, 1972), 16–57.

5. Arthur M. Schlesinger Jr., introduction to *The Age of Jackson*, The American Past. (New York: Book-of-the-Month Club, 1989), xix–xx.

6. Van Fenstermaker, *Development of American Commercial Banking*, table A-1, 111.

7. Ralph C. H. Catterall, *The Second Bank of the United States* (1902; rpt., Chicago: University of Chicago Press, 1960), 1–7.

8. "Speeches in the House of Representatives on Chartering the Second Bank," in Krooss, *Documentary History*, 1:412–55. During the War of 1812 the immediate purpose of many congressional advocates of a second national bank had been to provide money for fighting the war. Thus, wartime charter proposals had called for a large capital, up to fifty million dollars, composed of newly issued securities. Except for the unreformed Jeffersonian Republicans, who still resisted all banking, opposition to proposals for a new bank in this period concerned the size of the capital and the nature of the government securities. Six distinct attempts to establish a second Bank of the United States failed in Congress before the Treaty of Ghent. Catterall, *Second Bank*, 7–17. After the war the immediate need for cash no longer obscured regulation of the currency as the central purpose for a national bank.

9. "Speeches in the House," in Krooss, *Documentary History*, 1:412–19.

10. The Republican Party when the second Bank of the United States was founded was the party of Jefferson, though it included political leaders who did not see the world in wholly Jeffersonian terms. During the time frame covered

in this chapter, from Madison's through Jackson's presidency, the Republicans would divide into the Democratic-Republicans—Jackson's party and the direct precursor of today's Democratic Party—and the National Republicans. The National Republicans became the Whigs by the mid-1830s. The Whigs died out, their place in the two-party system assumed by today's Republican Party, which originated in the 1850s. Theodore J. Lowi and Benjamin Ginsberg, *American Government: Freedom and Power*, 4th ed. (New York: W. W. Norton, 1996), 459.

11. "State of the Union Message," December 5, 1815, in Krooss, *Documentary History*, 1:404.

12. "Annual Treasury Report on a National Bank," December 6, 1815, in ibid., 1:405–11.

13. "Veto of the 1814 Bill to Charter a Second Bank of the United States," January 20, 1815, in ibid., 1:401. Madison vetoed this particular bill in 1814 but invited one that met his objections to details.

14. The second Bank of the United States also did a limited amount of outright lending to state banks, but the "lender of last resort" technique was not a major regulatory tool in the United States at this point, though it was in England. In further contrast to Bank of the United States practice, the Bank of England was using reserve requirements, regulating how much credit a country bank could issue at the front end, as opposed to the American technique of regulating a bank by manipulating credit it had already issued.

15. Hammond, *Banks and Politics*, 211, 233.

16. Ibid., 243–44; Catterall, *Second Bank*, 21; Hofstadter, *American Political Tradition*, 42.

17. "Act to Charter Second Bank of the United States," in Krooss, *Documentary History*, 1:460–76.

18. Dallas to John C. Calhoun, December 24, 1815, Catterall, *Second Bank*, 19 n. 5.

19. Caterrall, *Second Bank*, 39–40.

20. On the bank under Jones, see ibid., 22–50; Hammond, *Banks and Politics*, 251–62, 268–72.

21. Catterall, *Second Bank*, 48–92; Hammond, *Banks and Politics*, 257–59, 262–63.

22. Thomas Payne Govan, *Nicholas Biddle: Nationalist and Public Banker, 1786–1844* (Chicago: University of Chicago Press, 1959), 76–78.

23. In the public administration classic *The Forest Ranger* (Baltimore: Johns Hopkins Press, 1960) Herbert Kaufman describes a technique for maintaining tight central control over policy and administration in a geographically far-flung federal agency. In the United States Forest Service the front line operator, the forest ranger, is rigorously trained in agency doctrine. The ranger is sent to locations in which he or she has no social support network and therefore comes to rely on the agency for such support. Compliance to centrally made policy is further ensured by rigorous requirements for reporting from the field and monitoring. This is precisely what Biddle did with the branch cashiers.

24. "Statement by Andrew Jackson on Removing Public Deposits from the Bank of the United States," September 18, 1833, in Krooss, *Documentary History*, 2:931, 935.

25. "Report from the House Ways and Means Committee on the President's Message," April 13, 1830, in ibid., 1:660–97; Albert Gallatin, "President of the National Bank of New York City, on the Banking System," 1831, in ibid., 1:738–56. Further evidence that policy makers supported the bank is to be found in the vote on charter renewal. Both chambers voted in favor, the House by 107 to 85 and the Senate by 28 to 20. For analysis by chamber and state, see Wilburn, *Biddle's Bank*, 9. Wilburn provides evidence that even the substantial majorities in favor of the bank understate its support: nine of the twenty senators who voted against renewal favored the bank but believed it more important to support the president. Ibid., 11–16.

26. Ibid., 49.

27. Ibid., 70.

28. Hammond, *Banks and Politics*, 300–323; Wilburn, *Biddle's Bank*, 70.

29. This sketch of Jackson's public philosophy is based on primary sources, including his eight annual messages, inaugural address, farewell address, bank veto, and "Maysville" veto. All are in James D. Richardson, ed., *A Compilation of the Messages and Papers of the Presidents: 1789–1897* (Washington, D.C.: GPO, 1896), vols. 2–3. I also relied upon two interpretations of Jackson's public philosophy by historians: Robert V. Remini, "Democracy," *The Legacy of Andrew Jackson: Essays on Democracy, Indian Removal, and Slavery* (Baton Rouge: Louisiana State University Press, 1988), 7–44; and Marvin Meyers, "The Restoration Theme: On Jackson's Message," *The Jacksonian Persuasion: Politics and Beliefs* (Stanford: Stanford University Press, 1957), 11–23. James Alexander Hamilton, in *Reminiscences*, made observations on Jackson's character and behavior, as well as his views, which also influenced my interpretation of the president's philosophy.

30. Jackson did share, with the founders, a wide range of experience in public and private roles in his own young country. He fought in the revolution as a boy. In private life he was a lawyer, planter, and land speculator in Tennessee. In public roles he had participated in Tennessee's constitutional convention, sat on the state Supreme Court, and served in the U.S. House and Senate. As a major-general in the state's militia and then the regular army, Jackson served in the War of 1812, led several decisive campaigns against native peoples, and was territorial governor of Florida. Richardson, *Messages and Papers*, 2:435–36.

31. Jackson's assertions that the founders intended direct democracy are quite extraordinary in light of the record we have that they did not. For example, he argued that "to the people belongs the right of electing their Chief Magistrate; it was never designed that their choice should in any case be defeated, either by the intervention of electoral colleges or by the agency confided, under certain contingencies, to the House of Representatives." "First Annual Message," December 8, 1829, in ibid., 2:447.

32. Ibid., 2:462; "Second Annual Message," December 6, 1830, in ibid., 2:528;

"Third Annual Message," December 6, 1831, in ibid., 2:558. Further evidence of Jackson's hostility to the institution from the beginning of his presidency appears in his personal correspondence. He wrote to James A. Hamilton on January 1, 1830, of his "opposition to a rechartering of the Bank of the United States." Hamilton, *Reminiscenses*, 153. And, upon withdrawing the government's deposits from the bank, Jackson told his cabinet that "the President's convictions of the dangerous tendencies of the Bank of the United States . . . were . . . overpowering *when he entered on the duties of Chief Magistrate*" (my emph.). "Statement by Andrew Jackson on removing the public deposits from the Bank of the United States," September 18, 1833, in Krooss, *Documentary History*, 2:926.

33. The argument that by 1832 there was far more support for the bank than opposition to it is most comprehensively made by Wilburn in *Biddle's Bank*. Wilburn gathered data to investigate support in Congress, among state banks, in state legislatures, and on the part of citizens generally. Analyzing the congressional vote on recharter, he found the majority of federal legislators from states throughout the West in favor as well as those in the middle states, with the exception of New York. Even there, in key votes in the state legislature, a majority of legislators in the western counties and New York City supported the bank. A majority from the Northeast also favored charter renewal, with the exceptions of New Hampshire and Maine. The South was the only region from which a majority of representatives of each state, except Louisiana, voted no. Analyzing memorials to Congress from state banks, citizens, and state legislatures, Wilburn found that state banks in most states, even in the South, actively supported renewal of the charter, as did citizens generally and most state legislatures. Less comprehensively, Robert Remini considered citizen memorials alone and viewed it as likely that popular support for the bank was overwhelming. *Jackson and the Bank War*, 41. In *Politics of Jacksonian Finance* McFaul focused on state bank support for the second national bank and concluded with Wilburn that it was strong across the United States.

34. Govan, *Nicholas Biddle.*

35. Remini, *Jackson and the Bank War.*

36. "Message by President Andrew Jackson Vetoing the Bank Recharter," July 10, 1832, in Krooss, *Documentary History*, 2:816–32; "Statement by Andrew Jackson on Removing Public Deposits from the Bank of the United States," September 18, 1833, in ibid., 2:926–41. In private correspondence as well as public remarks Jackson often charged the bank with political interference. He wrote to James Alexander Hamilton on June 3, 1830, that "the present hydra of corruption, [is] dangerous to our liberties by its corrupting influences everywhere, and not the least in the Congress of the Union." Hamilton, *Reminiscences*, 167. Also to Hamilton, on March 28, 1832, Jackson wrote, "When fully disclosed, and the branches looked into, it will be seen that its corrupting influence has been extended everywhere that could add to its strength." Hamilton, *Reminiscences*, 244. According to Remini, Jackson may have believed charges, never carefully investigated, that bank branches in Lexington, Louisville, Ports-

mouth, and New Orleans had thrown their weight against him in the presidential election of 1828. *Jackson and the Bank War*, 50–55.

37. Hamilton, *Reminiscenses*, 151; Remini, *Jackson and the Bank War*, 59–60; Sister M. Grace Madeleine, *Monetary and Banking Theories of Jacksonian Democracy* (Philadelphia: Sisters, Servants of the Immaculate Heart of Mary, 1943), 45–50.

38. "Second Annual Message," in Richardson, *Messages and Papers*, 2:528–29.

39. Jackson to Martin VanBuren, July 9, 1837, Hammond, *Banks and Politics*, 491; Jackson to J. A. Hamilton, February 1834, Hamilton, *Reminiscences*, 270.

40. "First Annual Message," in Richardson, *Messages and Papers*, 2:462.

41. "Report from the House Ways and Means Committee on the President's Message," April 13, 1830, in Krooss, *Documentary History*, 1:660–97.

42. Ibid.

43. Speaking of the government-controlled national bank the Ways and Means Committee supposed him to intend, Jackson wrote to J. A. Hamilton, June 3, 1830: "I have had no conversation with Mr. McDuffie on the subject of Banks; nor never did I contemplate such as in his imagination he has assumed." Hamilton, *Reminiscences*, 167.

44. William Gouge, *A Short History of Paper Money and Banking in the United States to Which Is Prefixed an Inquiry into the Principles of the System* (1833; rpt., New York: Augustus M. Kelley, 1968).

45. Gouge and his contemporaries did sometimes recognize that deposit credit could behave just like paper money, but deposit credit was lost from view more often than not, and the contemporary condemnation of banks was consistently leveled in terms of the evils of paper money.

46. Jackson to J. A. Hamilton, February 2, 1834, in Hamilton, *Reminiscences*, 269–70.

47. "State of the Union Message," December 5, 1836, in Krooss, *Documentary History*, 2:975.

48. "Farewell Address," March 4, 1837, in Richardson, *Messages and Papers*, 3:305–6.

49. "Act to Regulate the Deposit of the Public Money," June 23, 1836, in Krooss, *Documentary History*, 2:968–73.

50. "Act to Regulate the Value of Certain Foreign Gold Coins," in ibid., 2:1021.

51. "Devaluation Acts of June 28, 1834 and January 18, 1837," in ibid., 2:1040–49.

52. Hammond, *Banks and Politics*, 451.

53. "The Specie Circular," July 11, 1836, in Krooss, *Documentary History*, 2:1022–23.

54. "Message by President Martin Van Buren on the 'Economic Revulsion' of 1837," September 1837, in ibid., 2:1061–74.

55. "Two Speeches by Senator Daniel Webster [Massachusetts] Opposing the Independent Treasury Bill," January 31 and March 12, 1838, in ibid., 2:1075–91.

56. David Kinley, *The Independent Treasury of the United States* (New York: Thomas Y. Crowell, 1893), 30–33.

57. John J. Knox, *A History of Banking in the United States* (New York: Bradford Rhodes, 1908), 89.

58. Although national banks organized under the National Banking Act of 1864 could be designated by the secretary of the Treasury as public depositories or used as public fiscal agents, the Independent Treasury handled the bulk of the government's money. See Kinley, *Independent Treasury*, 69, 75, 83.

CHAPTER 4: FROM STATE BANKS TO NATIONAL BANKS

Qualitative and quantitative data on which this chapter is based were gathered from collections of primary material and from secondary works that both make a theoretical argument and display data. A major source of state banking data from the colonial period through 1900, including statutory and charter provisions as well as statistics, is Knox, "Banking under State Laws," pt. 2 of *History of Banking*. Van Fenstermaker gathered large numbers of bank charters and bank statements to create statistical series for the period 1782–1837 in *Development of American Commercial Banking*. Krooss includes state banking documents, including general and free banking acts and contemporary reports on free banking, in *Documentary History*, 2:1181–1239.

Major secondary works on state banking through the Civil War include William Gerald Shade's, *Banks or No Banks: The Money Issue in Western Politics* (Detroit: Wayne State University Press, 1972). For the states he studied—Ohio, Michigan, Indiana, Illinois, and Wisconsin—Shade examined qualitative and quantitative data, including the party press, ideas of party leaders as expressed in speeches, voting in state legislatures and constitutional conventions, and popular referenda. Larry Schweikart's *Banking in the American South from the Age of Jackson to Reconstruction* (Baton Rouge: Louisiana State University Press, 1987) includes extensive data for state banks in the Carolinas, Georgia, Virginia, Louisiana, Alabama, Florida, Mississippi, and Tennessee. Although the focus of Wilburn's *Biddle's Bank* is on the second Bank of the United States, it nevertheless provides valuable data on state bank circulation as well as material from state bank memorials to Congress and bankers' correspondence. Hammond discusses state banks throughout *Banks and Politics*; chapters 5, 7, and 17 focus on historical development.

1. The figure is computed from Van Fenstermaker, *Development of Commercial Banking*, tables A-1, A-6, A-7, and A-16.

2. Knox, *History of Banking*, 375.

3. "A Modest Enquiry into the Nature and Necessity of a Paper Currency," April 3, 1729, in Krooss, *Documentary History*, 1:24–30.

4. Knox, *History of Banking*, 595, 650.

5. Albert Gallatin, quoted in Hammond, *Banks and Politics*, 165.

6. Knox, *History of Banking*, 575; Schweikart, *Banking in the South*, 116–19.

7. Hammond, *Banks and Politics*, 166; Knox, *History of Banking*, 354–55.

8. Schweikart, *Banking in the South*, 127.

9. Knox, *History of Banking*, 564–65.

10. Schweikart, *Banking in the South*, 108.

11. Hammond, *Banks and Politics*, 166; Knox, *History of Banking*, 631–34.

12. Hammond, *Banks and Politics*, 559.

13. Knox, *History of Banking*, 365–68. Hammond, *Banks and Politics*, 549–56.

14. Ibid., 556–63; Knox, *History of Banking*, 399–407.

15. Van Fenstermaker, *Development of Commercial Banking*, table A-21, 163–64.

16. Ibid., table A-15, 146–49.

17. Ibid., table A-5, 115.

18. Schweikart, *Banking in the South*, 100.

19. Ibid., 122–23; Knox, *History of Banking*, 528–30.

20. Ibid., 543–61.

21. Ibid., 637–38.

22. Hammond, *Banks and Politics*, 609; Shade, *Banks or No Banks*, 28–33.

23. Knox, *History of Banking*, 694–95 , 698–99; Hammond, *Banks and Politics*, 618–21; Shade, *Banks or No Banks*, 183–85.

24. Ibid., 22–26, 34, 36.

25. Van Fenstermaker, *Development of Commercial Banking*, table A-1, 111.

26. "Commentary," in Krooss, *Documentary History*, 656.

27. Shade, *Banks or No Banks*, 40–50.

28. Daniel Webster, "Two Speeches Opposing the Independent Treasury Bill."

29. "Message by President Martin Van Buren on the 'Economic Revulsion' of 1837," September 1837, in Krooss, *Documentary History*, 2:1061–74.

30. George Brown Tindall with David E. Shi, *America: A Narrative History*, 3d ed. (New York: W. W. Norton, 1992), 1:418–22.

31. This argument is much indebted to Shade, *Banks or No Banks*, in which the central thesis is that banking became a partisan issue in the Old Northwest only in the 1840s.

32. "Albert Gallatin on Free Banking, 1841," in Krooss, *Documentary History*, 2:1194–1205; Hammond, *Banks and Politics*, 572–604.

33. To help relieve banks of the charge that they were privileged, the law referred to them not as corporations but as "associations." In short order, however, the New York courts decided that an entity with the government-granted privilege of limited liability, regardless of what it was called, was indeed a corporation.

34. Ibid., 573.

35. Issuing a paper currency was not dealing in money, in which the advantages of competition might be felt, Gallatin argued: it was making money. Gallatin went on to argue that fixing the value of money, along with fixing the standard of weights and measures, "are preliminary enactments which regulate and govern the freest possible trade" and are vested in the general government. "On Free Banking," in Krooss, *Documentary History*, 2:1196.

36. Shade, *Banks or No Banks*, 33. Shade wrote about the states of the Old

Northwest, but his conclusion regarding the rationale for supporting free banking is generally applicable.

37. James Willard Hurst, *The Legitimacy of the Business Corporation: 1780–1970* (Charlottesville: University Press of Virginia, 1970), 13–57.

38. James Willard Hurst, *Law and Markets in U.S. History* (Madison: University of Wisconsin Press, 1982), 47–50.

39. Morton J. Horwitz, *The Transformation of American Law: 1780–1860* (Cambridge, Mass.: Harvard University Press), 111–39.

40. Hurst, *Legitimacy of the Corporation*, 29.

41. Ibid., 33.

42. Of approximately $2.6 billion spent by the Union to fight the Civil War, taxation accounted for 21 percent, Treasury notes ("greenbacks") for 17 percent, and bonds for the balance. Tindall, *America*, 672.

43. "Annual Treasury Report, 1861," in Krooss, *Documentary History*, 2:1340–45; "Annual Treasury Report, 1862," in ibid., 2:1346–54.

44. "National Bank Act," February 25, 1863, in Krooss, *Documentary History*, 2:1381–82; "National Bank Act," June 3, 1864, in ibid., 2:1383–1411.

45. Before April 1865 purchases of government bonds by national banks under the National Bank Act accounted for only 3.6 percent of the borrowings of the government. Knox, *History of Banking*, 96.

46. Ibid., 312.

47. Ibid., 634.

48. Ibid., 387.

49. Ibid., 422.

50. Board of Governors of the Federal Reserve System, *Banking and Monetary Statistics* (Washington, D.C.: National Capital Press, 1943), 6, cited in Susan Estabrook Kennedy, *The Banking Crisis of 1933* (Lexington: University Press of Kentucky, 1973), 7.

CHAPTER 5: THE FEDERAL RESERVE BOARD

1. The concept of the "great chain of being" receives its classic scholarly treatment in Arthur Lovejoy, *The Great Chain of Being: A Study of the History of an Idea* (Cambridge, Mass.: Harvard University Press, 1964). A more recent discussion is E. F. Schumacher, *A Guide for the Perplexed* (New York: Harper Colophon, 1977).

2. "Annual Treasury Report, 1862," in Krooss, *Documentary History*, 2:1351.

3. Milton Friedman and Anna Jacobson Schwartz, *A Monetary History of the United States: 1867–1960* (Princeton: Princeton University Press, 1967), 17.

4. Board of Governors of Fed, *Statistics*, 6, cited in Kennedy, *Banking Crisis*, 7.

5. Fractional reserves behind state bank deposits could include the kinds of money which backed deposits in national banks, gold and greenbacks and, depending on state law, national bank notes as well.

6. Friedman and Schwartz, *Monetary History*, 17.

7. Robert Craig West, *Banking Reform and the Federal Reserve: 1863–1923* (Ithaca: Cornell University Press, 1974), 25.

8. *Statutes at Large*, 12:709, in Krooss, *Documentary History*, 2: 1334.

9. That departure from gold was intended as a temporary emergency measure is clear, for example, in Treasury Secretary Samuel Chase's annual reports in 1861 and 1862, in Krooss, *Documentary History*, 2:1340–54. Senator John Sherman of Ohio, chair of the Senate Banking Committee, articulated the same intent repeatedly during and after the war. See his speeches in the Senate of February 10, 1862, and February 13, 1862, in Krooss, *Documentary History*, 2:1312–21, 2:1355–80. The initial greenback and national bank statutes themselves anticipate a return to gold.

10. Irwin Unger, *The Greenback Era: A Social and Political History of American Finance, 1865–1879* (Princeton: Princeton University Press, 1964), 126–29.

11. Ibid., 120–26.

12. Atkinson to William B. Allison, April 12, 1874, Allison MSS, Iowa State Department of History and Archives, cited in ibid., 124.

13. "Speech by Senator John Sherman on Restoring Specie Payments," January 16, 1873, in Krooss, *Documentary History*, 2:1614.

14. See McCulloch's Annual Treasury Reports of 1865 and 1867, in ibid., 2:1457–82.

15. It was banking historian Lloyd W. Mints who labeled this theory the "real bills doctrine" in *A History of Banking Theory in Great Britain and the United States* (Chicago: University of Chicago Press, 1945), 1.

16. "View of George Coe, President of the American Exchange Bank, before the House Banking and Currency Committee," January 14, 1874, in Krooss, *Documentary History*, 3:1617.

17. Mints, *History of Banking Theory*, 9. In addition to the "most elegant" statement of real bills in the theory's history, Mints credits Smith with its first thorough exposition. Ibid., 25.

18. Adam Smith, *An Inquiry into the Nature and Causes of the Wealth of Nations* (1776; rpt., New York: Alfred A. Knopf, 1991), bk. 2, 265–72.

19. Mints, *History of Banking Theory*, 27.

20. Smith, *Wealth of Nations*, 257–67.

21. McCulloch had substantially contracted the money supply from 1865 through 1867, retiring $44 million in greenbacks and refunding $290 million in quasi-monetary interest-bearing securities. Unger, *Greenback Era*, 42–43.

22. Ibid., 41–67.

23. Ibid., 195–212.

24. "The Resumption Act," January 14, 1875, in Krooss, *Documentary History*, 3:1683–84. In addition to moving toward restoration of the gold standard, the Resumption Act bowed to the real bills doctrine. It repealed both the limit on total circulation of national bank notes and the geographic distribution requirements for those notes.

25. Unger, *Greenback Era*, 286.

26. Ibid., 208–12.

27. Richard Hofstadter, *The Age of Reform* (New York: Alfred A. Knopf, 1955).

28. Goodwyn, *Populist Moment*; George Brown Tindall with David Shi, *America: A Narrative History* (New York: W. W. Norton, 1992), 2:885–96.

29. Friedman and Schwartz, *Monetary History*, 41.

30. Ibid., 91.

31. "The Bland-Allison Act," February 28, 1878, in Krooss, *Documentary History*, 3: 1917–18.

32. "The Sherman Silver Purchase Act," July 14, 1890, in ibid., 3:1952–54.

33. *Sound Currency*, in Krooss, *Documentary History*, 3:2006–7 (my emph.).

34. "The Cross of Gold," July 8, 1896, in ibid., 3:2009–15.

35. Friedman and Schwartz, *Monetary History*, 137.

36. Thomas K. McCraw, *Prophets of Regulation* (Cambridge, Mass.: Belknap Press, 1984), 51.

37. Ibid., 97–98.

38. A trust company was a state-chartered financial institution similar to a bank but with broader powers and more loosely regulated than state banks.

39. The preceding description of what worried Democrats in regard to the money trust and the mechanisms via which they hypothesized that it operated is based on "Hearings before the Pujo Committee," 1912–13, in Krooss, *Documentary History*, 3:2107–42; and on the "Final Report from the Pujo Committee," in ibid., 3:2143–95.

40. H. Parker Willis, *The Federal Reserve System: Legislation, Organization and Operation* (New York: Ronald Press, 1923), 8–9, 12–13.

41. "The Gold Standard Act," March 14, 1900, in Krooss, *Documentary History*, 3:2016–22; Willis, *Federal Reserve System*, 13–15.

42. The process through which groups in the business and banking community developed their critique of the banking framework and began to promote that critique in the political arena has figured prominently in scholarly inquiry into the founding of the Fed since the beginning of such inquiry. H. Parker Willis, for example, treated it in his 1923 study, *Federal Reserve System*, 7–12. See also West, *Banking Reform*, 42–51. James Livingston, in *Origins of the Federal Reserve System: Money, Class, and Corporate Capitalism, 1890–1913* (Ithaca: Cornell University Press, 1986), argues persuasively that businesspeople and bankers, in association with mainstream journalists and academics, not only organized to develop an analysis and disseminate it broadly among themselves but also set out to "educate" the masses in their view and to move the political process. He maintains further that the business-based monetary reform movement was about more than monetary reform: it was the "matrix of capitalist class consciousness." That is to say, these groups self-consciously developed a culture within which to interpret the political economy. I would say that they worked out their public philosophy.

The conventional interpretation remains that establishment of the Federal Reserve System was a result of the business-based movement for currency reform. Business influence receives implicit approval in interpretations that have regarded monetary reform as a technical issue—that is, essentially as an inquiry into the scientific (natural) laws of money—and implicit or explicit disapproval in those that have seen it as a manifestation of the political or social power of capitalist interests. Livingston reviews the literature, ibid., 18–29.

43. Friedman and Schwartz, *Monetary History*, 168–69.

44. Friedman and Schwartz regard this second sense of inelasticity as confused because it failed to recognize fully the significance of deposits as money (which murky thinking was not new to this period) and because Friedman and Schwartz are critics of the real bills doctrine on which the concept relies. Ibid., 169.

45. Ibid., 156–57.

46. West, *Banking Reform*, 69–72.

47. Details of the governance structure included organizing subscribing banks into fifteen district associations. Each district association chose two members of the central bank's forty-six-member board of directors. Nine more directors were chosen based on stock ownership; four executive branch officials sat ex officio; two deputy governors were elected to the board by its other members; and the governor was selected by the president from a list given him by the board. A nine-member executive committee was to consist of five members chosen by the board, the two deputy governors (who had also been chosen by the board), the governor, and the comptroller of the currency.

48. Willis, *Federal Reserve System*, 83.

49. West, *Banking Reform*, 76.

50. Ibid., 148.

51. "Report from the Pujo Committee," Krooss, *Documentary History*, 3:2143–95.

52. Alfred Cash Koeniger, "'Unreconstructed Rebel': The Political Thought and Senate Career of Carter Glass, 1929–1936," Ph.D. diss., Vanderbilt University, 1980; Rixey Smith and Norman Beasley, *Carter Glass* (New York: Longmans, Green, 1939); Carter Glass, *An Adventure in Constructive Finance* (1927; rpt., New York: Arno Press, 1975).

53. On Wilson's public philosophy, see Arthur S. Link, *Wilson: The New Freedom* (Princeton: Princeton University Press, 1956); and Martin J. Sklar, *The Corporate Reconstruction of American Capitalism, 1890–1916* (New York: Cambridge University Press, 1988), 383–430.

54. Glass, *Adventure*, 68.

55. Carter Glass, introduction to Willis, *Federal Reserve System*, ix.

56. This is not to say that Glass and Willis were the first to propose a decentralized reserve system or district reserve institutions. The option had been discussed in the business monetary reform forums. In *Banking Reform*, 60–65, West ascribes its first systematic and published articulation to Victor Morawetz. My point here is that Glass was now proposing this particular structural innovation. It would seem unnecessary to insert such a note, but in the case of the Federal Reserve Act an enormous credit claiming brouhaha developed about ten years after the system was in operation. Initially after its passage, President

Wilson himself was given much of the credit for the legislation, but it appears to have been common knowledge among those involved that Glass and Willis authored the bill and integrated the compromises required for passage. At first business and bankers, unhappy about several major provisions in the new framework, were most interested in dissociating themselves from and criticizing features of Glass's proposal which diverged from the earlier Aldrich plan, which they had supported.

As the Federal Reserve System was actually built and statutorily ambiguous or unspecified details ironed out in ways that worked for them, bankers, business, and Republican politicians wanted credit to go to themselves and Paul Warburg, chief draftsman of the Aldrich plan, as apparently did Warburg, who wrote a book comparing the plans: *The Federal Reserve System: Its Origin and Growth* (1930; rpt., New York: Arno Press, 1975).

Considerable scholarly effort was then expended identifying the origin and development of the particular elements incorporated into the Federal Reserve Act. Scholars have established that Willis and Glass did not invent the Federal Reserve System on a clean slate; they worked with the elements that had been under discussion. There is no doubt that Willis used material from the Aldrich proposal as well as other proposals; he says that he did in *Federal Reserve*, 132. A sideshow in the credit claiming row occurred when a contemporary historian, Charles Seymour, published a piece claiming that Wilson's close advisor, E. M. House, was chiefly responsible for developing the Federal Reserve Act. Although the claim is absurd, Carter Glass was vicious in putting it to rest. The valuable legacy of an embarrassing bickering match is Glass's inside account of the development of the Federal Reserve Act, *Adventure in Constructive Finance*.

57. Ibid., 122.

58. For this preliminary proposal, see ibid., 81–82; Willis, "First Complete Draft of Glass Bill," app. 1 in *Federal Reserve*, 1531–53.

59. H. Parker Willis, Glass's staff expert, had been a graduate student of University of Chicago economist J. Laurence Laughlin—who had staffed or consulted with several private sector banking reform committees—and remained in cordial and frequent communication with his former teacher. Gabriel Kolko takes the relationship between Willis and Laughlin, and reliance by Glass and Willis on much of the diagnosis and analysis developed by private sector banking reform efforts, as definitive evidence that Glass's legislation served the private interest of big bankers. *The Triumph of Conservatism: A Reinterpretation of American History, 1900–1916* (1963; rpt., Chicago: Quadrangle Paperbacks, 1967).

60. Glass, *Adventure*, 73–92.

61. Among them, Livingston, *Origins of the Fed*, 215–34; Kolko, *Triumph of Conservatism*, 225–54.

62. William Jennings Bryan and Mary Baird Bryan, *The Memoirs of William Jennings Bryan* (Chicago: John C. Winston Co., 1925), 370–73; Link, *Wilson*, 206.

63. Ibid., 211–12.

64. Quoted in Glass, *Adventure*, 125.

65. Ibid., 199.

66. "First Draft of Glass Bill," 1538–39.

67. Glass told his fellows in the House: "Nearly every power conferred by this bill on the Federal reserve board . . . has been for half a century vested by the national-bank act in the Secretary of the Treasury and the Comptroller of the Currency. . . . Strictly speaking, the Federal reserve board performs no banking function; the banking business of the system is within the exclusive jurisdiction of the regional reserve banks, owned and operated by an aggregation of individual member banks." *Congressional Record*, vol. 50, pt. 5, September 10, 1913, 4644, cited in Lester V. Chandler, *Benjamin Strong: Central Banker* (Washington, D.C.: Brookings Institution, 1958), 11.

68. "Speech in the House of Representatives," December 22, 1913, app. A in Glass, *Adventures*, 317.

69. "The Federal Reserve Act of 1913," app. 6 in Willis, *Federal Reserve System*, 1667–96.

70. Hoover initiated the Glass-Steagall Act of 1932 primarily to protect the international gold standard. It permitted the Federal Reserve System to hold government bonds as backing for Federal Reserve notes, freeing up a portion of the gold that had been held for that purpose to meet an international drain. The law also made government securities eligible for rediscount at Federal Reserve Banks. Senator Glass opposed this measure, which violated his fundamental position that Federal Reserve Banks should only rediscount paper that arose from real commercial transactions—until Hoover convinced him that it was required to save the gold standard, the other natural monetary control mechanism in which Glass believed. Kennedy, *Banking Crisis*, 46–47; Koeniger, "Unreconstructed Rebel," 38–39; Friedman and Schwartz, *Monetary History*, 321.

The Emergency Banking Act of 1933 (in Krooss, *Documentary History*, 4:2697–2705) was passed in March immediately after Roosevelt took office. It retrospectively confirmed his authority to declare the bank holiday, specified the procedures for reopening the banks, and authorized emergency issue of Federal Reserve notes.

71. Kennedy, *Banking Crisis*, 233–35.

72. Ibid., 203.

73. Writing to Oliver J. Sands on December 16, 1931, Glass maintained that the banks were "responsible for the debacle which now oppresses the country." Quoted in Koeniger, "Unreconstructed Rebel," 32; see also 48–49.

74. "The Banking Act of 1933," in Krooss, *Documentary History*, 4:2751.

75. Kennedy, *Banking Crisis*, 212–13.

76. "Banking Act of 1933," 4:2755–60, 2768–69.

77. Ibid., 4:2726, 2749–50.

78. Officials of the reserve banks began the process of developing statutorily unanticipated practices and structures even as the system organized itself in 1914. They first set up a Conference of Governors, composed of the top officer, or "governor," of each of the twelve reserve banks. The group was a device for the governors to develop and disseminate among themselves approaches to ad-

ministering the organizations they were creating. Acting in concert to develop administrative procedure would seem unobjectionable, but the governors stumbled in the direction of coordinated monetary policy. In order to earn their own expenses, reserve banks were authorized by the Federal Reserve Act to buy and sell securities in the open market for their own portfolios. As they began to do this, two things became apparent. First, there was no ready market in some of the reserve districts for eligible short-term public and private instruments, so the reserve banks entered the New York money market. Second, when several of these big institutions were in the market, they distorted it. In response, the various reserve banks began to permit the Federal Reserve Bank of New York to buy and sell for them. In 1922, after the secretary of the Treasury had complained of the effects of reserve bank transactions on the market for the federal government's bonds, the governors conference set up a committee of five governors to coordinate open market operations, and by 1925 this committee was acting vigorously in pursuit of monetary policy objectives. Chandler, *Benjamin Strong*, 69–70, 210–15, 233–34.

79. Chandler, *Benjamin Strong*.

80. Friedman and Schwartz, *Monetary History*, 414–19. The name of the reserve bank's open market policy body changed a couple of times. It became the Federal Open Market Committee with the Banking Act of 1933 and remains so.

81. "Banking Act of 1933," 4:2732–49.

82. Ibid., 4:2750.

83. Kennedy, *Banking Crisis*, 214–20.

84. Marriner S. Eccles, *Beckoning Frontiers: Public and Personal Recollections* (New York: Alfred A. Knopf, 1951), 37, 51–53.

85. Ibid., 73–74.

86. Donald F. Kettl, *Leadership at the Fed* (New Haven: Yale University Press, 1986), 47. Eccles confirms Kettl's observation that he had never read Keynes's books in *Beckoning Frontiers*, 132.

87. Ibid., 37–38, 76–81.

88. Ibid., 166.

89. The major provisions of Eccles's bill as introduced are detailed in Koeniger, "Unreconstructed Rebel," 121–30, including a side-by-side comparison with corresponding provisions of the bill as it emerged from Glass's committee. Title II of the "Banking Act of 1935" is in Krooss, *Documentary History*, 4:2912–18.

90. Miller and VanHoose, *Modern Money and Banking*, 405–29. All three monetary policy instruments operate through depository institutions' reserves. In open-market operations the Fed increases and decreases the money supply by buying and selling U.S. government securities. When the Fed buys, depository institution reserves ultimately increase, thus credit can be expanded; when it sells, depository institution reserves decrease, and money tightens. Discounting is the process in which the Fed lends to depository institutions. Banks borrow from the Fed by temporarily selling eligible assets or by offering a promissory note based on U.S. government securities; the Fed pays the depository

institution by increasing its reserve account. The discount rate is the rate the Fed charges on its loans to depository institutions: a lower rate induces depository institutions to borrow more from the Fed, thus lend more, thus increase the money supply. A high discount rate has the opposite effect. Finally, the Fed can change reserve requirements for depository institutions. A lower reserve requirement means a bank can lend more, and a higher requirement means the bank must lend less.

91. The federal debt was less than a billion dollars when the Fed was created in 1913 but about twenty-seven billion dollars when World War I ended a few years later. Eccles, *Beckoning Frontiers*, 167.

92. "Testimony of Governor Marriner Eccles of the Federal Reserve Board on Banking," March 4, 1935, in Krooss, *Documentary History*, 4:2876–78.

93. Eccles, *Beckoning Frontiers*, 173.

94. Eccles, "Testimony," 4:2867.

95. Bentham, *Principles of Morals and Legislation*; Thomas A. Spragens, *The Irony of Liberal Reason* (Chicago: University of Chicago Press, 1981), 108–21.

CHAPTER 6: PROGRESSIVISM AND THE S&L FRAMEWORK

1. For an overview of the factors involved in the failure of the S&L framework, see National Commission on Financial Institution Reform, Recovery and Enforcement, *Origins and Causes of the S&L Debacle: A Blueprint for Reform*, Report to the President and Congress (Washington, D.C.: GPO, 1993). Scholarly studies offering reasons for S&Ls' failure include Thomas Romer and Barry R. Weingast, "Political Foundations of the Thrift Debacle," in *Politics and Economics in the Eighties*, ed. Alberto Alesina and Geoffrey Carliner (Chicago: University of Chicago Press, 1991), 175–209; Robert E. Litan, "Comment," in ibid., 209–14; James R. Barth, *The Great Savings and Loan Debacle* (Washington, D.C.: American Enterprise Institute, 1991); R. Dan Brumbaugh, *Thrifts under Siege* (Cambridge, Mass.: Ballinger, 1988); Lawrence J. White, *The S&L Debacle: Public Policy Lessons for Bank and Thrift Regulation* (New York: Oxford University Press, 1991); and Edward J. Kane, *The S&L Insurance Mess: How Did It Happen?* (Washington, D.C.: Urban Institute Press, 1989). Also helpful is U.S. Congress, Congressional Budget Office, *Resolving the Thrift Crisis* (Washington, D.C.: GPO, 1993).

2. Important works of philosophy and political economy foundational to progressivism include John Dewey, *The Public and its Problems* (Athens, Ohio: Swallow Press, 1927); Charles Sanders Peirce, "The Fixation of Belief," in *Pragmatism: The Classic Writings*, ed. H. S. Thayer (Indianapolis: Hackett, 1982); William James, *Essays in Radical Empiricism* (New York: Longmans, Green, 1916); John R. Commons, *Legal Foundations of Capitalism* (1924; rpt., Madison: University of Wisconsin Press, 1968); Thorstein Veblen, *The Instinct of Workmanship* (1914; rpt., New York: W. W. Norton, 1964); Herbert Croly, *The Promise of American Life* (1909; rpt., Cambridge, Mass.: Harvard University Press, 1965); Walter Lippmann, *Drift and Mastery* (1914; rpt., Englewood Cliffs,

N.J.: Prentice-Hall, 1961). Anderson's *Pragmatic Liberalism* is a current interpretation and elaboration of progressivism.

3. Critics of progressive thought and its institutional offspring, both public and private, include R. Jeffrey Lustig, *Corporate Liberalism: The Origins of Modern American Political Theory, 1890–1920* (Berkeley: University of California Press, 1982); Wendell Berry, *Unsettling of America: Culture and Agriculture* (San Francisco: Sierra Club Books, 1977); Sheldon Wolin, "The Age of Organization and the Sublimation of Politics," *Politics and Vision* (Boston: Little, Brown, 1960), 352–434; Theodore J. Lowi, *The End of Liberalism* (New York: W. W. Norton, 1979); Charles Lindblom, *Politics and Markets* (New York: Basic Books, 1977); Gabriel Kolko, *The Triumph of Conservatism* (New York: Free Press of Glencoe, 1963); E. E. Schattschneider, *The Semi-Sovereign People* (Hinsdale, Ill.: Dryden Press, 1960); Dwight Waldo, *The Administrative State* (New York: Ronald Press, 1948).

4. Joan Hoff Wilson, *Herbert Hoover, Forgotten Progressive* (Boston: Little, Brown, 1975); Lee Nash, ed., *Understanding Herbert Hoover: Ten Perspectives* (Stanford: Stanford University Press, 1987); Susan Estabrook Kennedy, *The Banking Crisis of 1933* (Lexington: University Press of Kentucky, 1973).

5. Among his positive efforts to address the Depression, Hoover provided leadership for establishment of the Reconstruction Finance Corporation and the Federal Home Loan Banks, initiated the Glass-Steagall Act of 1932 (an emergency banking measure), secured congressional funding for public works projects, and aggressively used the authority of his office to urge business leaders to voluntary responsive action.

6. My interpretation of Herbert Hoover's public philosophy is based on his philosophical works: *American Individualism* (New York: Doubleday, 1923); and *The Challenge to Liberty* (New York: Charles Scribner's Sons, 1934); his memoirs: *The Memoirs of Herbert Hoover: The Cabinet and the Presidency, 1920–1933* (New York: Macmillan, 1952); and *The Memoirs of Herbert Hoover: The Great Depression, 1929–1941* (New York: Macmillan, 1952); and certain public remarks : "The President's News Conference of December 11, 1931," *Public Papers of the Presidents: Herbert Hoover, 1929–33* (Washington, D.C.: GPO, 1976), 3:628–34; "Annual Message to the Congress on the State of the Union," ibid., 4:841–54. A secondary source on which I also draw for Hoover's public philosophy, as well as the consistency between his ideology and public action, is Wilson, *Forgotten Progressive.*

7. Friedrich A. Hayek, *The Constitution of Liberty* (Chicago: University of Chicago Press, 1960).

8. Hoover, *Memoirs: Cabinet and Presidency,* 92–96.

9. "Address to the White House Conference on Home Building and Home Ownership," in Hoover, *Public Papers,* 3:573.

10. "Statement on the White House Conference on Home Building and Home Ownership," ibid., 2:313–15; "Remarks to the Planning Committee of the White House Conference on Home Building and Home Ownership," ibid., 2:376–79; President's Conference on Home Building and Home Ownership, *Directory of*

Committee Personnel: December 2–5, 1931 (Washington, D.C.: Commerce Department, 1931); "President's News Conference of November 13, 1931," in Hoover, *Public Papers*, 3:538–42; "Statement Proposing the Establishment of the Home Loan Discount Bank System," ibid., 3:542–45; "Address to the White House Conference on Home Building and Home Ownership," ibid., 3:572–77.

11. Although they were most commonly called "building and loan associations," the same kind of organization also went under the rubrics *cooperative bank* in some states and *homestead association* in Louisiana. In New York and New Jersey by the 1930s they were already called "savings and loan associations."

12. The minutes of the meetings of the Oxford Provident Building Association of Philadelphia County throughout its first year are reprinted in Morton Bodfish, *History of Building and Loan in the United States* (Chicago: United States Building and Loan League, 1931), 37–57.

13. The original bylaws of the Oxford Provident are included in the minutes of its first meeting. Ibid., 37–43.

14. In Hoover's day encouraging home ownership and promoting thrift among low- and middle-income Americans are repeatedly stated as the two purposes of building and loan associations by leaders in the associations, the state building and loan leagues, and the U.S. League of Building and Loans. See Fred G. Stickel, New Jersey Building and Loan League, in House Committee on Banking and Currency, Subcommittee on H.R. 7620, *Creation of a System of Federal Home Loan Banks: Hearings on H.R. 7620*, 72d Cong., 1st sess., 1932 , 202; William Best, U.S. Building and Loan League, in ibid., 28; Morton Bodfish, U.S. Building and Loan League, Senate Committee on Banking and Currency, Subcommittee on Senate Bill 2959, *Creation of a System of Federal Home Loan Banks: Hearings on S. 2959*, 72d Cong., 1st sess., 1932, 79.

15. Horace Russell, *Savings and Loan Associations*, 2d ed. (Albany: Matthew Bender, 1960), 23; Bodfish, *Building and Loan*, 6–8, 11.

16. Ibid., 8–9, 13–14.

17. I generalize regarding the design of savings banks, but, like all of the banks considered in this study, savings banks were creatures of legislatures, and there was variation over time and from state to state in their constitution. For state-by-state analysis of savings banks at the beginning of the twentieth century, see Knox, *History of Banking*, 334–37, 358, 341–47, 369–70, 373–74, 388–89, 425–27, 439–41, 464–64, 468, 509–11, 536, 560, 571,688–90, 705, 752, 759, 774–77, 787–88. For a picture of mutual savings banks as late as the 1950s consistent with the generalization offered here, see American Institute of Banking, Section American Bankers Association, *Savings Banking* (New York: American Institute of Banking, 1951), esp. 6–8, 39–42, 448–68.

18. Russell, *Savings and Loan*, 23–30; Bodfish, *Building and Loan*, 75–120.

19. Thomas B. Marvell, *The Federal Home Loan Bank Board* (New York: Praeger, 1969), 14.

20. Ibid., 7.

21. "Excerpts from Building and Loan Annals, 1931," in Senate, *Home Loan Bank Hearings*, 81–82.

22. Other financial institutions, life insurance companies in particular, were also making mortgages that they referred to as "amortized" before the Depression. Outside of building and loans, however, *amortization* meant that some portion of the principle was paid over the life of the loan, but the loan was not fully paid upon expiration and required renewal.

23. President's Conference on Home Building and Home Ownership, *Home Finance and Taxation: Loans, Assessments and Taxes on Residential Property*, Reports of the Committee on Finance and the Committee on Taxation (Washington, D.C.: National Capital Press, 1932).

24. Russell, *Savings and Loan*, 23–28; Bodfish, *Building and Loan*, 100–115, 121–29.

25. Ibid., 122.

26. House, *Home Loan Bank Hearings*, 160.

27. This sketch of the impact of the Depression on building and loans, and on the markets for real estate and home mortgage credit, is based on testimony presented in 1932 during the House and Senate hearings on the federal home loan bank bill. See n. 14.

28. "News Conference of November 13, 1931: Home Loan Discount Bank System," in Hoover, *Public Papers*, 3:538–42; "Statement Proposing the Establishment of the Home Loan Discount Bank System," ibid., 3:542–45; "Annual Message to the Congress on the State of the Union," ibid., 3:589–90; "The President's News Conference of July 22, 1932," ibid., 4:329–31; "Statement about Signing the Federal Home Loan Bank Act," ibid., 4:331–34; "Radio Address to the Women's Conference on Current Problems," ibid., 4:446–47.

29. *Federal Home Loan Bank Act of 1932*, U.S. *Statutes at Large* 47 (1932): 725–41.

30. Hoover, *Memoirs: The Great Depression*, 86–95, 111–15; "Special Message to the Congress on Pending Legislation to Promote Economic Recovery," *Public Papers*, 4:1001.

31. R. Graeme Smith, Connecticut General Life Insurance Company, in Senate, *Home Loan Bank Hearings*, 274–75.

32. Senate Committee on Banking and Currency, Subcommittee on S. 6, *Proposed Repeal of the Federal Home Loan Bank Act: Hearings on S. 6*, 73d Cong., 1st sess., 1933.

33. *Home Owners' Loan Act of 1933*, U.S. *Statutes at Large* 48 (1933): 128–35.

34. For descriptions of the activity and impact of the Home Owners Loan Corporation, see the note to Franklin D. Roosevelt, "The Home Owners Loan Act Is Signed—the President Urges Delay in Foreclosures," in *The Public Papers and Addresses of Franklin D. Roosevelt* (New York: Random House, 1938), 2:233–37; and Josephine Hedges Ewalt, *A Business Reborn: The Savings and Loan Story, 1930–1960* (Chicago: American Savings and Loan Institute Press, 1962), 36–43.

35. Federal Home Loan Bank Board, "Regulation 3—Regulations Regarding Procedure to Be Followed in Connection with the Handling of Applications for Direct Loans to Individuals," in Senate, *Proposed Repeal*, 65–74.

36. An example of advocacy for federal chartering among building and loan leadership, before the Federal Home Loan Bank Act was passed, is provided by a speech delivered to the centennial convention of the United States Building and Loan League on August 13, 1931, by Charles O'Connor Hennessey, president of a New York building and loan association, reproduced in Senate, *Home Loan Bank Hearings*, 615.

37. Ewalt, *Business Reborn*, 75.

38. Ibid., 84–87.

39. *National Housing Act of 1934, U.S. Statutes at Large* 48 (1934): 1246–65.

40. House Committee on Banking and Currency, *National Housing Act: Hearings on H.R. 9620*, 73d Cong., 2d sess., 1934, 41; Senate Committee on Banking and Currency, *National Housing Act: Hearings on S. 3603*, 73d Cong., 2d sess., 1934, 207–8.

41. Ewalt, *Business Reborn*, 93–100; House, *National Housing Act Hearings*, 17.

42. Eccles, *Beckoning Frontiers*, 144–61; Harry Hopkins, Federal Emergency Relief administrator; Winfield Riefler, economic advisor to the Emergency Council; Albert Deane, National Recovery Administration; Marriner Eccles, assistant to the secretary of the Treasury; Frances Perkins, secretary of labor in House, *National Housing Act Hearings*.

43. Ewalt, *Business Reborn*, 91–108, 131–47.

44. Marvell, *Bank Board*, 32, 39–40.

CHAPTER 7: CREDIT UNIONISM AND POPULIST PUBLIC PHILOSOPHY

1. Senate Committee on Banking and Currency, Subcommittee on S. 1639, S. 1640, S. 1641, *Credit Unions: Hearings on S.1639, S. 1640 and S. 1641*, 73d Cong., 1st sess., June 1933, 19.

2. s&Ls had total assets of $8.8 billion dollars in 1930. Senate, *Home Loan Bank Hearings*, 81.

3. Credit Union National Association, Economics and Statistics Department, "Frequently Requested U.S. Credit Union / Bank Comparisons, 1997," photocopy, Madison, Wis..

4. The financial soundness of the institutions of the credit union framework has been confirmed since the late 1980s by observers outside the framework. See Deloitte and Touche, LLP, "Independent Auditors' Report," in National Credit Union Administration, *1997 Annual Report*; U.S. Department of the Treasury, *Credit Unions* (online) (Washington, D.C., December 1997, cited May 18, 1998); available at: <http://www.Treas.gov/press/releases/docs/cu_study .pdf>; U.S. General Accounting Office, "Credit Unions: Both Industry and Insurance Fund Appear Financially Sound" (GAO/T-GGD-94-142) (Washington, D.C.: GAO, 1994); U.S. General Accounting Office, *Credit Unions: Reforms for Ensuring Future Soundness* (GAO/GGD-91-85) (Washington, D.C.: GAO, 1991); Secura Group, *The Credit Union Industry: Trends, Structure and Com-*

petitiveness, Study Prepared for the American Bankers Association, Washington, D.C., 1989.

Steady growth of credit unionism in recent decades is evidenced in Secura Group, "Historical Trend—U.S. Credit Unions," fig. 2, in ibid., 14; and Thomson Financial Publishing Company, *Thomson Credit Union Directory* 12, no.1 (June 1998), R-18.

5. Secura Group, *Credit Union Industry,* 245–59.

6. During the Progressive Era the *Nation's* E. L. Godkin was typical of contemporary progressive intellectuals in describing populist thought and action as "the vague dissatisfaction which is always felt by the incompetent and lazy and 'shiftless' when they contemplate those who have got on better in the world," quoted in Goodwyn, *Populist Moment,* 210. Later historian of the Progressive Era Richard Hofstadter similarly viewed populist thinking as "an undercurrent of provincial resentments, popular and 'democratic' rebelliousness and suspiciousness, and nativism" in *The Age of Reform* (New York: Alfred A. Knopf, 1955), 5.

7. Examples of racist expressions among progressives include Herbert Croly, labeled the "chief philosopher" of the Progressive movement by historian Arthur Link, who maintained that "[Southern slave owners] were right, moreover, in believing that the negroes were a race possessed of moral and intellectual qualities inferior to those of the white men." *Promise of American Life,* 81. Link's reference in *Wilson: The New Freedom* (Princeton: Princeton University Press, 1956), 242. Historian John D. Hicks, author of the benchmark history of the populist program, commented gratuitously on the "gregarious instincts" and "characteristic shiftlessness" of negroes in *The Populist Revolt: A History of the Farmers' Alliance and the People's Party* (Minneapolis: University of Minnesota Press, 1931), 47. Woodrow Wilson, progressive policy maker and politician, presided over introduction of segregation in the federal civil service, permitted dismissal of negroes with civil service status, and replaced patronage appointees who were black with whites. See Link, *Wilson,* 246–48.

8. Kazin, *Populist Persuasion.*

9. Political theorist R. Jeffrey Lustig develops populism as systematic public philosophy in *Corporate Liberalism: The Origins of American Political Theory, 1890–1920* (Berkeley: University of California Press, 1982), 39–77. Historian Lawrence Goodwyn develops populism's institutional program in *Populist Moment* and recounts populism's struggle to include black people.

10. Lustig, in *Corporate Liberalism,* argues for the coherence of the public philosophy but views populism as having entirely lost out to progressivism institutionally. Goodwyn recognized functioning institutions constructed in terms of an inclusive populist paradigm but only for a historical "moment." Populism exists today, he laments, "primarily as a mass folkway of resignation. . . . People do not believe they can do much 'in politics' to affect substantively either their own daily lives or the inherited patterns of power and privilege within their society." *Populist Moment,* xiii.

11. Hicks, *Populist Revolt*, 60–74.

12. Ibid., 74–80.

13. Goodwyn, *Populist Moment*, 70.

14. Ibid., 20–27, 72; Hicks, *Populist Revolt*, 39–46.

15. Ibid., 21–22, 81–85.

16. Ibid., 55–57; Goodwyn, *Populist Moment*, 69–70.

17. Goodwyn makes the case for the central role of the Farmers Alliance in *Populist Moment*.

18. "St Louis Demands," app. A, in Hicks, *Populist Revolt*, 427.

19. Ibid., 430.

20. "Omaha Platform," app. F, in Hicks, *Populist Revolt*, 442.

21. Ibid., 441.

22. Roy F. Bergengren, *Crusade: The Fight for Economic Democracy in North America, 1921–1945* (New York: Exposition Press, 1952), 280–81.

23. David J. Gilbert, Walter S. Hilborn, and Geoffrey May, *Small Loan Legislation* (New York: Russell Sage Foundation, 1932), 53–54, cited in J. Carroll Moody and Gilbert C. Fite, *The Credit Union Movement: Origins and Development, 1850–1980,* 2d ed. (Dubuque, Iowa: Kendall/Hunt, 1984), 23; Arthur H. Ham, "Remedial Loans—A Constructive Program," *Proceedings of the Academy of Political Science* (New York: Columbia University Press, 1912), 161–69.

24. Ibid.

25. Moody and Fite, *Credit Union Movement,* 29.

26. Roy F. Bergengren, "The Historical Background of Our Credit Unions," *The Bridge,* June–July 1929, 5; Roy F. Bergengren, *CUNA Emerges,* 2d ed. (Madison, Wis.: Credit Union National Association, 1936), 8–18; Moody and Fite, *Credit Union Movement,* 3–37. Credit Union National Association, *People, Not Profit: The Story of the Credit Union Movement* (Dubuque, Iowa: Kendall/Hunt, 1993), 25–33.

27. Bergengren, *Crusade,* 141, 199–210; Moody and Fite, *Credit Union Movement,* 19–22, 36–37; CUNA, *People Not Profit,* 31–33, 45.

28. On the efforts of prominent Progressive reformers—including Charles W. Birtwell, John Sprunt Hill, William Howard Taft, and the Russell Sage Foundation—to encourage credit unions, see Bergengren, *CUNA Emerges,* 19–21.

29. Moody and Fite, *Credit Union Movement,* 49–54, 57–58; Bergengren, *Crusade,* 20.

30. Bergengren, *CUNA Emerges,* 4–5.

31. Ibid., 5.

32. For example, Bergengren wrote, "The people are capable of managing their own money." *Crusade,* 16.

33. Ibid., 17.

34. Bergengren, *CUNA Emerges,* ix.

35. Ibid., 19, 26–28. Four states had laws passed before CUNEB was established in 1921 which Bergengren regarded as "workable." Six more states had laws passed between 1913 and 1919 under which no credit unions had been

organized. Bergengren viewed these laws as containing provisions making them unworkable. With regard to the laws passed before his involvement with credit unionism, Bergengren regarded it his task to improve their workability.

36. Bergengren, *Crusade*, 218–35.

37. Prominent among credit union organizers in Bergengren's day were Charles Hyland, a firefighter from LaCrosse, Wisconsin; Thomas Doig, from the Minneapolis Post Office; Claude Orchard, recruited in the Armour meat-packing plant in Omaha; Joe DeRamus, Timothy O'Shaughnessy, and Earl Rentfro of the Rock Island railroad; and the Detroit schoolteacher Clarence Howell. Particularly beloved in the movement was the charismatic, polio-stricken Ralph Long. There had been outstanding women among the Alliance lecturers of the 1890s; so, too, there were women among credit union organizers from the beginning: Dora Maxwell organized farmers in upstate New York and immigrants to New York City, and Louise Herring organized credit unions in Ohio. Ibid., 73, 80, 87, 92–94, 109–11, 140, 173.

38. Ibid., 236–44; Bergengren, CUNA *Emerges*, xi, 32–33; Moody and Fite, *Credit Union Movement*, 123–46.

39. CUNA, *People Not Profit*, 101.

40. Moody and Fite, *Credit Union Movement*, 110–16.

41. Bergengren, *Crusade*, 222.

42. Ibid.

43. Roy F. Bergengren, "Federal Credit Unions," the *Bridge*, July 1934, 1–3; Senate, *Credit Union Hearings*, 1; Morris Sheppard, *Congressional Record*, 73d Cong., 2d sess., 1934, vol. 78, pt. 7, 7259–61. Moody and Fite, *Credit Union Movement*, 112–20; Bergengren, *Crusade*, 230; Bergengren, "Senator Sheppard," the *Bridge*, July 1934, 1.

44. Ibid.

45. Richard Ray Bailey, "Morris Sheppard of Texas: Southern Progressive and Prohibitionist" (Ph.D. diss., Texas Christian University, 1980). I have relied on Bailey's description of Sheppard's views but contend that these views are more accurately characterized as "populism," not, as Bailey does, as "progressivism."

46. Patman to Democratic Banking Committee members, June 8, 1934, cited in Moody and Fite, *Credit Union Movement*, 120.

47. *Congressional Record*, 73d Cong., 2d sess., 1934, vol. 78, pt. 11, 12225.

48. In the course of credit union hearings in 1969, Patman, then chairman of the House Banking Committee, declared his public philosophy: "I would rather be called a populist." House Committee on Banking and Currency, *To Create a Separate Agency for the Regulation and Supervision of Federally Chartered Credit Unions: Hearings on H.R. 2 and H.R. 8445*, 91st Cong., 1st sess., June, 1969, 23.

49. *Federal Credit Union Act of 1934*, U.S. *Statutes at Large* 48 (1934): 1216–22; *Federal Credit Union Act, U.S. Code*, vol. 5, sec. 1752(1) (1994).

50. Special Study Committee of CUNA International, "Regional Hearings on

Recodification of the Federal Credit Union Act" (Madison, Wis.: Department of Legislation and Governmental Affairs, CUNA International, Inc., 1969).

51. United States Forum of CUNA International, "Summary of Proposed Recodification of Federal Credit Union Act," photocopy, CUNA, Madison, Wis., May 1970 (my emph.).

52. Albert E. Burger and Tina Dacin, *Field of Membership: An Evolving Concept,* Study by Filene Research Institute, Center for Credit Union Research, School of Business, University of Wisconsin–Madison, February 1991, 1–8 (my emph.); Brief for the National Credit Union Administration, in the Supreme Court of the United States, in the cases of *National Credit Union Administration v. First National Bank & Trust Co., et al.* and *Credit Union National Association, et al. v. First National Bank & Trust Co., et al.,* 1996, 18–22.

53. From 1934 through 1977 amendments to the Federal Credit Union Act gradually increased the maximum amount of unsecured loans from fifty to twenty-five hundred dollars, the maximum term for unsecured loans from two to five years, and the maximum term for secured loans to ten years.

54. The minimal impact of amending the Federal Credit Union Act twenty times from 1934 through 1968 is summarized in Moody and Fite, *Credit Union Movement,* 301. Major features of law and regulation, as they stood in 1968, are summarized in United States Forum of CUNA, "Summary of Proposed Recodification."

55. Ibid.; Moody and Fite, *Credit Union Movement,* 306–31; Burger and Dacin, *Field of Membership,* 17–27.

56. There is an exception. A small class of "community development credit unions" is permitted to accept nonmember deposits. These institutions were designed in the 1960s in the context of the war on poverty, in conjunction with the Office of Economic Opportunity. They operate in low-income community development areas, providing services depending on member needs. They may provide check cashing and sell money orders, lend fifty dollars for two weeks, or provide small business start-up loans.

57. Burger and Dacin, *Field of Membership,* 17, 28–29; "NCUA Brief."

58. Burger and Dacin, *Field of Membership,* 2.

59. E. F. Callahan, NCUA chairman, to Fernand St. Germain, chairman of House Committee on Banking, Finance and Urban Affairs, October 28, 1983, cited in "NCUA Brief," 7–8.

60. Secura, *Credit Union Industry,* 58.

61. Drafts of original credit union bills introduced and letters of opposition from Treasury and the Federal Reserve are in Senate, *Credit Union Hearings,* 2, 10–13.

62. Bergengren, *Crusade,* 225.

63. Ibid., 105.

64. Moody and Fite, *Credit Union Movement,* 117.

65. Ibid., 121–22, 206.

66. Ibid., 206–7, 233.

67. Ibid., 233–34, 302.

68. Testimony of R. C. Robertson, president, CUNA, in House, *To Create a Separate Agency,* 39.

69. Ibid., 5.

70. Testimony of Robert Ball, commissioner, Social Security Agency, in House, *To Create a Separate Agency,* 6. For further evidence of department officials' view of the purpose of credit unions, see Robert H. Finch, secretary, Department of Health, Education and Welfare, to John Sparkman, chairman, Senate Committee on Banking and Currency: "This definition [of a federal credit union] ties the Federal credit union program directly into the programs of this Department. Many of the Department programs, as you know, are deeply and immediately concerned with the economic needs of the aged, the widowed, the disadvantaged, the disabled, the less well to do, and children—and so is the Federal credit union program." In Senate Committee on Banking and Currency, *Independent Agency for Credit Unions: Hearing on S. 2298 and H.R. 2,* 91st Cong., 1st sess., 1969, 7. See also Creed C. Black, assistant secretary, Department of Health, Education and Welfare: "We [within the Department of Health, Education and Welfare] feel that credit unions have an important role to fill in the implementation of this administration's commitment to help the poor and underemployed move toward self-sufficiency" (ibid., 16).

71. House, *To Create a Separate Agency,* 9.

72. Ibid., 18.

73. Ibid., 29.

74. Ibid., 10.

75. Ibid., 12, 14–15.

76. Ibid., 29.

77. Ibid., 4.

78. Ibid., 10.

79. Moody and Fite, *Credit Union Movement,* 320–22.

80. Senate Committee on Banking, Housing and Urban Affairs, Subcommittee on Financial Institutions, *Restructuring the National Credit Union Administration: Hearing on Title II of S. 1475,* 94th Cong., 2d sess., March 1976; Senate Committee on Banking, Housing and Urban Affairs, *Reorganization of National Credit Union Administration: Report to Accompany S. 3312,* 94th Cong., 2d sess., 1976, S.Rept. 94–751; House Committee on Banking, Finance and Urban Affairs, *Financial Institutions Act of 1978: Report to Accompany H.R. 13471,* 95th Cong., 2d sess., 1978, H. Rept. 95–1383; *Financial Institutions Regulatory and Interest Rate Control Act of 1978,* U.S. Statutes at Large 92 (1978): 3680–83.

81. Senate Committee on Banking and Currency, Subcommittee on Financial Institutions, *Federal Share Insurance for Credit Unions: Hearings on S. 3822,* 91st Cong., 2d sess., June 1970; House Committee on Banking and Currency, *To Provide Insurance for Accounts in State and Federally Chartered Credit Unions: Hearings on H.R. 18870,* 91st Cong., 2d sess., September 1970; Moody

and Fite, *Credit Union Movement*, 304–6, 309–10; GAO, *Credit Unions*, 54–57, 167–85; Treasury, *Credit Unions*, 31–61; Burger and Dacin, *Field of Membership*, 23; *Federal Credit Union Act*, secs. 1781–83.

82. R. C. Robertson, President, CUNA International, Senate, *Share Insurance*, 87.

83. Ibid., 85–98, 113–21; House, *Share Insurance for Credit Unions*, 55–63.

84. In 1970 about 240 of 23,900 credit unions belonged to NAFCU, but they had thirteen percent of total credit union assets and membership. Ibid., 65.

85. Senate, *Share Insurance*, 123–29.

86. Treasury, *Credit Unions*, 85–107; GAO, *Credit Unions*, 136–85; General Accounting Office, *Corporate Credit Unions: Condition, Issues, and Concerns* (GAO/T-GGD-95-15) (Washington: GAO, 1994); Moody and Fite, *Credit Union Movement*, 323; Burger and Dacin, *Field of Membership*, 23.

87. Moody and Fite, *Credit Union Movement*, 311–12, 322.

88. CUNA, *People, Not Profit: The Story of the Credit Union Movement*, by Ruth Witzeling (Dubuque, Iowa: Kendall/Hunt, 1993), 101–9.

89. Cited in Secura, *Credit Union Industry*, 4.

90. Credit Union National Association, "Credit Union Campaign for Consumer Choice" (online), cited September 2, 1998, available at: <http://www.cuna.org/data/consumer/whatis/campaign/cu_campaign.html>; Patrick M. Keefe, "Off and Running," *Federal Credit Union* (March–April 1997): 11–13.

91. Daniel A. Mica, "Statement of Daniel A. Mica, President and CEO of CUNA, following today's signing by President Clinton of H.R. 1151, the Credit Union Membership Access Act" (online), August 9, 1998, cited September 2, 1998, available at: <http://www.cuna.org/data/newsnow/spec_reports/hr1151/hr1151_mica.html>; Credit Union National Association, "Summary of Field of Membership Provisions in H.R. 1151: The Credit Union Membership Access Act" (online), cited September 2, 1998, available at: <http://www.cuna.org/data/newsnow/spec_reports/hr1151/hr1151_summary.html>; "Credit Union Membership Access Act" (online), August 1998, cited September 2, 1998, available at: <http://www.cuna.org/download/hr1151_enrolled.html>.

92. Michigan Credit Union League, "Focus: Operation Grassroots" (pamphlet), November 1990; John R. Cranford, "Administration Spells Out Plan to Reform Financial System," *Congressional Quarterly Weekly*, February 8, 1991, 357–61; Cranford, "Financial System's Wounds May Only Be Bandaged," ibid., February 2, 1991, 284–89; Cranford, "Banking Overhaul Bill," ibid., 23 March 1991, 733; "Jepsen Opposes Bill to Eliminate NCUA," *NCUA News* (February 1991): 1.

93. Quoted in Moody and Fite, *Credit Union Movement*, 327.

94. Albert E. Burger and Gregory M. Lypny, *Taxation of Credit Unions*, Study prepared for the Center for Credit Union Research, School of Business, University of Wisconsin–Madison and the Filene Research Institute, Madison, Wisconsin, October 1991, 3–7; Moody and Fite, *Credit Union Movement*, 323–26.

95. Ibid., 300.

96. See, for example, Eugene Johnson, "Banks vs. Credit Unions: A History of Conflict" (online), 1998, cited May 18, 1998, available at: <http://www.cuna .org/data/cu/cuna/pubs/specialreport/introconflict.html>.

97. Burger and Lypny, *Taxation of Credit Unions,* 9–14.

CHAPTER 8: WHITHER BANKING REGULATION?

1. Terry Moe, "The Politics of Bureaucratic Structure," in *Can the Government Govern?* ed. John Chubb and Paul Peterson (Washington, D.C.: Brookings Institution, 1989), 267–329.

2. A significant statement of the viewpoint is Friedman, *Capitalism and Freedom.*

3. Derthick and Quirk, *Politics of Deregulation.*

4. Robert E. Litan, *The Revolution in U.S. Finance* (Washington, D.C.: Brookings Institution, 1991); James R. Barth, R. Dan Brumbaugh, and Robert E. Litan, *The Future of American Banking* (Armonk, N.Y.: M. E. Sharpe, 1992); President's Inter-Agency Task Force on Regulation Q, *Deposit Interest Rate Ceilings and Housing Credit,* U.S. Senate, Committee on Banking, Housing and Urban Affairs (Washington, D.C.: GPO, 1979).

5. Thomas F. Cargill and Gillian G. Garcia, *Financial Deregulation and Monetary Control* (Stanford: Hoover Institution Press, 1982).

6. *The Report of the President's Commission on Financial Structure and Regulation* (Washington, D.C.: GPO, 1971), 9, cited in Cargill and Garcia, *Financial Deregulation,* 23.

7. As noted in chapter 5, interest rate ceilings on bank deposits had been introduced in the Banking Act of 1933 to limit competition among banks for deposits. The statute prohibited interest on demand deposits and gave authority to the Fed to regulate rates on time and savings deposits in member banks. The Banking Act of 1935 gave similar authority to the FDIC vis-à-vis nonmember banks. In the mid-1960s Congress and the regulators had begun to use rate ceilings for additional purposes: as a tool of monetary policy (to restrain the inflation triggered by Vietnam War expenditures), to maintain flows of credit into residential mortgages, and to protect the financial viability of S&Ls and banks from the threat of interest rates they could ill afford. It was in pursuit of these purposes that ceilings had been applied to S&L deposits for the first time, differentials were established permitting S&Ls to offer a slightly higher rate than commercial banks, and regulators engaged in ongoing rate adjustments. President's Inter-agency Task Force, *Deposit Interest Rate Ceilings,* 34–55.

8. A step backward is in order to clarify the interstate banking and branching issue. National banks were established in the National Bank Act in 1864 according to the free bank model of the time. Free banks did not have branches, and in the close interpretation of the National Bank Act given it by early comptrollers of the currency, national banks were not permitted to branch either. Most pre–Civil War state banks converted to national bank charters, and, as they did, branch systems broke up in the states where they had existed; state

bank branches came into the national bank system as separate national banks. By the time the expectation that all banks would convert to national charters broke down and states returned to chartering their own banks, the model of separately capitalized unit banks was strong at the state level as well as mandated at the national level.

The picture is complicated, however, for there were always some states that permitted their state banks to branch. There were even a few *national* banks with branches because state banks converting to national charters were permitted to bring their existing branches with them under an 1865 amendment to the National Bank Act, though few did. Comptrollers of the currency thus struggled with how to regulate a handful of banks with branches in a system of unit national banks. When the Federal Reserve was established in 1913, its membership included state banks as well as national banks; the Fed was then confronted with the problem of how to handle branching state banks in a system with national banks that could not branch. The McFadden Act of 1927 attempted to generate uniform treatment for state and national Fed member banks with regard to branching. It allowed member banks to keep branches established before 1927, but new branches could be opened only within the limits of the city in which the parent bank was located and only if state law permitted. The Banking Act of 1933 went farther toward uniformity and was more permissive about national bank branching, allowing national banks to establish branches to the same extent as state banks in the states in which they were located. There has thus been branch banking within some states since the Civil War, but branching across state lines remained prohibited almost everywhere.

Branching prohibitions led to the development of bank holding companies. A holding company is a corporation, formed according to the general incorporation law of a state, which owns stock in other corporations. Bank holding companies own the stock of banks; they function somewhat like large banks with branches, but the component banks in the system are separately chartered, separately capitalized banks with their own boards of directors. Bank holding companies developed after 1900, expanding until 1932. They declined during the Depression, but expansion picked up again in 1949. Holding companies were used to hold multiple banks both within a state and across state lines. When a holding company owns separate banks across state lines, its activity is called "interstate banking."

Federal regulators and some members of Congress were concerned because bank holding companies could control the policy and operation of state and national banks through ownership of the stock of those banks yet were largely unregulated. The Banking Act of 1933 required that holding companies that include a Federal Reserve member bank register with the Federal Reserve for a permit to vote their bank stock.

Efforts to establish clearer regulation of bank holding companies culminated in the Bank Holding Company Act of 1956, which put multibank holding companies firmly under the regulatory purview of the Federal Reserve Board and provided a legal framework for quasi-branch banking within states and to some extent across states. The use of holding companies to overcome restrictions on banking across state lines was quite limited, however, by the Douglas Amendment to the Bank Holding Company Act. The Douglas Amendment prohibited multibank holding companies from acquiring an out-of-state bank unless such acquisition was expressly permitted by the law of the state in which the acquired bank was chartered. No state permitted such interstate banking until 1975, but by 1994 all but Hawaii did, though about a dozen states limited it along regional lines.

The deregulatory objective of the 1990s with regard to interstate banking has been to remove the barriers that remained, thus permitting holding companies to acquire banks in any state, laying the basis for national banking networks. The 1994 Interstate Banking and Branching Efficiency Act accomplished this objective, though it included a provision for states to "opt out" by taking positive legislative action within a specified time period.

Beyond interstate banking the 1994 deregulatory legislation also permitted interstate branching. Although interstate banking—with separately chartered, capitalized, and managed banks—was broadly permitted by the 1990s, interstate branching remained essentially prohibited. (For a bank to branch means that it conducts banking business, taking deposits and making loans, at multiple locations. In interstate branching a bank would operate a branch outside its home state.) As branching restrictions fall away, bank holding companies can merge their separate banks into single banks with regional and nationwide branch systems. See Gerald C. Fischer, *Bank Holding Companies* (New York: Columbia University Press, 1961); Miller and Van Hoose, *Modern Money and Banking*, 212–13, 236–38, 247–48; "Banking Law Undergoes Revision," *Congressional Quarterly Almanac: 103d Congress, 2d Session, 1994* (Washington, D.C.: Congressional Quarterly, Inc., 1995), 93–100.

9. This summary of the Hunt report's recommendations for depository intermediaries follows Cargill and Garcia, *Financial Deregulation*, 22–24.

10. Task Group on Regulation of Financial Services, *Blueprint for Reform* (Washington, D.C.: GPO, 1984); John R. Cranford, "Administration Spells Out Plan to Reform Financial System," *CQ Weekly*, February 9, 1991, 357–61; Frank N. Newman, undersecretary of the Treasury, "Consolidating the Federal Bank Regulatory Agencies," Proposal Requested by the Senate Committee on Banking, Housing and Urban Affairs, Washington, D.C., November 23, 1993.

11. The laws were the Financial Institutions Reform, Recovery and Enforcement Act of 1989 (FIRREA), and the Federal Deposit Insurance Corporation Improvement Act of 1991 (FDICIA).

12. Daniel J. Parks and Lori Nitschke, "Clash over Community Reinvestment Threatens Senate Financial Services Bill," ibid., March 6, 1999, 548–49; Daniel J. Parks, "The House That CRA Built: Redlining Law Revisited," ibid., April 24, 1999, 938–44; Parks, "Where Gramm Draws the Line," ibid., 944.

13. Susan Hoffmann and Mark Cassell, "What Are the Federal Home Loan Banks Up To? Emerging Views of Purpose among Institutional Leadership" (pa-

per delivered at the 2000 Annual Meeting of the American Political Science Association, Washington, D.C., August 31–September 3, 2000).

14. Lori Nitschke, "GOP Touts 'One-Stop Shopping' as Key Benefit of Overhaul Bill," *Congressional Quarterly Weekly*, March 21, 1998, 728.

15. Canadian deregulatory moves in 1987 resulted in higher fees on consumer services and the closing of small-town bank branches, according to Emily Pierce, "In Canada, Consolidation Rules," ibid., 729.

16. Hoffmann and Cassell, "What Are the Federal Home Loan Banks Up To?" 7.

17. National Commission on Financial Institution Reform, Recovery and Enforcement, *Origins and Causes of the S&L Debacle: A Blueprint for Reform*, Report to the President and Congress of the United States (Washington, D.C.: GPO, 1993), 8.

18. Robert Kuttner, *Everything for Sale* (New York: Alfred A. Knopf, 1997), 159–90.

19. Ibid., 161.

20. John Kenneth Galbraith, *The Great Crash, 1929* (New York: Time, Inc., 1962).

21. Kuttner, *Everything for Sale*, 177–78.

22. An accessible explanation of how the Federal Reserve's monetary policy leverage was slipping is included in the testimony and report of Chairman William Miller, House Committee on Banking, Finance and Urban Affairs, *Monetary Control*, 96th Cong., 1st sess., 1979, 68–94.

23. Cargill and Garcia, *Financial Deregulation*, 45, 51–54; Miller and VanHoose, *Modern Money and Banking*, 238–41.

BIBLIOGRAPHY

American Bankers Association. American Institute of Banking Section. *Savings Banking*. New York: American Institute of Banking, 1951.

Anderson, Charles W. *Pragmatic Liberalism*. Chicago: University of Chicago Press, 1990.

Bailey, Richard Ray. "Morris Sheppard of Texas: Southern Progressive and Prohibitionist." Ph.D. diss., Texas Christian University, 1980.

Barth, James R. *The Great Savings and Loan Debacle*. Washington, D.C.: American Enterprise Institute, 1991.

Barth, James R., R. Dan Brumbaugh, and Robert E. Litan. *The Future of American Banking*. Armonk, N.Y.: M. E. Sharpe, 1992.

Bentham, Jeremy. *The Principles of Morals and Legislation*. 1789. Reprint. New York: Hafner Press, 1948.

Bergengren, Roy F. *Crusade: The Fight for Economic Democracy in North America, 1921–1945*. New York: Exposition Press, 1952.

———. *CUNA Emerges*. 2d ed. Madison, Wis.: Credit Union National Association, 1936.

Berry, Wendell. *Unsettling of America: Culture and Agriculture*. San Francisco: Sierra Club Books, 1977.

Bodfish, Morton. *History of Building and Loan in the United States*. Chicago: United States Building and Loan League, 1931.

Brumbaugh, R. Dan. *Thrifts under Siege*. Cambridge, Mass.: Ballinger, 1988.

Bryan, William Jennings, and Mary Baird Bryan. *The Memoirs of William Jennings Bryan*. Chicago: John C. Winston, 1925.

Burger, Albert E., and Gregory J. Lypny. *Taxation of Credit Unions*. Study Prepared for the Center for Credit Union Research, School of Business, University of Wisconsin–Madison. Madison: Filene Research Institute, 1991.

Burger, Albert E., and Tina Dacin. *Field of Membership: An Evolving Concept*. Study Prepared for Center for Credit Union Research, School of Business, University of Wisconsin–Madison. Madison: Filene Research Institute, 1991.

Caldwell, Lynton K. *The Administrative Theories of Hamilton and Jefferson: Their Contribution to Public Administration*. 2d ed. New York: Holmes and Meier, 1988.

Caporaso, James A., and David P. Levine. *Theories of Political Economy.* Cambridge: Cambridge University Press, 1992.

Cargill, Thomas F., and Gillian G. Garcia. *Financial Deregulation and Monetary Control: Historical Perspective and Impact of the 1980 Act.* Stanford: Hoover Institution Press, 1982.

———. *Financial Reform in the 1980s.* Stanford: Hoover Institution Press, 1985.

Catterall, Ralph C. H. *The Second Bank of the United States.* 1902. Reprint. Chicago: University of Chicago Press, 1960.

Chandler, Lester V. *Benjamin Strong: Central Banker.* Washington, D.C.: Brookings Institution, 1958.

Cohen, Michael D., James G. March, and Johan P. Olsen. "A Garbage Can Model of Organizational Choice." *Administrative Science Quarterly* 17 (March 1972): 1–25.

Commons, John R. *Legal Foundations of Capitalism.* 1924. Reprint. Madison: University of Wisconsin Press, 1968.

Cranford, John R. "Administration Spells Out Plan to Reform Financial System." *CQ Weekly,* February 9, 1991, 357–61.

Credit Union National Association. *People, Not Profit: The Story of the Credit Union Movement.* Dubuque, Iowa: Kendall/Hunt, 1993.

———. Special Study Committee of CUNA International, "Regional Hearings on Recodification of the Federal Credit Union Act." Madison, Wis., Department of Legislation and Governmental Affairs, CUNA International, 1969.

———. "Summary of Field of Membership Provisions in H.R. 1151, The Credit Union Membership Access Act." Online, cited September 2, 1998. Available at: <http://www.cuna.org/data/newsnow/spec_reports/hr1151/hr1151_summary.html>.

"Credit Union Membership Access Act." Online, August 1998; cited September 2, 1998. Available at: <http://www.cuna.org/download/hr1151_enrolled.html>.

Croly, Herbert. *The Promise of American Life.* 1909. Reprint. Cambridge: Harvard University Press, 1965.

Derthick, Martha, and Paul Quirk. *The Politics of Deregulation.* Washington, D.C.: Brookings Institution, 1985.

Dewey, John. *The Public and its Problems.* Athens, Ohio: Swallow Press, 1927.

Eccles, Marriner S. *Beckoning Frontiers: Public and Personal Recollections.* New York: Alfred A. Knopf, 1951.

Ewalt, Josephine Hedges. *A Business Reborn: The Savings and Loan Story, 1930–1960.* Chicago: American Savings and Loan Institute Press, 1962.

Fischer, Gerald C. *Bank Holding Companies.* New York: Columbia University Press, 1961.

Friedman, Milton. *Capitalism and Freedom.* 1962. Reprint. Chicago: University of Chicago Press, 1982.

Friedman, Milton, and Anna Jacobson Schwartz. *A Monetary History of the United States: 1867–1960.* Princeton: Princeton University Press, 1967.

Galbraith, John Kenneth. *The Great Crash of 1929*. New York: Time, Inc., 1962.
———. *Money: Whence It Came, Where It Went*. London: Andre Deutsch, 1975.
Glass, Carter. *An Adventure in Constructive Finance*. 1927. Reprint. New York: Arno Press, 1975.
Goodwyn, Lawrence. *The Populist Moment: A Short History of the Agrarian Revolt in America*. New York: Oxford University Press, 1978.
Gouge, William. *A Short History of Paper Money and Banking in the United States to Which Is Prefixed an Inquiry into the Principles of the System*. 1833. Reprint. New York: Augustus M. Kelley, 1968.
Govan, Thomas Payne. *Nicholas Biddle: Nationalist and Public Banker, 1786–1844*. Chicago: University of Chicago Press, 1959.
Ham, Arthur H.. "Remedial Loans—A Constructive Program." *Proceedings of the Academy of Political Science*. New York: Columbia University, 1912.
Hamilton, Alexander. *Alexander Hamilton's Papers on Public Credit, Commerce and Finance*. Edited by Samuel McKee Jr. New York: Liberal Arts Press, 1957.
Hamilton, James Alexander. *Reminiscences of James Alexander Hamilton: or Men and Events, at Home and Abroad, during Three Quarters of a Century*. New York: Charles Scribner's Sons, 1869.
Hammond, Bray. *Banks and Politics in America, from the Revolution to the Civil War*. Princeton: Princeton University Press, 1957.
Hartz, Louis. *The Liberal Tradition in America: An Interpretation of American Political Thought since the Revolution*. New York: Harcourt, Brace and World, 1955.
Hayek, Friedrich A. *The Constitution of Liberty*. Chicago: University of Chicago Press, 1960.
Hicks, John D. *The Populist Revolt: A History of the Farmers' Alliance and the People's Party*. Minneapolis: University of Minnesota Press, 1931.
Hoffmann, Susan, and Mark Cassell. "What Are the Federal Home Loan Banks Up To? Emerging Views of Purpose among Institutional Leadership." Paper presented at the 2000 Annual Meeting of the American Political Science Association, Washington, D.C., August 31–September 3, 2000.
Hofstadter, Richard. *The Age of Reform*. New York: Alfred A. Knopf, 1955.
———. *The American Political Tradition*. New York: Vintage Books, 1948.
Hoover, Herbert. *American Individualism*. New York: Doubleday, 1923.
———. *The Challenge to Liberty*. New York: Charles Scribner's Sons, 1923.
———. *The Memoirs of Herbert Hoover: The Cabinet and the Presidency, 1920–1933*. New York: Macmillan, 1952.
———. *The Memoirs of Herbert Hoover: The Great Depression, 1929–1941*. New York: Macmillan, 1952.
———. *Public Papers of the Presidents of the United States: Herbert Hoover, 1929–33*. 4 vols. Washington, D.C.: GPO, 1974–77.
Horwitz, Morton J. *The Transformation of American Law: 1780–1860*. Cambridge: Harvard University Press, 1977.

Hurst, James Willard. *The Legitimacy of the Business Corporation: 1780–1970.* Charlottesville: University Press of Virginia, 1970.

———. *Law and Markets in U.S. History.* Madison: University of Wisconsin Press, 1982.

James, William. *Essays in Radical Empiricism.* New York: Longmans, Green, 1916.

Jefferson, Thomas. *Basic Writings of Thomas Jefferson.* Edited by Philip S. Foner. Garden City, N.Y.: Halcyon House, 1944.

———. *The Writings of Thomas Jefferson.* Edited by Paul Leicester Ford. 10 vols. New York: G. P. Putnam's Sons, 1892–99.

———. *The Writings of Thomas Jefferson.* Edited by Andrew A. Lipscomb and Albert Ellery Bergh. 20 vols. Washington, D.C.: Thomas Jefferson Memorial Association, 1904.

Johnson, Eugene. "Banks vs. Credit Unions: A History of Conflict." Online, 1998; cited May 18, 1998. Available at: <http://www.cuna.org/data/cu/cuna/pubs/specialreport/introconflict.html>.

Kane, Edward J. *The S&L Insurance Mess: How Did It Happen?* Washington, D.C.: Urban Institute Press, 1989.

Katzmann, Robert A. *Regulatory Bureaucracy.* Cambridge: MIT Press, 1980.

Kaufman, Herbert. *The Forest Ranger.* Baltimore: Johns Hopkins University Press, 1960.

Kazin, Michael. *The Populist Persuasion: An American History.* New York: Basic Books, 1995.

Kelman, Steven. *Making Public Policy: A Hopeful View of American Government.* New York: Basic Books, 1987.

Kennedy, Susan Estabrook. *The Banking Crisis of 1933.* Lexington: University Press of Kentucky, 1973.

Kettl, Donald F. *Leadership at the Fed.* New Haven: Yale University Press, 1986.

Kingdon, John W. *Agendas, Alternatives and Public Policies.* 2d ed. New York: HarperCollins College, 1995.

Kinley, David. *The Independent Treasury of the United States.* New York: Thomas Y. Crowell, 1893.

Knox, John Jay. *A History of Banking in the United States.* New York: Bradford Rhodes, 1908.

Koeniger, Alfred Cash. "'Unreconstructed Rebel': The Political Thought and Senate Career of Carter Glass, 1929–1936." Ph.D.diss., Vanderbilt University, 1980.

Kolko, Gabriel. *The Triumph of Conservatism: A Reinterpretation of American History, 1900–1916.* 1963. Reprint. Chicago: Quadrangle Paperbacks, 1967.

Krooss, Herman E., ed. *Documentary History of Banking and Currency in the United States.* 4 vols. New York: Chelsea House, 1969.

Kuttner, Robert. *Everything for Sale.* New York: Alfred A. Knopf, 1997.

Lindblom, Charles. *Politics and Markets.* New York: Basic Books, 1977.

Link, Arthur S. *Wilson: The New Freedom*. Princeton: Princeton University Press, 1956.

Lippmann, Walter. *Drift and Mastery*. 1914. Reprint. Englewood Cliffs, N.J.: Prentice-Hall, 1961.

Litan, Robert E. *The Revolution in U.S. Finance*. Washington, D.C.: Brookings Institution, 1991.

Livingston, James. *Origins of the Federal Reserve System: Money, Class, and Corporate Capitalism, 1890–1913*. Ithaca: Cornell University Press, 1986.

Locke, John. *Second Treatise of Civil Government*. 1689. Reprint. Chicago: Henry Regnery, 1955.

Lovejoy, Arthur. *The Great Chain of Being: A Study of the History of an Idea*. 1936. Reprint. Cambridge: Harvard University Press, 1964.

Lowi, Theodore J. *The End of Liberalism*. New York: W. W. Norton, 1979.

Lowi, Theodore J., and Benjamin Ginsberg. *American Government: Freedom and Power*. 4th ed. New York: W. W. Norton, 1996.

Lustig, R. Jeffrey. *Corporate Liberalism: The Origins of Modern American Political Theory, 1890–1920*. Berkeley: University of California Press, 1982.

Madeleine, Sister M. Grace. *Monetary and Banking Theories of Jacksonian Democracy*. Philadelphia: Sisters, Servants of the Immaculate Heart of Mary, 1943.

March, James G., and Johan P. Olsen. *Rediscovering Institutions: The Organizational Basis of Politics*. New York: Free Press, 1989.

Marvell, Thomas B. *The Federal Home Loan Bank Board*. New York: Praeger, 1969.

McCraw, Thomas K. *Prophets of Regulation*. Cambridge, Mass.: Belknap Press, 1984.

McFaul, John M. *The Politics of Jacksonian Finance*. Ithaca: Cornell University Press, 1972.

Meyers, Marvin. *The Jacksonian Persuasion: Politics and Beliefs*. Stanford: Stanford University Press, 1957.

Mica, Daniel A. "Statement of Daniel A. Mica Following Today's Signing by President Clinton of H.R. 1151, the Credit Union Membership Access Act." Online, August 9, 1998; cited September 2, 1998. Available at: <http://www.cuna.org/data/newsnow/spec_reports/hr1151/hr1151_mica.html>.

Miller, Roger LeRoy, and David D. VanHoose. *Modern Money and Banking*. 3d ed. New York: McGraw-Hill, 1993.

Mints, Lloyd W. *A History of Banking Theory in Great Britain and the United States*. Chicago: University of Chicago Press, 1945.

Mishkin, Frederic S. *The Economics of Money, Banking, and Financial Markets*. 5th ed. Reading, Mass.: Addison-Wesley, 1997.

Moe, Terry. "The Politics of Bureaucratic Structure." In *Can the Government Govern?* Edited by John Chubb and Paul Peterson. Washington, D.C.: Brookings Institution, 1989.

Moody, J. Carroll, and Gilbert C. Fite. *The Credit Union Movement: Origins and Development, 1850–1980*. 2d ed. Dubuque, Iowa: Kendall/Hunt, 1984.

Nash, Lee, ed. *Understanding Herbert Hoover: Ten Perspectives.* Stanford: Stanford University Press, 1987.

National Commission on Financial Institution Reform, Recovery and Enforcement. *Origins and Causes of the s&l Debacle: A Blueprint for Reform.* A Report to the President and Congress. Washington, D.C.: GPO, 1993.

National Credit Union Administration. *1997 Annual Report.* Washington, D.C.: National Credit Union Administration, 1998.

Nitschke, Lori. "GOP Touts 'One-Stop Shopping' as Key Benefit of Overhaul Bill." *Congressional Quarterly Weekly,* March 21, 1998, 728.

Noll, Roger G., and Bruce M. Owen, eds. *The Political Economy of Deregulation.* Washington, D.C.: American Enterprise Institute, 1983.

Nozick, Robert. *Anarchy, State and Utopia.* New York: Basic Books, 1974.

Orren, Karen, and Stephen Skowronek. "Beyond the Iconography of Order: Notes for a 'New Institutionalism.'" In *The Dynamics of American Politics: Approaches and Interpretations.* Edited by Lawrence C. Dodd and Calvin Jillson. Boulder: Westview Press, 1994.

Parks, Daniel J. "The House that CRA Built: Redlining Law Revisited." *CQ Weekly,* April 24, 1999, 938–44.

———. "Where Gramm Draws the Line." *CQ Weekly,* April 24, 1999, 944.

Parks, Daniel J., and Lori Nitschke. "Clash over Community Reinvestment Threatens Senate Financial Services Bill." *CQ Weekly,* March 6, 1999, 548–49.

Peirce, Charles Sanders. "The Fixation of Belief." In *Pragmatism: The Classic Writings.* Edited by H. S. Thayer. Indianapolis: Hackett, 1982.

Pierce, Emily. "In Canada, Consolidation Rules." *Congressional Quarterly Weekly,* March 21, 1998, 729.

President's Commission on Financial Structure and Regulation. *The Report of the President's Commission on Financial Structure and Regulation.* Washington, D.C.: GPO, 1971.

President's Conference on Home Building and Home Ownership. *Directory of Committee Personnel: December 2–5, 1931.* Washington, D.C. Department of Commerce, 1931.

———. *Home Finance and Taxation: Loans, Assessments and Taxes on Residential Property.* Reports of the Committee on Finance and the Committee on Taxation. Washington, D.C.: National Capital Press, 1932.

President's Inter-agency Task Force on Regulation Q. *Deposit Interest Rate Ceilings and Housing Credit.* Washington, D.C.: GPO, 1979.

Reich, Robert, ed. *The Power of Public Ideas.* Cambridge: Harvard University Press, 1988.

Remini, Robert V. *Andrew Jackson and the Bank War.* New York: W. W. Norton, 1974.

———. *The Legacy of Andrew Jackson: Essays on Democracy, Indian Removal, and Slavery.* Baton Rouge: Louisiana State University Press, 1988.

Richardson, James D., ed. *Compilation of the Messages and Papers of the Presidents, 1789–1897.* 10 vols. Washington, D.C.: GPO, 1896–99.

Romer, Thomas, and Barry R. Weingast. "Political Foundations of the Thrift

Debacle." In *Politics and Economics in the Eighties*. Edited by Alberto Alesina and Geoffrey Carliner. Chicago: University of Chicago Press, 1991.

Roosevelt, Franklin D. *The Public Papers and Addresses of Franklin D. Roosevelt*. Vol. 2. New York: Random House, 1938.

Rossiter, Clinton. *Alexander Hamilton and the Constitution*. New York: Harcourt, Brace and World, 1964.

Russell, Horace. *Savings and Loan Associations*. 2d ed. Albany: Matthew Bender, 1960.

Samuelson, Paul A., and William D. Nordhaus. *Macroeconomics*. 14th ed. New York: McGraw-Hill, 1992.

Schattschneider, E. E. *The Semi-Sovereign People*. Hinsdale, Ill.: Dryden Press, 1960.

Schlesinger, Arthur M., Jr. *The Age of Jackson*. Boston: Little, Brown, 1945.

———. Introduction to *The Age of Jackson*. The American Past. New York: Book-of-the-Month Club, 1989.

Schumacher, E. F. *A Guide for the Perplexed*. New York: Harper Colophon, 1977.

Schweikart, Larry. *Banking in the American South from the Age of Jackson to Reconstruction*. Baton Rouge: Louisiana State University Press, 1987.

Secura Group. *The Credit Union Industry: Trends, Structure and Competitiveness*. Study Prepared for the American Bankers Association. Washington, D.C., 1989.

Shade, William Gerald. *Banks or No Banks: The Money Issue in Western Politics*. Detroit: Wayne State University Press, 1972.

Simon, Herbert. *Administrative Behavior*. New York: Macmillan, 1947.

Sklar, Martin J. *The Corporate Reconstruction of American Capitalism, 1890–1916*. New York: Cambridge University Press, 1988.

Smith, Adam. *An Inquiry into the Nature and Causes of the Wealth of Nations*. 1776. Reprint. New York: Alfred A. Knopf, 1991.

Smith, Rixey, and Norman Beasley. *Carter Glass*. New York: Longmans, Green, 1939.

Spragens, Thomas A., Jr. *The Irony of Liberal Reason*. Chicago: University of Chicago Press, 1981.

Staniland, Martin. *What Is Political Economy?* New Haven: Yale University Press, 1985.

Stigler, George J. "The Theory of Economic Regulation." *Bell Journal of Economics and Management Science* 2 (Spring 1971): 3–21.

Stokey, Edith, and Richard Zeckhauser. *A Primer for Policy Analysis*. New York: W. W. Norton, 1978.

Task Group on Regulation of Financial Services. *Blueprint for Reform*. Washington, D.C.: GPO, 1984.

Thomson Financial Publishing. *Thomson Credit Union Directory*. Vol. 12, no. 1. Skokie, Ill.: Thomson Financial Publishing and CUNA, 1998.

Tindall, George Brown, with David E. Shi. *America: A Narrative History*. 3d ed. New York: W. W. Norton, 1992.

Unger, Irwin. *The Greenback Era: A Social and Political History of American Finance, 1865–1879.* Princeton: Princeton University Press, 1964.

U.S. Congress. Congressional Budget Office. *Resolving the Thrift Crisis.* Washington, D.C.: GPO, 1993.

———. *Congressional Record.* 73d Cong., 2d sess., 1934. Vol. 78, pt. 11.

U.S. Congress. House. Committee on Banking and Currency. *Banking Act of 1935: Hearings on H.R. 5357.* 74th Cong., 1st sess., 1935.

———. *National Housing Act: Hearings on H.R. 9620.* 73d Cong., 2d sess., 1934.

———. *To Create a Separate Agency for the Regulation and Supervision of Federally Chartered Credit Unions: Hearings on H.R. 2 and H.R. 8445.* 91st Cong., 1st sess., 1969.

———. *To Provide Insurance for Accounts in State and Federally Chartered Credit Unions: Hearings on H.R. 18870.* 91st Cong., 2d sess., 1970.

———. Subcommittee on H.R. 7620. *Creation of a System of Federal Home Loan Banks: Hearings on H.R. 7620.* 72d Cong., 1st sess., 1932.

U.S. Congress. House. Committee on Banking, Finance, and Urban Affairs. *Financial Institutions Act of 1978: Report to Accompany H.R. 13471.* 95th Cong., 2d sess., 1978, H. Rept. 95-1383.

———. Subcommittee on Financial Institutions Supervision, Regulation and Insurance. *The Safe Banking Act of 1977: Hearings on H.R. 9086.* 95th Cong., 1st sess., 1977.

U.S. Congress. Senate. Committee on Banking and Currency. *Independent Agency for Credit Unions: Hearing on S.2298 and H.R.2.* 91st Cong., 1st sess., 1969.

———. *National Housing Act: Hearings on S. 3603.* 73d Cong., 2d sess., 1934.

———. Subcommittee on Credit Unions. *Credit Unions: Hearing on S.1639, S.1640 and S.1641.* 73d Cong., 1st sess., 1933.

———. Subcommittee on Financial Institutions. *Federal Share Insurance for Credit Unions: Hearings on S. 3822.* 91st Cong., 2d sess., 1970.

———. Subcommittee on Home Mortgages. *Home Owners' Loan Act: Hearings on S. 1317.* 73d Cong., 1st sess., 1933.

———. Subcommittee on S.6. *Proposed Repeal of the Federal Home Loan Bank Act: Hearings on S.6.* 73d Cong., 1st sess., 1933.

———. Subcommittee on Senate Bill 2959. *Creation of a System of Federal Home Loan Banks: Hearings on S. 2959.* 72d Cong., 1st sess., 1932.

U.S. Congress. Senate. Committee on Banking, Housing and Urban Affairs. *Reorganization of National Credit Union Administration: Report to Accompany S. 3312.* 94th Cong., 2d sess., 1976, S. Rept. 94-751.

———. Subcommittee on Financial Institutions. *Restructuring the National Credit Union Administration: Hearing on Title II of S.1475.* 94th Cong., 2d sess., 1976.

U.S. General Accounting Office. "Credit Unions: Both Industry and Insurance Fund Appear Financially Sound." Statement of Thomas J. McCool, House Committee on Banking, Finance and Urban Affairs, September 29, 1994.

———. *Corporate Credit Unions: Condition, Issues, and Concerns*. Washington, D.C., 1994, GAO/T-GGD-95-15.

———. *Credit Unions: Reforms for Ensuring Future Soundness*. Report to the Congress. Washington, D.C., 1991.

U.S. Treasury Department. "Consolidating the Federal Bank Regulatory Agencies." Proposal Requested by the Senate Committee on Banking, Housing, and Urban Affairs. Washington, D.C., November 23, 1993.

———. *Credit Unions*. Online. Washington, D.C., 1997; cited May 18, 1998. Available at: <http://www.Treas.gov/press/releases/docs/cu_study.pdf>.

Van Fenstermaker, J. *The Development of American Commercial Banking*. Monograph. Bureau of Economic and Business Research. Kent, Ohio: Kent State University Press, 1965.

Veblen, Thorstein. *The Instinct of Workmanship*. 1914. Reprint. New York: W. W. Norton, 1964.

Waldo, Dwight. *The Administrative State*. New York: Ronald Press, 1948.

Warburg, Paul. *The Federal Reserve System: Its Origin and Growth*. 1930. Reprint. New York: Arno Press, 1975.

West, Robert Craig. *Banking Reform and the Federal Reserve: 1863–1923*. Ithaca: Cornell University Press, 1974.

White, Lawrence J. *The s&l Debacle: Public Policy Lessons for Bank and Thrift Regulation*. New York: Oxford University Press, 1991.

Wilburn, Jean Alexander. *Biddle's Bank*. New York: Columbia University Press, 1967.

Willis, H. Parker. *The Federal Reserve System: Legislation, Organization and Operation*. New York: Ronald Press, 1923.

Wilson, James Q., ed. *The Politics of Regulation*. New York: Basic Books, 1980.

Wilson, Joan Hoff. *Herbert Hoover, Forgotten Progressive*. Boston: Little, Brown, 1975.

Wolin, Sheldon. *Politics and Vision*. Boston: Little, Brown, 1960.

INDEX

Jackson, Andrew: public philosophy of, 55–57; and second Bank of the United States 57–61, 68; and state banks, 65–66, 189
Jay, Pierre, 192
Jefferson, Thomas, 188, 189, 234; and first Bank of the United States, 37–40, 42, 56–57; public philosophy of, 24–25; views of: —contrasted to Glass, 119; —contrasted to Jackson, 56
Jeffersonians: reformed, 42, 48, 58, 74; unreformed, 43, 48–49, 85

Katzmann, Robert A., 252n. 13
Kaufman, Herbert, 258n. 23
Kazin, Michael, 19
Kelman, Steven, 252n. 15
Knights of Labor, 185–86, 187
Knox, John J., 262n
Kolko, Gabriel, 268n. 59

LaFollette, Robert, 142
Laughlin, J. Laurence, 268n. 59
liberalism, 10
limited liability, 63
Link, Arthur, 125, 276n. 7
Lippmann, Walter, 142
Livingston, James, 266–67n. 42
Lockean line, 45, 58–60, 93–94, 95–96. See also public/private boundary
Locke, John, 10, 98, 188, 234
loco focos, 85
Lustig, R. Jeffrey, 276n. 9

Madison, James: and first Bank of the United States, 21, 42, 47; and second Bank of the United States, second, 46–47, 69
McAdoo, William, 124
McCulloch, Hugh, 104, 106
McCulloch v. Maryland, 47, 255n. 29
McFadden Act (1927), 283n
McFaul, John M., 260n. 33

Meyers, Marvin, 259n. 29
Mints, Lloyd W., 105, 265n. 15
monetary policy: colonial, 27; criticized, 228; in DIDMCA, 246–47; enabling Federal Reserve Board for, 134–38; and Federal Reserve Banks, 130, 132; instruments of, 270–71n. 90
money trust, 113, 118–19, 120, 122, 123–24
Monroe, James, 52
Morawetz, Victor, 267n. 56
mortgage insurance, 175–76
mortgage structure, 156–57, 163

National Association of Federal Credit Unions (NAFCU), 213, 215
National Bank Act (1863/64), 85, 91–97, 136; criticism of: —business, 114–16; —populist, 111–13
national banks, 92–95
National Credit Union Administration (NCUA), 208–12, 215, 221–22
National Credit Union Share Insurance Fund (NCUSIF), 212–15
National Housing Act (1934), 173–77
National Monetary Commission, 116
nature, 8–9, 98–99; in classic liberalism, 10; in neoliberalism, 189–90, 236; in populism, 189–90; in progressivism, 145–46
neoliberalism, 12, 19–20, 96, 189, 234–38; reform agenda for depository institutions, 228–34; resurgence of, 226–28, 248
New England Bank, 80
New Freedom, 120
Nickerson, Herman, 211
Nixon, Richard, 210, 211
no-frills checking account, 239
Noll, Roger G., 252n. 14
notes, Federal reserve. See Federal Reserve notes
Nozick, Robert, 12